To my mother and father, for introducing me to books and for teaching me at an early age that the best way to learn anything was probably to explore it on my own.

About the Author

Warren Ockrassa is an authority on Director and Lingo. For more than 10 years, he has developed software for a wide range of clients, and has been the technical reviewer for several Director products.

Director® 8.5 Shockwave® Studio:
A Beginner's Guide

Warren Ockrassa

McGraw-Hill/Osborne

New York   Chicago   San Francisco
Lisbon   London   Madrid   Mexico City   Milan
New Delhi   San Juan   Seoul   Singapore   Sydney   Toronto

McGraw-Hill/Osborne
2600 Tenth Street
Berkeley, California 94710
U.S.A.

To arrange bulk purchase discounts for sales promotions, premiums, or fund-raisers, please contact McGraw-Hill/Osborne at the above address. For information on translations or book distributors outside the U.S.A., please see the International Contact Information page immediately following the index of this book.

Director® 8.5 Shockwave® Studio: A Beginner's Guide

1234567890 FGR FGR 0198765432

ISBN 0-07-219562-2

Publisher   Brandon A. Nordin
Vice President & Associate Publisher   Scott Rogers
Acquisitions Editor   Jim Schachterle
Senior Project Editor   Carolyn Welch
Acquisitions Coordinator   Tim Madrid
Technical Editor   Kerry Thompson
Copy Editors   Bob Campbell, Bill McManus
Proofreader   Susie Elkind
Indexer   Claire Splan
Computer Designers   Carie Abrew, Lucie Ericksen, Elizabeth Jang
Illustrators   Michael Mueller, Lyssa Wald
Series Design   Gary Corrigan
Cover Illustrator   Kevin Curry
Cover Series Design   Greg Scott

This book was composed with Corel VENTURA™ Publisher.

Contents

PART 1
Getting Acquainted with Director's Tools

PART 3
Unlocking the Power of Lingo

Object Oriented Programming

Acknowledgments

This turned out to be a bit more of a production than I thought it would be, and naturally there are several folks to credit for their effort and dedication in extracting this book from me.

First, there's Jim Schachterle, the Acquisitions Editor at McGraw-Hill/Osborne, who, in his search for an author to produce a Beginner's Guide for Director 8.5, looked over my Web site and decided to go with me anyway. His input and attention got this thing well enough in shape that it was able to get to the copyediting phase.

Then there's Tim Madrid, also at McGraw-Hill/Osborne, who provided useful feedback, commentary, and guidance on the production of this book.

Thanks also to my technical editor, Kerry Thompson, for not laughing hysterically when he heard I was working on this project and for actually being willing to go over the content and correct me, as necessary, whenever I was wrong. There were definitely places where I needed that.

From there I move on to the other brave souls at McGraw-Hill/Osborne, particularly the copy editors, who kept a sharp eye out for consistency and clarity; their efforts helped turn my sometimes abstruse syntax into something humanly readable, and that's not a bad thing, given this book's intended audience.

There are dozens of people—at least in the Director community—to whom I owe some gratitude as well. Chief among them are Macromedia and its great engineers, for without Macromedia there'd be no Director, and I'd likely be collecting cans somewhere for a living. Thanks also to the myriad inhabitants of the Director-related online community, none of whom I have actually met in person, for simply being a presence and, as often as not, a source of information when my explorations get me into trouble. Although I can't name all of them, I can at least provide a partial list (some of these folks are current or past Macromedians, by the way): Mark Castle, John Dowdell, Bruce Epstein, Colin Holgate, Minty Hunter, Tab Julius, Irv Kalb, Buzz Kettles, Alan Levine, Gretchen MacDowall, James Newton, Darrel Plant, Terry Schussler, Peter Small, Greg Yachuck, Brennan Young, and Alex Zavatone.

There are more people than I can easily name here and I've surely forgotten a few, so I'll have to trust you to know who you are. Try to keep the flame bulk to a minimum.

Stacks of thanks also to the Xtra authors who've turned Director into a lot more than a cartoon engine, including the creators of PrintOMatic, BuddyAPI, FileXtra3, FileIO, and the great MPEG handlers from Tabuleiro.

Thanks finally to Stan Pogrow for letting me get started with Director all those years ago.

Introduction

When it hit the digital scene last century, Director wasn't a heck of a lot more than an animation engine. With version 2, though, a scripting language was introduced, and an entirely different way of approaching computer programming hit the market.

Well, okay, maybe it wasn't *entirely* different, but Director did pull the concept of the Integrated Development Environment (IDE) more thoroughly into a developer's toolkit than anything else going at the time. It remains to this day a program capable of doing some genuinely spectacular 2-D animation (and now 3-D as well), while at the same time providing users with a set of rich and powerful programming tools—all while keeping everything fairly accessible and simple to modify.

For a while Director seemed like the ideal introduction to programming for designers and graphics experts, but as it grew in complexity some sacrifices were made to ease the initial learning curve. The way things are today, Flash is probably easier for relative novices to acquire (assuming no outside help), which is a key reason to have books such as this one.

I really believe in Director. I think it's a good tool and that it offers anyone willing to work at it a heck of a lot of bang for the buck. I hope that in reading this book and working with it, you'll come to the same conclusions.

Who Should Read This Book

First, perhaps your boss has just come to you and told you to learn Director, and to learn it now. You install the program, start it up, work through the Macromedia-provided tutorials, and have no clue where to go next. You're in the right place if you're looking for help. Or perhaps you are a graphics design professional and are interested in branching out some. Maybe you've seen how the programmers work with your art once you've produced it and you're looking for a better understanding of the other side of the shop, as it were. Or you might be in a supervisory position over people who work with Director, and want to have a somewhat better understanding of how it works and perhaps some idea what can be done with it. Maybe you've decided to punch up Web sites you've made using Shockwave, or are simply interested in learning about Director on your own. Finally, maybe you're a student and are enrolled in a course that teaches Director skills.

Whatever the case and whatever the reasons, if you're interested in gaining a functioning knowledge of Director, this is a great place to start. We move from the basics right up through object-oriented programming concepts, letting Director's own ease of use and power help us along the way.

What This Book Covers

This book is divided conceptually into four parts with a total of 15 modules, or chapters. If you are experienced with other languages (particularly OOP), you will probably only need to skim the first two parts. It's the last two parts—particularly the fourth part—that will get you into Director's way of doing object code.

If you're not all that familiar with programming, you'll really want to pay attention to the first two parts, which familiarize you with the tools you'll use most often in working with Director and basic programming concepts.

Parts 1 and 2 are designed specifically to help you get all the basic information you need to begin rolling your own software with Director; Parts 3 and 4 are there for you to enhance your skills once you've got a good grasp of the basics.

Part 1: Getting Acquainted with Director's Tools

Module 1 introduces you to the basic "physical" tools of Director, the items you will be using every day as you create programs. You'll become familiar with these tools partly by description and partly by direct use as you make a classic first-time program.

Module 2 covers Director's Library Palette, a collection of pre-packaged scripts called *behaviors*. The Library Palette is a great way to begin working right away with some fairly complex functionality without necessarily having to write a single line of code on your own; you'll have plenty of opportunities to have fun with the Library Palette in this module.

Module 3 introduces you to the basic anatomy of Lingo scripts including variables, handlers (or methods, functions, or subroutines, depending on what you're most familiar with), control structures such as **if…then** tests, Lingo's own keywords, and types of script available to you as a programmer. This is not an exhaustive (or exhausting) module, but rather is a description of the framework you use when you're creating scripts in Lingo.

Module 4 expands on the ideas of Module 3, explaining in more depth how to make your program code more readable and covering concepts such as good variable naming, internal documentation, and whitespace usage. A common problem with many Lingo scripts is that they might work very well but often tend to be difficult for a human to comprehend. This module helps alleviate some of that.

Module 5 covers the Debugger, a very powerful and useful tool often downplayed in the documentation. Here I will show you why it's a good idea indeed to be familiar with the Debugger, and why it's not just for tracking bugs in your scripts, either!

Part 2: Using Director to Create Programs

Module 6 covers the preparation involved in making a program, such as deciding who its target audience is, in what circumstances it will be used, how flexible it must be, and so on. These decisions all come into play in your design strategy.

Module 7 carries us into creating the program itself and includes such concepts as handling different user monitor settings and beta-testing your software. Covered also are suggestions for finding beta testers and ways to get good feedback from them on how your program is doing.

Module 8 describes in greater detail how to get Lingo to interact with items on the screen and vice versa—how, in short, to make your programs truly interactive.

Part 3: Unlocking the Power of Lingo

Module 9 introduces Director's lists, which are like arrays in other programming languages and can be thought of as a kind of internal database that can be used to store essentially any kind of information you want to keep. Lists are capable of holding information as mundane as the week's shopping or as mission critical as a user's business contacts. They can do a lot more than that, though, and this module will help illustrate that.

Module 10 introduces Director's capability of handling external files of various types, whether they be text, HTML, sound, digital video, or images. This module will help you understand how to integrate these items into your Director movies, expanding your program as you need to, when you need to.

Module 11 covers Director's Internet capabilities, both as a stand-alone item running from a computer's hard drive and as a Shockwave file playing in a browser window. In this module, as in the previous module, you learn that accessing information from remote machines is functionally identical to accessing it from the local system.

Part 4: Object Oriented Programming

Module 12 introduces object oriented programming (OOP) and describes its basic rationale. It explains why OOP is desirable, and why in some cases it can be seen as overkill, as more work than is necessary to achieve a desired result. In this module, we begin work on a project that we'll revisit for the rest of this book.

Module 13 is a recap of behaviors, this time from the perspective of OOP. We discuss the encapsulation of data into specific behaviors and explore further by building on the project we began in the previous module.

Module 14 discusses how to use other Director movies as movies-in-a-window (MIAW), which gives even more power to an OOP interface. From here, we continue to build our project we began in Module 12.

Module 15 discusses communication with and among MIAWs and talks about packaging "real" software for a final release version.

The appendix contains the answers to the mastery checks from all 15 modules.

How to Read This Book

You should read this book not simply by starting with the first word on the first page and sort of progressing from there. Although you can approach the text in the order it's presented—and you really should if you are absolutely new to Director in particular and programming in general—you may also take it in bits and pieces, dipping into specific topics as you need more information about them.

I strongly suggest that, wherever possible, you fire up a computer and actually work on the projects offered in this book. I also recommend, however, that you read through the step-by-step sections at least once before beginning any project to make sure you have at least a general grasp of where the project is going.

Special Features

Typographic conventions used in this book are relatively straightforward. Text in `monospace font` represents a code listing or a block of text the user types in to the computer; **bold text** is used for any individual set of commands or keywords being discussed. Words in SMALL CAPS represent keys you press on your computer's keyboard. Menu access instructions, rather than taking the form of "Choose Save from the File menu," appear as "Choose File | Save," with the vertical bar character indicating the menu or submenu option to be selected from the named menu item.

Throughout this book you will find tips, notes, and other informative sidebars, such as Ask the Expert sections, which allow you to further explore a topic without necessarily deviating from the main point in the text.

You can find additional materials for this text, links to sources of more information, online Director user support pages and mailing lists, sample files, and more at http://www.nightwares.com/director_beginners_guide/. Here, you'll also find the complete source code of all the project files presented in this book.

Part 1

Getting Acquainted with Director's Tools

Module 1

Director's "Physical" Tools

The Goals of this Module

- Learn a little about the history of Director
- Identify and grow familiar with the "physical" tools used most often in Director
- Use these tools to create a classic introductory program

Director, a programming and animation development environment sold by Macromedia, started out as something relatively easy to learn, but over time it has evolved into quite a mature product—complete with the kinds of capabilities (and problems) that usually are found in much more sophisticated (and much harder to learn) programmers' tools.

In this module, we'll explore the history of Director, touch on some of its basic capabilities, and get started right away with some painless programming.

When it was introduced in the mid 1980s, Director was called VideoWorks, and it was little more than a simple *animation engine*—a program used for generating cartoons of a type most like the "paper cutout" animations done by Terry Gilliam on the BBC series *Monty Python's Flying Circus*.

Upon its release as version 2, VideoWorks was renamed Director, a *scripting engine* dubbed *Lingo* was introduced, and for all practical purposes the Director we know today was created. What has followed has been quite a progression of enhancements, including:

- The capability to create and run programs on Windows as well as Macintosh (fully introduced with version 4; Director was originally a *Mac-only* program). This has obvious advantages, for a properly written Director *movie* (file) will work on either Mac or Windows, even if that's not where it was created.

- *Bytecoded* Lingo, also introduced in version 4, which resulted in a tremendous enhancement of speed whenever scripting was used. Later versions resulted in even greater speed of Lingo execution, to the point that some Lingo written in Director 8 can run as much as three to five times faster in Director 8.5, released only a year or so later. Bytecoded Lingo vastly improved speed of calculations; among other things, this has permitted the introduction of 3-D computer modeling "live" in Director programs (that is, without exclusive reliance on external software to produce them).

- Movie in a Window (MIAW), allowing you to run multiple different Director files at once (another version 4 improvement); this has allowed expansion of the basic engine well beyond the original design intent. MIAWs can include simple items you put onscreen to get more information from the user; things you create just for your own use as a Director programmer (these are known as *MIAW Xtras*); little navigation "remote controls" that let users move around in your programs more easily; and so on. Anything you can do in a regular Director program can also be done in a MIAW, though in many cases what you do in a MIAW has an ancillary or supplemental purpose.

● True *object-oriented* scripting/programming (really full-blown by version 5); OOP is the core of the best programs made today, including Director itself. OOP programming is an interesting, if nebulous, subject, and one we'll cover in depth in Part 4.

● *Dot-syntax* Lingo—very similar in concept to the models used in such languages as Java, debuting in version 7. While Macromedia's application of dot syntax is still inconsistent in places, it's generally preferred as the, ahem, *lingua franca* of Lingo by most Director programmers. In some ways, this syntax can be hard to grasp, so I'll make sure to explicate it throughout this book. I will also be sure to point out places where it *does not work* yet; these can be pretty frustrating pitfalls, even if you're *experienced* with Director.

● With version 8.5, the addition of 3-D *polygon casting* and rendering for creating stunning animated games every bit as complex—and challenging— as such C++-based titles as *Tomb Raider*. To no small degree, this represented a doubling of the power available to Director programmers, but unfortunately an exploration of 3-D in Director is beyond the scope of this text. Happily, James Newton has written an Osborne advanced guide for Director users, and just as soon as you're finished with this book, you'll be ready to tackle his.

Don't worry if you're not familiar with what all this means. By the time you're finished with this book, it'll all make sense to you. If your instinct is to conclude that Director's come a long way and evolved into a sublimely powerful programming environment, your instinct is correct.

Scripting? What's Scripting?

Scripting is considered—by some—to be a form of simple programming, but you should not be deceived by the term *simple,* and you should definitely understand that it *is* programming.

Many Director users, some of whom I know to be quite superb programmers, feel a certain sense of inferiority toward people who work with "real" programming languages such as C++; and to be fair, *some* such "real" language users look down on anyone who uses a scripting language, the implication being that it's so simple a chimpanzee with its brain removed could do it (and thus, by extension, the Director programmer is such a primate).

I think that's just jealousy, because a good Director programmer can often do, in a few weeks' time, what it takes a good C++ programmer several *months* to complete (which really annoys the C++ programmer). Besides, many of those same C++ programmers don't hesitate to use tools like Perl or Java, both of which are *also* scripting languages!

What might *start* as a pretty basic method for moving from one screen to another can rapidly develop into something much more closely approximating a full-fledged programming environment, and this is what indeed has happened with Director and its scripting engine, Lingo.

What makes Director stand out as compared to scripting environments such as Java, Perl, or Python is the fact that it comes packaged with an exhaustive— to many new users bewildering—array of *rich-media* components and controls.

These components include tools for placing text onscreen, for creating graphics right inside Director itself, for manipulating digital video (Apple's QuickTime is an example of this), and for handling sound effects such as music or narration. They also provide the ability to play back and respond to commands from animations made in Macromedia Flash.

By the end of this part, you'll be familiar with many of these components, and you will know enough about the rest to be able to work with pretty much all of them. In fact, by the end of this part, you'll be quite capable of putting together some very interesting Director programs, to the point you might consider starting your own business doing so, or at least enhancing your current income by doing some smaller jobs on the side. I say go for it!

Other Scripting-Style Programming Environments

1

Other packages out there allow you to do something similar to Director, of which the major contenders currently include MetaCard and AuthorWare. However, AuthorWare uses a *flowchart* approach (icons connected by lines) to placing things onscreen and controlling interaction with users, and it does not allow as direct access to its scripting tools as Director does; MetaCard, while it gives you more ready access to its script engine, is built on a card-stack approach (similar to the one HyperCard uses).

Many people, including me, find such modes of working to be difficult once the really heavy programming starts happening, which is why I've found Director's method to be preferable. To be sure, both the card-stack and flowchart approaches are pretty easy for many newcomers to get the hang of, but after a few years they've more or less exhausted their possibilities for enhancement, and that might leave the programmer hankering after something a little more meaty.

By contrast to these other programming packages, Director's script engine, Lingo, is actually so powerful that you can use it to *permanently* modify Director files—or even create *new* Director files without using *any* of the items that are provided to you by Macromedia. (A Director file is a collection of text, graphics, and other interesting media objects, packaged with Lingo scripting, which is used by Director to put things onscreen—in short, a program.)

Note

A file made using Director is called a *movie,* and is to Director what a document file (such as a letter or term paper) is to a word processor program. This can be somewhat confusing out of context, because (for instance) things made in Flash and QuickTime are also called movies. In this text, when I use the term *movie* I am describing a program file made using Director, unless I explicitly say otherwise.

Such techniques are often referred to as working *on-the-fly*, meaning that you might start with only a set of commands you've created in Lingo, and end up with a complete Director movie you've made out of nothing at all. (That sounds pretty complicated, and believe me, it is. Don't worry; you won't have to tackle anything that involved here, but it might really intrigue you to know that you *can* do it. And once you're done with this book, you will have all the knowledge you need to begin experimenting along those lines yourself.)

When Lingo elevated its power over Director movies to its current level, at about version 4 of the Director program, the software became fractally more sophisticated than it had been in previous versions. (*Fractal* levels of sophistication are effectively bottomless—regardless of how deep you go, there's always more you can do.) Director was the first multimedia engine ever to allow self-altering code to this extent, and the concept of self-altering code is itself so involved that you can do entire doctoral dissertations in computer science on just *one* element of its implications. Prior to this change in the Director engine, no multimedia scripting environment that I know of afforded anything like this degree of power to its programmer (you, of course!).

Not bad for a "flash-and-glitz" engine that "just" uses scripting, that's "only" used to make games. (So much for *those* myths!)

With the modern Director engine, you can make something as simple as a text editor, as prosaic as a World Wide Web browser, as useful as a file indexer, as fun as a finger-painting program, or as thrilling as a 3-D action/adventure game. Furthermore, Director's power lets you include the ability to change these programs after you have written *and distributed* them, or even let the user make *his own* changes—and thus *permanently* alter the way the program runs. It is this combination of relative ease of use for the programmer added to a *lot* of power that can be made available to end users that I think is the single most exciting thing about Director.

So now that you're slavering after some of this power for yourself, it's time to break into the world of programming with Lingo and Director. We'll begin our foray by looking over the most obvious things you see when you run Director—the things you'll end up using the most.

Director's Primary "Physical" Tools

"Physical" tools are, for the purpose of this book, tools you can directly access, view, and manipulate on the screen using the mouse. I put the term *physical* in quotes because, of course, nothing that appears on your computer's screen is an actual real-world physical object, but you can often do things with it in a more or less straightforward fashion that feels like you're working with an actual physical object as opposed to just some stuff happening in memory. An example of a "physical" item of this type might be a program icon, a folder, or a document scroll bar.

Let's begin by looking over some of the most commonly used tools in the Director programming suite. We'll start with the most obvious ones you see when you run Director for the first time.

If you have not already done so, install, locate, and run your copy of Director now. If you do not have a copy yet, you can download a demo version of it for free right from Macromedia's Web site. (The demo expires in 30 days from its first use, and there's no way to unexpire it short of formatting your hard drive, so don't get a copy, install and run it, and then forget about it for a month; you'll be disappointed. The good news is that if you purchase the demo, you'll be the proud owner of a fully licensed version of Director and will be able to use it any time you like, for as long as you like, to make any programs you can imagine doing.)

The first time you run Director, you should see something a lot like what you see in Figure 1-1. This is the Macintosh version of Director. The Windows version has a similar appearance to it.

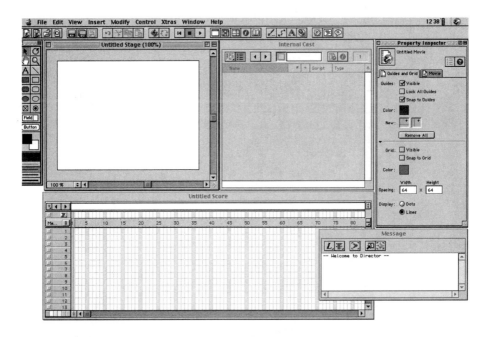

Figure 1-1   The first time you run Director, your screen should look a lot like this.

Indispensable Tools

We'll begin by studying the *indispensables*—the core set of Director tools, items you will want to have available onscreen at all times while you are working in Director, because you will be using them the most.

The Stage

The first thing you're likely to notice is a largish expanse of blank screen space toward the upper left of your computer's monitor. This space might remind you of the blank page a word processor starts with, or perhaps an empty canvas in a paint or drawing program. In reality it's a little of both, plus quite a few other things.

Figure 1-2 displays the Stage as it generally appears when you begin running Director: a sort of blank canvas awaiting your command to make things appear onscreen.

This *Stage* is Director's way of representing to you the space onscreen where your program will be visible to the user. Anything placed on the Stage will be visible to the user when the program you've created runs. In a way, it's

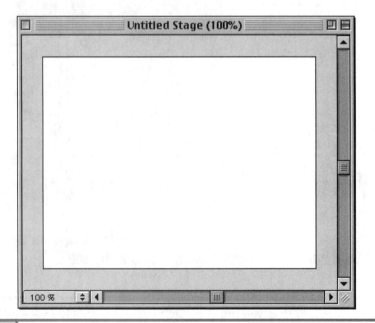

Figure 1-2 The Stage, where most of your program's functions take place onscreen

1

Director's model of the user's computer monitor, most often employed for just that purpose. You use the Stage in much the same way you would use a document window in a program such as Adobe's Illustrator: You create and place graphics, titles, interactive buttons, and so on with which your users will interact; the Stage is the place where—as far as users are concerned—your final program will happen on the computer's screen.

The Stage's name is rather apt; it does represent a place onscreen where you can add "actors" (which are actually Director Cast members—more on those soon) that perform or interact with the user in ways you can control, including such things as how far to the left or right they show up, how they are aligned relative to other Cast members on the Stage, and so on.

The performance you create may be nothing more interesting than simply having something animate from one part of the Stage to another, or it might be an intricate series of commands, which, once fully packaged by you for distribution, is indistinguishable from programs written using languages such as C++ or VisualBasic (except inasmuch as it didn't take you as long to make your program, and probably yours will be a lot more interesting visually).

It's important to understand that the Stage is not exactly meant to represent the end user's computer screen, but it often is used for that purpose. You can use the Stage to represent how your final program will look on your user's full-screen monitor, *or* you can use it to construct things that happen in a window on that monitor, *or* you can use it as a sort of animated drawing canvas to do things that happen in part of your user's screen while other things happen elsewhere on the screen (this last is often the way Shockwave files are created for use on the World Wide Web).

Right now, it's not so important to think of the Stage as being exactly equal to your user's monitor. It's better to think of it in terms of how you will present things to your user in a given space on the screen, regardless of *where* that space on the screen might end up.

What you do on the Stage is your choice.

1-Minute Drill

● What is a Director movie?

● What is the Stage for?

● A Director movie is any program file made using Director.

● The Stage is the place in Director where you do visual composition of your program, placing items such as text or images that will appear on your user's computer when he or she runs your program.

The Score

Underneath the Stage, you'll likely see a window stretching most of the way across your monitor, filled with many little blank rectangles, called *cells*. It will probably remind you, more than anything else, of a spreadsheet, though that is not exactly what it is. Figure 1-3 shows this window as it appears in Director.

This is the *Score,* the most direct means by which you control many aspects of your Director movies, including:

- The length of time something might appear on the Stage

- What actually does appear

- In what order things appear (both in terms of what comes before what, and what appears on top of something else)

- What happens when something is going to disappear

A simple way to think of the Score's relationship to the Stage is that the Stage controls *where* things happen on the screen, while the Score controls *how, when,* and in *what order* they happen.

Note how there are numbers in this Score, starting at 1 toward the upper left and increasing as you move down vertically. These are *channels,* which display, in inverted order, how things stack on top of each other onscreen.

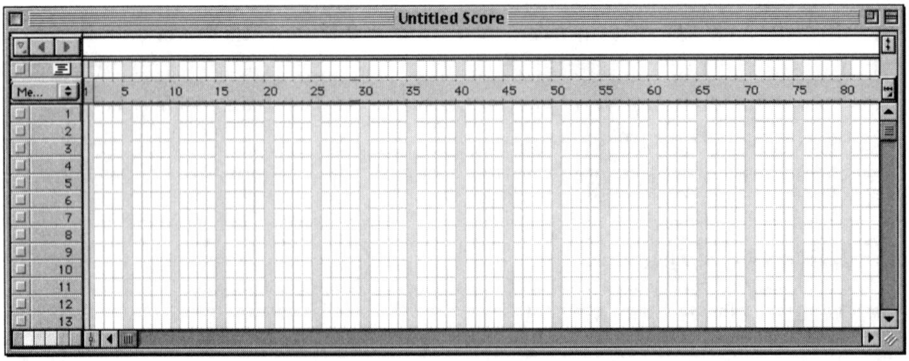

Figure 1-3   The Score, a visual way to understand layering and order in time in your Director files

Thus, a Cast member placed in channel 1 of the Score would appear *behind* another Cast member placed in channel 2. The member in channel 2 appears, onscreen, as being on *top* of the member in channel 1. (If you have used PhotoShop, this is very analogous to the way layers work in a PSD file, but inverted relative to the way they appear in PhotoShop's layer window.)

Tip

When you place a Cast member on the Stage, by the way, it is referred to as a *sprite.* That's not to confuse you. It's called a sprite because, way back when computers used 16KB of RAM and you had to *type* in all your commands to get anything done, items that were made to appear and animate onscreen as graphics were called sprites. Thus, Director's sprites are directly conceptually linked to their ancestors from the Dinosaur Age of computing, also known as the 1970s and 80s. Welcome to Jurassic Programming Park.

Note another set of numbers starting at 1 toward the upper left and increasing as you move to the right in the Score. These are *frames,* which can be understood to represent and control the flow of *time* in a Director program. Generally, something placed in frame 1 of the Score will appear, in time, before something placed in frame 2; if you think of it in movie terms, where 24 frames of pictures taken in rapid succession compose one second of projected image, frame 1 of the Score is like frame 1 of the film, frame 2 of the score can be seen as being frame 2 of the film, and so on.

You can also use frames to create animations, making things move across the screen by controlling where they first appear on the Stage itself, then changing that location in a different frame, causing the item to move across the screen as you go from frame to frame.

You will probably also note a red rectangle sitting over frame 1 on a gray bar near the top of the Score window. This is the *playback head,* which is Director's way of showing you which specific frame of your Score is currently being displayed on the Stage.

Figure 1-4 illustrates frame numbers (the numbers across the top of the Score), channel numbers (the numbers to the left), and the position of the playback head (which frame in your Director movie is currently being displayed). In the background you can see the Stage, with a text sprite placed on it. The bar-shaped item in the Score represents that sprite as it appears on the Stage.

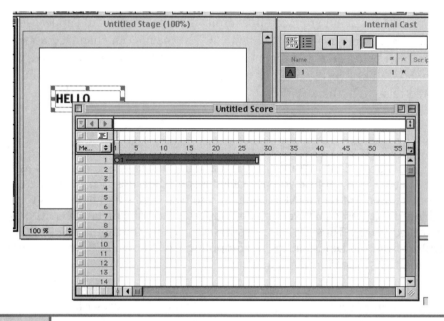

Figure 1-4   Key Score components, including frame numbers, channel numbers, and the playback head

You can make the playback head jump from one frame to another by clicking the gray bar over the frame you want. You can also drag the playback head back and forth to force Director to manually move from frame to frame; this is one great way to preview animations you're making right as you're making them.

Another thing you should understand is that, while frames in the Score can represent frames in animation, you do not have to place a sprite on the Stage 24 times in a row in order to make it appear for one second on the screen. Later in this book, we'll get into the idea of setting *tempo*, or how fast an animation plays, and we'll also learn a *lot* about how the Score is *not* like movie film. For instance, you can make your Director program "pause" on a single frame in the Score for as long as you need to, until the user clicks a button or does something else to make the program continue running; you can also make Director jump from one frame to another, completely different one. The Score is not just a time line. It is actually a very powerful tool for controlling user experience and program operation.

For now, it's most important for you to understand that, generally, what appears in frame 1 of the Score will show up on the Stage *before* what appears in frame 2, that what appears in frame 2 will show up before the contents of frame 3, and so on.

1-Minute Drill

- What is a sprite?
- What elements of the Score represent time?
- Does an item in channel 2 of the Score appear on top of or underneath an item in channel 1?

The Cast

To the right of the Stage (probably) is another blank window calling itself the *Cast*. The Cast window is really very little more than a database, but it's not like the kind you might have used to look up someone's phone number. This database can contain things such as rich text, images, sounds, and Lingo script elements, all of which you bring together in the Score to present on the Stage. (As you can see, Macromedia has carried the Director-as-a-moviemaker metaphor right through a lot of the principal tools—Stage, Score, Cast, script.... Even Director files, saved to disk, are referred to as *movies*. Are you beginning to feel like Steven Spielberg yet?)

Figure 1-5 shows you what the Cast window will look like the first time you run Director.

The Cast is kind of a bucket into which you can drop pretty much anything—any kind of file Director can recognize—and from which you can grab things to put into your Score (and thus onto your Stage).

Once you've put a file into the Cast (or created a Cast item yourself using Director's built-in tools), it is available to you to use anywhere you want to in your Director file, as many times as you want to use it in that file, and to a very great degree you can control almost every aspect of its existence, both as a file in the Cast and as an entity (*sprite,* remember?) on the Stage.

If you want a Cast member to be a sprite on the Stage in different places, by the way, you do not have to make multiple copies of it in the Cast. All you have to do is place it right on your Stage wherever and whenever you want it to appear;

- A sprite is any item (button, graphic, text) placed on Director's Stage.
- Frames represent time. They begin at 1, farthest to the left, and increase horizontally.
- Channels represent space or stacking layers, starting at the top with 1, which is the lowest channel. Thus, an item placed in channel 2 would appear to be layered on top of something in channel 1.

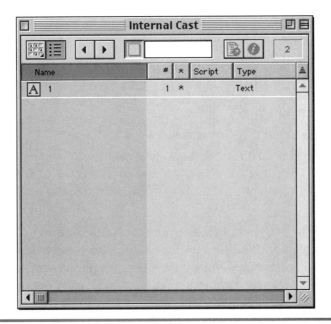

Figure 1-5 The Cast, where you store the items you'll be placing on the Stage in your Director file

you can actually use the same Cast member as a sprite an essentially unlimited number of times in a given Director program. And if you remove that sprite from the Stage, it's still there in the Cast, waiting for you to use it again.

The best way to think of the Cast might be in terms of your kitchen "junk drawer." You can throw pretty much anything into it, and by pulling something out and putting it on the counter you can make arrangements of things like paring knives, apple corers, tape dispensers, candles, or just about anything else you want to use.

Note

The kinds of files Director can recognize automatically is a constantly growing list. The ones most commonly used are bitmaps (images such as JPEGs); digital video (such as QuickTime or AVI movie files); sound files (such as WAV, AIFF, or MP3); Flash files (these must currently be SWF format, not FLA); and several varieties of text, namely RTF, HTML, and "plain vanilla" ASCII. Your Director manual will include a complete list of the kinds of files that Director can import into your Cast; consult that book for more information.

I'd like you to look at your Cast window now. Toward the upper left, odds are that you will see a little square box that looks like a tiny view of a bullet list, and it probably appears recessed into the Cast window frame. This is to indicate to you that your Cast window is currently in *list* view. (If you leave your cursor over this icon for a moment, you should see a ToolTip appear containing the words "Cast View Style.")

I'd like you to click that so that your Cast window turns into a bunch of numbered square boxes. (If your Cast window already looks like that, you're okay.) I'll discuss the reasons for this in Part 2, but for now understand that you can *toggle* (or change) your Cast view to be either a list, like what you see in a folder list view on your computer, or an icon view, which is (to my mind) a more effective way to actually organize your Cast members.

1-Minute Drill

● What is the main purpose of the Cast?

● What kinds of media can you store in the Cast?

The tools given you in the Cast, Score, and Stage hold, among them, the answers to all the basic questions for putting things onscreen and turning them into a program: *who* (Cast members), *what* (the kind of Cast member it is), *when* (location in the Score), *where* (location on the Stage, channel position in the Score), and *how* (order of appearance, actions taken onscreen, etc.).

You can move all the tools around onscreen and set them up any way you like, and you can make any of them disappear (you can always make them reappear later) if they are getting in the way. For the time being, I don't advise you to do that. Wait until we get into Part 2 before you start making substantial changes in your tool layout; by then you'll have a pretty good idea what items you're using the most, where you're most comfortable having them, and how to relate them to each other in the Director programming environment.

● The Cast is a sort of catch-all container in which you store all the media types supported by your copy of Director. These types can include QuickTime files, images, text, sounds, and so on. Your Lingo scripts are also stored in the Cast. The items stored in the Cast are available for you to use throughout your Director file.

● You can store any media type Director supports in your Cast. Out of the box, this includes several digital video formats, several sound formats, several text formats, and several image formats. Flash files can also be added to the Cast.

One More Indispensable

The final indispensable tool you *must* have at *all* times when working with Director is the Lingo manual. That book (two books, for Director 8.5; the second one does not merely describe what's new, as its title implies) is far more than simply a dictionary of all the Lingo commands, keywords, and other functions you can use; it is also a pretty thorough encyclopedia, which documents—not always perfectly, granted, but overall quite well—the methods for *using* those Lingo commands, and which often includes examples of those commands in operation (though the examples, if you are still new at programming, might actually confuse you *more* than the explanations given!).

The Lingo manual is there for you to read, consult, abuse, mark, note, underline, and draw in, and I fully expect you to get into the habit of referring to it with great regularity. If you have not already done so, take a few minutes now to look through it and become familiar with its general layout and means of presenting information to you. By the time you're done with *this* book, you'll also be pretty familiar with that one—I guarantee it.

Looking at that manual now, you might feel like experimenting with some of the Lingo commands you see in there, and find that you encounter a lot of script error messages when you try to use them in Director. This is because the example code presented in the Lingo manuals is actually a terse form of notation, intended to be read and assimilated by someone with a foregone experience with Lingo (ideally) or at least programming using something other than BASIC. In that sense, the examples are like algebraic formulas.

For instance, if you know that, in a right triangle, the square root of the sum of the squares of the shorter sides equals the length of the hypotenuse, the Pythagorean theorem $a^2 + b^2 = c^2$ makes perfect sense. Furthermore, in examples that show this formula in use, little explanation is required, because there is an assumption you understand the fundamental tenet.

Of course, if the word *hypotenuse* makes you think of a big fat river-dwelling mammal, you're hosed.

Well, the Lingo manual is written from this same understanding: that you have enough basic experience with programming in general—and Lingo in particular—that the examples given make sense to you. What you see in the examples is there just to show you general usage guidelines; it is not meant to describe how you work it from keyword to literal.

If you're new, the explanations probably won't be very illuminating, and that's no reason to feel inferior or frustrated. That's why you have this book, why you have *me*—to get you to the point that the Lingo documentation as

1

produced by Macromedia actually makes sense to you, or at least doesn't appear to be total Greek.

However, if you swear you are using your Lingo correctly, and the docs may be in error, you might be right. The Lingo manual is, after all, written by humans and so cannot always be entirely correct. There are Web sites dedicated to highlighting and correcting errata and lacunae in the Lingo documentation. Those sites are worth a surf if your tail is really in a crack.

The Almost-Indispensables

From our whirlwind tour of the Director gotta-haves, we move on to the things you'll use enough that it behooves you to both be aware of and make space for them on your monitor.

While, by and large, you do not *have* to have these items around every minute of every day you're programming in Director, I use them frequently enough that I think I can safely advise you to keep them handy.

The Control Panel

This probably is not open right now on your Director program screen, so select it via Window | Control Panel to make it appear. Figure 1-6 displays this Control Panel.

It looks a lot like the control buttons you might see on a VCR, doesn't it? Here is a description of the major function buttons. As you point your mouse to these three buttons in the Control Panel, you will see a ToolTip appear naming each one.

- **Rewind** This moves Director's Score playback head to frame 1 in your Score. It "rewinds" your Director movie to its beginning.

- **Stop** This stops your Director movie playback. It also (in most cases) terminates execution of any Lingo scripts that might be running at that

Figure 1-6 The Control Panel

point, as well as exiting any *breakpoints* that might have appeared in the Debugger. In Module 5, we'll explore the Debugger in great depth.

● **Play**   This begins playback of your Director movie starting from whatever frame the playback head is currently on. (It does not start over from the beginning; to do that, click Rewind first, then Play.)

The Tool Palette

Toward the left edge of your screen you should see a tall, skinny box filled with hieroglyphs. This is called the Tool Palette, though the number of really relevant programming tools that remain on it has dropped considerably with Director revisions. That's not to say Macromedia has removed anything from it; quite to the contrary. However, over the last several version releases, enough enhancements have taken place to other aspects of Director that this palette of items has fallen somewhat into disuse. Figure 1-7 shows what the Tool Palette looks like in Director.

Figure 1-7   The Tool Palette, home for lots of the basic items used in making sprites appear on the Stage

1

Ask the Expert

Question   If no one really uses these tools much any more, why have them around?

Answer   They're still very useful. While the button and line controls you find there, for instance, are not especially sophisticated by modern terms, they are still quite functional, and if you need to rough out a quick and dirty interface as a proof-of-concept that something you have in mind is even technically feasible, the items in the Tool Palette are probably the first things you'll grab.

Another common use for Tool Palette objects is as *placeholders*—items that take space on your Stage (and Cast, and Score) meant to be occupied later by more-finished-looking images or files created by professional graphic artists.

This is a great strength of Director, in fact. By using placeholders in this fashion, you're *theoretically* able to write the logic and structure of your entire program before your client has even selected a color scheme. That's a great way to get ahead of the curve.

Placeholders also allow you to show your client a working model of your program in its early design stages, which can help you isolate potential trouble spots in your design before they become "hard-coded" into graphics expensively made.

Finally, it's a good way to show your client that you *are* making progress on the program he's paying you a lot of money to create.

Most of the items you can click in the Tool Palette represent things you can place on your Stage, such as buttons, text and field items, and other shapes. Some of them, however, represent things you use to manipulate sprites that already exist on your Stage.

The icons in the Tool Palette, by the way, affect your cursor only when it is over the Stage. They don't change it anyplace else, because the Tool Palette is meant only to apply to the Stage.

From upper left to the right, then down, these icons represent the following:

Arrow Cursor   Select this item in the Tool Palette to turn your computer's cursor into the standard arrow pointer. This is particularly useful if you have chosen one of the other items from the Tool Palette and want to turn your cursor back to normal.

Rotate and Skew Tool   If you've selected a sprite on the Stage by clicking it with the arrow cursor, and you then select this tool, your mouse pointer will change to a circle when it is over the selected sprite, and to a parallelogram when it's over the sprite's edge.

When the cursor is circle-shaped, clicking and dragging your sprite will cause it to *rotate* on the Stage. When the cursor is a parallelogram, clicking and dragging the edge of the sprite will cause it to *skew*, or slant.

This is a fun tool. Until Director 7 was released, there was absolutely no way to make sprites rotate or skew "live"—that is, right on the Stage. You had to go through a rather involved series of steps with the Cast in order to make something like this happen.

This tool won't work in the same way with all sprites. For instance, you can't rotate or skew Flash sprites, and you can't rotate or skew digital video sprites. Furthermore some sprites don't look very good when they're rotated or skewed, particularly images (such as JPEGs) or anything containing text.

Hand Tool   Use this to drag the Stage around when you need to change the part of the Stage you can see in its window. (You'd use this in place of the scrollbars that normally appear alongside the edges of the Stage.)

When you click this tool, your mouse pointer changes to a hand when it's over the Stage. Clicking then will let you "grab" the entire Stage and drag it around in its window.

This is especially useful in conjunction with the zoom tool.

Zoom Tool   Click this, then click the Stage, to magnify the view. OPTION-click (Mac) or ALT-click (Windows) to zoom out.

Why zoom in or out on the Stage? For many of the same reasons you'd zoom in or out in a paint program, or a graphics editor such as FireWorks or PhotoShop: to enlarge your view to the point you can see individual pixels. Such views are quite useful for aligning sprites onscreen, for instance, or zooming out and getting a sort of "wide angle" view of your overall layout.

Note

Pixel means picture element, and represents the tiniest point of light your computer can "paint" to the screen. There are about 72 of them per inch on a standard computer display—both across and down. If you do the math, you'll find this means there are 5184 individual pixels in each square inch of computer display. (Well, more or less. In Module 7, we'll find out that this is one of those rules of thumb that often gets mashed by the hammer of reality, as it were.) When you've zoomed in on the Stage, you'll see those pixels in a magnified form as large blocks.

Text Tool   Click this and your mouse pointer changes again, this time to a large crosshair. Click and drag across the Stage to create a rectangle there. Into this rectangle, you can enter any text you wish.

If you try this now, you will see the rectangle appear on the Stage, you will see an item appear in your Cast window, *and* you will see a bar appear in the Score that will probably fill 28 frames.

This is because by making a text sprite appear on the Stage, you have automatically caused it to appear in channel 1 of the Score (with a *span,* or duration, of 28 frames). Furthermore, since your text sprite has to be stored someplace in the program (other than just on the Stage), Director has created a slot for it in your Cast.

To enter text, you can either double-click the rectangle on the Stage or double-click the Cast slot that the text sprite is occupying in your Cast. If you double-click the item in your Cast, a window will open that resembles nothing more than it does a regular word processing window.

There is a lot you can do with text, and we'll revisit this powerful tool many times throughout this book.

Line Tool   As you may well guess, you use this tool to draw lines on the Stage. Click and drag to draw a straight line in any direction you like. SHIFT-click and drag to constrain the line to 45° diagonals.

Rectangle Tools   These (both the square-cornered and rounded varieties) allow you to draw a basic rectangular shape on the Stage, much as you did when you made a rectangle with the text tool. The rectangles can be filled with a solid color or pattern, or they can be hollow boxes.

Click and drag to define the rectangle. SHIFT-click and drag to constrain the shape to be a square instead.

Ellipse Tools   Similar to the rectangle tools, these tools let you draw an oval onscreen. You SHIFT-click and drag to make circles with these tools.

Checkbox Tool   This tool allows you to create a simple control on your Stage, a *checkbox*. (You've seen these in programs before. Anytime you check items in a computer screen, you're using checkboxes.)

Radio Button Tool   *Radio buttons* are so named because they usually come in groups, and only one can be selected at a time from a given group. In this way, they work like the buttons on car dashboard radios.

   Both the checkbox and radio button tools allow you to enter text to use as a *label*—a brief definition of the function or meaning of the control. We'll be using these controls in Part 4 of this book..

Field Tool   This one might get confusing. You click the field tool button to define a space on the Stage where you can enter text.

   Déjà vu!

   In this sense, the field tool and the text tool appear to behave in the same fashion, but they are in fact almost entirely unrelated.

Ask the Expert

Question   Why have two different tools that seem to do exactly the same thing?

Answer   Because they only *seem* to do the same thing. Field Cast members are quite different from text Cast members in many ways.

   Originally, you could only make field Cast members; this changed with the introduction of Director 6, when the text Cast member made its debut.

   Text members allow you to make use of both rich text and HTML-style text, and, in fact, if you copy and paste HTML code into a text Cast member, it will even let you use *hyperlinks*—those colored text labels that let you know to click a word or phrase to make something happen.

Field members basically give you plain old letters, numbers, and words, without all the fancy styling or functionality of either RTF or HTML text.

In Part 2, we'll look into this in depth. To sum it up now, a field Cast member is to a text Cast member as a program like WordPad or SimpleText is to Microsoft Word or Corel WordPerfect. One is used for relatively basic operations, while the other is a pretty fancy package with which you can accomplish a lot more. (Also, field members take less space on disk and less memory to draw to screen than text members.) Because of this, and because you can do different things with the field tool and with the text tool, Macromedia left both in the Tool Palette.

To minimize confusion, I will use the special terms *#text* to indicate a text Cast member, and *#field* to indicate a field Cast member. I use the pound sign because this is the way the Director program itself refers to these Cast member types. For this reason, when I refer to #text members, I am speaking of items made using the text tool item, just as #field members are made using the field tool item.)

This is important because—again—#text and #field Cast members are not the same, and with very few exceptions, the Lingo script commands you use with them and the things you can do with them are discrete.

Button Tool   As its name implies, you use this tool to define regular buttons on your Stage. You type the label right into the button, and when you click it, some script or other you've entered is executed.

Foreground and Background Color Chips   You use these to define foreground (line or border) colors and background (fill) colors for lines and shapes you have made on your Stage.

To use these chips, click a shape or line sprite on your Stage, then click one of the color chips. A color selection palette will pop up, letting you pick the color you like for your shape.

If you've clicked a shape that has no fill, the background color chip will have no effect on that shape.

You can also define custom colors in the selection pop-up.

To change the foreground and background colors in a #text or #field member, double-click the member's sprite on the Stage to activate it, and then drag your mouse across the text whose color you want changed. You can now set those colors too, using the color selection chips.

Ask the Expert

Question Why do I have only about 300 colors to choose from? My computer is supposed to be able to show *millions!*

Answer Director's approach, since it was created, has been to use *palletized* color, meaning you have a palette of predefined system-standard colors from which you can choose. Over the years, of course, computer displays have come a long way, but Director still uses this palletized approach in its default color selection windows.

In Part 2, we'll explore color palettes more and discuss ways you can work with them.

Pattern Selector You use this as you would the color chips on your shape sprites. You can choose a fill pattern here, from lines to dots to a 50 percent *scrim* (one pixel the foreground color, the next the background color) and so on.

Line Thickness Tools Use these to set the thickness of lines and of shape borders. The dotted line at the top means no border. To change the border thickness on a shape, first click the shape and then click the thickness tool you want.

1-Minute Drill

● What tools would you use to place words on the Stage?

● How do you move the Stage's view around?

● How do you rotate or skew a sprite?

● The #text and #field tools.
● Either select the hand tool and use it to drag the Stage, or use the Stage scrollbars.
● First select the sprite, then the rotate and skew tool. When the cursor is over the sprite, it becomes circular and you can drag the sprite to rotate it; when the cursor is over the sprite's edge, it becomes a parallelogram and you can drag the sprite to skew it.

1

The Debugger

In the Bad Old Days, before version 6, when your Lingo scripts began malfunctioning it could get really hard to figure out how and why, because there was no ready way to pause the program scripts and step through them line by line to see how they were operating, what variables were changing, and so on.

This changed completely when Macromedia introduced the Debugger, quite probably the single most useful innovation made to the program with version 6.

I must confess that I did not like it at first. I thought it was more confusing than other methods I had (such as using the **put** command to send output to Director's Message window—more on that following), and I didn't really know how to make use of it fully.

Now I look back and think I was probably nuts.

It *is* confusing, but it is also extremely powerful, and that is why I've devoted all of Module 5 to discussing the Debugger window.

This is another one that probably will not be present when you first run Director. To make it appear, select Window | Debugger and give it a once-over.

Don't worry too much about any of the icons you see or what they mean, but let your mouse hover over each of them for a few moments and look at the ToolTip names that appear. The ones you will probably use most are the *script stepping* buttons and the *go to handler* button.

Figure 1-8 shows what the Debugger looks like when you first open it.

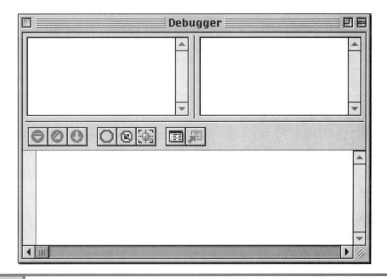

Figure 1-8   The Debugger

The Property Inspector

The Property Inspector (PI) is a very handy way to get at a lot of the *properties*—attributes—of many of the things you'll be using in Director, from the "movie" (Director file) itself to the most miniscule placements of sprites on your Stage.

As you click different windows, Cast members, and sprites in Director, you'll note that the information presented to you in the Property Inspector changes. Here you get lots of feedback about the characteristics of the indicated thing, and here too you can set all sorts of options.

Rather than try to introduce you to and describe all the variable items in the Property Inspector right at this moment, I'll point things out as we go along, letting you know when and how you can view and set various attributes in the Property Inspector. This is because there really is a lot of ground to cover there, and I don't want this first module to be 200 pages long. (Neither, I'm guessing, do you.)

To make things easier on all of us, from now on I will refer to the Property Inspector simply as the PI in this text.

Figure 1-9 shows one view you can get in the Property Inspector.

The Message Window

The Message window is not a way for you to retrieve e-mail; rather, it is something you can use to send messages to and retrieve messages from Director as it's executing your Lingo scripts.

The Message window can be a very handy way to get a sense of what your program is doing while it's running, can be used to test single lines of Lingo code, and can be a way to preview more complex functions you've created in a script window.

The Message window is another one you don't normally have open when Director first loads. You can get to it by selecting Window | Message. Figure 1-10 shows you the Message window.

Go ahead and open the Message window now. I'm going to help you make Director perform a silly trick with it.

Click in the text area of the Message window, so you see a blinking line cursor. Into it type the following text:

```
ALERT "Hello, world!"
```

You need to use the main keyboard's RETURN key because in Director it has different functionality from the keyboard's ENTER key.

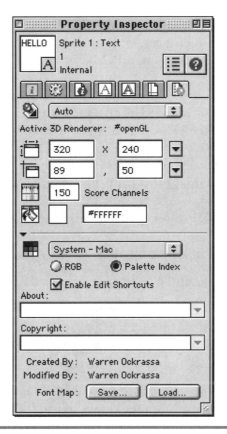

Figure 1-9 The Property Inspector displaying movie properties

Figure 1-10 The Message window

What just happened? A window appeared on the screen. (In technical terms, this is known as a *dialog box.*) It should contain a triangular yellow icon with an exclamation point in it, a button labeled OK, and the text you entered in the Message window.

I'd like you to take note of something. While the dialog box appeared, the text it displayed was *not* surrounded by quotation marks, and surely you noticed it didn't have the word *ALERT* in it. This is because the word ALERT is a Lingo *keyword*—a special term used to give commands directly to Director's Lingo *interpreter,* the part of Director that reads commands you have entered as script and interprets them into things that happen on your computer's screen. What follows in quotation marks is a *string,* or a line of text.

What happens inside Director's Lingo interpreter is something like this:

1. You type in **ALERT**, followed by a brief quoted sentence, and press RETURN.

2. The interpreter looks at the text you just entered before pressing RETURN.

3. The interpreter sees that the text begins with a keyword, in this case **ALERT**. This causes the interpreter to say to itself, "Aha, I'm supposed to put up an alert dialog box, containing whatever string of text my programmer has entered for me to read right after this keyword."

4. The interpreter then looks at the rest of the line and sees an opening pair of quotation marks. At this point, it says to itself, "This is the beginning of the stuff I'm supposed to put into the dialog box."

5. It then looks for a pair of closing quotes. When it finds them, it says, "Okay, this is all the text."

6. The interpreter then packages your string into information that it displays when it places the dialog box onscreen.

Now I'd like you to get back into the Message window and remove the final pair of quotation marks, then press RETURN again.

What happened this time? You got a *script error* message. This is because Director's Lingo interpreter was looking for a final pair of quotes to indicate your string was closed, that you had no more for it to put onscreen. It didn't find those quotes, and so it got confused.

You will see a similar message if you remove the opening pair of quotes instead of the closing pair. This is because quotation marks are, in the Lingo interpreter, *string delimiters*—they indicate to the interpreter where the beginning and end of a given string are meant to be. Without those string delimiters, Lingo will try to interpret text you enter as being programming instructions (variables, keywords, and so on).

I mention this because it's sometimes easy to forget to add the quotes when you're entering text for Director to display onscreen like this, particularly if you're unsure *why* you even have to in the first place, or *when*.

A handy way to remember is that, in writing, anything enclosed in quotation marks is meant to be understood as being a literal, direct quote—something read and presented as literal content, not subject to interpretation.

Similarly, when you are entering text into Director scripts like this, what you're telling the program is "Take this as a literal thing. Don't interpret it. Don't try to do any programming with it."

Often, quoted text like ours is referred to as a *string literal*. You should note, by the way, that these string literals are defined using double quotation marks (")—not by using two single quotation marks in a row ("). If you do the latter, Director will not understand at all what you intend.

Tip

You might have learned that you can use l and O in place of 1 and 0. While that works for typing, it does not work in programming. This is because the computer-level interpretations of these symbols, called ANSI (or ASCII) values, are very discrete from each other. The computer sees them as ell and oh, not one and zero. So if that's a habit you got into at some point in the past, it's time to break it.

Ask the Expert

Question   I see you've entered the Lingo keyword "alert" in all caps. Do I have to do that, too?

Answer   No. To a large extent Lingo is not *case-sensitive*—it doesn't usually care whether things you type in go in UPPERCASE, lowercase, or Anything eLSE.

However, I've always used the convention of entering the **ALERT** keyword in all caps. This is because it is entirely possible for a program to become alert-happy: to require so much user interaction from standing dialog boxes—which often completely interrupt the user's flow of work—as to be almost impossible to employ in a productive fashion. (In general, I keep keywords initially lowercase to distinguish them from any custom terms I've entered myself.)

Think about it. If you're concentrating hard on some work you're doing, and the program you're using keeps kicking up a bunch of dialog boxes you have to read and respond to before you can continue, don't you get to the point where you say to the machine, "Enough already! Shut up and let me get some work done!"?

Well, I surely do.

How this relates to entering *ALERT* versus *alert* is simple. If it is inconvenient for you, as a programmer, to remember this little rule in coding your **ALERT** dialog boxes, odds are pretty good you'll think about whether you really *need* them when you're writing a program.

Remember, with an **ALERT** dialog in Director, everything your user—and your program—was doing grinds to a complete halt until he or she responds to it.

Earlier I mentioned the **put** keyword. Here's a chance to try it out now. Into the Message window, type

```
put "Hello, World!"
```

and press RETURN.

That was sure exciting, wasn't it? But what you just saw was an example of how you can send messages through the Message window. This is one way to peek into your Lingo scripts while they're running.

For example, if you're unsure what the *value* of a variable might be—in other words, if you're not sure what a given variable might have in it at some point—you can use the **put** keyword in your script at that point to cause Director to place that variable's contents into the Message window.

1-Minute Drill

- What is one way to make Director display text on the screen?
- How do you define a string literal in Director?
- Look up the terms **ALERT** and **put** in your Lingo dictionary.

What's Left?

There are doubtless other tools you've noticed included in your copy of Director. These include:

- The Vector window, used for creating and editing vector shapes. A *vector shape* is a form of computer graphics that uses mathematical formulae to define areas on the screen that are meant to be filled with color. Vector shapes generally look smoother onscreen than bitmap graphics such as JPEGs.

- The Paint window, used for creating or editing bitmap images in your Cast. If you import a JPEG into your Cast, for instance, you can open and change it in the Paint window.

- The Real window, used for previewing content made using Real Media, a format for delivering highly compressed audio and video over the Internet.

Additionally, there is a pretty complete suite of tools used for creating, importing, and modifying 3-D content. I'd love to be able to take you through that, but unfortunately it's beyond the scope of this book.

- There are two ways we covered via Lingo, to use either an **ALERT** or a **put** statement. You can also place a #text or #field sprite on the Stage and enter text into it directly.
- String literals are delimited by opening and closing double quotation marks.

Fortunately, James Newton has written an advanced guide for Director users that covers all the 3-D tools and commands you have available to you, so that's probably the book you're going to want to read after this one!

Of course by the time you've finished with this text, you'll be ready to tackle his.

Project 1-1: Creating a Classic Program

Finally! You get to take some of your new skills and create a program!

Traditionally, the program used to introduce a programming language is called "Hello, World," because that is what you make the computer say. It doesn't sound especially fascinating, nor very practical, but it's still got its uses.

With our "Hello, World," we will use several of the Tool Palette tools we covered in this module. We'll also step through the basic steps needed for compiling a program—creating a simple, ready-to-run application that can work on your computer without needing to run inside Director.

The goals for this project are as follows:

- Understand how to use the text tool and the button tool.

- Create a simple set of Lingo scripts.

- Understand how to create a stand-alone program.

Step-by-Step

1. Open a new Director file. Do this by selecting File | New | Movie.

2. Click the #text icon in the Tool Palette. (This is the icon with the A in it, not the word *field*.)

3. Drag your cursor across the Stage to create a rectangle for your #text sprite.

4. Double-click the Cast member (not the sprite on the Stage) that was just created. At the top of the member's window, there is a space where you can type in a name. Type in *hello*.

Tip

You use member names to refer to items in the Cast window through your Lingo programming. You can name members almost anything you want, but beware of having two or more members with the same names. If that happens and you later use member names in your Lingo, Director will grab the first member it finds that has that name. This can definitely lead to headaches.

5. Close the #text Cast member window, and click the button tool on the Tool Palette.

6. Drag this across the Stage to create a button.

7. If you do not see a flashing text insertion cursor blinking in the middle of the button sprite, double-click the button sprite to activate it, and type in the word **Quit**.

8. Your button Cast member should now be in Cast position two. Click once on that Cast member, then click the *script icon* in the upper-right portion of the Cast window frame. The script icon looks like a little white sheet of paper with tiny lines of text on it, and a little arrow in a circle in the lower-right corner.

9. A *script window* opens automatically, containing the following text. There should be a cursor blinking between the lines:

```
on mouseUp

end
```

10. Where the cursor is blinking between the two lines in the script window, type **quit** and close the script window by clicking its close box. What you have just done is define a *mouse event,* meaning that when the user clicks your quit button (**on mouseUp**), the program will quit running (**quit**).

11. Double-click the first cell above the gray frame number bar in the Score window.

12. Another script window will open, containing text like this:

```
on exitFrame me

end
```

13. Again, where the cursor is blinking between these lines, type *go to the frame* and close the script window. This is a *frame event,* and it tells Director that, as it's playing your file, each time it comes to the end of this specific frame (**on exitFrame**), it should *return* to that very same frame (**go to the frame**). This is one way you can "pause" your Director file so that playback remains on a given frame until the user does something to make a change. (We'll get to the term **me** later.)

14. You should now have three items in your Cast: an empty #text member that you have named *hello,* a *quit* button with a script attached, and a slot where your frame script is being kept. Your program is almost, but not quite, finished; you want to put some text into the #text member, don't you? This is where the programming really starts to get interesting!

15. Click the empty Cast member at position number 4 in your Cast window, and then select Window | Script. A new script window will open, called "Movie Script 4." Into this window, type the following:

```
on startMovie
 member("hello").text = "Hello, World!"
end
```

16. Close this script window as well. What you have just done is tell Director that, when the program first loads (**on startMovie**), it is to take the string literal "Hello, World!" and put it into the Cast member named "hello." (More accurately, it is to set the *text* contents of that Cast member to "hello"; there are quite a few attributes you can set with a #text member, not just the actual text it contains. Those attributes include color, font, location on screen, and more.)

?—*Ask the Expert*

Question What does *member("hello").text* mean, anyway?

Answer This is a perfect example of one of the more convoluted script styles of Director, *dot syntax.* Briefly, it can be thought of in terms of *big thing.little thing.tiny thing,* where *big thing* is the main category, *little thing* is a subcategory of the big thing, and *tiny thing* is another subcomponent of the big thing, in the little thing group.

If you keep extensive tax records, you might have a drawer containing everything for 2000. In that drawer, you might have a folder for a given month, within which is another folder for charitable donations, and in that charitable donations folder, you might have receipts for that given month.

So if you want to tell someone where a specific receipt is, the long version might be "The charity receipt to the Old Programmers' Home, for March of 2000"; the dot-syntax version of that would be "2000.March.Charity.Old Programmers' Home." It is inferred by context that you are describing the location of a receipt.

In our preceding example script, you could also type

the text of member "hello" = "Hello, World!"

but the dot syntax version is shorter and is also more likely the type you'll find in use in others' Director files.

17. Now that you have entered your Movie script code, click the Rewind button on the Control Panel, then click the Play button. You should have seen the words *Hello, World!* appear in the #text member onscreen.

18. Select File | Save and name your file something useful, probably "hello.dir." Save it someplace convenient, where you can get to it later on.

Tip

The *.dir* is a *file extension,* used to denote that this is a Director file. It might seem confusing or unnecessary to you to use extensions like this if you're on a Mac, but it's really pretty useful once you get the hang of it, since there is never any ambiguity when you're looking at a file regarding what program was made to use it.

19. Now select File | Create Projector... and locate the hello.dir file you just saved. Select it in the left-hand side of the dialog box and click Add, then click the Options... button. In the projector options screen, click the Center checkbox and, for Macintosh, uncheck the Use System Temporary Memory option. (System temporary memory, a Mac-only option, is really for the system, not programs, and a good-sized Director program can end up taking up a lot of memory that it shouldn't, so it's probably best to leave this option permanently unselected.)

20. Click the Create... button. Note that Director has given the program a *default* name, Projector. I changed mine to Hello! instead, because I think it's a nicer name. Once you've given your program a name, click the Save button.

21. Director will begin creating the projector. Once it's finished, it will be a self-contained, *stand-alone* program that can run on any computer of your platform type. (Thus, if you create a projector on a Mac, you can run it on other Macs; if you do it on Windows, the projector will work on other Windows machines, even if they don't already have a copy of Director installed.)

22. Quit Director, locate your "Hello" projector, and double-click it. Congratulations! You've rolled your own program!

Project Summary

To summarize, you have just

- Created a #text member with *variable* content, meaning that your Lingo programming controls what will be put into that #text member. Naturally, you do not have to make text appear onscreen in this fashion. You could just as easily have typed the words into the Cast member yourself and forgotten about all that *startMovie* stuff. But where's the fun in that?

- Created a *quit* button that does exactly what you expect it to do.

- Created a Director file that loads and remains on a specified frame until the user does something to make that change.

- Made a stand-alone, self-contained program.

☑ *Mastery Check* ───────

1. Do movies created in Director work on Macintosh only, Windows only, or both?

   _____

   _____

2. Define projector and movie, and describe their differences.

   _____

   _____

3. Define the Stage, the Score, and the Cast, and describe their purposes in creating programs.

   _____

   _____

4. Define frames and channels, and describe their uses.

   _____

   _____

5. Describe one method for getting words to appear on the Director Stage. (This is not the same thing as using **ALERT**!)

   _____

   _____

6. Name at least two Lingo keywords and describe their uses.

   _____

   _____

7. Describe the basic steps required to create a simple, stand-alone program in Director.

   _____

   _____

Module 2

The Library Palette

The Goals of this Module

- Become familiar with Director's Library Palette
- Learn what a *behavior* is
- Learn how to use the behaviors in the Library Palette
- Learn how to modify the behavior library yourself

D irector's complexity—as you have probably discovered by now—necessarily prevents it from being immediately usable if you're unfamiliar with programming. For this reason, Macromedia introduced the Library Palette with version 6. Now that you've gotten your feet wet with simple scripting, it's time to explore this tool further.

Director's Library Palette

In the last module, you learned that quite a few tools are available for your use in Director, tools intended to make your job as a programmer easier.

To this suite of tools we can add the Library Palette, an innovation first brought to the Director toolset with version 6. The items you will find in the Library Palette are intended to be *drag-and-drop* additions to the Director script engine—items you can grab, place, and use in your Director movies without having to know a whole lot about Lingo scripting—or, sometimes, about programming in general.

Well, that's the *theory* anyway; in practice, of course, things turn out to be a little more complicated than that.

Let's start by opening the Library Palette. Run your copy of Director and select Window | Library Palette. What you'll see onscreen is a small window with icons running down the left side, brief titles to the right, and little scroll arrows you can use to get a view of icons not currently visible. Figure 2-1 shows you what the Library Palette looks like on a Mac; it'll be similar for Windows.

Drag the corner of the Library Palette to enlarge it a little. Probably you'll end up revealing quite a few other icons apart from the ones initially shown. If you haven't opened the Library Palette before, you should be looking at a set of related behaviors called *actions*. These are prepackaged Lingo scripts that have been introduced to support the new suite of 3-D functions Director now makes available to you.

In the upper-left corner of the Library Palette is a square icon that looks a lot like one of the icons you see in your Cast window. If you click that icon, a pop-up menu appears containing (probably) the following:

2

- **3D**, with Actions and Triggers submenus

- **Animation**, with Automatic, Interactive, and Sprite Transitions submenus

- **Controls**

- **Internet**, with Forms, Multiuser, and Streaming submenus

- **Media**, with Flash, QuickTime, RealMedia, and Sound submenus

- **Navigation**

- **Paintbox**

- **Text**

Each one of these items, when selected, changes the list of icons displayed in the Library Palette, and each icon in each set represents a *behavior*—a piece of preengineered Lingo scripting—that you can drag from the Library Palette and drop right onto a sprite on your Stage to assign it a specific set of functions, and you can probably guess by now why these functions are called *behaviors*.

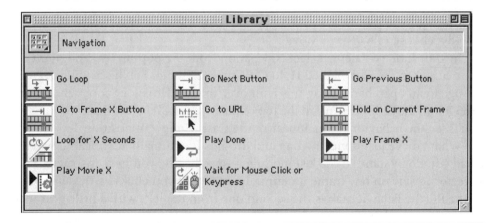

Figure 2-1   Director's Library Palette

They change the behavior of the targeted sprite, transforming it from a static item that simply sits onscreen to something that offers a pretty high degree of interactivity.

By now you're canny enough to suspect that, as simple as the preceding description sounds, in practice it's never that easy, and you're right; we'll find out what that means in the next couple of pages. Now, though, the first thing I want you to do is hover your cursor over every single behavior icon in the Library Palette and read the description in the window that pops up. It doesn't matter if it doesn't all make sense to you now. I just want you to look over your Library Palette and get a feel for what's there.

1-Minute Drill

● Why are items in the Library Palette called behaviors?

● How do you learn more about what a behavior can do?

Exploring Behaviors

Okay, now that you've looked over your Library Palette contents, it's time to start trying them out. Begin with a new Director movie; if you haven't done so already, choose File | New | Movie.

In your Library Palette, select Navigation from the pop-up list, and point your cursor to the icon named Hold On Current Frame. You'll see your cursor change to an open hand. Drag this icon over to your Director Score window and drop it into the script channel at the top of that window. If you've done it correctly, you'll see the behavior's icon appear in the Cast window in position 1.

What you've just done, by drag and drop, is functionally identical to what I had you do by hand in the last module —specifically, you have instructed Director to stay on one frame indefinitely. In fact, if you click the Behavior tab of the PI (the Behavior tab is the second one from the left, with a little gear icon in it; and remember PI means *Property Inspector*) and then click the Script button

---

● They're called behaviors because they affect the behavior of sprites onscreen.
● You can hover your mouse over a behavior's icon to see a ToolTip describing, briefly, its functions.

(this has a little document icon with an arrow superimposed over it), you will see that the script prepared for you in this behavior is basically like the one you entered by hand before.

Of course, if you *do* actually open the script window for this behavior, you'll see a whole lot of extra stuff in there. For the time being, you really don't need to worry about what all that extra content is—it's programmer documentation (some of it), and some of it is special commands used to determine how Director itself interacts with this behavior. We'll be exploring both of these things throughout this book; for now, just be aware that such things exist and are relatively commonplace.

Now I'd like you to click the #text tool in your Tool Palette and drag it across your Stage, creating a rectangle for you to enter something. Type whatever you want; perhaps you could simply type in **Hi there** for this short example.

From there, choose Animation | Automatic from the Library Palette pop-up, and drag the icon named Fade In/Out directly on top of the #text sprite you have created on your Stage. A highlight rectangle will appear around the sprite when you've done this correctly; release the mouse button at that point.

Wow! What just happened? Out of nowhere you got a dialog box asking you all kinds of questions!

The box, titled Parameters For "Fade In/Out," includes an interesting mix of questions and controls. This is a kind of fill-in-the-blank questionnaire that you use to tell Director how to manage this little animation effect. Figure 2-2 shows what this dialog box looks like.

First is the item labeled Fade In Or Out, which has a pop-up menu alongside it. There are two choices there—*In* and *Out*. *In* is selected by default; go ahead and leave it there.

Underneath that is a slider control labeled Maximum Fade Value, which should be automatically set to 100. Although it's not completely obvious, this is a *percentage*—how much opacity the sprite you're setting up should have for its maximum. This you can also leave at 100 for now.

Beneath the Maximum Fade Value slider is another one for Minimum Fade Value; as you have probably guessed, this denotes how much *minimum* opacity the sprite should have, or how transparent it will be once it's fully faded. The default here is 0, for zero percent opacity. You can guess that this means, when the sprite has reached its minimum opacity, it will be completely invisible.

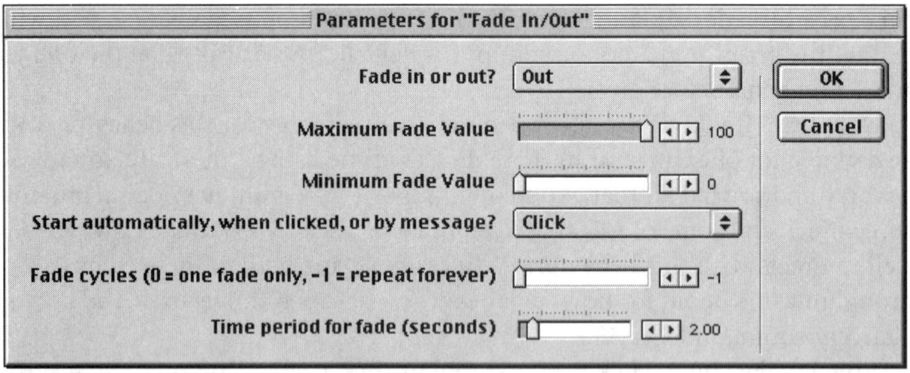

Fade in or out?	Out
Maximum Fade Value	100
Minimum Fade Value	0
Start automatically, when clicked, or by message?	Click
Fade cycles (0 = one fade only, −1 = repeat forever)	−1
Time period for fade (seconds)	2.00

Figure 2-2   The dialog box for the Fade In/Out behavior

Below this is another pop-up labeled Start Automatically, When Clicked, Or By Message? Leave that set to *Automatic* for the moment.

Under this is an item labeled Fade Cycles (0 = One Fade Only, −1 = Repeat Forever), and its default value will be 1. This is not enough to show the real effect of this animation, so set the slider so that its value is −1. You can do this by either dragging the slider thumb all the way to the left or clicking the left arrow to the right of the slider until it's set to −1.

Finally, you see an item labeled Time Period For Fade (Seconds), with a value of 2.00. Again, you can leave this setting alone for the moment.

In order to close this dialog box and have Director accept your settings, all you have to do is click the OK button.

Now what? Now you test your file to see what happens. Click the Rewind button in Director's Control Panel, then click Play.

Okay, maybe that isn't the most exciting thing in the world—you have a sprite that sits there on the screen and fades in and out. Hard to win any awards with that one. But I'd like you to consider something. You have done by a simple drag and drop, plus a few clicks, what can take quite a few frames of Score to achieve otherwise using sprite opacity controls. And you did not have to write a single line of Lingo code to do it!

2

⊥*Tip*

If you're feeling really adventuresome, open the script window for the "Fade In/Out" behavior in your Cast. It should be in slot 3. Now take a deep breath. That's a *lot* of Lingo for one relatively simple little trick, isn't it? And aren't you glad you didn't have to write that stuff? And does it excite you to know that, by the time you're done with this book, you'll be *able* to write stuff like that yourself? (Or does that thought require you to take several more deep breaths?)

1-Minute Drill

● How do you get a behavior into your Director movie?

● How do you change the way a behavior acts on the Stage?

Seeing as how you've cut your teeth a little on behaviors, double-click your #text sprite in your Stage and replace its current text with the words "Click me." You might be able to guess what's coming next.

Click the Behavior tab in your PI; you should see one item in the little window list underneath—the "Fade In/Out" behavior. Click that to highlight it, then choose the button in the PI that looks like two gears meshing. This is the Parameters button, which will cause the behavior's dialog box to open again.

First, under Fade In Or Out?, choose *Out*. Then, under the Start Automatically, When Clicked, Or By Message? label, choose *Click*, then click OK.

Now rewind your Director file and click Play again. What happens? Nothing at all—until you click your #text sprite, that is.

Now play around a little with this fade behavior. Try different settings and different options, and see how those settings make the fade on your #text sprite change according to what you have entered.

⊥Note

In the Start Automatically, When Clicked, Or By Message? pop-up, you'll notice that if you choose *Message,* nothing appears to happen. Director is not broken. The behavior is waiting to receive a *message* to begin its fade. We'll talk about sending messages among Behaviors in Part 4, where such discussions are more germane.

● Drag and drop it from the Library Palette onto the sprite (or script channel) you want to affect.
● You change its settings in its parameters dialog box.

You may have noticed that when you selected the behavior in the PI, a list of items opened in the PI window. (If you do not see the list of items, click the black arrow in the bottom-left corner of the PI frame to expand the list.) Upon inspection, you might notice that the items listed there are the same as the ones listed in the Parameters dialog box, but you don't have to actually open the Parameters dialog box to get to them. Try using those controls to change settings on your fade behavior. Most of the time, you'll probably want to use those controls to set options for behaviors, but there will also be times when you'll use the Parameters dialog box instead. Figure 2-3 displays this list of items as they appear in the PI.

Now that you've had a moment to explore the Fade In/Out behavior, why not make your program a little more interesting?

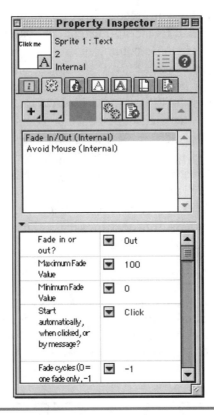

Figure 2-3 Another way to set behavior parameters: through the Property Inspector

From the Library Palette pop-up, choose Animation | Interactive. Locate the icon named Avoid Mouse and drag it on top of your #text sprite (the same sprite that has the fade behavior attached). In this behavior's dialog box, you're asked to set the following; however, I'd advise you to leave the default values in place and run the file before you go back and try to make any changes:

- **Distance**, or how far the sprite will try to move from the cursor

- **Speed**, or how fast it moves away

- **Active At Start** (whether the avoidance is active immediately)

- **Limit To Stage Area** (this will keep the sprite from moving off the Stage)

Now play your movie and try to catch the sprite!

What you've just learned is that it is possible to attach more than one behavior to a given sprite. In fact, I know of no theoretical upper limit to the number of behaviors you can attach, but I can assure you that you don't want to get too behavior happy. Director does require memory and a certain amount of access to your computer's CPU for each behavior it has to process on a frame, so there can definitely be too much of a good thing. Too many behaviors in one frame can make your Director movies run *very* slowly.

Practical Uses for Behaviors

Okay, now that you've had a chance to play around with a silly computer trick, let's try something a little more practical.

You may have noticed that your Director Library Palette includes a set of behaviors for something called a "paintbox." This sounds a little interesting, so let's go ahead and see what we can do with it.

If you hover over the various behaviors included in the Paintbox set, you see a few references to "bitmap" members. You might recall that a bitmap is really a kind of image file, and it's possible to make those image files directly inside the Director program.

First start with a new Director file by choosing File | New | Movie. You can save your previous file if you want to.

The first thing we need is a *canvas* bitmap—a plain, solid rectangle that you can use to paint in. We need to use some of Director's tools to make this and other components for our paintbox file.

Ask the Expert

Question I copied a sprite and pasted it right into the channel beneath it, and I see that my behaviors are attached to this second sprite as well. Does this mean that if I change parameters for the behavior on one sprite, they'll also be changed on the other sprite?

Answer No. Behaviors are specific to one sprite for its channel and duration in the Score. This means that if you have two separate sprites in the same channel (say one sprite from frames 1 to 10, and another sprite at frames 15 to 25, both in channel 1), any behaviors you add to the first sprite will not affect the second one, and vice versa.

Oh, well, okay, there is of course one exception, and that's when you choose to make a sprite completely invisible—that actually affects the visibility of the entire channel and has the same effect as if you click the little square next to the channel number on the left-hand side of the Score window. (That little square, called the *mute* button, can in fact be marked for any channel, including script, transition, sound effects, and so on.)

But by and large, any one behavior affects only the one sprite to which it's attached, for the duration of that sprite's life onscreen. This is sometimes referred to as the sprite's *duration* or *span*, and each behavior so attached to a sprite is often called an *instance*.

Thus in your current program, you have two behavior instances attached to one sprite (until you copy and paste); then you have two sprites with two behavior instances each.

Question How do I set parameters for a whole bunch of sprites at once, then? I don't have to go through a dozen dialog boxes, do I?

Answer First, set your sprites up more or less as you want them to appear onscreen, and then SHIFT-click to select all of them in the Score. Then, in the PI window's Behavior tab, click the + button and choose the behavior you want to attach. From there, just set the options you want all your sprites to share in the PI's behavior parameters list, just beneath the behavior list window itself.

Question I've tried adding other behaviors too, but not all of them seem to work. Why?

Answer Look at the ToolTip that appears next to a behavior's icon in the Library Palette after you've hovered your mouse. You might see that some behaviors say they work with "Flash" or "Vector shapes" or some other specific sprite types. These behaviors actually can't work with any other sprite type, and rather than allow you to assign a nonfunctional behavior to an unsupported sprite type (which could result in all manner of errors later), Director instead simply won't let you attach a behavior to that sprite in the first place.

Choose Window | Paint and, in the window that opens, click the filled rectangle tool. Using this tool, create a roughly square shape in the Paint window, about the size of your Stage. It will probably be filled with black, which is not exactly ideal. (After all, we want to be able to paint in it, and if it's solid black, well, it might be hard to find any lines we draw.)

So click the bucket tool once, then click the foreground color selector chip in the Paint window. From the pop-up that appears, select a very light shade of gray. Then click the rectangle to change all of its color at once to the color you just selected.

Tip

If you choose white, the Paint member will vanish from your Cast! This is because of a minor frustration in the Director bitmap handling engine—it considers the color white to be an excludable part of the image, meaning that Director assumes you don't want white around the edges in a bitmap, so it cuts out the white automatically. The problem there, of course, is that if you fill your *entire* rectangle with white, Director will assume it can cut out *all* of the image, and it does so—making your entire bitmap disappear.

Now that you've got your off-white rectangle in the Paint window, name it "canvas" in the Cast member name field and close the Paint window. Drag that Cast member to the Stage; Director will make a sprite space for it in channel 1.

Ask the Expert

Question I see that in the Canvas behavior dialog box there is a reference to RGB color. What in the world does that mean?

Answer Director now prefers to refer to colors in RGB values—amounts of red, green, and blue, ranging from 0 to 255 for each color. Thus, 0 red, 0 green, and 0 blue make black; 255 red, 255 green, and 255 blue make white. All other color shades come from combinations of these values.

Question So how do I determine what these values are for something? For instance, suppose I want the color turquoise. What's its RGB value? How am I supposed to know?

Answer That is not an easy question, unfortunately. However, for your canvas behavior, the PI comes to your rescue. After you've closed the canvas dialog box, click your canvas sprite on the Stage and then click the Behavior tab in the PI. In the text list that appears underneath the behavior window, you see the settings list I described earlier in the module. In that list, you'll see two tiny color selection chips; you can use these as you do any other color selector anywhere else in Director to set the foreground and background colors you want.

Now, from the Paintbox submenu of the Library Palette, drag the Canvas behavior on top of the canvas sprite you just placed on the Stage. The behavior parameters dialog box that appears holds some things you can alter; for the time being, go ahead and leave them as they are.

If you click the Play button now, you'll notice that your canvas rectangle turns white; we'll explore the reasons for that a little bit later in this module. However, you will probably also notice that your playback head (in the Score) zooms along to the end of the canvas sprite's span, then jumps to frame 1 again. This is not desirable behavior; we actually want our playback head to stay parked on one frame (because, of course, when we make a *projector* —a self-running program, you may recall—out of this file, we want the head to hold on one frame, not go right through to the end. Letting it do that in a projector will result in your program quitting).

You can either choose the Hold On Current Frame behavior from the Navigation library submenu or type the script into frame 1 yourself using the technique I described in Module 1. The choice is yours.

When you click and drag around your canvas as your movie is playing, you'll see a black circle appear that follows the cursor for as long as you drag. Well, black is not the most exciting color in the world; it would be nice to allow the user a few more choices for this paintbox.

In the Tool palette alongside your Stage, click the filled rectangle tool. (Note that this looks exactly the same as the filled rectangle tool in the Paint window; the important difference, however, is that in the Paint window you are working with *bitmaps,* whereas on the Stage you are working with simple shapes—often referred to as *QuickDraw* shapes—Director can place right on the Stage for you.) Somewhere along the bottom edge of your canvas sprite, create a small black rectangle. Then, in the Score, copy that rectangle and paste it into the Score three more times, moving each instance of the rectangle sprite over a few pixels so that there's space between them.

Now, click the second shape sprite and, from the color selection pop-up in the Tool palette, choose red. Note that, when you do so, Director changes just the color of that one sprite, not all four of them. From this you may infer that color is a per-sprite characteristic for shapes made on Director's Stage from its shape tool.

Repeat this process for the third and fourth rectangles, coloring them green and blue, respectively.

Now drag across all four of their sprite spans in the Score, thus highlighting all four of them at once, and from the Paintbox submenu drag the behavior named "Color Selector" onto the four sprites. In this particular instance you will have no dialog boxes appear, because this behavior is not designed to require any settings from you.

You will notice that, by this gesture, you have automatically assigned the "Color Selector" behavior to all four sprites, which is exactly what you wanted to do.

Now rewind your movie again and click the Play button. Your paintbox will begin drawing with the color black, but if you click one of your color selector chips, the brush color will change to the one you have chosen.

After you've had a few minutes to play around with this, go ahead and save your file, then create a Projector of it using the techniques you learned in Module 1. Then run the Projector and tinker with it a bit more.

Depending on your personality, you might now be thinking either *so what* or *wow, this is cool*—and I hope it's the latter you've got in your brain, because you've just had your first real taste of how you can use Director to create practical, useful programs. Sure, your paint program doesn't save files, and it doesn't let you open files for editing, but that doesn't really matter right now. You've laid the framework for making later, more interesting programs that actually can do some useful things, and you managed to do it in just a few minutes.

A couple pages back I mentioned we'd explore why your canvas bitmap turns white when you run your Director movie. Find the script for the Canvas behavior in your PI, then click the Behavior tab.

In the list that appears in the lower half of the PI, you see a label called Background Color (If Opaque):, along with a color selection chip. Odds are (unless you've changed this value) that the chip is white. This is the color that happens to end up being used for your actual paint canvas member, and it is an illustration—albeit a rather brief and incidental one—of how much power Lingo gives you over virtually anything in Director. You can even change the colors of images! (It might interest you to know that, using a set of special commands collectively called *Imaging Lingo,* you can actually create entire images from nothing at all except Lingo scripts. That's far beyond the scope of this module, though, and is almost another book in itself.

You can pick different colors from this chip, and each time you do, when you hit the Play button in the Control Panel, the canvas color will change to reflect the new shade you've chosen.

If you *really* want to see the Lingo behind this, I can tell you that the color for the canvas is set in the **Canvas** script under the section "**on initialize(me),**" and that **initialize** is called from within "**on beginSprite(me).**" What all this means is probably mostly Greek to you now, but that's okay, because by the time you're finished with this book, you'll understand how this works and will have had some first-hand experience writing Lingo that resembles these commands. By the end of Module 4, in fact, you should be able to make some educated guesses.

1-Minute Drill

● What happens to the white edges in a bitmap in Director's Cast?

● What is RGB color?

A Taste of 3-D

For our next exploration in this module, we'll play around a little with some of the 3-D behaviors, which are a new and exciting extension of the Director tool set.

The purpose of this is not to provide you with an extensive introduction to working in 3-D, which often is a very complex process, worthy of a book—actually several books—all its own; rather, it's just to give you a little taste of how quickly you can begin exploring this interesting new set of Director controls. James Newton's book would be a terrific place to continue your explorations of 3-D in Director.

Start with a new Director file, and then create a #text member on the Stage with the word "Hello" in it. Using the Text Inspector (choose Window | Inspectors | Text), set its justification to centered, then, under the Text tab in the PI, choose *Fixed* from the Framing pop-up. This will cause the #text member's sprite area on the Stage to be hard-set to whatever size you give it using the mouse. Drag the #text sprite's rectangle so that it fills the entire Stage area.

Now, again under the Text tab in the PI, choose *3D Mode* from the Display pop-up.

Wow, what just happened there? Suddenly your flat, dull "Hello" has turned into an *extruded* 3-D object—it's no longer a simple little word, but rather something that looks like it's zooming out of the Stage. Figure 2-4 shows what you might see after performing this step.

Explore this more. Choose different sizes for your font, and different fonts too, and play around with the settings in the 3D Extruder tab of the PI. There are a lot of different things to experiment with here, so I'll let you know that the ones you'll probably be most interested in right away include the Smoothness and Tunnel Depth sliders, the Bevel Edge pop-up and Bevel Amount slider, the Director Light pop-up, and the Diffuse color selector chip.

● Director assumes the white edges in a bitmap are undesirable and removes them from bitmaps in its Cast. This can have the unfortunate effect of making all-white bitmap shapes disappear from your Cast.

● Color defined as amounts of red, green, and blue mixed together, in values from 0 (fully off) to 255 (fully on).

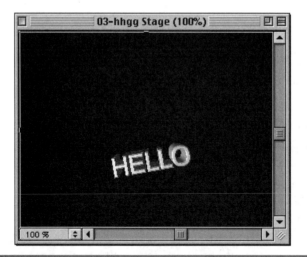

Figure 2-4 The joys of one-click 3-D

Don't get too wrapped up in this, though, since we're going to be attaching some behaviors as well.

Now that you've got your "Hello" extruded and colored the way you like it, let's make it a little interactive.

In the Library Palette, choose 3D | Actions, then drag the Drag Model To Rotate behavior on top of your #text member. Leave the Sensitivity slider where it is for now, and in the box asking you about which group the behavior belongs to, type **hello**.

You're not quite ready yet—you may have noticed from its ToolTip that this dragging behavior requires a *trigger,* meaning that there's another segment of behavior you must add before you can actually make anything interesting happen. Fortunately, those triggers are already there for you to use.

In your Library Palette, choose 3D | Triggers, and from there select the Mouse Left behavior, dragging it atop your #text member. It's okay to leave all the behavior's parameters at default for now.

Now click the Play button and try dragging your "Hello" text.

Once again you see that it's pretty easy to put together some interesting effects using only the tools provided for you with Director, though naturally you can't exactly build a complete program with any of them. In this way, the behaviors in the Library Palette are kind of like Lego toys—premanufactured items you can plug in to each other and, using some foresight and imagination, use to build some pretty useful stuff without having to do a lot of the programming yourself.

There are lots of other fun things you can do with this 3-D behavior set; for instance, you could try removing the mouse actions and use keyboard input instead. I played around a little and made a 3-D flythrough that's also a little tribute to one of my favorite series of novels. You can find an online version at **http://www.nightwares.com/director_beginners_guide/2/hhgg.dir**. Use the up and down arrows to control your flight; pointing the mouse at the 3-D text will get you moving in the first place.

You can actually save this file right to your hard drive and look at the settings I gave to the behaviors and the #text member in the PI if you want to; just open it as you would any other Director file once you've saved it to disk.

If you can't figure out how to save the movie in your browser, enter the following in Director's Message window:

```
goToNetMovie (
"http://www.nightwares.com/director_beginners_guide/2/hhgg.dir" )
```

This will cause the file to load into your Director program; you will then be able to save it as a movie anyplace you want to on your drive.

Behaviors That Collect Information

For our final bit of behavioral experimentation, we're going to be working on the Internet itself, creating a little Director movie that retrieves some HTML-formatted text (which resides someplace on the Internet, rather than is something you've got on your hard drive now) that I've set up for you.

Start with a new Director file and place a #field sprite in channel 1. The default span for the sprite will probably be 28 frames. Drag the box at the end of the sprite's span all the way to the left, causing its duration to now be just one frame.

In the #field member, type **Welcome to the Internet Introduction**.

Now use the Tool palette to create a button tool, and place it on your Stage somewhere below the #field you just made. Shorten its sprite span to one frame as well, and into it type the word **Continue**.

Now drag the Hold On Current Frame behavior from the Navigation submenu of the Library Palette into the script channel over frame 1.

Finally, create a *marker* by clicking the white bar at the top of your Score window. Click right above frame 1. This will cause a small black inverted triangle to appear with the text New Marker alongside it. Into that text area type the word **intro**. Type it so that it replaces the *New Marker* text.

A *marker* is a way to label the beginning of a sequence of frames in your Director movies. Markers may be accessed directly via Lingo, telling Director to navigate from one marker to another by name using the Lingo command **go to label "*markerName*"**, where *markerName* is the name of the marker you made. (And yes, you do have to use quotes when referring to a marker name in this fashion.) This is a much more convenient way of doing things than telling Director to move to a different frame number via **go to frame *someNumber***; after all, as you create more and more complex Director movies and begin to move things around in your Score, frequently the frame numbers will change, which will make your frame number references cease to function as expected. Using markers eliminates this source of possible troubles and is a great way to organize your Score data into logical chunks, sort of like visual chapters in a digital book.

You're not quite ready yet. At about frame 10 of your Director file, drop your Cast's Hold On Current Frame behavior again (note you do not have to drag another copy from the Library Palette; the one you have in your Cast now is just fine), and place another marker above that. Name this marker *getText*.

Tip

You don't have to have your playback head positioned at a frame where you want to create a marker. You can create new markers anyplace in your Score just by clicking the white marker area over the frame you want the marker to be.
If you create a marker someplace other than over the frame where you want it, you can just drag the marker so that it's seated over the frame you intended.
If you accidentally click in the marker area and create a marker you don't want, you can get rid of it by dragging the marker (not its text label) downward toward your Score.

Figure 2-5 illustrates what I mean and shows you what your Score should now resemble.

Now create a #text sprite (not a #field sprite) on that frame of your Score, and use the PI's Text tab to set its Framing pop-up to *Scrolling*. This gives you a #text sprite that includes scroll bars and arrows, just like the ones you see on

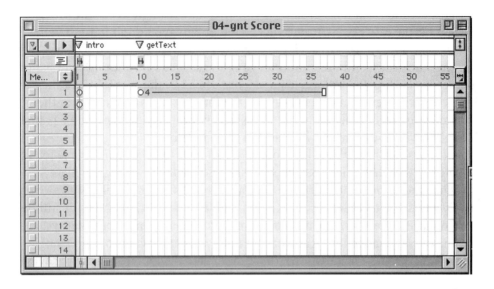

Figure 2-5 The Score after creating two markers, naming them, and placing some
sprites and scripts

the right edges of a word processor document. They work exactly as you would
expect them to, allowing you to scroll text when there's too much to see at once.
Size the #text sprite so that it more or less fills your Stage.

Now select the Text submenu of the Library Palette, and drag the behavior
named Get Net Text atop your #text member. In the Behavior Parameters
dialog box, enter **http://www.nightwares.com/director_beginners_guide/2/
sample.htm** for the URL. After doing so, make sure to select *frame* from the
Activation pop-up menu (this will cause Director to begin loading the text as
soon as the program jumps to this frame), then click OK.

Now return to frame 1 and, from the Navigation submenu of the Library
Palette, drag the behavior named Go Next Button on top of your "Continue"
button. This behavior will automatically make Director jump to the next frame
with a marker in your Score—and that will be the frame that contains your
#text sprite, which is set to retrieve some HTML content right off the Internet.

Note that to proceed, you must have an active Internet connection. If you
normally have to dial a modem to get e-mail or surf the Web, you should go

ahead and connect to the Net now. If you are lucky enough to be *hardwired*—perhaps at the office, or at home via cable modem—you don't have to worry.

Once you're connected, click the Play button and, once your movie has begun playing, click the Continue button on your Stage. A couple of things will happen at once here: Director will move its playback head to the "getText" marker, and it will begin retrieving information from the Internet that is contained at the location you typed in before in the Get Net Text property dialog box. Be patient; it might take a few moments for the load to complete.

Once it's finished, you will be looking at some HTML content I made for you to peruse. Note that, once your #text sprite has filled with enough content, its scrollbar and arrows automatically became active. Director handles that for you.

Of course, you can also package this movie into a projector; it will still be able to retrieve the HTML on any computer you copy it to, provided that system also has a Net connection. And you did it all without having to type a single line of Lingo code, a fact that can sometimes make the Library Palette behaviors extremely useful. The most complicated thing you had to do was create some markers and place some sprites.

The reasoning behind this one should be pretty obvious; suppose you have a client who wants to release a catalog of products but periodically needs to change descriptions for the products (or simply wants to be able to change the price when there's a sale on). If you create a Director program that has all of that information simply entered as text right in Director, you'll be creating a nightmare for yourself each time you want to update that information. You'd have to provide download options, or perhaps remake the CD you release, or produce occasional update packages—all of which are difficult and, in many cases, considerably expensive. Since the goal of being a computer programmer is to make the computer work for you, this approach is not the very best one possible.

By providing a central repository for information that can be retrieved online, however, you allow your client's software to be updated anytime it's required, simply by retrieving updated text information right off the Internet. Another advantage of this approach is that the same HTML pages your program retrieves can also be used on the Web itself, allowing the client's Internet site to hold exactly the same information as his or her CD-ROM. This is the kind of intercommunication the Net brings to you, and it's the kind of thing that can be included in Director programs relatively painlessly, as you've just learned.

2

Ask the Expert

Question   Since I can accomplish so much, and so rapidly, using behaviors, why would I even want to consider reading the rest of this book? Who cares about all that Lingo stuff if behaviors are good enough?

Answer   Behaviors aren't good enough. They're often ways to get started, and they're ways to string together some relatively complicated actions without having to do a lot of programming, but in order to create anything genuinely interesting, you can't constrain yourself exclusively to premanufactured behaviors, for much the same reasons that using a paint by numbers kit is not the same as making new art all your own, or that you can't make a great new novel by copying and pasting passages from public-domain texts like *Leaves of Grass*, *Moby Dick*, or *The Raven*. You have to be able to both take general code and create new, exciting stuff of your own to really make a compelling Director program.

This is so largely because behaviors are meant to work within the context of a single Director movie, and even then, with some details filled in by you. They generally don't take into account the possibility of interacting with other Director movies, with the user's hard drive or operating system, and so on—and for that reason they are often inadequate for performing these kinds of tasks (which tasks are at the heart of creating genuinely powerful and satisfying programs, as we will really explore in Part 2).

Certainly the behaviors provided to you by Macromedia fit this description, and by and large the ones available online, written by your fellow Director programmers, are equally constrained. Partly this is true because the more complex a behavior gets, the more likely it is to be something that cannot simply be lifted from one Director movie and dropped into another and have its functionality remain valid within that new context; and partly because—justly so—some Lingo programmers aren't comfortable with simply giving away free code that might have taken days or even weeks to perfect. (And in many cases, proprietary issues completely prevent their being able to do so.)

Ultimately, most behaviors are meant to serve as *starting points* for you. They get you going in the right direction, but you're expected to make whatever changes are necessary to get them to work well in your own programs. That fact is one of the reasons this very book exists.

Changing the Library Palette

Having the Library Palette at your disposal can be, as we've seen, extremely handy—but what if you want to add more behaviors? Fortunately, Director makes this relatively easy for you. In Director's program folder—the place where you first installed it to your hard drive—you will see a folder called Libs. Inside that folder, you'll see files that have names that correspond to the library choices available to you in your Library Palette, and you can probably guess what they contain!

Each of these items is actually a Director Cast file. When Director first loads, it reads the contents of this folder, then sets up those files for display in your Library Palette.

All you have to do to add more behaviors to this palette is create a new Cast file, place the behaviors you want into it, and then put it in the Libs folder inside Director's program folder. You can give your custom library files any name you choose, and you can organize them however you like. Folders, for instance, *inside* the main Libs folder become main navigation menus you use in the Library Palette, and any individual Director Cast files are considered menu palettes in the Library Palette. Figure 2-6 shows you what my Libs folder looks like on my Mac. Your Windows version should look more or less the same.

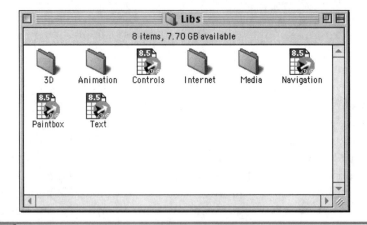

Figure 2-6   The contents of Director's "Libs" folder. Cast (.CST) files are library choices. Folders are submenus that contain other Library choices.

Any Director Cast file you place into this folder will automatically be added to the Library Palette the next time you run Director, and any changes you have made to those Cast files will be reflected in your current Library Palette.

This is good to know because some extremely useful code *extensions* to Director—outside programs that make Director more flexible and powerful, such as the OSControl Xtra suite by peghole.com—include a complete set of behaviors you can use with those extensions. It's nice to be able to just drop those Cast files into your Libs folder and have their behaviors automatically added, forevermore, to your Director tool set.

Tip

You can't actually change anything contained in the Libs folder using Director itself; you must first *copy* the library file you want to change out of the Libs folder. This is because Director is actually accessing these items whenever it's open, and it won't let you edit them directly. To edit an existing Cast file in the Libs folder, first drag it outside of Director's Libs folder, then open it for editing in Director by double-clicking it.

After you've edited the preexisting file's copy, quit Director and move the modified library file back into the Libs folder. (Your computer may ask you if you want to replace the existing file with the one you are moving; click OK.)

In order to prepare a new document to be a Library Palette item, select File | New | Cast... In the dialog box that appears, give it any name you like and click the External radio button ("Internal" means that Director will try to store the Cast file inside the main Director movie, something you don't want—you want this to be an *external* file, something you can use anyplace). Once you've done this, click the Create button.

To enter a new behavior directly into a new Cast member, choose Window | Script. Into this window you can either type the behavior text by hand or—more conveniently—just paste it right into that window.

For example, you might have found some behaviors online someplace that look interesting. You can copy the behavior's text right from your Web browser's window and then paste it into the script window you've opened in Director.

However, this still does not make the behavior a behavior. The default script type for Director is actually what's called a Movie Script, which is not at all the same as a behavior. (We'll discuss script types in greater depth in Module 3.) In order to change the script type from Movie Script to Behavior, just click the

Script tab of the PI and select *Behavior* from the Type pop-up menu. Figure 2-7 shows you what the Script tab in the PI looks like when you're changing a script's type from *Movie* to *Behavior*.

Then just close the script window, save the new Cast library you just made, quit Director, and place the Cast file into Director's Libs folder. The next time you load Director, your Library Palette will include the new behavior submenu and any behaviors you've added—ready to drag and drop into your Score, just like any others.

Getting Your Library Card

In closing, let me suggest you revisit your Library Palette from time to time as you work through this book. The more practice you get with Lingo, and the more experience you have creating programs using Director, the more likely it will be you can find interesting things tucked away in your Library Palette, things you can use to add a little extra functionality or zip to your programs.

I'd also caution you not to go overboard. Having all sorts of interesting animation and fade effects might be fun from a programming perspective, but there is such a thing as overkill with the eye candy. In many ways, programming with Director is about finding a balance between really cool ways to convey information and to cause visual effects to happen, and *actually being able to convey meaningful, useful information.*

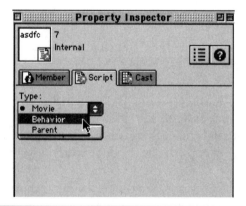

| Figure 2-7 | Changing the script type in the Property Inspector |

Ask the Expert

Question   I tried copying and pasting some behaviors I found online into a new Cast file I want to use in my Library palette, but Director is giving me error messages about some funny-looking character (¬) being in the script. What does that mean?

Answer   With the change to version 8, Director also changed its *line-continuation* symbol, a special character you enter to indicate that the end of a line of Lingo in the script window is actually meant to be continued on the line following. (Ordinarily, when you press RETURN, Director assumes you are done entering a line of Lingo and are ready to move on to the next. For a lot of reasons, sometimes you want to *break* a line for script display onscreen, but you don't want Director to believe you are entering a whole new line of Lingo. This is why line continuation characters came into existence.) Line continuation characters in Lingo act a lot like hyphens in printed words when you reach the margin of a printed page: They serve to let you know that the broken word continues at the next line of text. With Director, they tell the Lingo interpreter that the broken line of *Lingo* continues just below.

This continuation character used to be ¬, something it was very hard to enter in Windows (remember, Director used to be Mac only, and the keystroke for the ¬ character on Mac is just OPTION-RETURN, while on Windows it's one of those four-number ALT-key combinations that's impossible to remember). So Macromedia changed it to a backslash (\), which is easy to find, located as it usually is just above the main keyboard RETURN or ENTER key.

The problem with that is that many, many hundreds of thousands of lines of Lingo have been created using the old-style continuation symbol, and while the Director Lingo engine is smart enough to *recognize* that these symbols still exist, it was not programmed, with version 8.5, to automatically *replace* them when it encounters them in scripts.

To remedy this, open the offending script and copy one of the old-style ¬ symbols, then choose Edit | Find | Text... In the Find field, paste the ¬ character, then enter \ into the Replace field underneath. Click the All Casts radio button and check the Wrap-Around checkbox, then click the Replace All button. Director will warn you that you can't undo the replace; click OK.

This will make Director search through all the behavior scripts you've entered and replace the old ¬ character with the new, updated \ character. After that, you should find your scripts behave properly.

For the record, I almost never use line continuation characters, partly because I don't like the implicit logical break (one line equals one block of logic to me, and so what if it has to wrap in the script window?), and partly because they're kind of annoying to use, I think.

For example, I'm sure that, in surfing the Web, you've come across some truly ugly pages by now—they are either laid out poorly, or unnavigable, or (because of a pink background with green text) actually unreadable. Take care not to let your own Director movies fall into that trap. Just because you *can* do something does not mean you always should.

Project 2-1: Exploring Library Behaviors

This is an exploratory project. What you need to do is use some of the behaviors available to you in Director's Library Palette to add some interesting interaction to a movie, then create a projector from that movie and see how it works.

Use any behaviors that seem of interest to you!

The goals of this project are to

● Become more familiar with the behaviors in the Library Palette.

● Learn ways you can explore approaches to getting work done in Director.

Step-by-Step

1. Start with a new Director movie.

2. Place a Hold On Current Frame behavior in Script channel 1.

3. Place some sprites on the Stage. Use #field, #text and button sprites, shape sprites, graphics, or anything else you care to try.

4. Begin experimenting with the behaviors available to you. For instance, try some of the 3-D text effects, and then add some 3-D navigation behaviors to see how they work.

Project Summary

After experimenting with the Library Palette for a while, you should be a little more familiar with some of the prewritten behaviors available to you, and perhaps you will even have thought of ways you can use some of them to make interesting programs. At the very least, you should have a better idea of the offerings in the Library and how you can use them in your Director movies.

Mastery Check

In this Mastery Check, I'm not going to ask you too many questions. Rather, I want you to go back to the paintbox Director movie you made, and add some more functionality to it. Explore the rest of the "Paintbox" items available in the Library Palette, and try incorporating some of the other tools and controls contained in the Library.

Also, try poking around on the Internet for a while and see if there are other behaviors you can add to the Library, items that will enhance not just your paintbox program, but that may enrich your entire Director programming toolset.

☑*Mastery Check*

1. Define the Library Palette.

_____

_____

2. What is a way to get a behavior from the Library Palette into your Director movie?

_____

_____

3. How do you change the contents of your Library Palette?

_____

_____

4. Why are Library Palette behaviors often not enough to create a complete Director program?

_____

_____

Module 3

Code Tools

The Goals of this Module

- Learn about variables
- Learn how to use operators
- Learn how to use control structures
- Explore lingo keywords
- Write and understand handlers
- Learn about various script types

In addition to the "physical" tools discussed in Module 1, Director provides a rather exhaustive set of *code tools*—means of sending instructions to the computer, causing it to behave or display things in a certain fashion. In short, programming. These tools were used to create the Library Palette behaviors you explored in the last module, and we'll be using them throughout the rest of the book, beginning now.

In this module, you will learn about some common code tools and how they interact with each other in creating programs.

Preparing for Adventure

The feeling many relatively new programmers have, when they first begin to delve into the real "guts" of their programming language, is probably somewhat like how Hansel and Gretel must have felt when they realized they were truly deep in the woods, and it was going to be rather difficult—to put it mildly—to get back out again.

To this feeling I think can be added a sense of legitimate frustration, for you often know that a particular thing *can* be accomplished, and are sure of your ability to do that thing if only someone were to provide you with a clear and precise set of instructions for doing so.

Don't bother looking to the Lingo Dictionary; unfortunately, the lucidity you require just isn't there to be found. Macromedia, for some reason, has always seemed to produce less than optimal documentation for Director, which is probably one of the greatest reasons that the Home for Deranged Programmers' population has been growing exponentially in the last decade.

The Lingo Dictionary is useful for guidance when you want to get some syntactic suggestions for using various commands in Director, and it's generally good at defining them, but there are errata in the existing definitions and sufficient lacunae to make the reference primarily an exercise in frustration for anyone just getting started with Director, and that's really unfortunate.

Macromedia provides sample files as well on the Director installer CD, but these samples are not always outstanding examples of well-written Lingo, and the very nonlinearity of Lingo itself can make these examples quite hard to follow.

(By nonlinear I mean that Lingo does not proceed as with BASIC, starting at line 1 and running through to, say, line 100—often Lingo scripts jump all over the chart, making references to themselves, other scripts, and external code functions, and often those scripts do not have a lot of internal documentation to help anyone in figuring out exactly what is going on at a certain point, or why, or what's going to happen next.)

We're going to start getting a little technical here, and it's what you might call a necessary evil if you want to ever get beyond simply using Library Palette behaviors to create Director programs.

Before we go any farther, I must insist that you take a few moments to drop all of your emotional baggage. Every bit of it. Don't for one second shake your head or cringe and certainly never think *This is going to be hard, I don't know if I can do it.* If you find yourself plagued by doubts, write all of them down on a piece of paper, one right after the other—every single negative message you send yourself about your ability to comprehend … well, anything—and then take that piece of paper outside, put it on the barbecue grill, and *set fire to it.* I'm not kidding. Burn those doubts, destroy them, take them out of yourself and render them to nothing. Be free of them; then you will be ready to proceed.

Variables Are Just Containers

How programs store information is actually pretty simple—they store it internally (in variables) and externally (in files). That's it. Those are really your only two options here.

Consider your word processor, for instance. When you select some text in it to copy and paste someplace else, that text is copied to a variable—a storage container the word processor has created in your computer's memory—and when you paste the text, it's taken out of that storage container and inserted in a new place in your word processing document.

Similarly, when you save your word processor file to disk, everything you've done is written to your computer's drive as magnetic information (something like how audio or video cassettes store sound and images).

We'll tackle variables here, because I believe you've worked with your computer enough by now to understand the idea of opening and closing files in a given program.

Run your copy of Director and, if its Message window is not already open, choose Window | Message. Into that window, type the following:

```
myVariable = "Hello"
```

followed by the RETURN key. You've just done it—you've created a variable, and stuffed something into it.

A variable, in all the world of computing, is a beast that never really changes. It is a container that is used to store something, and that can be read (or accessed, or looked into) at pretty much any time thereafter, allowing you (or your program) to actually see its contents.

Immediately after the line you just typed into Director's message window, type the following:

```
put myVariable
```

followed, again, by RETURN. What happened? Director did this:

```
-- "Hello"
```

The **put** command is used to tell Director to take the contents of a variable and put those contents into the Message window, where you can see them. In this little example, it simply acts as proof that Director did, in fact, correctly store the "Hello" you put into the variable **myVariable**, and that it's still there in memory, waiting for you to access it.

Now quit your copy of Director entirely, and run it again. Reopen the Message window, and into it type the following. Before you press RETURN, though, I want you to try to guess what will happen.

```
put myVariable
```

What happened this time? Director should have done this:

```
-- <Void>
```

This is Director's way of telling you that **myVariable** is empty. More than that, it's telling you that **myVariable** never, in fact, had anything in it to start with.

Wait a minute, you're surely thinking—*I just gave it a value a minute ago; I put the word "Hello" into it.*

Aha, but in the meantime you also quit Director and reopened it, causing it to completely forget everything you did before.

This is referred to as *volatility*. It means that any variables you create, and anything you put into them, will all be forgotten when the program quits. The storage space the program sets aside in your computer's memory is volatile. Anything in there gets completely wiped out every time a program exits, or every time your computer restarts. If you think *you* have bad short-term memory, well, your computer has none at all.

This is, of course, why it's important for programs to be able to save things to files on disk periodically. When a program saves a file, it is writing information to a hard drive that has been specifically *formatted*—prepared—so the program can reconstruct the work you have done next time you open it. Without this ability to store information, computers would really be no more useful than pocket calculators, most of which also forget everything you were doing as soon as you turn the power off.

Thus, work you do in Director itself, as you go along, is stored in your computer's memory as a (rather complicated) set of variables. When you save your Director movie to disk, all that information gets written to your drive in a formatted way that permits Director to *restore*—come back to—the place you left off when you quit the program.

Tip

Variables, in Lingo, can be one word only. You can't have a variable named **my variable**; Director won't understand. You can, however, have one named **my_variable**, but not **my-variable** (because Director will read that as 'the value of **my** minus the value of **variable**'). Variables also cannot begin with an initial number; you can't have a **2Variable**. However, you can have a **Variable2**.

In addition to the generic ability to create variables, put things into them, and find out what they contain, there are the issues of *scope* and *persistence*. Scope generally refers to how "available" a given variable is, and persistence generally refers to how long it lasts in a program.

Let's do a quick demonstration here. Start with a new Director file and use the Tool Palette to create a button sprite on your Stage, giving it any text you want.

Next, open the script window for the button Cast member by selecting the button in the Cast, then clicking the little document with an arrow in it.

You will see the following:

```
on mouseUp

end
```

with a cursor blinking between the two lines. Into that space, type the following:

```
myVar = myVar + 1
put "My variable is:" && myVar
```

If you've done it properly, it'll look like this:

```
on mouseUp
  myVar = myVar + 1
  put "My variable is:" && myVar
end
```

Note, by the way, that Director automatically indented the lines for you. Why this is interesting will be discussed a little later in this module.

Here you have created a simple script—a very brief program—which tells Director to do something. Line by line, this is what the preceding code means:

on mouseUp

This tells Director that it is supposed to do whatever follows this line whenever the button containing this script has been clicked with the mouse. Every time the user clicks this button, its **on mouseUp** script is activated.

myVar = myVar + 1

This tells Director to take the current value of the variable **myVar** and add 1 to it. This might seem a little confusing because **myVar** appears on *both* sides of the equal sign, and that's just the way it works with most programming languages. Everything on the *right* side of the equal sign generally gets stuffed into whatever is on the *left* side of the equal sign. We'll explore this a bit more later in this module.

The equal and addition signs are *operators,* or symbols that tell the computer to behave in a certain fashion. Typically, mathematical operators are the kinds you're likely to see and use most. The other common ones are – (subtraction), / (division), and * (multiplication).

put "My variable is:" && myVar

You've seen the **put** command already. What we're doing is telling Director to place the text "My variable is:" into the Message window, followed by the value of **myVar**. We know we're putting the *value* of **myVar**—what the variable actually *contains*—into the Message window instead of simply the word "myVar" because we have *not* placed quotation marks around **myVar**.

The double ampersand is deliberate, by the way, not a typo. This tells Director to put the value of **myVar** after the phrase "My variable is:" *and* to put a space *between* the two when it dumps the entire line into its Message window. We add the space to make the output a little more readable.

end

This tells Director that this is the end of this script—there's nothing else for it to do, so that's the end of the mouseUp script for this button.

Now go ahead and click the Play button. Each time you click your newly scripted button, you might *expect* to see the following output in the Message window:

```
-- "My variable is: 1"
-- "My variable is: 2"
-- "My variable is: 3"
-- "My variable is: 4"
-- "My variable is: 5"
```

That is, you might expect the value of **myVar** to increase by 1 each time you click your button, because that's presumably exactly what you wrote the program to do.

Of course that's *not* what you see at all. What you discover, in fact, is that no matter how many times you click your button, the value of **myVar** never, ever exceeds 1.

This is because Director actually *forgets* the **myVar** variable just as soon as it's done running the script. This means that the variable's *scope*—how available it is to the rest of the program—is limited only to this script; its scope is said to be *local*. Furthermore, its *persistence*—how long the contents of the variable actually stay in memory—is limited to a single run of the script. The result, of course, is that its persistence prevents it being remembered even from mouse click to mouse click.

Every time the script runs, then (that is, each time you click your button), it starts with **myVar** being <Void>, or completely brand new and containing no value whatsoever. By adding 1 to its value, you have set the contents of **myVar** equal to 1. As soon as the script is finished, Director completely forgets everything it just did, forgetting the variable, its contents, what you did with it—everything.

1-Minute Drill

- What does volatility mean?
- Define scope.
- Define persistence.

You can actually prove this scope and persistence limitation to yourself by changing your button script a little:

```
on mouseUp
  myVar = myVar + 1
  put "My variable is:" && myVar
  myVar = myVar + 1
  put "My variable is:" && myVar
end
```

This will force Director to add 1 to the variable *twice* each time you click the button, and then put its description into the Message window after doing so.

What do you think will happen when you click Play now, and then click your button a few times?

Try it and see if the results are what you expected.

There is a way to increase the persistence and scope of your variable, thus giving it a life beyond the script that contains it, and that is to use the special Director keyword **GLOBAL**. If you first *declare* your variable as global—meaning

---

- Volatility refers to the tendency of information in computer memory to be erasable.
- How widely available a variable is.
- How "permanent" a variable is.

you specifically enter an extra line of Lingo at the beginning of your button's script—the scope and persistence of the variable will no longer be limited to just that script. It will become something you can "see" and use anywhere else in your Director movie.

Here's the modified script:

```
on mouseUp
  GLOBAL myVar
  myVar = myVar + 1
  put "My variable is:" && myVar
end
```

Note the extra line, where we use the keyword **GLOBAL** before **myVar**.

Now try running your program and clicking your button. See what's happened there?

Persistence of Memory

A variable with global scope really *is* global. This means that its contents can be peeked into from any other part of your Director movie where you also reference the same global variable. Of course, the contents can also be changed, as we'll see here.

Duplicate your first button in the Cast window (the fastest way to do that is to click once on the button in the Cast window, then press CTRL-D, or CMD-D on Mac), and then place that second button on your Stage alongside the first. Rename it if you want. Into its script window, enter the following:

```
on mouseUp
  GLOBAL myVar
  myVar = myVar + 10
  put "My variable is:" && myVar
end
```

Do you see the difference? It's that we're adding 10 to **myVar** in this script instead of 1.

Now try running your program. What do you think will happen when you click the two different buttons? When you do it, are the results what you expected?

This happens because both scripts are actually accessing—and changing—the *same* global variable. This is one way in which you can get into trouble if you're not careful; you could inadvertently end up changing a variable's contents or value without realizing it or meaning to.

But there's another way you can get into trouble, and that is to *forget* to reference a global variable when you really meant to.

For example, change your second button's script so that it now looks like this:

```
on mouseUp
  myVar = myVar + 10
  put "My variable is:" && myVar
end
```

Notice that we've removed the line GLOBAL myVar.

What do you think will happen now when you run your program? Try it, click your buttons, and see if what happens is what you thought would happen.

This might have really surprised you, because *both* button scripts are accessing variables that have exactly the same name. However, in the first script, the variable is set to global scope by use of the **GLOBAL** keyword, whereas in the second script, its scope is local.

Director assumes that, unless you explicitly tell it otherwise, any variable you make or use in any given script is meant to be local in scope and have a persistence only for the life of that particular script.

This can be a really nasty surprise for many novice Director users, and it is probably responsible for an accumulated time loss in debugging of at least five thousand years. As you might well guess, it's important, pretty early on, to be able to tell the difference between global and local variables, and it's really important to pay attention to how you name them. In Module 4, I will lay the groundwork for you to become an organized programmer, which will greatly reduce the number of hours you end up spending trying to catch almost unnoticeable mistakes like this.

Script Anatomy 101

After your whirlwind tour of variables, it's time to look at Lingo script structuring a bit more deeply.

Ask the Expert

Question Why doesn't Director tell me an error happened in cases like this?

Answer Because an error didn't happen, at least not technically. Both scripts are perfectly acceptable syntactically. That the results you obtained are not necessarily the ones you expected really is not the fault of Director; it's what's occasionally referred to as a *wetware error,* said wetware being the creature at the hardware trying to instruct the software to do something.

There's very little Director can do to help guard against these kinds of error conditions. The nature of Lingo is such that it's a relatively loose language, meaning it lets you get away with a lot of relatively informal ways of writing programs, without complaining about that informality. While this is very convenient, the negative side is that errors like this become considerably more likely and cannot really be blamed on Lingo or Director itself.

The only way around situations like this is to pay attention.

You recall your button scripts began with **on mouseUp**, and ended with **end**. Though your mouse scripts are examples of *event* scripts (meaning that they execute when a specific event occurs—in this case, a mouse click), they are also nice little templates that serve to illustrate how all scripts are generally written.

You probably recall from Module 1 that you entered another script to change the text in a #text member on your Stage, and that this script began with **on startMovie**. As you've probably guessed by now, a **startMovie**() script is another example of an event script. (I'll more fully explain the parentheses I used here later in this part; they're there to help distinguish handler names from standard Lingo keywords.)

Well, naturally Director allows you to create your own scripts. These are known as *handlers,* and they are essentially to Director what a function or subroutine is to many other programming languages. You write a handler with the purpose of grouping a related set of programming instructions, which are meant to cause the computer to behave in a certain way. You can almost think of handlers being to programming what paragraphs are to writing.

For the quickest, least painful introduction to creating handlers, let's modify your "click me" button movie a little further.

Open a new blank script window in your button movie by selecting Window | Script, or by pressing CTRL-SHIFT-U (CMD-SHIFT-U on the Mac). In the window that opens, enter the following:

```
on ButtonClicked
  put "You clicked the button!"
end
```

Now close this script window and open your button member's script. Modify it so that it resembles this:

```
on mouseUp
  GLOBAL myVar
  myVar = myVar + 1
  put "My variable is:" && myVar
  ButtonClicked()
end
```

Take a look at this button's script. What do you think will happen when you run your movie and click your button now? Well, run it and try it!

You saw both the button's variable and the **ButtonClicked** script's output appear in the Message window, and I hope you noticed that the button's variable output appeared *first* each time. Looking at the button's script, you can surely infer why, and this tells you something important about how Lingo handles things.

Now move the **ButtonClicked()** call from the bottom of the button script to the top, so that it looks like this:

```
on mouseUp
  ButtonClicked()
  GLOBAL myVar
  myVar = myVar + 1
  put "My variable is:" && myVar
end
```

?Ask the Expert

Question Can I make one handler call a second, which calls a third, which calls a fourth, and so on?

Answer You certainly can, and in fact you can make your very last handler call your second handler by mistake, ensuring yourself you will be caught in an infinite loop of handlers—like the famous woodcut by M.C. Escher that shows water flowing through a canal, down over a water wheel, and back into the canal that feeds it.

The only real difference with computers is that this event—called *infinite recursion*—is not only literally possible but something that happens to pretty much everyone at least once.

You're not really programming, I guess you could say, until you've had at least one accidental case of infinite recursion. It sure makes things exciting, watching your program grind to a halt and possibly even freeze up your computer entirely, particularly when you realize, all in a flash, exactly why it happened, and end up smacking your forehead.

Run your movie again, and note how the output in the Message window has changed. Did it change in a way you expected? Did you expect Director, for instance, to run just the **ButtonClicked** script and ignore the rest of the button script?

It's important to realize that calling a handler as we're doing here does *not* actually stop a script from working; it just makes Director jump out of the current script for a moment to run the one being called. Once the second script is finished, Director picks up where it left off in the first script.

This is a nice way to make programs that are easier to understand and write. Any time you have a repetitive set of operations, you can put them into a handler, and rather than having to copy and paste all those operations over and over, you can just call the handler whenever you need it. You also have the advantage of having to make only one change to affect your entire program's operation, rather than having to go in and make change after change in individual bits of code you've entered all over your Score. Just change the one handler, and you're done.

1-Minute Drill

- How do you make handlers call other handlers?
- Why would you want to do so?
- When Director calls one handler from within another, does it skip the rest of the contents of the first handler?

Now let's get a little more crafty with our button script and handler combination. We'll start by giving the button a name, and passing that name along to the **ButtonClicked** handler so that it can change the text it displays.

Reopen your button script and change it so that it resembles the following:

```
on mouseUp
  buttonName = "Click Me"
  ButtonClicked( buttonName )
end
```

Here, of course, we have created a new local variable, **buttonName**, and placed the value "Click Me" into it. Note, also, that when we call the **ButtonClicked** handler this time, we include the variable we just made in the parentheses following.

This is called an *argument,* and when we include an argument with a handler call we're making, we *pass* that argument as a *parameter* into the handler that we're calling.

However, you need to change the ButtonClicked script a little so that it can actually *accept* the parameter being passed. Open your movie script (remember, that's CTRL-SHIFT-U, CMD-SHIFT-U on Mac) and modify your **ButtonClicked** script so that it looks like this:

```
on ButtonClicked button
  put "You clicked the" && button && "button!"
end
```

- By referencing any valid handler from within another handler.
- To place commonly used program instructions into one central location where they can be easily modified if necessary.
- No, it pauses execution of the first handler to run the second, then resumes the first where it left off.

Notice that the **ButtonClicked** handler name has been modified such that there is now a term trailing after it, **button**. This is the part of the handler definition that will accept the parameter we pass when we call the script. Note too that this parameter acceptor does *not* have the same name as the variable being passed—in point of fact, it's not necessary for it to.

Tip

A *passed* parameter is always a local variable that has been sent from one handler to another. There's no need to pass global variables as parameters, since globals are available anywhere to any handler that accesses them.

The best reason to pass parameters is that you don't actually need to declare extra globals to make them work; you can have a handler act on one specific passed parameter without also needing to declare it as a global. This makes your code much easier to read and change relatively safely.

Overuse of globals in Lingo scripts is a common tendency among many relatively new programmers; this leads to what is often called "Global soup," a term that accurately describes a script (or set of scripts) that contains dozens of globals. That's usually too many to really be efficient.

Now run your movie and click your button a few times. Not very thrilling, of course.

Well, duplicate your button a couple of times and place the duplicates on the Stage along with the first one, then change each button's **buttonName** variable to make them easier to tell apart. For instance, the first button script might now look like:

```
on mouseUp
  buttonName = "Click Me #1"
  ButtonClicked( buttonName )
end
```

the second button's script might be:

```
on mouseUp
  buttonName = "Click Me #2"
  ButtonClicked( buttonName )
end
```

...and so on. What do you think will happen when you play your button movie and click the various buttons now? When you actually *do* play the movie, do you get the results you expected?

This is an example (arguably an inane one) of how passing parameters can affect the way a handler behaves; in this case, the text the handler puts into the Message window is changed to reflect which button has been clicked, because the parameter you pass from each button script is slightly different from the rest.

Now let's do a little something with variables, too. We're going to add a counter to tell the user how often he's clicked the buttons in the movie.

Before you read farther, do you think we want to use a global variable here, or a local one? And do we want those variables in the button scripts, or in the movie script?

Here's a hint. We want the count to persist for as long as the movie is running; does that mean we want a variable with local scope and per-handler persistence, or do we want a variable with global scope and longer persistence?

Also, if the variable is global, should we put it in the button scripts or in the movie script? Remember that a global handler can be accessed from anyplace, and that the point of calling handlers is to reduce the number of times we must enter the same set of commands in individual scripts.

So, here's what your movie script should look like now:

```
on ButtonClicked button
 GLOBAL clicks
 clicks = clicks + 1
 put "You clicked the" && button && "button!"
 put "You've clicked this program's buttons" && clicks && "times!"
end
```

Was that more or less the way you thought the changes should be made?

Run your movie and click the buttons a while to get the idea of how it works. As you do, reflect on how easy it was to make this last set of changes. You didn't have to alter any of the button scripts at all—all you had to do was change the one handler they all access in order for all your changes to be made at once.

This is the power of handlers in Director when they are combined with variables. This basic combination is the root of all programming—not just in Director; in all programming languages.

1-Minute Drill

● What's the difference between passing a parameter and using a global variable?

● Why would you pass a parameter rather than use a global variable?

Making Decisions

3

It's not enough to have the computer simply do things when you tell it to. One of the points of programming is to teach the computer how to figure things out for itself and do something special based on conclusions it reaches on its own.

It's not as simple, of course, as simply typing in some plain-English instructions, but Director makes some of the most common instructions pretty easy to read.

Any set of instructions that causes the computer to make a decision based on current conditions is called a *control structure*, because it controls the way in which a program executes.

Go back to your button movie again. We're going to add some code to the movie script, so open its window and set things up so that they look like this:

```
on startMovie
 GLOBAL clicks
 clicks = 0
end

on ButtonClicked button
 GLOBAL clicks
 clicks = clicks + 1
 put "You clicked the" && button && "button!"
 put "You've clicked this program's buttons" && clicks && "times!"
 if clicks > 10 then
  put "Aren't you getting bored?"
 end if
end
```

Before you run your button movie, look things over and see if you can guess what the program will do after you've clicked the buttons more than a few times.

● A parameter is a local variable passed from one handler to another; a global variable exists with or without any given set of handlers.

● Doing so reduces the number of global variables used. This makes program code easier to read, understand, and edit without running too much risk of destroying a program completely.

Now play the movie and see if it does what you expected.
Let's take a look at the new parts of the movie script.

on startMovie

You probably remember this from Module 1. This is a special Director script, and it is run whenever your Director movie first runs (with a projector, it runs when the program first loads; when you're working with the movie in Director, it runs whenever you click the Play button).

GLOBAL clicks
clicks = 0

Here we're declaring the global variable **clicks** and setting its value to zero. Thus, every time this movie first runs, its **clicks** variable is set to zero regardless of what it might have been before.

Down in the **ButtonClicked** script, you surely noticed some extra lines, too.

if clicks > 10 then

You've seen > (greater than) and < (less than) symbols before, in math classes. This line is the beginning of an **if...then** control structure, and it is testing to see if the value of **clicks** is greater than 10. If it's not, the rest of the control structure—everything up to the **end if**—is ignored. Skipped. As though it were never there. However, if **clicks** is greater than 10, the Lingo script you entered within the control structure is executed, and then (generally) the rest of the handler is run as well.

Tip

If you're having trouble remembering that < is less than and > is greater than, think of the < as being a kind of bent letter L. Since less than starts with L, that can be a handy clue.

put "Aren't you getting bored?"

This script, inside the **if...then** control structure, is executed when and only when **clicks** is greater than 10. What may have surprised you is that it continues to be executed *every time thereafter,* because of course once clicks gets above 10 it never is less than that amount again, until you stop your Director movie and click the Play button to cause the **startMovie** handler to run again.

3

You might also have been surprised when you saw **clicks** became equal to 10, and the computer's rather testy message didn't appear right away. This is because we're testing to see if **clicks** is *greater than* 10, and when **clicks** was 10, it was *not* greater than 10. It was equal to 10, which is of course not the same thing. This might seem like the kind of technicality you'd see in a TV show about lawyers, but computers are extremely technical beasts.

end if

This is very, very important. It tells Director that it's reached the end of the **if…then** control structure. You must *always* close an **if…then** with an **end if**. Director will not permit you to do otherwise, and will refuse to accept any Lingo you enter until the situation is corrected. An **end if** must always be matched with an **if…then**, just as an opening parentheses must be matched with a closing one (like this). Not like this), and certainly (not like this.

Note

It is possible to put the entire if…then structure onto one line and not use an end if when you do so, like this:
if clicks > 10 then put "Aren't you getting bored?"
but this is a *very bad idea.* Sometimes—not always, but often enough to be a problem—Director will completely fail to recognize **if…then** structures that are built into one line of Lingo.

The Lingo script window actually gives you visual cues relating to this. If you have not properly closed a control structure, the indentation in your Lingo scripts will vanish from the offending point downward in the script window. Every line of Lingo will appear flush left and will remain there until you've properly closed your open control structure. (In Module 4, we'll look into how to deal with this, and I'll show you a nifty trick there as well to make Director's habits with indenting a little easier to handle.)

Tip

Director allows another structure, the **case** statement, which behaves, more or less, like the **if…then** statement. It's preferred (but not required) in situations where there are a lot of possible conditions to test; for simple decision structures there's no benefit to using **case** rather than **if…then**. I mention this not because I expect to use it in this book, but to let you know it's out there and that it's not uncommon. For those of you familiar with other programming languages, **case** is analogous to **switch**.

The basic grammar for an **if...then** control structure is:

```
if something then
  doThisStuff
else
  doThatStuff
end if
```

The **else** is optional. You can also tack on other **if...then** statements after the **else**, or stack them within each other, and sometimes you have to. I don't generally recommend it if it's avoidable, though, because often such logic can be very hard to follow.

Here's a way you can modify your button movie script to see an **else** statement in use:

```
on ButtonClicked button
  GLOBAL clicks
  clicks = clicks + 1
  put "You clicked the" && button && "button!"
  put "You've clicked this program's buttons" && clicks && "times!"
  if clicks > 10 then
    put "Aren't you getting bored?"
  else
    put "Keep clicking..."
  end if
end
```

Again, before you run this, try to guess what it will do. Then go ahead and play the movie and watch how the output in the Message window changes. Did you notice that the command in the **else** statement stopped executing after a while? This is because, once **clicks** became greater than 10, the first half of the **if...then** statement began running. Until **clicks** was more than 10, however, only the second half ran.

This is an example of programs being taught how to make decisions based on circumstances. I'll grant you it's not HAL-level intelligence, but it's real, and a lot of programming is basically using control structures more or less like these.

1-Minute Drill

● What is the purpose of an **if...then** control structure?

● Why are the words **end if** important in Lingo?

Do This That Many Times...

So you've mastered the **if...then** statement; now it's time to take a look at *counter loops*.

Counter loops are structures wherein a given set of events is made to happen a specific number of times. This can be useful in Director, for as we've seen, the Score is a series of frames and channels. Often counter loops are used in Director to affect or test the state of sprites in the Score, and rather than have to enter the same line of code up to one thousand times to hit all the channels, it's more useful to just do a counter loop.

There are lots of different types of counter loop names in the world of programming, the most common being **for...next**. Director, however, uses **repeat with**.

The basic grammar is:

```
repeat with counter = someNumber to someOtherNumber
 doSomeThing
end repeat
```

Open your button movie script and make a few more changes to it:

```
on ButtonClicked button
 GLOBAL clicks
 clicks = clicks + 1
 put "You clicked the" && button && "button!"
 put "You've clicked this program's buttons" && clicks && "times!"
 if clicks > 10 then
```

● These allow decisions to be made according to the state of the Director program at any given point.
● Each **if...then** must always be closed with an **end if**. If this pairing does not take place, the Lingo script is not acceptable to Director and will fail to work.

```
   put "Aren't you getting bored?"
 else if clicks > 15 then
   put "That's enough; I'm bored now."
   repeat with spriteNum = 1 to 4
    sprite(spriteNum).visible = FALSE
   end repeat
 else
   put "Keep clicking…"
 end if
end
```

Did you see what I did there? Not only did I add a **repeat with** structure; I altered the **if…then** control set to add another condition.

Take a look at this Lingo and think about what it might do, then go ahead and run your button movie for a while.

Well… after you clicked the buttons more than 15 times, something interesting seemed to occur on your Stage. All the buttons vanished!

Looking at the changes we've made, here's why:

else if clicks > 15 then

This, of course, executes when there have been 16 or more clicks to the buttons. Did you notice that this line was also skipped whenever **clicks** was less than 10? And that it only executed once—when **clicks** was more than 15? Why? Because of what follows:

repeat with spriteNum = 1 to 4

Here we're defining a counter, **spriteNum**, and automatically beginning its count at 1. This is a **repeat with…** structure that executes four times. As you might infer, the counter variable **spriteNum** is incremented (1 is added to it) each time the **repeat with…** loop cycles. Director handles the incrementing for you, which is handy.

Tip

If you want to count from a higher number down to a lower one, you simply have to use **down to** instead of **to**. For instance, to count back from 100 to 1, you would enter **repeat with someNumber = 100 down to 1**.

sprite(spriteNum).visible = FALSE

3

Oh no, more of that dot syntax stuff. Well, consider what you're telling Director here. We know that as the **repeat with…** loop runs, **spriteNum's** value increments, beginning with 1. So what do you think the computer's seeing here?

Since **spriteNum** is a variable, it's looking at the variable's *contents*—in this case a number—and from that is determining which *sprite* is being affected.

It then assigns a value to one of a sprite's properties, as you can tell by the **sprite** keyword at the beginning of the statement. Any time you want to refer to a given sprite on the Stage, you refer to its channel number; from there you use dot syntax to determine which specific property of the sprite you want to affect.

Note

In non-dot syntax, this line would instead be "set the visible of sprite spritenum to FALSE." That might be a little more understandable, but it takes longer to type.

There are quite a few properties you can set with a sprite; for now, we're just interested in the **visible** property. You saw what happened when this **repeat with…** loop ran, so you can probably guess what **setting sprite(n).visible** to **FALSE** does.

This is why the **clicks** value never goes past 16. All the buttons become invisible and can't be clicked any more!

end repeat

This is another one of those must-haves, like **end if**. Without it, Director has no way of knowing you've reached the end of the **repeat with…** loop.

Without this **repeat with…** loop, our code would have looked like this instead:

```
else if clicks > 15 then
   put "That's enough; I'm bored now."
   sprite(1).visible = FALSE
   sprite(2).visible = FALSE
   sprite(3).visible = FALSE
   sprite(4).visible = FALSE
```

I think you can agree that the **repeat with…** loop is much better, especially if you want to set a couple hundred sprites to invisible at one go.

If you want to be a real smarty, you can consider how to make your buttons visible again. I'll offer you a hint: You'd want to do it in your **startMovie** handler, and you don't need to do any **if…then** testing to make it happen.

Do This Until...

The last control structure we'll look at here (there are only three in the world of Lingo) is similar to the previous **repeat with...** example; this is a **repeat while...** loop.

The basic grammar:

```
repeat while someConditionExists
  doSomeThing
end repeat
```

These can be tricky monkeys. They cause your computer to loop endlessly in a process while a condition being tested for is not met, and if that condition is never met, the loop is never exited. This causes lockups and is a definite no-no.

I'll give you an example of how this loop works by altering the **ButtonClicked** handler again:

```
on ButtonClicked button
  GLOBAL clicks
  clicks = clicks + 1
  put "You clicked the" && button && "button!"
  put "You've clicked this program's buttons" && clicks && "times!"
  if clicks > 10 then
    put "Aren't you getting bored?"
  else if clicks > 15 then
    put "That's enough; I'm bored now."
    spriteNum = 1
    repeat while spriteNum < 5
      sprite(spriteNum).visible = FALSE
      spriteNum = spriteNum + 1
    end repeat
  else
    put "Keep clicking..."
  end if
end
```

Well now, that's a little different, isn't it?

spriteNum = 1

We have to do this to initialize the **spriteNum** variable; that is, if we don't set it to 1 initially, Director will complain that a variable was used before a value was assigned to it. This was taken care of automatically for us in the **repeat with…** loop, but for this **repeat while…** loop we have to do it ourselves.

repeat while spriteNum < 5

Ah, another math operator. This is less than, of course (remember, it's a bent L), and it's telling Director to perform a set of operations for as long as the variable **spriteNum** has a value less than 5.

It's less than 5, by the way, because we want this operation to happen *four* times. If we tested for **spriteNum** being less than 4, the **repeat while…** loop would stop when its value was 3. That would leave one button on the screen, the one in channel 4.

sprite(spriteNum).visible = FALSE

You know what this does.

spriteNum = spriteNum + 1

This one's important to add, because in this **repeat while…** loop, **spriteNum** is *not* automatically incremented by the loop's own internal command structure. If you don't add this line, Director will never exit the **repeat while…** loop, because **spriteNum** will never be greater than 5. In fact, it will remain 1 forever.

Try it now. Remove the line **spriteNum = spriteNum + 1**, then run your button movie. After the sixteenth click, what happens? Nothing, apparently. Actually, what's going on is that Director is stuck in the **repeat while…** loop.

Press CTRL-PERIOD (CMD-PERIOD on Mac) to stop Director (this will not cause Director to quit; it'll just get you out of the loop). Ha! You've just had your first infinite loop. Congratulations, you are now a real programmer.

I can't tell you how regularly you can get into trouble with repeat loops that never exit, particularly **repeat while…** loops that test for a condition that never turns out to be true.

Keywords

So much for control structures; now we'll look at some Lingo keywords in greater depth. A *keyword* is a predefined term that Director understands to be part of its built-in Lingo functionality.

One keyword you already know: **sprite**. This is used, as we saw before, to refer to sprites on the Stage. Other keywords include **on** and **end**, **if**, **then**, **else**, **GLOBAL**, **FALSE**, and so on. In fact, the Lingo dictionary is full of keywords.

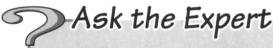

Ask the Expert

Question   If repeat while… loops can't be broken out of (at least in some cases), why use them at all? Isn't that dangerous?

Answer   Not if you're careful. There are plenty of times when, for instance, you might want to repeatedly try a handler call, giving up only when it's been run a certain number of times or when it's been executed successfully; a **repeat while**… loop is a great way to construct such programming.

There are ways you can build in a second test; for instance, you could count the number of times the loop has actually occurred, and then break out if it's past a certain maximum number. This is called a *kickout,* and they're nice to remember to program in, particularly if the condition you are testing is heavily reliant on things beyond your control (such as the condition of the user's computer system; for instance, if the user is not connected to the Internet but you want to get something done that requires a Net connection, you could use a **repeat while**… loop to test for that connection and, once your number of tries got past a certain amount, you could kick up an **ALERT** telling the user that without an Internet connection, your program can't keep going).

By now I'm sure you've noticed that, as you enter Lingo scripts, your text changes colors. This is called *syntax highlighting,* and it is pretty handy to have around. It allows you to see, by the colors alone, whether you might be using a Lingo keyword or not.

The reason that's important is because it's not generally a good idea to use, as a variable or handler name, something that happens to also be a Lingo keyword. Unpredictable things can happen.

Here's an example. Try entering this as a script:

```
on StartClock
  ticks = 0
  repeat while ticks < 100
  put "ticks are" && ticks
  ticks = ticks + 1
  end repeat
end
```

Director won't complain when you run this script through the Message window, but you're actually using *part* of a Lingo keyword *set* here, the full set being **the ticks**. Ticks are increments of time equal to 1/60th of a second, and there are plenty of times in programming when you will want to gain access to **the ticks**. Using a script like the preceding one could result in something not working correctly in your program, and it might take forever to figure out why.

This is why it's really a good thing that Director highlights syntax as it does. Any time you're entering some Lingo and you see a variable (whose name you chose) you've entered change colors, it's not a bad idea to see if it's listed in the Lingo dictionary. If it is, do yourself a big favor and change the name of your variable. In Module 4, I'll offer you some suggestions on creating variable names that have no chance whatsoever of being Lingo keywords.

And of course, you can really get into trouble by choosing a handler name that happens to be a keyword. For instance, suppose instead of **StartClock** you named your handler **StartTimer**.

That can really muck things up, because any time you tried to enter the Lingo keyword **startTimer** in one of the scripts in that same file, the Director Lingo timer would not start as it is supposed to. You'd get your handler running instead.

Here's another example:

```
on Put text
 ALERT text
end
```

You know already, from your experience with the Message window, that the **put** keyword sends text into that window. This handler is one way to short-circuit that. Enter it in a movie script, and into the message window type

```
put "This message has been redirected."
```

You can, of course, do something a little more insidious, the kind of "practical joke" on a fellow programmer that's likely to land you a serious dental bill, by entering this in a script someplace:

```
on Put
 nothing
end
```

Every time your hapless victim uses a **put** statement, nothing at all will happen. Nothing will get sent to the Message window, and there'll be no really obvious reason why (unless your victim is smart enough to fire up the Debugger, which we'll be exploring in Module 5). Or, you could just get downright *horrible* with your **put** rerouting, and send your victim to an Internet site, or cause his program to quit, or whatever. I wouldn't recommend doing that, though, unless you have both comprehensive medical coverage and absolutely no desire to remain gainfully employed.

Keywords, then, are parts of the Lingo command set, and they really should not be used as anything but valid Lingo commands, or all manner of strange behavior may take place. The only real way to know what's a keyword and what isn't, barring syntax highlighting, is practice and a willingness to dig through the Lingo dictionary. It's one of those things that comes with time.

1-Minute Drill

● What is one way to determine if you're using a Lingo keyword?

● Why should you not use Lingo keywords for variable or handler names?

Types of Lingo Script

Finally, we come to script *types*, of which there are several.

In your button movie, you entered scripts for the buttons themselves to execute when they were clicked, you entered a set of handlers, and you placed a frame script in your Score; however, unless you used a behavior for your Score's frame script, every kind of script you entered was of the type called a *movie* script.

Tip

Adding scripts directly to Cast members, as you did with your buttons here, is not particularly recommended any more by Macromedia; there's a strong inference that they will eventually be unavailable. I've used them here for convenience, but there are better ways to do things, and we'll be using those better ways in the rest of this book.

● The Lingo script you are entering will change its colors as you complete the keyword.
● Doing so will short circuit those keywords, in some cases causing minor annoyances, and in other cases causing a total program malfunction.

In general, a movie script is a kind of catch-all container wherein you can dump any set of handlers you want made available anywhere in your Director movie. Just as there are global variables, you can think of these as being global scripts. They're available to anyone.

Another type of script is the *behavior,* which—as you saw in Module 2— alters the way sprites do things on the Stage. Generally, behaviors are considered *encapsulated,* which means that the behavior affects only the specified sprite it's attached to (or perhaps a few others), but that its handlers and variables are pretty much the exclusive domain of the behavior itself.

Behaviors are pretty useful in this regard, because you can have several *instances* (copies in memory) of the same behavior running at once on the Stage without having to worry that they'll get confused with each other, inadvertently sharing variables or what have you. As we progress through the modules in this book, I'll be using more and more behaviors, as opposed to Cast member scripts, but I don't think you'll mind the transition, and by the time you're through with me, you'll be swearing by them (as opposed, of course, to *at* them).

The third type of script in Director is called the *parent* script, and we'll really be looking into these in Part 4. What I can tell you now as a preview is that parent scripts are the places where you write large-scale *object-oriented* routines, meaning that you enter some really complex stuff into them that you can use to vastly extend the reach of your Director movies' capabilities without having to bother too much with all the details.

You can see what any script's type is by looking at its properties in the PI. Click a script in any Director Cast window, then click the "Script" tab in the PI. You can see—and set—a script's type with the "Type" pop-up menu.

If you're feeling a little brave, go back to your button movie and change its main script's type to something other than movie, and then try running the program again..

What happens when you click a button this time? Director gives you a "handler not defined" error message—this is because each button in your movie is trying to make a call to **ButtonClicked**(), but because **ButtonClicked**() is no longer in a movie script, Director can't find it.

Most of the time, when you're creating your own handlers, you'll probably be in a movie script. Second to that, you'll likely be working with behavior scripts; parent scripts are for relatively specialized applications, and generally once you've got one going you don't need to modify it very much, assuming it's been well designed.

Project 3-1: Getting a List of Files

All right, so now we've gone over the wiring, and you've had a real peek into the stuff that really makes Director work—Lingo keywords and control structures, variables and operators, handlers and script types. Time to apply some of that knowledge.

For this module, we'll be creating a Director movie that gets a list of files in a folder. There are plenty of reasons, of course, why you might want your programs to know what files are resident on a given computer, and this little project will show you a basic way of getting it done.

With this project, you should learn, among other things,

● How to apply a **repeat with...** control structure in a meaningful way.

● How to learn a little information about the environment in which a Director movie is running.

● In a general sense, how Director movies can be programmed to interact usefully with the computers on which they are running.

Step-by-Step

1. Start, as always, with a new Director file. We're going to do this one a little differently than previous ones by starting the scripting right away.

2. Open the main movie script window by pressing CTRL-SHIFT-U (Mac CMD-SHIFT-U). This simultaneously opens and creates a new movie script. Into it enter the following:

```
on startMovie
 GetFiles()
end

on GetFiles
 lastFile = the maxInteger
 member("fileList").text = ""
 repeat with fileNumber = 1 to lastFile
  thisFileName = getNthFileNameInFolder ( ( the moviePath ), fileNumber )
  if thisFileName = "" then
   exit repeat
  else
   put thisFileName & RETURN after member("fileList")
  end if
 end repeat
end
```

Got that? Good. As you can see here, your **startMovie** handler calls another handler, **GetFiles()**. That's where it gets a little interesting, but hopefully you can look at the Lingo and get a feel for what's happening:

> **lastFile = the maxInteger**

Here, **lastFile** is a limit—the highest number we want to count to (we have to stop eventually, after all). We want to set it to a sufficiently high number, though, because we don't know exactly *how many* files there might be in a given folder. So we set its value to **the maxInteger**, which is the largest integer number Director can store. (It's a very high number—over two billion.)

> **member("fileList").text = ""**

This Cast member does not actually exist yet, because we haven't created it. But we know we're going to, so we're just planning ahead a little. When the movie runs, it will automatically empty the **fileList** member's text contents.

> **repeat with fileNumber = 1 to lastFile**

Remember, this is a **repeat with...** loop, not a **repeat while...** loop, so **fileNumber**'s value will automatically iterate each time the loop runs. We've set it here to stop at the highest integer value Director recognizes.

> thisFileName = getNthFileNameInFolder ((the moviePath), fileNumber)

This looks a little funny. **getNthFileNameInFolder** is a Lingo keyword that instructs Director to get the name of a specific numbered file in a folder list.

We have to tell Director *where* to look, so that's what **the moviePath** does—it tells Director to look in the folder the movie is actually playing from (where the movie file itself is located on the hard drive).

We also have to tell it which file *number* to read in that location, so the second thing we pass is our **fileNumber** variable.

This causes Director to retrieve the name of the file numbered **fileNumber** at **the moviePath** location of the hard drive. We then take that name and put it into another variable, **thisFileName**.

> **if thisFileName = "" then**
>
> **exit repeat**

Here we test to see if **thisFileName** is empty. If it is, it's because we've reached the end of the list of files in the folder, and so we just **exit** the repeat loop right away, rather than making Director count all the way up to two or so billion.

else

put thisFileName & RETURN after member("fileList")

end if

Here we add the name **thisFileName** to the contents of our text member, followed by **RETURN** to give the list a line break (otherwise, it'd all just flow together and look pretty messy). We do this, of course, only when **thisFileName** is not empty.

3. Now construct the rest of the movie file. Create a #text sprite on the Stage, and use the PI to set its type to Scrolling (this will give you a scrollbar on the #text sprite, which is handy for looking at long lists). Don't forget to name the #text member **fileList**.

4. Add a frame script that keeps Director on a given frame; you remember this from Module 1:

```
on exitFrame
  go the frame
end
```

5. Finally, add a *quit* button. To do that, use the button tool in the Tool Palette to make a button sprite on the Stage, and for its script enter the following:

```
on mouseUp
  QUIT
end
```

Now you're ready to run your movie! Save it and click Play.

6. Here's where it gets to be fun. Create a projector like the one you did in Module 1, then move your projector around from folder to folder on your drive.

Note

On Windows, it's important to make sure you're moving the *program,* not creating a *shortcut* (which is the default way Windows does things). To do that, instead of left-clicking the projector to drag it to another folder, right-click and, when you release the mouse button on the place you want the projector moved to, select Move Program from the pop-up list of choices.

7. After you've moved the projector to another folder, double-click it to run it. As you can see, the #text sprite's contents change according to where the projector is running; Director is capable, as you've just proved, of reading file lists inside folders. *Any* folders.

Project Summary

With this project, you have

- Learned a constructive purpose for a **repeat with...** control structure.

- Learned that Director movies can be aware of the environment in which they operate.

- Become aware of some of the concepts you will use as a programmer to create genuinely interactive software.

There are ways to make this program more interesting, and we'll be returning to the concept in Part 4 of this book. With this movie, you've actually begun to lay the conceptual groundwork for a legitimately useful program—one we're going to write together. The program, by the time we're done, will be able to create a list of image files in any folder, then make an HTML index of those images in thumbnail view, complete with clickable links, that can be loaded in any browser. We'll also throw in some nice features, like a slideshow option, just to make things a little more nifty (and because we can). You've seen these programs before, surely; they're *image cataloging* utilities and can be handy to have around if you have a lot of photos or whatever on your system. Usually they're available online as shareware programs, with a requested fee of $30 or more. The difference is that ours will be free!

Meanwhile, though, consider once again how easily Director lets you do things, and revel a moment in the fact that you already know *everything you need to know* to take on large programming projects in Director. All the basic skills you need have been covered in these first three modules; the rest of this book is about enhancing and refining your skills.

☑ *Mastery Check*

1. What is a variable?

_____

_____

2. What is a handler?

_____

_____

3. What is an **if...then** control structure?

_____

_____

4. What is a **repeat with...** loop?

_____

_____

5. What is a **repeat while...** loop?

_____

_____

6. What is a keyword?

_____

_____

7. What is important about **end if**?

_____

_____

☑ Mastery Check

8. What is important about **end repeat**?

_____

_____

9. How do you make one handler run from another handler?

_____

_____

3

Module 4

Well-Written Lingo

The Goals of this Module

- Learn the anatomy of handlers
- Understand variable names: good, bad, and ugly
- Understand the precepts for good script (program) writing
- Understand good command structure
- Learn to use internal documentation and white space to make your code more readable

Director's relative ease of use permits one to begin programming almost immediately—however, a certain degree of planning ahead and self-discipline are required to make the experience of writing a program something truly enjoyable, rewarding, and successful.

There's More to Programming than Typing Commands

Up until now I've really shown you only little pieces of program—relatively simple handlers and scripts that don't perform overly complex operations. Hopefully, you've been able to follow this and are also able to gather that the creation of complex programs is really very little more than stringing together some fairly simple scripts into what can turn into a pretty exciting piece of software.

In Part 2, we'll go through this process in depth—the steps involved in planning, considering, testing, and executing different types of scripts to construct software that is capable of remarkably powerful operations on the computer.

Before we do that, though, I believe it's essential to have a good, solid set of fundamentals in place. By this, I don't mean knowing every possible Lingo keyword. Rather, I mean knowing how to write well-constructed Lingo scripts in the first place.

In the previous modules, I avoided using those principles, largely for clarity. From this point on, however, I shall employ them with absolute consistency, as I believe that once we're well into Part 4, you'll have a definite understanding of the merits of my approach.

How to Handle Yourself Properly

To begin, we'll consider good handler construction. It's not really sufficient to simply have an **on something…end** and call it a handler; good handler names and a relatively rigorous *convention* are extremely useful.

4

Director has several handler-type keywords that actually are used to construct handlers all the time; **startMovie** is, as you've already seen, one of them. Contrast this to the handler we made in Module 3, **ButtonClicked**, and I think you'll notice an immediate difference.

Initial capitalization of handlers and handler calls, in scripts, is not absolutely necessary, but I believe it helps distinguish calls to custom script names from calls to Director's built-in handler events. This is especially useful when you make use of external code objects constructed for the purpose of making your job easier. And since we will be making calls to such external objects, it won't hurt to get into the practice now.

Tip

Director is not case sensitive, with one exception, but never as far as handler names are concerned. This means that buttonclicked, Buttonclicked, buttonClicked, BUTTONclicked, etc., are all considered by the Lingo interpreter to be the same thing. This is why it's a good idea to adopt and stick to one convention for capitalization. It makes things just a little more clear than they would be to someone who's used to languages that are case-sensitive.

Also, it's a good idea, when you place that final end at the close of the handler, to add the handler name again. Doing so is, again, not strictly necessary, but when you are scrolling through several screens, it can be most frustrating not to know precisely where one handler may have ended and the next begun. (Sometimes it can be very hard to tell.)

So rather than this:

```
on startmovie
 -- some code goes here
 myHandler
end

on myHandler
 --more code
end
```

Ask the Expert

Question   Thinking of conventions gives me the kind of headache I usually get if I've eaten a pint of ice cream in five seconds. Why do we need to cover this stuff?

Answer   A standardized approach to a particular task is enormously useful. Consider musical notation. If someone had not formalized the diatonic scale, had not defined rhythm notation, treble and base clefs, and so on, you'd be able to enjoy neither Bach nor Britney Spears. (Okay, so maybe formalized systems are not always good, but you'd also be missing out on every kind of music you like, probably, and most likely every song you've ever enjoyed.)

Lingo's script interpreter is very loose, meaning that it doesn't insist on particularly rigorous rules for creating programs. This is both good and bad, since an informal approach to programming can allow you to get things done quickly—including getting yourself into a lot more trouble than you would if you were working with a more formal, rigorous language.

I'll go into more details later, but one definite example I can give now is Lingo's rather frustrating habit of defaulting to integer math operations, even when you *want* decimals; a more formal language would allow you to declare variables as floating-point from the beginning, and would not *coerce* (change) them into integers unless you explicitly told it to do so.

in the interests of both consistency and a good general look to your scripts, this would be preferred:

```
on startMovie
  -- some code goes here
  MyHandler()
end startMovie
```

```
on MyHandler
  --more code
end MyHandler
```

This version is considerably easier to read. You get a very clear demarcation between handlers and can tell in the first one where the second one is being called; the parentheses make it very clear.

You've surely noticed by now that I add parentheses when referring to a handler as a handler.

Note

This is important! It is not always obvious when a handler is being called, just by context or inference. There are handlers—and we'll be writing some ourselves in the course of this book—that *return values,* meaning that they perform a set of operations and pass back a variable when they're done. If you don't make it obvious you're calling a handler when you use such structures, it can look simply as if you are setting one variable equal to another—a misleading conclusion.

Why this special attention? Because handlers are the primary means of program construction in Director (and, in fact, all modern languages have some derivation of them, be they called functions, subroutines, or what have you) and are not meant to be confused with keywords, variables, or any other kind of element you can gain access to or program via Lingo. For this reason, treat handlers as unique articles. Not only will this help you better understand the process of programming; it will make your programs easier for others to read.

Neatness Counts

These are not hard and fast rules, by the way, in that they are not required of you by Director. But they *are* important for giving your code a good structure.

When you're writing a letter, for instance, you want it to have proper grammar, capitalization, punctuation, and spelling, and you want to express yourself clearly and fluently. Understanding English rules is crucial to this process.

Similarly, if you want to write lucid code that does its job efficiently and can be understood by others (including yourself in six months' time), you will pay serious attention to what I am saying here.

Here is an example. This is poorly written Lingo (extremely poorly written), but it is perfectly acceptable and valid to Director.

```
on startmovie
  global x,y
  x=0
  y=0
  addnums x,y
on addnums x,y
  x=x+y
  y=y+1
  if x>y then x=y
```

If you were working for me and turned in code like that, I'd give you half a day to either clean it or your desk up. Not only is it sloppy; it is excessively hard for any human being to read. It would also be very hard to maintain and update such code in the future, and nearly impossible for another programmer to simply pick up and begin working with.

Unfortunately, it's far too easy for Director programmers to allow themselves to get lazy while working, and the result is (very often) stuff that looks at least as bad as the preceding code, if not worse.

One reason is that often there's little *peer review* in the Director programming community, which means that you don't have to actually try to get your Lingo approved by a colleague. Another reason is that the Lingo compiler itself is pretty loose; it doesn't require a lot of the more particular things that many other interpreters do. A third reason is the real dearth of well-written Lingo example code.

And when things need to be fixed or changed—as they always do—producers of such slipshod programs often end up taking several times as long to get the job done, if they are capable of even doing it in the first place.

Better done, the preceding example would be:

```
on startMovie

  GLOBAL x, y
```

```
x = 0
y = 0

AddNums( x, y )

END startMovie

on AddNums x, y

  x = x + y
  y = y + 1

  if x > y then
    x = y
  end if

END AddNums
```

While this does not absolutely follow my recommendations for white space and internal documentation, I believe you can already see quite an improvement in the readability and comprehensibility of the Lingo code.

Thus, the best shape for any handler to have is this:

```
on ThisHandler
  -- Some code goes here
end ThisHandler
```

That is, **on** followed by the **name** of the handler itself, initially capitalized (this is really optional with Director keyword–styled handlers such as startMovie, as syntax highlighting sets them apart as well), followed by the **code** contained in the handler, terminated with **end** and a recapitulation of the handler **name**.

Oh. You've noticed that Director indents things for you automatically when you do **repeat** or **if** prefixes. This gets annoying, because all your Lingo becomes flush left until you've closed that structure with the appropriate **end** keyword.

The nifty trick I promised in the last module is simply to do this.

When you begin one of these control structures, hit RETURN a few times and close it with the **end** that it needs, then use the arrow keys on your keyboard to move your cursor into the space between and happily proceed with entering your **if** or **repeat** code.

This allows you to continue to enter commands as you need to, without having the peripheral visual annoyance of the Lingo interpreter trying to do weird things with your indenting (namely, slamming everything into the left margin).

This also ensures that you never have an open **if** or **repeat** structure, which as you know now is not a good thing.

Finally, it lets you deal with the internal logic of your Lingo without having to wonder if the flush-left implies an error in the code you've entered so far, or whether it's just the Lingo interpreter being characteristically literal with you.

Note

For those trying to work out what the Lingo actually does, the answer is nothing, really; **AddNums()** simply adds any two numbers handed to it, sets them equal if the first is larger than the second…, and then promptly forgets everything. Why? There's no **GLOBAL** declaration, and there is no value returned from **AddNums()**. It's pointless code, just there as a sample. Of course, the first example of this very code makes it nearly impossible to see that fact, even if you're relatively experienced.

1-Minute Drill

● Why is good structure in your Lingo scripts important to have?

● What is the recommended basic structure of a handler?

Toward a Taxonomy of Variables

Another thing you have surely noticed from our earlier example is that there are two variables, **x** and **y**, and there's no readily obvious way to know what it is they are supposed to contain. Numbers, presumably—but numbers representing what? GNP versus national debt? Miles versus gallons? Amount

---

● It allows code to be human readable; it enhances maintainability; it enhances discipline in the thinking of the programmer.
● on handlerName, followed by the code in the handler, terminated by end handlerName.

of chocolate ice cream versus days required to eat it? Or just coordinates on a polar axial system?

There's no way to know, at least not from the variable names, and that is terrible, *terrible* Lingo design. Lingo does not require you to limit variable names to just six or eight characters, and there is no reason whatsoever to use terse variable names unless you are writing a very short program and won't have a lot of data to keep track of. And even then, it's bad design, so do not do it.

But there's more to variable names than just the *names* themselves. Actually, I'm about to launch another vector here on a debate that has been going on for years regarding a variable naming convention known as *Hungarian Notation*.

Hungarian Notation holds that you can add single initials to the beginning of a variable's name that help describe its *contents* (such as **n** for integer, **s** for string—as in a person's name—etc.), its *scope* (**l** for local, **g** for global), its *persistence* (**t** for temporary, **s** for static), and so on.

Of course, in some languages you can have several *types* of types (or subtypes) of variable (such as long unsigned int as opposed to short signed int), and Lingo allows superglobals—more on those in the next few pages. Many languages permit at least some variable types to be *coerced* to other types (integers converted to decimals and vice versa, for instance, but not integers to strings).... Well, you can go more than a little nuts using Hungarian Notation to an extensive fault. You might have noticed, for instance, that we had **s** for both string *and* static, which implies that if you want to get really particular, you begin dealing with character position as well in the variable's name prefix (second **s** from the left is static, fourth is string...)—and it is quite possible to end up with a dozen letters, not all of them different from each other, preceding a variable name before you actually get to the name of the variable. That's ridiculous, of course, and represents Hungarian Notation taken to its worst extremes.

Since Lingo is a relatively simplified language, I prefer to use a simplified form of Hungarian Notation to name all my variables.

Yes, *all* of them—and I can hear some C-type programmers grunting in frustration here—even my throwaway integer counters (**n** or **i** is not enough). There is no reason not to. A 15-character variable name in Lingo takes up exactly the same amount of memory as a one-character name, with the advantage that you can look at the longer variable name and have a clue what it's doing.

4

So my variables will begin with different letters:

- **n** for integer: 1, 2, 3, etc.

- **f** for floating-point (decimal): 1.121, 3.14, etc.

- **s** for string (even if it's one character): "Hello"

- **y** for symbol (a string converted to a quasi-numeric value): #hello

- **b** for Boolean (true or false, never anything else): TRUE or FALSE, 1 or 0

- **l** for list (we'll get to those in Module 9, at the beginning of Part 3)

- **m** for member (as in Director Cast member, of course)

- **o** for object (a code object of some kind or other; much more on those in Part 4)

- **x** for a parameter being passed that could be any one of the preceding types, to be determined by code testing—these are pretty rare

There may occasionally be minor divergences from the foregoing list, but only where noted.

Furthermore, there is the question of *scope,* which I'm sure you recall from Module 3. You will remember reading about local and global variables, as well as properties of behavior or parent scripts. For scope, I tack on either a **g** for a global variable, a **p** for a property, or nothing at all for local scope.

Thus, you can guess at both the contents and the scope of all the following variables, given their names alone:

gfPercentageIncomeTax

nNumberOfDays

psUserName

gbWonTheGame

sThirdCatsName

I know this is a little strange if you've never seen it before, and it might take some getting used to—however, when your Lingo scripts start approaching ten thousand lines in length, you will be very, very glad you've adopted something like this convention.

Understand, too, that you do not have to follow exactly the recommendations I have here, as long as your choices are absolutely consistent, and as long as you include copious notes—in the form of internal documentation—describing your variable naming conventions.

As far as actual placement in your scripts goes, it's best practice to *initialize*—prepare your variables for use—at the top of any handler that is going to use them. Lingo allows you to initialize variables on the fly, but I think it makes your code a little more tidy to do it at the top of the handler itself, rather than down somewhere in its logical bowels.

I mentioned *superglobals* a little while back. These are global variables defined outside of a handler:

```
GLOBAL gnTimesPlayed

on startMovie

 gnTimesPlayed = 0
 IncrementTimesPlayed()

end startMovie

on IncrementTimesPlayed

 gnTimesPlayed = gnTimesPlayed + 1

end IncrementTimesPlayed
```

This might seem a little odd, since the global **gnTimesPlayed** is declared outside either **startMovie()** or **IncrementTimesPlayed()**, yet the obvious inference is that both handlers know about it and what to do with it. Such global variables, declared outside handlers, are called superglobals, and in practice they are the only kind of global variables I personally use. The same set of handlers, rendered without the superglobal, would be:

```
on startMovie
```

```
GLOBAL gnTimesPlayed
gnTimesPlayed = 0
IncrementTimesPlayed()

end startMovie

on IncrementTimesPlayed

GLOBAL gnTimesPlayed
gnTimesPlayed = gnTimesPlayed + 1

end IncrementTimesPlayed
```

As I think you can see, superglobals reduce the amount of typing you need to do to grab variables, and using them makes your globals truly *global*. So I just don't use any kind of global except the superglobal. I believe it reduces confusion.

So let's do something relevant with our better understanding. In the last module, you created a program that got a list of files in any particular folder. You might recall its Lingo looked like this:

```
on startMovie
 GetFiles()
end

on GetFiles
 lastFile = the maxInteger
 member("fileList").text = ""
 repeat with fileNumber = 1 to lastFile
  fileName = getNthFileNameInFolder ( ( the moviePath ), fileNumber )
  if fileName = "" then
   exit repeat
  else
   put fileName & RETURN after member("fileList")
  end if
 end repeat
end
```

As you can see, this code just doesn't follow the recommendations I've made in this module. So the obvious thing to do is update it so that it does.

4

Ask the Expert

Question   If there are no Lingo requirements apart from some pretty simple basics, why define "standards" here? Isn't that a little hubristic?

Answer   Hey, you're welcome to write a book defining your own standards too. Yes, I know it seems a bit conceited, but I have *got* to impose some kind of structure on Lingo to wrestle it into a shape I can express to you meaningfully.

Since no real standards have ever been defined (apart from the fact that Bruce Epstein and others do advocate using **g** as a prefix for global variables, and **p** for property variables), it's fair for me to apply some of my own.

You are free to accept or reject any of them, but don't do so until you've worked with them enough to know exactly what you don't like about them, and why you don't like it.

Please don't go farther before trying this yourself. I'd like you to revise the code on your own first, drawing on your understanding of what I've said so far, before looking at my own version of it that follows.

Done? Okay, here's what I came up with. Don't worry too much if what's here isn't exactly like the revisions you made. As long as it's close, and the program still works, we'll be able to get along.

```
on startMovie

  GetFiles()

end startMovie


on GetFiles

  nLastFile = the maxInteger
  member("fileList").text = ""

  repeat with nFileNumber = 1 to nLastFile
```

```
sFileName = getNthFileNameInFolder ( ( the moviePath ), nFileNumber )

if sFileName = "" then
  exit repeat
else
  put sFileName & RETURN after member("fileList")
end if

end repeat

end GetFiles
```

You'll probably note, first, that the variable names have changed a little to reflect my simplified Hungarian Notation. You might also note some extra carriage returns between some lines; this is called *white space,* and we'll cover that a little later in this module. However, before we do we need to talk about internal documentation.

1-Minute Drill

● Define the following as they pertain to variables: n, s, f, g.

● Describe the scope and likely contents of the following: gnCurrentYear, sDayOfWeek, pfSalesTaxRate, gsHolidayWishList.

Read the (Built-in) Manual

First, *internal documentation* is often the last thing thought of by most programmers. Many of them utter the phrase "Good code is its own documentation," which is as rotten an excuse for laziness as any I've ever come across. Furthermore, it has implicit the assumption that the programmer in question is capable of writing good code. Too often, that is not at all the case.

● These are prefix designators for integers, strings, floating-point numbers, and a global scope indicator.
● A global integer for the current calendar year; a local string for the day of the week; a property for sales tax rate (a floating-point number); and a global string containing some kind of holiday wish or shopping list.

Note

Program code is a lot like cursive handwriting. Everyone thinks his or her own is perfectly readable. Obviously, this is an erroneous belief. It takes literally years of practice and a lot of concentration—every time you're doing it—to have such completely lucid penmanship. I assure you it's no different at all with programming. However clear it is to you, it won't be to anyone else.

Lingo allows you to use the double hyphen (--) to indicate the beginning of a *comment*. It's general practice to add these at the beginning of a line, but they can also be appended to any line of Lingo without getting you into trouble, as long as you understand that everything to the right of the comment marker, right up until you hit a carriage return, will be considered a comment. It will be ignored completely by the Lingo interpreter; Director will behave as though those lines of text did not exist at all.

All programs need internal documentation, really, and the ratio should be about 1:4—that is, for every four lines of program, one line should contain some documentation regarding what the program is actually doing at that point.

This is important for many reasons. For starters, any novices attempting to read your code (perhaps to study it and learn from it) will be eternally grateful. Second, if you should happen to get run over by a cement truck, *someone* is going to have to take up where you left off, and the person filling your seat will definitely appreciate the boost in understanding your logic (otherwise, she'll probably end up thinking a cement truck was too good for you).

Of course, a year from now, when you yourself are trying to edit or improve your code, you'll pat yourself on the back for having planned to help yourself along by adding reminders all over the place in your program of what it's doing and how—a sort of trail of bread crumbs through your own thought processes at the time.

Finally, and perhaps most importantly, adding internal documentation makes you stop and think about the code you've written as part of explaining it to yourself. In doing so, you will very often find a much better, more efficient way to do what you had been doing, and will be able to rewrite some of your own Lingo to match a newer, faster, more efficient model because of that—in the process, perhaps identifying and trapping for possible error conditions that might have arisen otherwise. And that never hurts.

Naturally, actually adding documentation as you go is likely to be tedious and somewhat cumbersome, so I don't think it's necessary to stop and write the comments as you're writing your active code. But you should reserve perhaps an hour each day of eight to just go over what you've done and document it. This will enhance your Lingo programming skills, increase the readability and stability of your Lingo code, and allow you to create more reliable, more expandable Director programs.

Depending on the size (and especially complexity in the Lingo) of your Director project, you might need only a little internal documentation. At the very least, your first movie script should contain a brief description of what your program is meant to do, what (if any) external code objects or other Director movies or casts it uses (these are often referred to as *external dependencies*), and any variable naming conventions you care to define (actually, *always* define your variable naming convention, as there is no "standard" among Lingo programmers).

Ask the Expert

Question   Come on. I wrote that code myself. I'm not going to forget how it works. Besides, how often will I actually have to go back and revise anything I've done before?

Answer   You would be amazed how much you can forget after a while, especially when you're doing really complicated projects. It's possible to start a project and—three months later, when it's almost finished—to have to go back and revisit, and possibly revise, some of your early work. If it really is a complicated project, you need to be careful, since the wrong kind of revision might turn the entire thing into one giant unworkable mess.

This kind of stuff happens all the time when you're writing code for a client, so be assured it can and likely often will happen to you.

As far as going back and revising closed projects goes: Ever hear of upgrades? Version 2? If you've satisfied a client, you *will* get repeat business—which might well mean doing exactly that: going back and reworking a previous project.

At times like those, lucid code, good structure, and rigorous internal documentation will be the only things that keep you from deciding to take up a career collecting aluminum cans someplace.

For the first two parts of this book, the foregoing will be quite adequate. Later, however, you're going to want to get considerably more involved with your documentation, to the point that in certain cases your Lingo scripts almost document themselves. (I'll show you how to do that when we get there; there are a couple of handy tricks we can use.)

Also, it's a very good idea to begin each handler definition with a line or two of comments to describe what the handler is meant to do in your code, and what (if any) result it is supposed to return once it's finished doing its thing.

Again, none of this is strictly necessary for Director to handle your Lingo; in fact, if you pay attention to the indenting in Lingo scripts, you'll see Director itself take care of the minimums for you. You don't do these things for Director, which really doesn't care. You do it for others, and you do it for your own sense of achievement and accomplishment. Well-written code is a lot like a well-written essay: It makes sense, is capable of maintaining a coherent theme, and above all follows proper structure conventions, such as initial capitalization, indenting, and so on.

Back to our Lingo from Module 3. You saw what I did to it a few pages back; now consider how you would add your own comments to your own code, and see if what I've entered here seems to be too little, too much, or just about right:

```
-- This program gets a list of files from whatever folder it's
-- running in, and places that list of files into a #text member
-- onscreen.

-- Variable names are simplified Hungarian. A 's' prefix indicates a
-- string; an 'n' indicates integer.

-- This program depends on no external code objects and should be
-- able to work in a Shockwave environment.

on startMovie

  -- Begin retrieving the file list
  GetFiles()

end startMovie


on GetFiles
```

```
-- This handler retrieves a list of files from the current folder
-- on the drive, and places that list in a text member onscreen.

-- Local variable init
nLastFile = the maxInteger      -- Max number to which we can count
sFileName = ""                  -- Temp container for each file name
member("fileList").text = "" -- Empty the file list onscreen

repeat with nFileNumber = 1 to nLastFile

  -- Retrieve file number nFileNumber's name
  sFileName = getNthFileNameInFolder ( ( the moviePath ), nFileNumber )

  if sFileName = "" then
    -- If it's empty we're at the end of the file list, so kick out
    exit repeat
  else
    -- Otherwise we add the file name to the list and keep going
    put sFileName & RETURN after member("fileList")
  end if

end repeat

end GetFiles
```

Here, of course, my ratio is not 1:4; it's more like 1:1.3 or so. This is for a couple of reasons. One, I wanted to show you the various ways in which you can insert comments into your Lingo scripts. Two, I wanted to show you how much clearer Lingo can be when it's exhaustively internally documented.

The preceding code is a great example of the kind of script that could be read and understood by anyone with no knowledge of Lingo whatsoever, but at least a general gloss of programming. I don't expect you to get this particular with every single script you write; there is such a thing as documentary overkill. However, I do want you to get into the habit both of looking for (and reading!) comments in code and of planning for and writing your own comments in your scripts.

Looking over the preceding code, you can see I've included

● A description of the program itself—what it's intended to do

● A description of variable name conventions

- Notes regarding external dependencies

- Explanations of handler calls

- Descriptions of what a given handler is meant to do

- Descriptions of variables, including a notation of scope

- Explanations of the logic of my control structures

Please, please, please take the time to add comments yourself. If you do not, eventually you will be in a position of writing something pretty complicated, and being utterly unable to fathom its structure—let alone describe it to anyone else.

1-Minute Drill

- What's one good reason to include comments in your Lingo scripts?
- What's a good ratio for internal documentation to active lines of code?

A Clean, Well-Lighted Script

At last we come to white space. Hemingway hated it; Melville tried to harpoon it. We're going to make it our close companion.

White space refers to extra blank spaces inserted into your code lines. It's there exclusively and only to make your code more readable to other human beings. The computer does not care about white space. As long as you create Lingo that Director can understand, you could jam it all together into one hideous mass of logical spaghetti (as we have seen).

Some languages—notably C++—don't even require you to add line breaks. They just use semicolons, parentheses, and braces. In such languages, you can actually write an entire program on *one single line,* if you really feel like doing it, and there are even contests to see who can produce the most *obfuscated* program code.

- It allows others to understand your logic; it allows you to revisit your logic months after having written a program; it causes you to consider what you've written and think of ways you might simplify it.
- About 1:4 is a good ratio to try to hold.

Don't even think of trying this with Lingo. For one thing, Lingo actually does require line breaks in a lot of (most) situations; for another, your goal is *not* to create bad code that confuses. Your goal is to create perfect code that is entirely lucid and comprehensible.

Again, we're talking partly about adopting your own methods, and partly about doing things as I recommend them, at least until you get the hang of things enough to develop your own means. For the time being, please use what I recommend, and certainly expect all my code listings to use this convention themselves.

The simplest form of white space, the carriage return, is what I use most often. I include three between handler definitions, and two from the start of the definition to the first line of Lingo it contains. I also add two before the end of the definition.

Control structures always get an extra line of white space, to distinguish them visually even further than the standard indentation does.

Contiguous lines of code—that is, several variable initializations, for instance—don't get any extra white space.

Your choice of font is important; don't pick a font that tries to look like handwriting or cursive. Those get very hard to read after a while. You can set your script font to be anything you want by selecting File | Preferences | Script…. I generally prefer some version of Courier, since it's *monospaced* (has a fixed width), which means that any white space I insert between a variable initializer and the comment I add describing it will align from one such line to the next.

The one major downside of Courier is that it can sometimes be hard to distinguish l (ell) from 1 or O (oh) from 0, and of course computers care about the difference, quite a lot. Another inconvenience is the serifs across the bottom of Courier characters, which can make them run together visually onscreen (though this helps make them more distinct when printing your scripts out). If you have Courier New, try that one—it represents an improvement over the original typeface.

Note

It's actually rather ironic that many computer screen fonts don't clearly make the distinction among one, zero, ell and oh, since all information stored on a computer is binary—composed entirely of ones and zeros. Given their high degree of importance, you'd think it'd be easier to tell them apart onscreen.

That said, here's the final incarnation of the code from Module 3 that we've been reworking. Note all the blank lines. This use of white space might seem excessive here, where we don't have a whole lot of code to break up, but I guarantee you that it will make things look a lot neater as we move along in this book.

```
-- This program gets a list of files from whatever folder it's
-- running in, and places that list of files into a #text member
-- onscreen.

-- Variable names are simplified Hungarian. An 's' prefix indicates a
-- string; an 'n' indicates integer.

-- This program depends on no external code objects and should be
-- able to work in a Shockwave environment.



on startMovie


  -- Begin retrieving the file list
  GetFiles()


end startMovie



on GetFiles


  -- This handler retrieves a list of files from the current folder
  -- on the drive, and places that list in a text member onscreen.

  -- Local variable init
  nLastFile = the maxInteger   -- Max number to which we can count
  sFileName = ""           -- Temp container for each file name
  member("fileList").text = "" -- Empty the file list onscreen

  repeat with nFileNumber = 1 to nLastFile

    -- Retrieve file number nFileNumber's name
    sFileName = getNthFileNameInFolder ( ( the moviePath ), nFileNumber )
```

```
  if sFileName = "" then

    -- If it's empty we're at the end of the file list, so kick out
    exit repeat

  else

    -- Otherwise we add the file name to the list and keep going
    put sFileName & RETURN after member("fileList")

  end if

 end repeat

end GetFiles
```

So as you've seen, we took a really short script that filled maybe a dozen lines and at least doubled its size overall. This might represent a waste of space to you, but computer storage is cheap—particularly where text is concerned—and the Lingo interpreter completely ignores the blank lines and comments, so they don't add any *overhead* to the program (meaning they don't make it run more slowly).

What this does do, of course, is make your scripts considerably easier to read—an important goal for any programmer.

Project 4-1: Text Editor à la Lingo

On to the Project du Jour. Today we're going to make a simple *text editor*—a program that permits you to copy, paste, and edit text as you would in an application such as SimpleText or Notepad. (It won't save any external files; we'll get to that in Part 3, after we've tackled some of the more involved parts of Lingo.)

This time, we're going to do things a little differently than before, because we're going to make a *two-part* file.

What I mean by this is that there will be a main part of the program, which is the actual text editor; and a loader, which does nothing except load the text editor movie.

We're doing it this way so that you can easily save text changes you've made in the editor—you'll be saving the changes inside the text editor movie itself.

Thus, you'll learn one way in which Director files can actually be changed at run time (that is, without using Director itself at all) *and* one way in which to get one Director file to open another.

Upon finishing this project, you will have learned:

- How to make one Director movie open another.

- How to apply that with a projector as well.

- How to save changes made in a movie even though you've loaded it in a projector rather than in Director itself.

Step-by-Step

1. We'll start with the loader Director movie. Begin, as always, with a brand new Director file, and place a #text sprite onscreen containing a message along the lines of "Loading text editor... Please wait."

The reasons for this are twofold. One, it will take a few moments for your projector to load the editor file; and two, by adding a #text member to this loader file, you force Director to include some Xtras (external resource files) that are necessary to allow your text editor to work. Paired pheasants, single stone.

2. In frame 1 of your loader file, add the classic frame script:

```
on exitFrame
  go the frame
end
```

3. Now open a movie script window and enter the following:

```
-- This loader file opens a simple text editor made in Director.
-- The file has no external dependencies apart from the editor itself.



on startMovie


  -- Load the editor Director movie
  go to movie "editor"
```

```
end startMovie
```

What this code does is really very simple. When this Director movie loads—whether you've clicked Play in Director, or double-clicked a projector made from this movie—it instantly looks for and tries to open another Director movie named **editor**.

Note

You do not have to include the **.dir** extension in order for your loader movie to find your editor movie. In fact it's a good idea *not* to, for reasons we'll explore in Part 2.

4. Save your loader movie as anything you want to name it; it doesn't matter, really. That's it for the first part—you're now ready to make your editor.

5. Again, start with a new Director file, and put a #text sprite on the Stage (déjà vu all over again). This time use the PI to turn it into a scrolling #text member, mark it as being editable, and resize it to fill your Stage. Make sure to leave room on the right side for the scrollbar.

6. Frame 1 gets another **go the frame** script; then open a movie script window and do the following:

```
-- This text editor is called by a loader file.
-- Without the loader file this will only work in Director itself.




on stopMovie

  -- Called whenever someone quits the program

  -- Save changes made to the #text member
  saveMovie


end stopMovie
```

4

7. Close your script window again. That's it for the editor portion; save it to disk with the name **editor**, right alongside your loader movie.

All this movie does is allow a user to type things into a text window onscreen, and save any changes automatically whenever the user quits the program.

You need to do the saving in a separate, external Director movie because, on Windows, Director projectors can't make internal changes to themselves (they can on a Macintosh, but such behavior is not really considered ideal, as self-altering programs might be considered as viruses by some virus-stopping programs, which means any program that does try to alter itself might be blocked from doing so, and so your text editor would not, in fact, save changes).

8. Now go ahead and create a projector from your loader movie, setting things in the options screen so that it's not full screen and shows its title bar. (This will give you a standard system window with a close box in it, allowing the user an obvious way to exit the program).

Your loader projector must have the editor file alongside it to function; beyond that, it's a self-contained program that you can use like many other text editors.

When you run it, you can copy text from your editor by selecting the text and pressing CTRL-C (CMD-C on the Mac); you can paste text into your editor by pressing CTRL-V (CMD-V on the Mac). Anytime you click the close box, the editor quits; note, however, that text you've entered and changes you've made are still there next time you run the program.

Project Summary

With this simple text editor program, you've seen how you can do the following:

- Allow a user to copy and paste text, type new content, and even save changes.

- Program one Director movie to open another Director movie on the computer's hard drive.

- Save changes made in a Director movie even though it's running within a projector rather than within Director itself.

That's it for the fourth module of this book. The next module, the final one in Part 1, will describe using the Debugger, a great tool in the Director suite. From there, we'll move on to Part 2 and start writing some really beefy programs.

☑ *Mastery Check*

1. Categorize the following as variable names or handler references:

sContents

ValueOfItem()

gnValueOfItem

2. If you were writing a program, what names would you give to the variables that contained the following information?

The user's name, employed throughout the program

A session ID number, employed once and accessible no place else in the program

Local sales tax, used frequently for calculating prices

3. What is the purpose of white space in a program's code?

_____

_____

4. What set of characters does Lingo use to denote the beginning of a comment?

_____

_____

5. Is the "end" strictly necessary at the conclusion of a handler definition?

_____

_____

6. If "end" is not strictly necessary, what is one good reason to include it anyway?

_____

_____

Module 5

The Debugger

The Goals of this Module

- Learn about the Debugger
- Learn how to correctly set breakpoints
- Learn how to use the Debugger to follow (step through) Lingo scripts
- Learn how to find and fix possible problems in your Lingo programming

S ince its advent with version 5 of Director, the Debugger has proved to be one of the greatest single tools in a programmer's arsenal. With careful use, the Debugger can turn hours of potential frustration into only a few minutes' reasoned exploration and troubleshooting.

The Three Choices in Script Errors

If you've had them happen to you by now, you know that Director's script error reports are contained in a dialog box with three buttons, such as the one shown in Figure 5-1.

As you see, there are three options here; the first is to Cancel, or exit the handler that has malfunctioned. Unfortunately, this also has the effect of stopping playback of your Director movie, which you might not always want, and unless you know exactly where in your Lingo the trouble spot might be, this will do you little good.

The second button, Script..., is great if you actually do happen to know where the error is, because (unless you're doing some of the more complicated programming in Director) clicking this button will cause a Lingo script window to open where the trouble arose. This also stops your movie from running, though.

The third button, Debug..., is what we're going to pay attention to in this module, because it opens the Debugger window and lets you see not only the lines of Lingo causing the trouble, but also the contents of the variables that existed in memory at the time the error occurred. This is tremendously useful information, because you get an inside peek at the *state* of your program, meaning you can see exactly what's being passed around, and you can even step back through your code's commands to see where things went wrong.

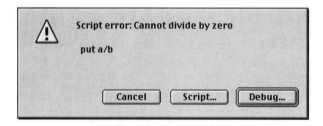

Figure 5-1   A typical script error dialog box

Messing Up on Purpose

Before we can really explore the Debugger, we need to deliberately create an error condition; that is, we have to write some Lingo that will malfunction when it runs. That's actually rather hard to do, because the basic errors you might think of making are all tested for by Director itself. It won't let you make obvious mistakes, in other words, so you need to do something subtle.

Start with a new Director movie and, in frame 1, place a **go to the frame** script in the script channel. Then use the #field tool in the Tool Palette to make two new #field sprites on the Stage. Name the #field members "num1" and "num2" in the Cast window. Use the Field tab in the Property Inspector (PI) to set their types to editable, and then create a button labeled "Divide".

Now create a new behavior for the Divide button:

```
on mouseUp me


  nFirstNum = value( member("num1").text )
  nSecondNum = value( member("num2").text )

  ALERT "The result was" && string ( nFirstNum / nSecondNum )


END mouseUp
```

Here's what this code does:

nFirstNum = value(member("num1").text)

First, we get whatever text has been typed into the #field sprite named "num1" in the Cast, and then we try to convert it to a number with the **value** keyword.

nSecondNum = value(member("num2").text)

Here we're doing the same thing with the text typed into "num2".

ALERT "The result was" && string (nFirstNum / nSecondNum)

And finally, we divide the two numbers, convert that result to a **string** so that it will be treated as text once more, and put the result into an **ALERT** box. (This is a very simple program, of course.)

Now click the Play button and enter 1 for the first number and 0 for the second, and then click your Divide button. You will get a script error saying you cannot divide by zero (which is true; in mathematics, division by zero is *undefined,* or an operation that yields no known result). Don't click Cancel or Script... though; instead click Debug.... You should get a window resembling the one in Figure 5-2.

There are three panes to this window. In the upper-left corner is the *stack* of handlers you've passed through to arrive at this point. Since the **mouseUp** handler was the only one used here, that's the only handler listed.

To the right is a list of all the variables currently in use in this handler. As you can see, the Debugger is showing you the values for **nFirstNum** and **nSecondNum**.

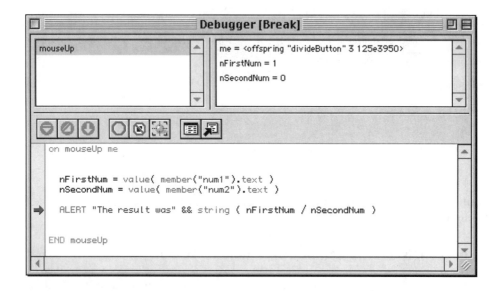

Figure 5-2 The Debugger displaying a line of Lingo where an error has occurred

Note

The **me** variable refers to the behavior script itself. We'll be discussing **me** in depth in Part 4.

Underneath you can see the Lingo you entered, complete with an arrow pointing to the **ALERT** line. This is the place where your program stopped working. Something is happening in this line of Lingo that Director does not like, and by looking at the list of variables you can see that the problem is the value for **nSecondNum**, which is zero.

Well, that's a little obvious, but it's a quick introduction to how you can get a peek into the way your program believes it should be running. There are more effective uses for the Debugger, which we'll be covering in the very next section.

1-Minute Drill

● What happens if you click the Debug... button in a script error dialog box?
● What does **value** do?

Stepping Through Code

Sometimes you might not know exactly *where* something is going wrong, and so you need to deliberately invoke the Debugger to see what's happening in your program.

For instance, click Director's Stop button. (Note that when you do so, everything in the Debugger disappears.) Open a new Movie script and enter the following:

```
on DivideNumbers n1, n2


  nResult = n1 / n2
```

● The Debugger opens at the point in your Lingo where the script error occurred, enabling you to see the variables, handlers, and so on as Director sees them.
● It attempts to convert text to some kind of mathematical or variable value that Director will not treat as text any longer; as in converting the typed number "5" into the mathematical value 5.

```
ALERT "The result was" && string ( nResult )


END DivideNumbers
```

This, of course, is not very different from the code you wrote for the Divide button, by which you may infer we are going to change that script a little and call this handler from the button's behavior, passing along the two numbers entered in the #field sprites as parameters:

```
on mouseUp me


  nFirstNum = value( member("num1").text )
  nSecondNum = value( member("num2").text )

  DivideNumbers( nFirstNum, nSecondNum )


END mouseUp
```

Now, click Play again and enter 1 for the first number and

6 + 3 * (–2)

for the second, paying attention to the parentheses. Click Divide. Well, you got the same script error as before, because 6 + 3 * (–2) is zero, again, and since Director calculates mathematical operations when it takes the **value** of a field, you're still dividing 1 by 0.

However, you will notice that there are now *two* names listed in the handler stack in the upper-left pane of the Debugger, the bottommost one being your **DivideNumbers** handler. As the arrow in the Debugger shows, the place where the program stopped working was with the line

nResult = n1 / n2

inside that handler. And as you can also see, **n2** has a value of 0.

Of course, you know already why this is happening, but you can actually step *back* through your handlers to see where those values came from.

To do that, click the **mouseUp** handler listed in the upper-left pane of the Debugger window. What happens? Director does two things:

● It steps you back into the **mouseUp** script.

● It displays the variables associated with that **mouseUp** script, specifically **me**, **nFirstNum**, and **nSecondNum**.

Here again you can see that **nSecondNum** turned out to be zero, which is how **n2** got its zero value when the variable was passed to it in the **DivideNumbers** call from the **mouseUp** script. ˙

You can also step *ahead* into the **DivideNumbers** handler once more, and as you can see from this example, the Debugger lets you roam through the previous handlers that ran before the one that malfunctioned. In this way, you can see not only the place where the actual script error occurred, but also the events leading up to it—which often will tell you what went wrong, and where.

Okay, click the Stop button again and notice that, once more, the Debugger clears. Then, click Play again and enter 1 for the first number as before, but 7 / 3 for the second, and then click Divide.

Now that was probably unexpected. Director told you the result was 0!

Why? Let's see if we can use the Debugger to find out.

Open your button's behavior script and click in the gray bar on the left-hand side just under the **mouseUp** handler. A red dot should appear there, resembling the picture in Figure 5-3.

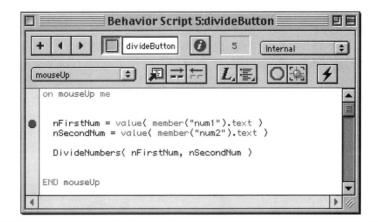

Figure 5-3   Setting a breakpoint in a Lingo handler

This is a *breakpoint,* or place in your Lingo where you are deliberately telling Director that you want it to pause and open the Debugger window. In other words, you want the program to show you at that point what's going on, so you set a breakpoint to cause that to happen.

Now, click Play again and, with 1 for the first number and 7 / 3 for the second, click Divide.

As you can see, the Debugger window becomes active at that point, with the **mouseUp** script listed in the stack pane in the upper-left and the variable list to the right. Note that **me** has a value, but that **nFirstNum** and **nSecondNum** are defined in the Debugger as **<Void>**. This simply means that they don't have any values assigned to them yet.

Note also that there are some green buttons below the stack list that have become active: a downward-pointing arrow with a line above it, another arrow like that but pointing to the lower right, and a third solid arrow pointing straight down. Figure 5-4 shows you these arrows in close-up.

Left to right, these arrows allow you to

- Step *through* the current lines of Lingo, meaning you can watch the Lingo execute one line at a time.

- Step *into* another handler being called from the current one, meaning you can follow your Lingo as it moves from one handler to another.

- *Run* the rest of the code until the next breakpoint is hit, meaning you can shoot right through every line of code.

We want to step through this Lingo to try to figure out why Director thinks that 1 divided by 7/3 is 0, so click the leftmost step button.

When you do that, you see that the variable **nFirstNum** receives a value of 1, which is exactly what should happen according to the Lingo you entered.

Then, when you click the step button again, you see that **nSecondNum** gets a value of 2. Two? That's not right. Seven divided by three is two and

Figure 5-4   The Step Script, Step Into Script, and Run Script buttons in the Debugger

one-third, or 2.333…. So it's obvious that there's one thing that needs fixing in our code already.

┤Note

You'll have to click the step button twice here to see the changes made to **nFirstNum** and **nSecondNum**. This is because Director is first reading the text contained in your #field sprites before assigning the values to the variables.

But that still doesn't answer the question of why Director gives us a final answer of 0, so we need to follow the program into the **DivideNumbers** handler.

With the break arrow pointing to the line that reads

DivideNumbers(nFirstNum, nSecondNum)

click the *diagonal* arrow, which is the Step Into Script arrow. If you're a little lost, look at Figure 5-5.

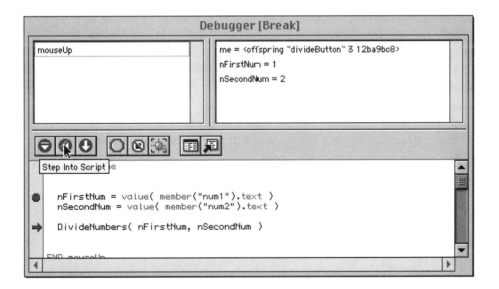

| **Figure 5-5** | The Debugger just as we're ready to step into a second handler from the main one |

Once you do that, you'll see that the Debugger has carried you into the **DivideNumbers** handler—you've jumped into it, following the Lingo in the same order that Director itself follows it. You can see that the handler stack in the upper left now has the **DivideNumbers** handler listed, and that to the right **n1** and **n2** are shown with values of 1 and 2, respectively. **nResult** shows a value of **<Void>**, which you remember means it just hasn't been given a value yet.

So now if you click the step button, you see that the division operation takes place, but that **nResult**'s value is 0, which is strange, because one divided by two is one-half, or 0.5.

1-Minute Drill

- What is a breakpoint?
- What do the three leftmost arrow buttons in the Debugger window do?

Now we've found what is happening—our numbers are not working as decimals—but the larger question of *why* is still unanswered.

It's happening because Director defaults to *integer* math operations when performing many different mathematical functions, which means that while 7 divided by 3 is 2 1/3 (or 2.333...), Director *truncates* the trailing decimal, giving us an incorrect result of 2.

What's worse, Director now assumes that this 2 value is meant to be an integer. So when it divides 1 by 2, it assumes the result is supposed to be an integer too, and 0.5 gets truncated to zero.

In order to fix this, we must explicitly tell Director that we want it to perform math calculations with decimals by using the **float** keyword. This forces Director to work with decimals, even if it would normally work with integers only.

To change things, we need to rewrite some of our code, beginning with the Divide button's script:

```
on mouseUp me
```

- A point set in Lingo scripts that causes Director to pause and load the Debugger.
- From left to right: step through the code a line at a time; step into a handler as it's being called; and run the rest of the script.

```
fFirstNum = float ( value( member("num1").text ) )
fSecondNum = float ( value( member("num2").text ) )

DivideNumbers( fFirstNum, fSecondNum )


END mouseUp
```

Here you can see we've added the keyword **float** to the **value** operations we're getting for our variables. We've also changed their prefixes from **n** to **f**, to indicate we're not working with integers any more, but rather floating-point numbers.

Then we need to rework the **DivideNumbers** handler a little too:

```
on DivideNumbers f1, f2


  fResult = float ( f1 / f2 )

  ALERT "The result was" && string ( fResult )


END DivideNumbers
```

Technically, this second **float** specification is redundant, since the two variables that have been passed into this handler are already floating-point numbers. It's been included here because it's not a bad practice, when you're writing Lingo scripts, to specify the format you want a given variable to have as Director manipulates and displays it. After all, as we've just learned, if we don't do so, unexpected or weird things can happen.

Note too that we've changed the **n** prefixes here to the letter **f**, just as we did in the **mouseUp** script, and for the same reasons.

Now does it work? Go back into your **mouseUp** handler and make sure the breakpoint is still in place, then close the script window and click the Play button. By the time you're through seeing the value for **fSecondNum** being set, you'll see that it seems to be working, so you can simply click the third arrow (the run script arrow) in the Debugger's window, which will cause the rest of your Lingo to execute. And there you are; you learn that the result of your calculations is 0.5, which is *still* not what we expected.

Now, 1 divided by 2.333... is *not,* in fact, 0.5; if you do this in the Message window:

```
-- Welcome to Director --
put 1.0 / 2.333
```

You see the result is less than one-half:

```
-- 0.4286
```

Run your program again and pay attention to the value given to **fSecondNum** as it appears in the Debugger. Though the variable is given a decimal, the division operation on the equation in the field is being handled *before* the **float** keyword, which means that we're getting the *integer* **value** of 7 / 3, or 2.0—not the 2.333... we actually want.

Here the Debugger has shown us a fundamental error in the way the program operates, demonstrating that it's not really our Lingo that is at fault any more, but rather a basic hitch in the way Director handles math. Unfortunately for this one, there is no easy fix, because there's no simple way to force the text the user enters into floating-point values as it is being entered.

Since this particular issue is a little too thorny for us to handle easily right now, we'll let it rest and continue exploring other things we can do with the Debugger.

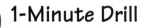

1-Minute Drill

● What does float do?

● Why is it important to use float?

More Debugger Features

Alongside the three script buttons in the Debugger, you'll see another triumvirate of icons, as shown in Figure 5-6.

● It forces Director to work in floating-point (decimal) math, instead of integer math, which is its default.
● If you don't explicitly declare variables and math calculations as floating-point, decimal numbers might get truncated, giving incorrect results.

Ask the Expert

Question   There's no way at all to fix this?

Answer   No, there are ways, but they're complicated if you're relatively new to programming.

The quickest alternative would be to make sure the user does not enter anything except numbers, which you can achieve by attaching the following behavior to both #field sprites on your Stage:

```
on keyDown me

  if "0123456789" contains the key = FALSE then

   dontPassEvent

  else

   pass

  end if


end keyDown
```

Essentially, what we're doing here is making sure that the key pressed is a number, and letting it get entered into the #field if it is. Otherwise, we don't let it through.

In Part 4, we'll look at handling text—as the user types it—in much greater detail; feel free to look up **dontPassEvent** and **pass** on your own if you want to before then.

This approach has its own limitations, though, because it allows only numbers, not decimals; and it doesn't let the user press DELETE or BACKSPACE to clear out mistakes. This is not something we really need to worry about at this point in our progress with Director, so rather than allow our discussion to be diverted, we should proceed to cover the other functions of the Debugger.

5

Figure 5-6 | The Toggle Breakpoint, Ignore Breakpoints, and Watch Expression buttons in the Debugger

These buttons allow you to

- *Toggle* a breakpoint at the current line of code, which means you can cause a breakpoint to come into existence where the script is currently running if there isn't one there, or remove one if there is.

- *Ignore* breakpoints, which will cause Director to behave as though there are no breakpoints at all anywhere in your Lingo.

- *Watch* an expression, which will cause a variable to be added to Director's Watcher window.

Let's continue with the divide movie we've been practicing with. Make sure you've still got a breakpoint set in the **mouseUp** script, then click Play and, when the Debugger window loads, highlight the **fSecondNum** variable in the script pane as I have in Figure 5-7.

Having done so, click the **Watch expression** icon in the Debugger's window. When you do that, a new window, the Watcher, will open, resembling the one shown in Figure 5-8.

As you can see, **fSecondNum** has been entered in this window, with its value being displayed as **<Void>**. Now go back to your Debugger and step through the script, paying attention to the value of **fSecondNum** as it is displayed in the Watcher.

As you do so, you will see **fSecondNum** being given a value in the Watcher window. This is a very nice way to see what given variables might contain at particular points in your Lingo code, sort of turning a spotlight onto them as you step through your scripts in the Debugger.

Note also that the Watcher has Add and Remove buttons; you can add variables to this window by hand by typing their names into the field at the top of the Watcher and clicking the Add button, or you can remove any variable from the Watcher list by clicking it in the large scrolling field in the center of the Watcher and then clicking Remove.

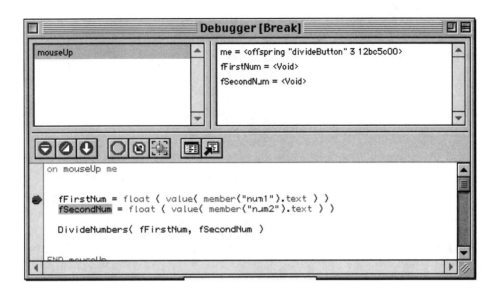

Figure 5-7   Highlighting a variable so that it can be added to the Watcher window

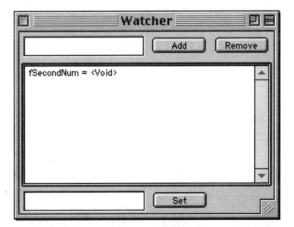

Figure 5-8   The Watcher window can be used to get and set a specific variable's value as it changes over time in your Lingo scripts

5

Ask the Expert

Question   Why use the Watcher to look at variables if I can see them in the Debugger's variable list?

Answer   There are a couple reasons:

- Sometimes a variable might be too large to easily be shown in the Debugger's window, so the Watcher is a great place to look at it.

- If you've written a complex program, you might have dozens of variables listed in the Debugger, which gets distracting when you only want to look at one.

   Besides, you can use the Set button in the Watcher to change a variable's value easily if you need to.

Question   Why does fSecondNum stay <Void> in the Watcher?

Answer   It doesn't really; when it does have a value, that value appears. However, since fSecondNum has only *local* scope, it's considered by Director to have a value only when you're in the handler that uses it. Thus, most of the time its value as displayed in the Watcher will be <Void>. This will be true for any local variables you add to the Watcher window.

Finally, if you are stepping through code in the Debugger and want to change the value for a variable you have listed in the Watcher, you can click its name in the list, then type the value you want the variable to have into the field at the bottom of the Watcher window and click the Set button. That way, you can manually override variables sometimes—quite useful if you want to deliberately test some variables you might get by random values. In Figure 5-9, you can see that I've changed **fSecondNum** to 2.3333 in this way.

Now go ahead and click the Run Script button to let your Lingo run through to the end, and click Divide again after dismissing your **ALERT** dialog. This breakpoint is getting annoying, isn't it? You can remove it by clicking the Toggle Breakpoint button in the Debugger, which will cause the breakpoint to disappear from your script. From that point on, you'll be able to run it just as though it wasn't there.

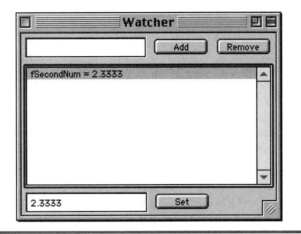

Figure 5-9 Manually changing the value for a variable using the Set button in the Watcher window

─┼─*Tip*──────────────────────────────
You can also remove a breakpoint directly by opening the script that contains it and clicking it in its gray bar to the left; this will cause it to vanish in the same way.

1-Minute Drill

● What does the Watch Expression button do?

● What does the Toggle Breakpoint button do?

The Other Debugger Controls

Figure 5-10 shows the other two buttons in the Debugger window. These buttons are there to

● Cause the Watcher window to open (if it's not already).

────────────────────────────────

● It causes a variable to be added to the Watcher window.
● It allows a breakpoint to be set or cleared in code while the Debugger is running.

| Figure 5-10 | The Watcher and Go To Handler buttons |

- Allow you to jump right to the script you're currently seeing in the Debugger, even to the point of having the text cursor appear near the current line of Lingo.

This latter feature is a great way to quickly gain access to the one line of code that's going wrong out of your entire Director movie, make the change or changes required, and then run your program again to see if the problem's been fixed.

Now, you might be tempted to use the Debugger a lot to see how Lingo works, and I think that's a great idea. Try it on some of the Library Palette behaviors you've added to your movies, for instance, seeing how the scripts are run and how variables are set dynamically as the Lingo goes through its routines.

There are some places, though, where you won't want to set breakpoints, necessarily. A big one is in any frame script, because every time an **enterFrame** or **exitFrame** script takes place, the Debugger will jump up and pause your movie until you step through.

Other places breakpoints won't work well are with **mouseWithin** scripts or any scripts that use **mouseDown** or **mouseUp** to get the actual coordinates of the mouse pointer, since the coordinates won't work when the Debugger appears. That's because you'll have to click one of the step buttons to keep the program going, which will mean the mouse is no longer over the thing you clicked.

Tip

You can also use the function keys on your keyboard to step through your code in the Debugger; F5 will run your script, F8 will allow you to step into scripts, and F10 will step through scripts.

Finally, you might not want to set a breakpoint in a repeat loop if your loop is supposed to count to a really high number, since you'll have to step through the loop a line at a time until everything's finished. If your counter is supposed to go to one million, that would take a while.

1-Minute Drill

● What are some places not to set breakpoints?

Using the Debugger to Understand Others' Programs

As handy as the Debugger can be for looking for trouble in your programs, it can also be pretty useful if you want to see how others have constructed their Director movies.

As you grow in expertise and skill with Director, you will want to make use of others' behaviors, for instance, to expand the functionality of your own movies.

However, not all behaviors are perfect, and some of them are extremely confusing if you're just looking at the Lingo, trying to figure out what's supposed to be happening simply by reading through the handler and variable names. This is where the Debugger can really shine through, letting you set breakpoints at strategic locations in those behaviors and see what's happening (or meant to be happening) at any given time in the behavior's existence.

In this way, the Debugger can act as a kind of interactive guide, letting you move through another person's set of code a few steps at a time until you feel you've got a reasonably good grasp of what's happening. If you ever find yourself in the position of having to maintain or upgrade Lingo written by someone else, and that Lingo is not well documented, the Debugger might be the only way for you to meet your needs.

● With frame events, generally, or with mouse events. Counters and repeat loops are bad, too.

Project 5-1: Stepping Around Town

For this module, I want you to create some Director movies that use Library Palette behaviors, then use the Debugger, the Watcher, and breakpoints to step through those behaviors and see how they work.

The goals of this project include:

- Increasing your familiarity with the Debugger
- Gaining an insider's perspective on how Director handles Lingo

Step-by-Step

1. Find a Director movie on your hard drive.

2. Place a breakpoint in one or more scripts.

3. Run the movie and use the step controls in the Debugger to see how the scripts operate.

4. Place some Library Palette behaviors onto some sprites on the Stage as well, and use the Debugger to see how they operate and respond to different events (both keyboard or mouse events and events that happen as the Director movie is running).

A good place to start might be the programs we've made so far. Try different things, adding variables to the Watcher or toggling breakpoints here and there, stepping into and out of handlers, moving around in your handler stack, and so on.

Project Summary

In doing this little exploratory project, you will have gotten a very good feel for how the Debugger operates, which will serve you in excellent stead as you move on in your Director knowledge.

The Debugger may also help you to understand some of the more complicated scripts we'll be creating in Parts 3 and 4, if you happen to feel a little lost by my explanations, since you can set breakpoints anywhere and move through those programs one line at a time.

Summary

In this module, you've had a chance to look over the functionality of the Debugger. I've just given you the basics here, because odds are pretty good that as you write Director programs, you'll have ample opportunity to work with it on your own.

Tip

What that means is you'll likely get script errors now and then. You're not really programming if you don't get errors from time to time!

5

Do use it, and do get comfortable with it, because it is often your first line of defense in figuring out what's going wrong, and in fixing problems in your Director movies when they arise.

That's it for Part 1 of this book. You now have a feel for all the basic tools Director provides you; in Part 2, we'll begin really using these tools in concert to create some more interesting programs.

✓ Mastery Check

1. Why click the Debug button when you get a script error?

2. What is a breakpoint?

3. What results will you likely get from the following mathematical operations in Director?
3 / 4
2.0 / 7
2.0 / 3.0

4. How do you force Director to work in decimal arithmetic?

5. What does the Watch expression button do?

6. How do you change a variable's value in the Watcher?

7. How do you toggle a breakpoint while the Debugger is running?

☑ Mastery Check

8. How do you step into another handler in the Debugger?

_____

_____

9. How do you step out of a handler into previous ones in the Debugger?

_____

_____

5

Part 2

Using Director to Create Programs

Module 6

Preparing to Create a Program

The Goals of this Module

- Learn how to plan for your program's target audience
- Learn how to plan for the possible release platforms involved
- Learn how to determine what tools to use in creating your program

In Part 1 of this book, you learned about the basics of using Director and the tools it provides you to create programs. This is important to know, as even a relatively simple Director-based animation will use at least some programming knowledge. In this part, we will begin expanding your knowledge to explore some of the more interesting aspects of programming.

Glamour?

As you've no doubt surmised by now, programming—even with a tool as relatively easy to use as Director—does not simply involve sitting down at a computer and banging out some Lingo by poking randomly at keys, then dashing off to complete your next assignment. This is the kind of role programmers are often handed by Hollywood, which is sort of good, as you can use that image to intimidate squirrelly clients. However, this image is also harmful, as it fosters a totally unrealistic notion of what programming actually is.

Thomas Edison once stated that genius is "One percent inspiration and ninety-nine percent perspiration," probably because he didn't understand decimals very well. It's actually more like 99.44 percent perspiration, with 0.56 percent being that rare *aha* moment you get that lets you create something unique, or at least radically different from the norm. Most of the programming you will ever do will not be that interesting, or it will be something done in support of something that started out being interesting. There is much drudgery to be found in programming, which could be why so many programmers favor energy foods such as caffeine-laden sweetened fizzy liquids and chips loaded with unnaturally shaded cheezish substances. (My personal favorite is a mix of salted nuts and pretzel sticks. It doesn't do much to keep me awake, but it does keep me crusty enough to hammer at the code for as long as I need to.)

But you will find this general fact to be true with any creative endeavor. Whether you are a poet, an artist, a dancer, or in fact one of any of the members of the creative professions, you will find that it's all about planning, preparation, and practice. Expertise in a field does not come naturally; even prodigies cannot reproduce something until they have first seen or heard it. In this part, we'll be discussing the aspects of skill you need to create programs, beginning with this module, where we discuss what you need to do before you even really begin writing the program at all.

Finding Your Audience

In my experience, when discussing preliminary program design with clients, I am often struck by how little the client him- or herself even knows about what the final goal is to be. Presumably, if someone is willing to fork over five or more figures' worth of fees for a product, that person is going to have some clue what the desired product actually is.

Not so.

In trying to gain a handhold on the elusive goal, I've found that considering the release market is one of the best things you can do early in the stages of a program's evolution. For whom is the program being written? What is the desired user base? Is this program intended to be used by law enforcement officers in the field? Is this program a video game for 13-year-olds? Is this program meant to help octogenarians research their family histories? Is the program meant to help hearing-impaired individuals appreciate the works of Mozart? Or is it just intended to teach fourth graders the fundamentals of multiplication? (That last possibility, by the way, is by far the hardest kind of program to write.)

Let's take the educational angle for a minute. Consider the possibility that a client comes to you and wants you to write a program that teaches decimal arithmetic operations via some series of sessions that are not meant to be simple rote-practice "drill-and-kill" exercises. That is, your user will have to be stimulated to maintain interest in what is happening at all times, will be required to show increasing skills in dealing with decimals, but should never at any time feel that the program is unbeatable, that she or he is "too dumb" to keep up.

Oh, your client mentions casually, and it has to be interesting to ten-year-olds, but it might also be used in adult-education or remedial high school education settings.

Now here you might be tempted to walk out of the meeting. How can you possibly write a program that will be interesting to anyone within an age range from preadolescence right through full adulthood? Can it even be done?

Well, consider a few things. Consider, for instance, Pixar's movie *Toy Story*. Consider *Star Wars*. Consider *The Simpsons,* or *Harry Potter* (the books). Or Sherlock Holmes or *Lord of the Rings* (again, the books). What do these movies and stories have in common? They have an appeal across an absolutely vast range of ages. Eight or eighty, they attract most comers. Between them all, they manage to attract everyone, or virtually everyone. So yes, it is possible for your

6

program to have a wide appeal base, and, in fact, I submit it will be harder to get kids to like it, because they don't have the patience an adult might have with things that are less than wholly engrossing.

But that, of course, is just one consideration, just one possibility. You might also get a client who manufactures hydraulic compressors, and who wants to create a CD-ROM-based troubleshooting matrix that allows mechanics to rapidly diagnose likely sources of problems. Or, you could have that same client wanting you to create an "online" version of the company's 500-page parts catalog, without any conception on the client's part of what exactly is meant by the word "online," and without any comprehension of the fact that receiving the documents in Quark format will not be sufficient for the purpose.

Or, you could end up creating a piece meant for Internet distribution that is intended to show visitors to the local Community College's library how to use the card catalog.

Some of these might seem like interesting challenges, and some are. Many of the jobs you'll end up doing are not particularly interesting, though, and still they will require your full time and attention to assure the task is completed on time and correctly. In all cases, the final product is clearly important to consider in your approach to the question of preparation.

For example, your client might be absolutely certain that the program is never going to be used outside a given arena, and while such assurances are sincerely given, they might well not be true. I'm not suggesting you get a disclaimer, necessarily, but if you feel your client might change the venue of a product without necessarily telling you of that decision beforehand, you could find yourself in the nasty predicament of having to retool significant portions for free.

To this confusion, you can add the fact that often a program will have to bear several aspects of different kinds of release to be truly effective. For example, an educational program will probably have to have some entertainment value; and a utility program might have to include some instructional elements to really be useful to many people. In general, however, we'll be discussing four main categories of programming here, and each has its own approach to getting the task done.

1-Minute Drill

● What's an important thing to consider before beginning to write a program?
● Why can educational programs be hard to write?

● What the purpose of the program is, and who the target audience is.
● It can be challenging to develop a program that holds the interest of a wide age range of users.

Entertainment

Entertainment programs don't just include video games, though this is the commonest genre of the entertainment subset, and it could be the entire reason you are reading this book. Perhaps right now you're feeling a little lost, wondering how any of the rest of this stuff is relevant, thinking *C'mon, I just wanna make a blast-the-aliens game.* Okay, so how do you propose to do that without even knowing how programs are written?

You should know, by the way, that most of the really hot entertainment titles have not been made using Director. Odds are reasonably decent they use polygon-casting engines created in C or C++ and have been assembled using Metrowerks' CodeWarrior product. This shouldn't deter you, as there are lots of really interesting Shockwave games on the Net, and *all* those games were made using Director.

All entertainment games, if they are well done, will include factors of simplicity, cleverness, and powerful user interaction. Take as one example the wild success of the video game Tetris late last century. This was a game with very, very simple rules and controls, but it was one of the most addictive things ever unleashed on the human population, at least for a while. Its simple rules and almost childish shapes hid a surprisingly captivating motive. Close contenders have been games such as Lemmings and the Chu-Chu series.

By far the greatest game, though, in the entire entertainment genre, is likely to be Myst, which really was not a shoot-em-up game at all, but rather a more or less complete vision of another world brought to computer screens using HyperCard, Apple's scripting engine, which had been more or less the conceptual precursor of Director. I mention these titles not to discourage you. Each one of them is well within the technical capacity of Director to produce. All it needs is for some clever Director programmer—perhaps you—to put in that 99.44 percent work to back up that one *aha.*

But in going with entertainment, you have to keep some rules in mind. You can't make the controls too bewildering; you can't make your clues too obscure; and you shouldn't tell just anyone all your cheat codes. (Those really are there to allow testing of higher levels, not to let dishonest adolescents rack up impossible scores.) While you might not need to consider such factors as ADA compliance (more on that in the Education section), you do have to at least try to make your game accessible to a relatively wide range of people.

In this light, probably the only major consideration you'll have is ensuring that your keyboard usage is more or less standard. This is not as easy as it might sound, for the layouts in Germany will not be the same as they are in the U.S.,

6

and if your have navigation keys that rely on positions on the board to make sense, you could get into trouble.

Education

Education, as I suggested earlier, is probably the hardest genre for which to write software. Apart from the fact that you must balance a learning experience with entertainment—thus keeping your user *productively* riveted through the entire program—you must also consider special-needs users, something not generally encountered when working on other kinds of programs.

For example, you might think that creating a memory game wherein cards that have already been chosen are given a different color than the rest sounds like a good idea until you consider the needs of color-deficient individuals— these are people who might not easily see the difference in colors that to you is completely obvious.

Or, you might think nothing of creating a program that has entirely mouse-driven navigation, meaning that moving from screen to screen will be accomplished by pointing and clicking. But consider how a person with little or no control of the hands or arms might be able, then, to get around; worse, consider someone who has only partial control of those extremities, but who is not capable of the fine motor coordination required to do precision point-and-click work.

And, given the fact that computers are highly visual devices, it might surprise you to know that a significant minority of computer users are also legally blind. If you are presenting a lot of information onscreen that must be read to be assimilated, you could get into trouble pretty quickly here.

A few years back, the U.S. legislature passed the ADA—Americans with Disabilities Act—which requires public institutions to have equipment and resources in place that meet some pretty intensively defined minimum standards. For computer programmers, the standards that are of most interest include provision for alternative means of navigating through a program (be it via keyboard, speech activation, or other means of control) and provision for visually impaired users, meaning you might have to create a program that can read itself aloud.

For this reason, if you are contemplating producing an educational title, it is vitally important that you ask early if it has to be ADA compliant, and make sure your client knows this means added expense and (probably) a longer development phase. This might also mean that some of your ideas for making the program more interesting will have to be passed over.

Sales Support

PowerPoint is dead, and pretty much everyone except Microsoft knows it. What started out as a handy way to augment or enhance a presentation has rapidly turned into a hideous beast that often ends up being the presentation itself.

Market-minded businesses know this and are always interested in talking about creating a newer, more interesting product presentation using cutting-edge tech. Often what they end up with is just a rehash of their PowerPoint slides, but that's generally more the fault of the "creative" designers of the program than it is anyone else's.

However, sales support doesn't just mean digital commercials. It can also mean catalogs, training manuals, even Web sites integrated with released desktop software. Of all the clients you are likely to have, it is the ones in this genre that are likely to be the most intractable (and the highest paying). They have a clear image for their product and their company, and they tend to be overly critical of anything that is in any way at variance from that vision, however slightly. To some extent they have that right, of course, but it's also not uncommon for business clients to become used to abusing their vendors. Knowing the difference between a legitimate complaint about a program and what's actually more properly defined as *scope creep* is something we'll discuss a little more fully in Module 7. How to handle such issues comes down to the question of how willing you are to risk throwing the sale versus how genuinely unreasonable the client is being.

6

Utility

This isn't as dull as it sounds. Antivirus software is utility software. A lot of Internet access software is utility software. Clocks that know what time it is in different time zones, the text editor we made in Module 4, even the program that makes lists of files in a folder from Module 3 are utility programs.

Without a decent working knowledge of how to look for, open, read, and save files on a user's disk, there is little purpose in writing any software at all. Why bother, if it can't actually do anything? Ultimately, you end up with blinking lights and beeping.

So even if utility code doesn't thrill you, it's going to comprise the bulk of our efforts in this book. The latest Tomb Raider would not be able to save level progress—or even play sound effects—without generous dollops of utility code in the mix.

1-Minute Drill

- What are things to consider when writing educational software?
- What is one benefit of writing utility software?

Determining Your Release Platform

After deciding which of the preceding four types of program (or combination thereof) you're going to be creating, the next question to ask is one of *platform*— on what type of computer your software is to be distributed, and how that distribution is to take place.

Code written for release on a CD-ROM will naturally be quite a lot different from code intended for Shockwave distribution, for example, and necessarily so. A CD can hold up to 700 megabytes of data, which would take days to receive off the Net. Obviously, the Shockwave environment is not suited, then, for full motion, full-screen video.

However, even something as apparently innocuous as going with one platform for distribution has its dangers, as we'll see considering the following.

Windows Only

This sounds simple enough until one considers that no major release of Windows has ever been the same as its predecessors. The jump from 3.1 to 95 alone was quite significant, and Win98 is itself rather variant from 95. With the release of NT, Microsoft began pulling support for MCI calls, which unfortunately formed the bedrock of many rich media playback environments for years previous. Windows 2000 furthered the trend, and ME has continued it. XP promises to be visually interesting and programmatically hideous, for if one cannot even count on the dimensions of control windows and buttons to remain constant, one cannot meaningfully create recyclable program components.

This inability for programs to port across platforms within the Windows environment itself is profoundly exasperating. For the most part, a Director programmer will not have to consider these issues, but you should know that it's *impossible* to guarantee that something that works on one version of

---

- Whether ADA compliance will be a factor (and to what degree); what kinds of special-needs users might be running the software; the approximate age range of the target audience.
- You may learn how to perform functions such as opening and saving external files, or similar system-related activities that can enhance all the programs you write.

Windows will necessarily work on any other version—or even that *same* version, with just a few hardware differences thrown into the mix.

Macintosh Only

Mac has had its changes too, though none of them (with the exception of the change to OS X) have been as drastic as what Windows went through. In general, if your program works on one Mac, it probably will work on just about all of them.

In both of these scenarios, never, ever believe a client if he or she tells you that your program will never have to port to the other platform. In my experience, this has never been true. It doesn't matter how sure your client is that your program will always run under Windows. You are almost guaranteed that you'll get a call about three weeks before the completion deadline, and in that conversation will learn that yeah, maybe you should make it run on Mac after all.

For this reason alone, I strongly recommend against your using Xtras (external code objects) that harness you to one platform exclusively. For instance, many Director programmers have happily touted the virtues of using ActiveX components to make their Windows Director movies do interesting tricks—happily, that is, until the client begins demanding similar tricks on Mac, which does not support ActiveX, leaving the suddenly unhappy programmer wishing he'd just kept it simple and not relied on too many embedded system calls.

6

Shockwave

Shockwave distribution combines the caveats just cited with its own set of peculiar problems, specifically (as implied before) file size; and tight restrictions on access to the end user's hard drive. A Shockwave file, obviously, cannot afford to be huge, and so you need to take into account some space-saving considerations, such as not using high-color bitmap graphics, avoiding digital video, and trying to keep sound effects to an absolute minimum.

You must also remember that Shockwave can run on either Mac or Windows, which means you have to be really careful about any Xtras you use. In fact, it's generally best to create Shockwave files that use few or no Xtras at all.

Coupled with this, however, is the constraint specific to Shockwave that does not allow you, under any circumstances, to simply open any old file on the user's system. This means there's no simple way for you to allow the user to open or import files into a Shockwave presentation, and there's no simple way for you to save anything significant. Thus, Xtras such as FileIO are strictly forbidden, so don't even bother to try.

Furthermore, printing in Shockwave is nearly impossible, so my recommendation is don't try it unless you really know what you're doing.

Finally, using lots of large graphic images, such as 800 × 600 pixel bitmaps, is not a good idea for Shockwave files. It takes quite a while for those images to be received via modem through the Internet, and many people simply won't have the patience to wait for them, resulting in your program never even being seen.

Multiple Platforms

This is where it can get tough, especially if you also have Shockwave to consider. Just porting across Mac to Windows can be pretty tricky, but if you include the limitations of size and external resources imposed by Shockwave, you end up with a program that's almost hamstrung from the moment it's created unless you rely on program quality rather than media richness to create a satisfying experience.

You can make a program that works well on Mac or Windows if you remember a few things:

- Always use embedded fonts; don't rely on system fonts for consistent look and feel.

- Try to keep reliance on Xtras at a minimum, and when you do use them, make sure they are available for both platforms. The Print-O-Matic and OS Control Xtras are good examples of this.

- Digital video must be QuickTime, no exceptions. QuickTime is a better-looking format than AVI, and is not subject to the same whimsical changes. MPEG-1 is workable, but most Windows systems are still incapable of handling it properly unless QuickTime has been installed anyway (or you use an Xtra), and MPEG-2 requires special video hardware to play back. It's least painful to simply stick with QuickTime for both Mac and Windows.

- Port early, port often. I cannot stress this enough. Check how your code works on the other platform regularly. If you are doing your job properly, you will be able to code on either platform without any difficulty, and your program will work on both.

The major plus of Director is that a properly created file will function interchangeably under Mac or Windows. The greatest frustration of Director is that you do have to buy another copy of the program for the other platform. You can't use your Mac version to make Windows programs, and you can't use your Windows version to make Mac programs. There are workarounds, such as creating a "stub" projector that loads any Director file; or creating a Shockwave file; but the former approach lacks the flexibility you get from being able to make your own distribution program (including adding custom Xtras you might have); and the latter suffers from enough restrictions that it's useful only in emergencies as a bellwether.

Ask the Expert

Question   So what's the one thing I really need to know about porting my Director movies?

Answer   The cardinal rule for working on multiple platforms is port early, port often. Test your program as you go, particularly if you are creating a Shockwave release. You have to do this, and you have to do it a lot, to make sure that what you *think* you're doing is in fact what the end result will be.

Question   Well, if porting is such a headache, why worry about it, especially if my client tells me it's never going to happen anyway?

Answer   Clients change their minds, a lot. Always plan for porting to a different platform, even if your client insists it's never going to happen. The halls of Director history are filled with frantic requests for help from desperate programmers told, in the eleventh hour, that a file they've been designing for Windows-only release, which relies extremely heavily on Windows-specific functions, has now been designated by the client for release on Mac as well, or in Shockwave format, or both. These poor souls are faced with the most terrible alternative any programmer can consider, that of the *top-down rewrite,* meaning that weeks or perhaps months of work will have to be discarded to achieve the required goal.

Besides, code that is portable is also generally more robust. It's not subject (extraordinarily) to changes in the platform for which it's written, meaning that if most or all of the rules on a platform have been remade by the newest release version of the operating system, properly portable code is less likely to cease functioning, and it will probably require only relatively minor changes to make sure it continues working.

6

Don't let this scare you off. Multiple-platform ports are relatively simple to accomplish with Director, as long as you plan ahead. One of the things we'll keep addressing in this book is this very issue, so don't feel that you have to go it alone or that it's some kind of deep, arcane mystery to which very few people have any of the solutions.

Choosing Your Tools

As you've seen, Director can—and very often does—make use of Xtras when creating programs. Some of these Xtras are "standard" with the Director release, and you might not even be consciously aware of them. These Xtras include items that handle vector and Flash shapes and Xtras that allow text to be drawn on the Stage. Many Director programs make use of FileIO as well, at the very least to request from the user a location of a target external file, or to save files out to a specific place on the user's drive.

My advice to you is to strive, as much as possible, not to use Xtras that are not standard with the Director package. This is not because you cannot trust the makers of these Xtras; rather, it is because over-reliance on external code objects can endanger the success and quality of your programs. For example, many media-handling Xtras for Windows rely on ActiveX components as their core engines for doing their work. The problem is that there is no such thing as "standard" ActiveX on Windows, and in fact older versions that used to be installed on Win95 now are not available at all on systems such as Windows 2000. This means that some Xtras that relied on those older ActiveX cores will not function at all on newer Microsoft systems.

If you must use Xtras, try to use ones that are available for both Macintosh and Windows. This is important because the dual-platform nature implies that they are written independent of any embedded operating system features, which implies in turn that they will continue to function properly regardless of the kinds of changes that may be made to that operating system. Examples of this kind of Xtra include FileIO (released by Macromedia and included in your Director package), Print-O-Matic (which allows you to create really high-quality printouts from virtually anything in your Director Cast), and the OSControl set, which lets you add standard-looking system components to your Director movies such as buttons, pop-up menus, labels, and so on that are not included at all in the current Director control suite.

The other thing to consider with Xtras, though, is that not all of them will function correctly with Shockwave. FileIO is a very particular example of this and is one of the things that catches quite a few novice Director programmers unawares.

The scenario typically is one in which a programmer happily creates a nice Director program that uses FileIO to save settings, or text files, or high scores, to the user's hard drive. This programmer is then shocked and dismayed to learn that FileIO absolutely will not work in Shockwave, no matter what tricks he tries.

This is because FileIO poses a profound security risk in a browser setting, and if you think about it for a few moments you'll realize why. Consider the chaos that could be wrought by a program, running in a browser window off the Internet, which is capable of randomly opening, changing, or even *deleting* any particular file on an end-user's computer. Since FileIO permits precisely that kind of operation to take place, obviously it cannot be permitted to run in a browser environment. There's too much risk that some individual with malicious intent could create a program that does tremendous damage to any computer that tries to run it.

ActiveX components also are not good to use in Shockwave files, because of course there is no way for Macintosh computers to run them. This might seem a small consideration to some, but I should point out that there is a chance there'll be a Director (and Shockwave) for UNIX-based systems at some point in the future, and the combination of Mac and UNIX markets is quite large—much larger, in fact, than the share held by Windows.

Furthermore, it is rather selfish to create programs that can be seen and appreciated only by users of one particular operating system, and, of course, it simply adds to the disproportionate saturation Microsoft has in the desktop computer market now.

There are other things to consider regarding Shockwave, such as the fact that movie-in-a-window (MIAW) Director files will not function at all.

So in determining which tools to use, you must have a very good understanding of the kind of release you're considering: whether you plan to do a desktop install, perhaps from CD; whether that desktop install will be for only one type of operating system; whether you're going Shockwave only; or, whether you are going for a combination of desktop install and Shockwave access.

6

1-Minute Drill

- Why is it unwise to rely too heavily on Xtras?
- What is important to know about FileIO when considering Shockwave file release?

Internal Tools

These are always the most reliable, since they are packaged into the Director engine itself, even if (as with #text) they take the form of Xtras. Internal tools are the ones we've seen and used up to this point, tools that let you create buttons, lines, and shapes on the screen, or that let you use bitmap or vector graphics from your Director Cast. Internal tools will always work the same on either Mac or Windows and pose no major issues with Shockwave.

There are three caveats to consider for Shockwave distribution where internal tools are concerned:

- If you have imported digital video, such as QuickTime, that movie is not in fact *embedded* into your Cast. It is actually *linked to* it. Thus, if you put your Director file online as a Shockwave file but don't upload the QuickTime file alongside it, your Shockwave file will not play the video. It can't. We'll discuss ways to handle external files such as these in the next few pages, and we'll cover them in greater depth in Part 3.

- If you are using a lot of bitmap graphics (such as images created using PhotoShop), you'll probably want to *dither* the color down into Director's Web 216 color palette. This is because a bitmap graphic file gets very large (in terms of disk usage) when it is displaying lots of colors. Typically, an 8-bit image is quite sufficient; this displays up to 256 colors and is the way that GIF image files are shown onscreen. However, many images show 16 bits of color per pixel, which is around 65,000 possible colors; some go up to 24-bit, which is about 17 million colors, and some go as high as 32-bit, which is 17 million colors plus 256 levels of transparency effects per pixel. Why does this matter? Because the number of bits an image displays per pixel has a direct correlation to the size that image occupies on disk, and large image files take much longer to download in a Shockwave environment.

- Some Xtras assume that an operating system will remain constant, which means if the system changes or you port to another platform, your program probably will not work any more.
- FileIO cannot be used in Shockwave files.

Of course, preparing a Director movie for Shockwave release does compress bitmaps, which can reduce their size by up to 90 percent. This would mean a 1.8MB bitmap could end up getting squeezed down to a mere 180KB, which might take on the order of five seconds to retrieve from the net. However, compression in bitmaps tends to seriously degrade image quality. At its highest settings, Shockwave compression of a graphically rich 24-bit image is probably not going to give you an acceptable result, especially if your client is expecting very high quality visuals.

This is the reason you'll want to try to keep your images really low in bit depth if you can, and why you will probably want to dither them into the Web 216 palette. Then they end up using just 8 bits of information, with the added advantage that the Web 216 palette built into Director allows you to show these images on either Mac or Windows without worrying about what might happen to the rest of the computer's display on certain machines. We'll explore the Web 216 palette and dithering bitmaps in the next module.

6

- Sounds, particularly high-quality stereo sounds, are really large, for much the same reasons that bitmaps can be large. When using sound in Shockwave, start with 22 kHz monaural sound at a 16-bit sample depth. This is not CD quality, but computer sound systems are not manufactured by Polk Audio either. For the most part, users are listening to sounds play back on speakers that bear a close resemblance in size and quality to those found in telephones. You do not have to have CD-quality audio in your Shockwave files, and you rarely will need it in any of your Director programs.

You can compress these sounds massively using Shockwave as well. If you go with the second-highest quality setting for the Shockwave compression and a mono mix, what starts out as a 1MB sound file could be reduced to a few dozen kilobytes, with virtually no detectable degradation in audio quality.

Note

Shockwave audio compression uses the same scheme as MPEG layer 3 (MP3) compression, with slightly different information at the start of the audio file that distinguishes the two formats. In fact, Director can now import and play MP3 audio files, so if you have a client that wants a lot of sound and is planning to provide it to you in the format of your choice, suggest MP3.

Ask the Expert

Question   What exactly is a bitmap?

Answer   Bitmaps work by creating and storing a literal map of each pixel of data an image contains (remember, there are 72 pixels in one inch on most computer displays).

This means that a simple 10 × 10 pixel bitmap onscreen is the representation of one *hundred* individual items of data on disk. The computer must have full color information for every single pixel that is stored in a bitmap, and for that reason bitmap files can get quite large. Contrast this to vector shapes, where there is simply a calculation of a geometric formula and a "recipe" given for the kind of color fill that is to occupy that geometric space, and you can guess why vector images tend to be much smaller files on disk than do bitmaps.

The key advantage of a bitmap is that you can get highly detailed information stored in them, which is why images such as photographs are always stored in bitmap format, while things such as circles or rectangles are better created as vectors.

Question   How can I predict whether a bitmap is too large to be practical?

Answer   There are 8 bits in a byte of computer data, there are 1024 bytes in a kilobyte, and there are 1024 kilobytes in a megabyte. Thus, to calculate the size a bitmap image file might occupy on disk, you use this formula:

width in pixels × height in pixels × bit depth ÷ 8 ÷ 1024 ÷ 1024

If I have an 800 × 600 pixel 32-bit image, then, we get

800 × 600 × 32 ÷ 8 ÷ 1024 ÷ 1024 = 1.83MB

This is a very large bitmap. It would take a 56K modem approximately 30 seconds to retrieve it, assuming the maximum speed available was in fact the speed at which the image was being downloaded. In reality, it would probably take a minute or more, during which your user will be wondering exactly what is taking so long. (Do *you* have the patience to stare at a browser window for a minute, waiting for a single image to download?)

Apart from these factors, internal tools and internal media in your Cast will work more or less the same on a Mac, on Windows, or in a Shockwave setting. For the sake of simplicity, then, it's best to limit your initial programs to these internal tools and formats, until you've had some practice working with Director and feel reasonably sure you've got a good grasp of how it handles these items in various situations.

External Files

There are two chief types of external files you're likely to use most in Director:

- Media files, such as digital video or sound

- Other Director files, accessed using **go to movie**, **play movie**, or **movie-in-a-window**.

6

External Media Files

As I mentioned a couple pages back, some files you use in Director programs are not actually contained within those movie files, digital video being the key example of these. (Though you can also link to other external files—images, HTML content, and so on.) When you're going to use external media files, it is most important to plan ahead and gather them into one location that will remain the same, from the moment you start working on your Director program until it is actually being seen by your end users.

My usual habit is to create an external folder named media, and to place it alongside my Director movie file. Into this folder go all my externally linked media files, such as QuickTime movies. Then, when I create a projector (or upload a Shockwave file), that media folder and everything it contains go along with it. Thus, my final Director program "knows" that all the external material is still contained in the media folder, and the media folder is where the program expects it to be, right alongside the program itself.

A word of caution about filenames. If you're planning a Shockwave release, you cannot use filenames that contain spaces. This applies to any Director movies you make as well as to any external files you plan to use. Furthermore, all files you use must have the appropriate extensions attached so that they'll be recognizable on different systems.

Examples of valid filenames include:

- familyvideo.mov—a QuickTime movie
- happy-birthday.mp3—a song
- my_dog.mpg—an MPEG movie

These filenames will not work correctly in many situations where Shockwave is involved:

- familyvideo—there's no file extension
- happy birthday.mp3—this one has a space in the name

Additionally, Macintosh computers can't recognize filenames containing more than 31 characters. So if you're working on Windows and planning for a Mac release, a sound file with a name like

Pink_Floyd_singing_The_Wall_live_at_Coventry_Gardens.mp3

is not going to work on the Mac.

The practice I've gotten into is to never use capital letters, to substitute hyphens for spaces, and always to include a file extension in any name—and I do all my main work in Director on a Macintosh, which doesn't require any of those things. However, this habit has helped me over the years to be sure that anything I do will work on Windows and in the Shockwave environment, so I'd suggest you take up the practice as well. I do this with all my files, by the way, not just ones I'm working with in Director. That reinforces the habit.

Here's a list of common file extensions and what they mean, for the edification of both Mac and Windows users; again, I strongly recommend you get into the habit of using and understanding extensions regardless of the kind of computer you're using:

- .exe—executable, a program
- .dir—a Director movie file
- .cst—a Director Cast file
- .mov—a QuickTime movie file
- .mp3—an MPEG layer 3 sound file
- .psd—a PhotoShop image file

- .jpg—a JPEG image file
- .gif—a GIF image file
- .wav—a Microsoft WAV audio file
- .bmp—a Microsoft bitmap image file
- .txt—a plain ASCII text file
- .rtf—a rich-text format text file, which usually contains extra information that allows it to display special fonts, formatting, and so on
- .htm or .html—an HTML Web page file
- .fla—a Flash file that can be edited in the Flash program
- .swf—a Flash file that can be uploaded to the Web or imported into a Director movie

6

Tip

Windows users might be wondering where the file extensions are. With the introduction of Win95, that system began hiding the filename extensions. The extensions are still there, but Windows does not display them by default. To change Windows to show the file extensions, open the My Computer icon and select View | Files, then uncheck the item labeled "Hide extensions for known file types." This will let you see things like .dir, .txt, and so on associated with every file on your system.

We'll go into pretty great depth about external media files in Part 3; here, I just want to give you some idea of the kinds of things you have to consider when using them in your Director programs.

External Director Files

There are two types of external Director files, specifically other Director movie files loaded with calls such as **go to movie**; and external Cast files, which can be handy places to store common resources if you are using several different movie files in the creation of a larger program experience.

What you do with those files is pretty much up to you. You can have them right alongside your main movie file, or you can place them into a folder if you like, as with the preceding media example. Where you put them is not as important as ensuring that they are in the same relative location when you actually make your projector or upload your Shockwave file.

External Cast files and movie files you load using **go to movie** or **play movie** will work fine on Mac or Windows and will also work in Shockwave; however, external Director files you load as movies in a window will not work at all in Shockwave. While using MIAW files can be a really great way to modularize a program, grouping logical sets of functions into their own separate windows, there's no way currently for this to function in the Shockwave environment. Thus, don't do it for anything but desktop-installed programs.

We'll be discussing MIAWs and their uses in Part 4.

You might also, on occasion, import one Director movie into another. This is referred to as a *linked Director movie,* or LDM. This might sound somewhat convenient, but it's not as nice as it might seem at first. You have not actually imported the items in the Director move, but rather references to those items. Thus, the movie you've imported must still be present in order for the program to work, much as with digital video files. LDMs are another way to get one Director movie to play another without resorting to **go to movie** or MIAW commands.

If you're planning to use external Director or Cast files in Shockwave, remember that the rules regarding filenames are the same. No spaces, and remember to use the appropriate file extension (.dir for Director, .cst for Cast).

Xtras

As I mentioned several pages back, you will probably eventually have occasion to use Xtras (other than the standard suite provided by Macromedia) in your Director files. There are yet more things to consider here, chiefly whether the Xtras in question will function on both Mac and Windows; and whether the Xtras can be used in Shockwave.

Single-platform Xtras might make sense if there were only one computer operating system in the world. However, there are several, and for that reason it is a very bad idea to use Xtras designed to function on only one OS.

Partly this is because (as I suggested earlier) at some point or another you might want your Director movie to play back on other operating systems. It's always best to start from the assumption that you will eventually want to do this.

Partly, too, you must consider that even the one operating system you might be using will change over time, and your Xtra might no longer work as expected (or at all) if it has been designed in such a way that it makes extensive use of special features of that one operating system or one version of the system.

Of course, that's just half of what you must consider. Whether an Xtra can work in Shockwave is very important in deciding to use it or not to use it, if you anticipate going to Shockwave at any point in the future with your Director movie. Such so-called *Shockwave-safe* Xtras are more or less acceptable, but you must also consider that if you use an Xtra that is not part of the standard Macromedia package, your end user will have to download that Xtra from someplace. Generally, the download and installation process is automatic—which is quite helpful—but it still takes time, and if you have an impatient user you've probably lost her already.

Media types that are safe—that work with the standard Xtras Macromedia ships with Director, and that will work in Shockwave, include:

● Any internal #text type, including RTF and HTML

● QuickTime, provided the end user has QuickTime installed

● Any internal sound, including MP3

● Internal Flash and vector shapes

Xtras that are *not* Shockwave safe include:

● FileIO

● MUI (Macromedia User Interface, a utility for creating dialog boxes)

● BuddyAPI (a profoundly useful tool)

and any other Xtras that might allow you to alter the data or contents on a hard drive in any significant fashion. A rule of thumb to follow is that if the Xtra lets you change data on a computer's disk or settings on a user's computer, it won't be Shockwave safe.

There are, naturally, Shockwave-safe Xtras that are not standard and must be downloaded to be used; these include:

● OSControl

● TreeView (which lets you display hierarchical menus of information)

● MPEGXtra (which lets you play back MPEG movie files on Windows) as well as various other Xtras that let you play different media types or display information or images onscreen.

Usually, an Xtra's distributor will indicate prominently whether the Xtra is Shockwave safe. If there's no indication whether it is or not, you should ask before you plan to make any use of it in a Director movie you intend to release as a Shockwave file.

 ## 1-Minute Drill

● What does *Shockwave safe* mean?

● What are some examples of Xtras that are not Shockwave safe?

Decisions, Decisions

In summary, Director lets you use a lot of different external media, file, and tool types to increase the flexibility of programs you can write and enrich the environment for your end user, but this expansion carries with it a certain amount of risk that you could end up trying to do some things that simply are not possible under all situations.

Wherever it's conceivable, keeping your media and tool types internal will go a long way toward ensuring your programs will work anywhere. If you can't do that, at least try to use external media and tools that will work on the widest possible range of computers and operating systems, as the flexibility your Director movies will inherit will make them considerably more likely to be able to continue working well into the future.

By the time you've finished this book, you should have a pretty good grasp of working with several different external media and file types, and you should be able to make some good educated guesses about the likely consequences of working with other such files in the future.

● An Xtra is Shockwave safe if it's allowable to use it in Shockwave files. Xtras that cannot be used in Shockwave files are not Shockwave safe.

● FileIO, BuddyAPI, and any other Xtra that can make significant changes to a computer's hard drive or system settings.

Project 6-1: Making an ASCII Key Utility Program

This module's program is an example of the flexibility I mentioned. I originally wrote it using Director version 4, back in about 1993. Apart from periodic updates of the movie file to new versions of Director, this same program has remained fundamentally unchanged since I wrote it.

I call it Keyster, but you can name yours anything you want. It's just a little program that displays the ASCII and Director keyCode values for keys you press. This is useful for detecting whether the user has pressed some keys that don't have any alphanumeric equivalent—the arrow keys, page up, page down, and so on. Since you might want to check for and respond appropriately to those keys sometimes when the user presses them, knowing what their numeric representations in the computer are can be pretty handy.

We're going to do something a little different with this file. We're going to turn it into something called a *MIAW Xtra,* which is a fancy way of saying it'll be a utility we can have access to any time we're working in Director (after all, that's when you're most likely going to need it). So rather than turn it into a stand-alone program, in this module we're going to make it a utility file we can use ourselves.

With this project, you will

- Learn how to read and display the ANSI (ASCII) value for a given key the user presses.

- Learn how to extend the flexibility of your copy of Director by creating an Xtra you can use whenever you're programming a Director movie.

6

Step-by-Step

1. Start, as always, with a new Director file. In the Movie tab of the PI, select 160 by 120 for the Stage size from the pop-up list. This program does not need to be very large.

2. In frame 1, place the standard **go the frame** script, and then open a movie script window. Into it enter the following:

```
on startMovie

  the keyDownScript = "DisplayCodes"
```

```
end


on DisplayCodes


  member("keypress").text = the key
  member("ascii").text = string ( charToNum ( the key ) )
  member("keycode").text = string ( the keyCode )


end
```

Line by line, here's the new stuff:

the keyDownScript = "DisplayCodes"

This, as you might infer, tells Director that whenever a key is pressed, it is to run a specific handler (script). The handler it is to run is named **DisplayCodes**.

In the **DisplayCodes** handler you see the following:

member("keypress").text = the key

This tells Director to put (if it's able) the actual key that was pressed into a #text or #field member named **keypress**. I say "if it's able" because some keys, such as the ENTER key, won't show up in the **keypress** member.

member("ascii").text = string (charToNum (the key))

You can guess what the Lingo on the left-hand side of the equal sign is doing, but the part on the right might be confusing. Here we're taking **the key**—which, again, was the actual key pressed—and converting it from its key-ish nature to *ASCII,* or the number that the computer uses to understand which key it actually was. All computers use ASCII values to understand keypresses, and for all intents and purposes those ASCII values never change.

Note

ASCII is short for American Standard Code for Information Interchange and is pronounced ask-ee.

This ASCII value is then converted from a number to a string (since text is a string, and since we want to put text into the **ascii** Cast member); this step is not technically necessary, but stipulating formats in this fashion is a good practice.

member("keycode").text = string (the keyCode)

This puts Director's own number for the key pressed into a third Cast member. Director's **keyCode** is usually quite different from the ASCII value. The **keyCode** call was introduced to Lingo before there was a ready way to obtain ASCII values, and for the most part **keyCode** isn't used any more. It's here mainly for those rare times when you might encounter it in others' Director movies.

3. Now, of course, you have to make the appropriate #text or #field members in your Cast and name them as implied previously, then place them on the Stage, perhaps with some labels to provide you with information regarding what each sprite's contents are.

4. Set up your Stage in any way that appeals to you. This is a simple utility program, so you don't really have to go nuts making it look really pretty.

5. Save the file, then click the Play button and start pressing keys. Pretty neat, huh?

6. Now that you're done playing, quit Director and drop the movie you just made into Director's Xtras folder, the one located right alongside the main Director program on your hard drive, and then run Director again. Click the Xtras menu. What do you see? The movie you just made is there, ready for you to access it!

6

Ask the Expert

Question   I entered everything as you described, and I'm pretty sure I've got it all right, but when I click Play and start pressing keys, nothing happens. What's wrong?

Answer   If nothing seems to be happening in any of the sprites on the Stage, this is probably because the Stage does not have *focus*. What this means is that the keypresses you are making are not being recognized as something the Director movie itself needs to notice and respond to. In order to "wake up" the Stage, click it once with the mouse; then start pressing keys again.

This, by the way, is a common situation many Director programmers encounter, so don't feel silly.

Figure 6-1 Getting a look at my Keyster

Go ahead and select your movie from the Xtras menu. Note that it loads in a window; that you can move, resize, or close it; and that it still displays the key, the ASCII value for the key, and the keyCode for anything you press. Figure 6-1 shows you what my MIAW Xtra looks like when it's running on my Mac.

Congratulations—you've just made a MIAW Xtra, a handy little utility you'll probably end up using quite a lot as you continue working with Director.

Project Summary

As you've seen, Director's flexibility gives you a lot of options for handling all manner of media, external resources, and tools, and these options can have a great impact on the kinds of things you can do for various distributions of your program. For the most part, the built-in functions are the least likely to give you trouble for multiple distribution platforms, but if you're reasonably careful and plan ahead—and given some experience and a willingness to try different things—you'll find that this flexibility can tremendously enhance both your own experience as a programmer and the way users enjoy your finished programs.

In the next module, we'll go into greater depth regarding actually creating programs for wide distribution, not merely planning for them.

☑ *Mastery Check* —————

1. When preparing to create a Director program, what are some considerations for the audience you must have?

_____

_____

2. What's an important consideration if you're creating software for educational purposes?

_____

_____

3. What does the term *port* mean as it pertains to making programs in Director?

_____

_____

4. Describe one way in which choice of Xtras can affect portability of a Director movie.

_____

_____

5. What is an important consideration regarding Xtras when you're planning a Shockwave distribution?

_____

_____

6. Can external media files be used in Shockwave?

_____

_____

Module 7

Creating Programs

The Goals of this Module

- Learn how to plan for different monitor types
- Learn how to test your software
- Know when your software is ready for release
- Learn how to package your program

I n Module 6, you discovered that there are many different factors to consider when you're preparing to create a program using Director. (And in case you're curious, it's much harder with other programming languages.) In this module, we'll go into further detail regarding the creation of software.

Screen Testing

Believe it or not, monitors are one of the more difficult things you'll have do deal with when you're using Director to write programs.

This is because there are hundreds of different possible configurations for monitors. Some are capable of showing relatively few colors, and a relatively small image area, while others can handle more colors than the human eye is actually capable of seeing, and display them over a very large desktop space.

The absolute rock-bottom configuration for a monitor you'll likely ever need to consider will be capable of showing only 256 colors in a 640 × 480 pixel area. That's pretty confined, and for the most part such configurations are pretty rare. Modern desktop systems can do much better than that.

However, portable PCs can still be pretty severely limited. Most can show about 65 thousand colors over an 800 × 600 pixel area, which sounds a bit like an improvement, but 800 × 600 pixels is not a lot of space. Sure, the number of colors has improved, but an 800 × 600 pixel window is not a whole lot of real estate.

When we speak of the amount of image data that can be shown on a monitor, we are talking of its screen resolution. This is not a description of how large a monitor is; rather, it is a description of how much data can be displayed on it at once.

A monitor that can display 800 × 600 pixels is capable of showing 35 percent more data than is a monitor that maxes out at 640 × 480. This does not mean the monitor is 35 percent larger, but that it can squeeze just that much more information into its image area.

And actually, we shouldn't speak of monitors here at all, but *video cards*—the devices inside the computer to which the monitors are attached. It's the video card that really determines how much information can be sent to the screen at once.

Some cards are capable of displaying multiple resolutions. Often these cards are capable of at least 640 × 480, 800 × 600, and 1024 × 768 pixel images. Naturally, the higher the numbers go, the smaller things appear to be on the monitor. This is, of course, because if you want to display more information on a screen of fixed size, the only way to do it is proportionally shrink the information you're attempting to display.

Ask the Expert

Question   So what's the difference between a 15-inch monitor, a 21-inch monitor, and a video projector?

Answer   How large the image being displayed appears to be. This might not make immediate intuitive sense, but the physical size of the monitor bears no relationship whatsoever to what it's actually capable of showing.

Think of the movie *Lawrence of Arabia*. This film was shot on 65 millimeter film and projected in theaters as a very wide screen, 70-millimeter presentation. In some theaters, the image was surely 60 or more feet wide.

But the movie, playing back on your TV through your DVD player, is not 60 feet wide; it's perhaps one-thirtieth that, unless you've dumped a lot of money into your entertainment system. Still, you have not lost any of the image data contained in the original movie; you've simply shrunk the size of the image being displayed.

Similarly, a 15-inch monitor set to display 800 × 600 pixels will show exactly the same amount of visual information as a video projector set to display 800 × 600 pixels, even if the projector is throwing an image ten feet wide.

7

If you are writing software for a client, you'll want to have discussions about minimum system requirements anyway; just make sure display resolution is one thing you discuss at length. Macromedia publishes minimum specification information in the documentation that came with your copy of Director, so make sure that your client's systems are going to at least be on a par with the description listed under "playback requirements."

You *can* get away with running your Director movies on systems that have less power, but you have to reduce the number of colors you use, limit the amount of animation you do, and try to keep things like video or Flash to a minimum. The programs we've written so far in this book will work fine on machines that fall well below the minimum specifications stipulated by Macromedia, but that's because we're not really doing anything taxing with any of them.

This really becomes a factor when you start creating programs that might end up anywhere, such as Shockwave files. You have no way of predicting what the end user's configuration is going to be, so you don't know if you're going to overload his or her system by trying to display too many graphics, animations, and so on at one time. You also have no way of knowing what the maximum resolution of the display will be, so you could end up writing a program that can't be entirely seen on some monitors.

There are some ways around that last concern, the simplest being to create a "safe" area in your program where you'll put all the controls. If you're assuming most users will be running at 800 × 600, you can set up your Stage to be that size, and you can certainly fill that space with graphics. However, you should put all the controls and critical information a user will need to run your program into the center of that space, so that when the program loads, even if the user's display is set to 640 × 480, all the important parts of your program will be visible. (Unless you simply want to insist on a minimum resolution of 800 × 600; however, that will significantly reduce the number of public schools that can run your programs, if that's an issue, as many schools can't afford to upgrade their video cards to the point they can handle anything past 640 × 480.)

Additionally, if you're really unsure what kind of system your software will be loaded onto, try to keep the graphics down to 8-bit (256 shade) color, and avoid using huge images, since a rule of thumb is that if a display's color depth can't go past 8 bits, it's probably running in a slow system with very little memory or speed to spare.

Next in this module, we'll be discussing testing and ways you can help ensure your program will function more or less as expected on a wide range of systems.

1-Minute Drill

- If one monitor is 15-inches diagonally and another is 17 inches, which monitor can show the greater number of pixels?

- Why does display resolution matter?

Knowing How You're Displaying Yourself

There are two nice little features built into Lingo now that let you get a sense of the kind of color depth and desktop size (monitor resolution) you're dealing with before your Stage even becomes visible on the screen. The keywords involved are **the colorDepth** and **the deskTopRectList**.

the colorDepth

The keyword **the colorDepth** returns an integer that can be used to determine how many colors can actually be shown on a given display, using its current settings. It does not tell you what the maximum number of colors might be; that's a function of the display card itself; it tells you only the number of colors that are being shown when the command is issued.

Possible values returned by **the colorDepth** are as follows:

- **1** A 1-bit display depth, this is a true black-and-white screen. The original Macintosh models used 1-bit graphics. On 1-bit displays, any

7

- Neither. Maximum pixels displayable is a function of the video card, not the physical dimensions of the monitor.
- If your end user's display can't show all the pixels you've set your Stage to fill, parts of your program will not be visible.

pixel is either on or off, and there are no shades available. The odds of your ever encountering a 1-bit display are practically zero.

● **4** Four-bit displays can show 16 colors. Early color Macs used 4-bit displays, and this was the maximum color depth that Windows could achieve for a very long time, until video card technology became relatively cheap and the number of colors that could be displayed went up as a result of that. You might encounter 4-bit displays in very old PCs that have been upgraded to Windows 95, but that have not had a video card upgrade. Many public schools in less affluent neighborhoods may have this kind of configuration.

● **8** Eight bits, as you know by now, translates to 256 colors. This is the lowest color depth you're likely to encounter on any machine capable of running your Director movies in the first place. 8-bit color is increasingly rare, but it is still seen from time to time. 8-bit color is also called *palletized* color, because it draws its 256 colors from one of several possible *color palettes* stored either in the computer or in the software running on it.

● **16** At 16 bits, you can display around 65,000 colors. This is also called "high color" on some Windows systems. It's often referred to as "thousands of colors" as well, for pretty obvious reasons.

● **24** 24-bit color shows around 17 million shades, which is about 11 to 12 million more than a human eye can perceive. This is sometimes called "true color," which is somewhat misleading. This color depth can show any shade, but that doesn't necessarily mean the shade being shown is the genuine color of the thing being depicted.

● **32** 32-bit color displays the 17 million available in 24-bit but also includes 256 levels of transparency and effects for each pixel in a separate channel called the *alpha* channel. Alpha-channel effects are one thing that allows PhotoShop to display interesting glows, soft-edged drop shadows, and so on. Director is also capable of handling graphics that contain an alpha channel, and, in fact, it is currently the only programming environment of its type that can do this. It's very common for modern Macintosh computers to be set to 32-bit color depth, and this setting is becoming increasingly popular on Windows systems as well.

You can see **the colorDepth** in action by entering the following in the Message window:

```
put the colorDepth
```

Odds are you'll get 24 or 32 as the result.

As mentioned previously, the lowest color depth you're likely to contend with is 8-bit. If you're pretty sure a lot of the systems that will run your program are capable only of 8-bit color, you'll want to make sure not to exceed that when you're writing your program. I'll explain how to handle that in the next section.

If you absolutely *must* have a minimum color depth for your program to work, you can include a test in your Director movie that looks for a colorDepth lower than the minimum value you want, and that prevents the program from running.

For instance, suppose you have to have at least 256 colors and want to make sure no one's trying to run your program at a lower color depth. You might then include a script like this in your Director movie:

```
on startMovie


  if the colorDepth < 8 then

    ALERT "Sorry, but this program requires a monitor set to
display 256 or more colors."
    QUIT

  end if


END startMovie
```

Here's the stuff you may not have seen before:

if the colorDepth < 8 then

Tests to see if the colorDepth value for the monitor display is less than 8 bits. If this turns out to be the case, the next two lines of Lingo are executed:

ALERT "Sorry, but this program requires a monitor set to display 256 or more colors."

Ask the Expert

Question Should I put that kind of test into every Director program I write? It seems pretty useful.

Answer I personally believe it's rather presumptuous to simply quit a program under these circumstances. It's entirely possible the user knows what she's doing, more or less, and wants to see the program anyway, even knowing the images might look terrible in 4-bit color.

I'm a user like that, in fact. I want the program to run anyway, even knowing it might not work very well, or at all. For this reason, I'd suggest taking a different approach, one that doesn't make the program stop running but simply warns the user that performance might be seriously degraded. For that, you'd change your message a little:

```
on startMovie


  if the colorDepth < 8 then

    ALERT "This program is designed for a monitor set to
display 256 or more colors. You may continue running the
program, but be aware that performance or image quality may
suffer."

  end if


END startMovie
```

Here you let the user go on if he wants to, but you've at least given a warning that conditions are less than optimal. That way, if the program fails to function correctly or crashes, you're covered as far as disclaimers go, but there's also a chance it will function anyway. This makes everyone happy. (Well, at least it can minimize complaining, which sometimes is the best you can aim for in the world of programming.)

Kicks up a system-standard alert box containing a warning message.

QUIT

Forces the projector to quit at this point.

If you know for a fact you're looking at a minimum color depth of 8 bits for your end users, you're going to have to make sure your Director movie is designed to work at that depth. In order to do this, you have to prepare by reducing your monitor's color depth so that it's no greater than 8 bits either.

This is because of the way Director handles color. It creates and handles graphics on the author side at whatever color depth value your monitor is using at that point. So in order to create a Director movie that automatically works in 8 bits, your monitor has to be set to 8 bits while you're creating the program.

On Windows you can do this by right-clicking your desktop and selecting Properties from the context menu that appears. Click the Display tab and select 256 colors from the pop-up menu, then click Apply. You may have to give "final approval" to the setting change before your display color depth is reduced to 8 bits.

For Mac, it's a little easier. Open the Monitors Control Panel and choose the 256 color setting.

Then run Director and begin creating your program from a new file.

This still leaves you somewhat at a loss for handling the actual color palette settings, since Director has several different 8-bit palettes available to it. The default will always be the 8-bit palette appropriate for your system, which means if you're on Mac the color palette will be the System—Macintosh palette. For Windows, of course, it will be System—Windows. You can choose the default movie palette by clicking the palette pop-up menu in the Movie properties tab of the PI.

However, if you experiment a little with these choices, you will see that not all the colors match. This can become seriously problematic, because some of the places where the colors are different between the two palettes are reserved for system use.

This means that if you are running a Director movie that uses a Macintosh palette on a Windows system running at 256 colors, some of the standard components of the Windows desktop will end up looking awful. Colors will get very wrong, dialog boxes (such as those used by ALERT or FileIO) will have incorrect color shading, and in some of the worst cases you'll end up with images that look like a Jimi Hendrix album cover—psychedelic funk.

Similar things can happen on the Mac when you're running a Director movie at 8 bits that uses the Windows palette.

Fortunately, there is a way to avoid this situation completely, and that is to set the Web 216 palette as your default whenever you are authoring a movie for 8-bit color. The Web 216 palette was specifically engineered to never interfere with standard system colors for either Mac or Windows, while at the same time leaving you a relatively large number of alternate shades from which you can choose. (As the palette name implies, there are 216 of them.) Running a Director program that uses this palette on either Mac or Windows will give you consistent and appropriate results in all cases, without the funky psychedelic side-effects.

This palette, as its name indicates, is also ideal for creating Shockwave movies that may be seen on relatively low-color systems.

The one major disadvantage to setting your palette to 8 bits is that any bitmap you import will likely have to be *dithered,* or reduced, to the palette you've chosen. This can result in images becoming a little grainy in appearance, because when an image is dithered down in color it's also given a kind of blur that tries to make the visual effect of color reduction less obvious. (Nondithered images when reduced in color depth tend to show a lot of "banding" where there are lots of color changes; dithering tries to minimize this banding effect but can make the graphic look somewhat blurry.) This suffering in image quality is not necessarily a bad thing, but if you've got a client who's a real stickler, you will want to do some test imports and run your results by him before you proceed with the rest of your program. Some people really object to the way a dithered image looks, while others don't even notice or, if they do notice, don't care. It seems to be largely a question of how particular you want to get over the issue.

The only other alternative is to use *custom* palettes, which bear with them all the risks inherent in using either of the system palettes for Mac or Windows, and which also then require you to use one specific palette for any set of images you want to put on the Stage at one time. You will probably also have to muck about with *palette transitions,* which allow you (more or less) to change palettes *on the fly,* or while your program is actually running. All these considerations are really beyond the scope of this text, but I can tell you that in all the years I've worked with Director, I did this kind of thing only once, and I hated every minute of it. I don't recommend doing it if you can avoid it.

Ask the Expert

Question   Don't I have any other alternatives? Suppose a user just doesn't know how to change the display settings, but she's running a video card that can handle everything I want to throw at it?

Answer   Some Xtras let you change the user's color depth or display resolution when your movie loads. On Mac, you can even set your movie to change color depth without an Xtra by changing a setting under File | Preferences | General.

I advise against it. If for some reason your program terminates abnormally (a polite term for "crash"), the changes you put into effect will not be removed, which means your user's display will be messed up relative to what it had been before she ran the program. This is not a good thing to do to any user.

In general, it's unwise to change system settings, at least partly because there are so many variables in different systems that you can't be sure of consistently getting those changes to work. It's especially bad to change them without even asking. It's better to simply write a program that can handle highly variable situations without much difficulty. Flexible programs are generally more stable, and the programs themselves are usually easier to port and upgrade. You may have to sacrifice some image quality, but that's a much better choice than making a user believe you've done some kind of damage to her computer.

What I'd suggest is including some instructions somewhere that tell the user how to change her video settings on her own. That way if she wants to, she can, and perhaps you'll be able to educate her a little about her computer in the process.

7

Another option you can consider when planning for 8-bit systems is simply trusting Director to be able to dither back automatically if it's necessary. It already does this with a high degree of success when a movie made at 24- or 32-bit depth is playing back on a 16-bit display; the results for 8 bits are not much worse. The disadvantage here is that the program will run more slowly and will probably end up using more memory. However, if you're pretty certain that your movies are not going to be playing back on many 8-bit machines, this option might be the best one for you to choose.

1-Minute Drill

● What is the least likely value for **the colorDepth** to have on modern computers?

● What is the advantage of using the Web 216 palette for 8-bit color depth?

the deskTopRectList

This is a Director list containing descriptions of the pixel area covered by the display card or cards on the current system. The descriptions are defined as rectangles with minimum and maximum values; the difference between those values lies in the representation of the dimensions, in pixels, of the data being displayed onscreen.

There is no way to fully predict what **the deskTopRectList** will return, because any system might have its display resolution set to any setting, and quite a few desktop systems today have more than one monitor attached at a time. So the best place to start is with your own computer, by entering into the Message window the command

```
put the deskTopRectList
```

When I do that on my iBook, here's the result:

```
-- [rect(0, 0, 1024, 768)]
```

This is a funny-looking response, because of the parentheses and brackets. The brackets are special characters that denote a list, something we'll be exploring quite thoroughly in Module 9. Inside those brackets is a Lingo-flavored description of nothing more nor less than a rectangle.

The basic format for a rectangle is

rect (left, top, right, bottom)

where **left** is the left edge or coordinate of the rectangle, **top** is the top, **right** is the right edge or *width* of the rectangle, and **bottom** is the bottom edge or its *height*. Thus, by the response I got we can determine that the screen on my

---

● 1-bit, or true black and white.
● It does not interfere with reserved system colors on either Mac or Windows, which means it won't cause the user's display to show odd color effects.

iBook is set to display 1024 pixels across by 768 pixels down. This isn't bad for a portable.

Note

Rect coordinates in Director are *always* given in terms of pixels, not inches or centimeters or anything else. Remembering how rectangles are defined in Lingo can be tough, since if you muddle the left, top, right, and bottom dimension order, the rectangle you define will not have the shape you expect. For this reason, you might want to use a mnemonic device, as with the old standby for musical scales, *Every Good Boy Deserves Fudge.* For rects you could try *Lingo Takes Reading Books* (or *Lingo Tasks the Really Bright*); or *Logic Tests Rational Boundaries;* or maybe even *Litotes Take Real Brilliance.*

Where it can get pretty nasty is if the user has more than one monitor attached, because this is generally treated as being an *extension* of the primary monitor. If I had an external monitor attached to my iBook, I might have seen something like this:

```
-- [rect(0, 0, 1024, 768), rect(1024, 0, 2048, 768)]
```

Oh brother. Here we can infer that the second monitor is in fact serving as an extension of the main one—but how to make Director aware of that, if we should have to?

One of the things you can do when working with lists in Director is gain access to specific values by their *index position* in that list. Fortunately for us, Director has been programmed in such a way that the primary monitor on a computer—the main one that has all the system controls on it—is always the *first* entry in **the deskTopRectList**. So in all cases, I just modify my call a little bit:

```
put the deskTopRectList[1]
```

which tells Director to send the item at index position 1 of **the deskTopRectList**, and what I get is this:

```
-- rect(0, 0, 1024, 768)
```

Aha! The brackets are gone! That's because we simply grabbed the first item in the list all by itself, which is a rectangle describing my monitor dimensions.

7

Why does any of this matter? Suppose you've written a program that has to run at 800 × 600 or more. Using **the deskTopRectList**, you can determine immediately, as you did with **the colorDepth** before, whether a user's display settings are proper for running your program:

```
on startMovie


  if the deskTopRectList[1] < rect(0, 0, 800, 600) then

    ALERT "Sorry, but this program requires a display set to
show 800 by 600 or more pixels."
    QUIT

  end if


END startMovie
```

The new stuff is just one line by now, since you're getting used to Lingo:

if the deskTopRectList[1] < rect(0, 0, 800, 600) then

This determines whether the rectangle defined in position 1 of **the deskTopRectList** is smaller than 800 × 600 pixels. If it is, the rest of the **if…then** control structure is executed. An **ALERT** is displayed and the program quits. Otherwise, the program proceeds as normal.

Again, don't let the apparent weirdness of lists, such as **the deskTopRectList**, trouble you. We'll definitely be going over them in Module 9, and by the time you're done with that, you'll not only understand them, but you'll probably be able to apply them with great success throughout your programming career. In fact, you'll likely end up using them a lot, as they are fantastic ways to assemble such things as databases. Any decent programming language has them; in C++ and related languages, they are called *arrays*.

There are other uses for **the deskTopRectList**. You can actually figure out how many monitors your user has attached, for example, and if you want to have some fun, you can use that understanding to "launch" MIAWs into those other monitor spaces. You can also create programs that expand automatically to fill multiple screens, or you can offer the ability to "remember" where the

Ask the Expert

Question Are you trying to tell me that this really powerful programming language can't automatically resize the Stage to fit whatever monitor it's running on?

Answer Director *is* capable of scaling its Stage up or down to fill a screen appropriately via some commands you use through MIAW, and it will scale everything on the Stage except for #text and #field sprites. However, when it does that, image quality tends to suffer greatly.

Resizing bitmap graphics, for instance, will generally give you "crunchy" images that have noticeable square or rectangular artifacts in them; these are the actual pixels in the image scaled up or down in size. Graphic manipulation programs such as PhotoShop can do this with relative ease, but they're dedicated to that one task. Director is not.

In situations where you might want to have a scalable Stage, then, it's best to use vector graphics and Flash animations, since they'll resize smoothly regardless of how large or small you want to make them. (Remember, they're vector shapes.)

program appeared onscreen the last time it ran and place it in that location again, while still being able to restore it to its default screen location if it happened to be dragged onto a monitor that is no longer attached to the computer. (This happens quite often with portables.) But at the very least, as we've seen, you can use it to make sure that your program will be able to fit into the display your user is operating.

1-Minute Drill

● What is the order of dimensions as defined in a rect?
● If I look at the value for **the deskTopRectList[1]** and get rect(0, 0, 1280, 1024), what does this tell me about my display?

● Left, top, right, and bottom.
● That it's set to a resolution of 1280 × 1024 pixels.

Testing, 1, 2, 3...

After the last dozen or so pages on monitors, perhaps you're ready for something a little less rigorous, less prone to high variability. Unfortunately, this isn't it.

After you've got your program working more or less as you and the client want it to be, you've got to test it.

There are two real phases for program releases prior to the final, the *alpha* and the *beta*. Alpha releases are generally worked on only by you and represent the initial stomping you give your code to make sure it's functioning more or less as you expect it to in various circumstances. Beta testing is handing the code to *others* and having them do the same thing. It's not a good idea at all to begin distributing a program of even moderate complexity if you have not passed it through beta testing first.

Alpha Testing

This is primarily your task as the programmer. You need to go through your code and make sure it does what you intend it to and what the client is paying for. Alpha testing is not sufficient to ensure that any program of reasonable complexity will function. Just as you really can't spell-check your own writing, you really can't test your own software.

The reason for that is pretty simple. You already know what the program is supposed to do and how users are supposed to interact with it, so you're not likely to do something that will cause the program to malfunction, accidentally or otherwise. Alpha testing is moderately capable of seeing that a program behaves as expected—but only when it's used as expected.

Things to try when you're alpha testing:

- Set your computer's color depth and display resolution to all the different combinations it supports and run the program to see how it behaves.

- Run a whole lot of other programs in the background and then try yours, to see if it completely dies under low-memory situations or where there's a pretty high load on the processor already. (You have to expect it to slow down; however, it really shouldn't crash.)

- If you're doing anything with Internet calls involved, try them with different network configurations (if it's feasible) such as Ethernet, dial-up access, or DSL. Also, try different firewall and proxy configurations if you can to see how things will work.

- If you're doing a Shockwave release, try it in different browsers. If you are planning on doing a lot of Shockwave work, you will want to have several browsers and versions installed, including IE3, 4, and 5 and Netscape 4.5, 4.7, and 6. This may seem excessive, but when you see the differences that may emerge in the various browsers, you'll understand the wisdom. Make sure to also try your Shockwave program with other programs running, and at different display resolutions and color depths.

Also, make sure to check your spelling thoroughly. Don't laugh. This gets overlooked a lot, and sometimes with rather embarrassing results.

At this point, you will also want to make sure, if you're working on a Mac, that your projector is getting enough memory to run properly. Macintosh programs (for any system less than OS X) are designed to grab only a certain fixed amount of memory when they load, which the program will then use to operate under. You or anyone else can view and change this amount of memory through the program's *info* window.

To see what the memory allocation is for a projector, click its icon *once* in the Mac Finder, then select File | Get Info | Memory. A window will open describing, among other things, the minimum and recommended memory sizes for that projector. Figure 7-1 shows you what such a window might look like.

As you can see, the projector is set to get a minimum of 8197KB of memory, with a maximum of 12,293. (This translates to roughly 8 to 12MB of RAM.) While this is adequate for many situations, if you're going to be loading a lot of really large images, or you plan to play a lot of sounds or Flash files, you'll probably want to increase those settings somewhat. You can click those fields and type in other numbers; a good place to start is 20480 for the minimum setting and 40960 for the max, which is between 20MB and 40MB. If you don't do this, your program might end up running very slowly, and in some circumstances it might even crash because it runs out of memory entirely.

You can get a feel for how much memory your program is actually using by going to the Finder and selecting About This Computer from the Apple menu. You will see a window something like the one in Figure 7-2, giving you

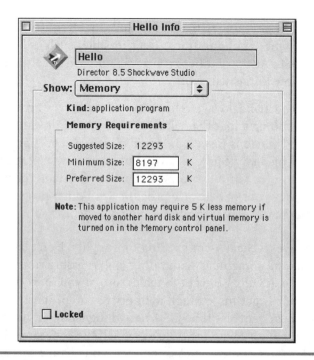

Figure 7-1 The Memory info window for a projector on the Macintosh

a graphical description of the amount of memory various programs are using on your system, including your projector. You can fine-tune the amount of RAM you allocate by looking at those graphical bars and making adjustments as necessary.

Beta Testing

This is the hard part, because you have to endure the critiques of others. Your beta testers should be checking for two primary things: program *functionality* (that it works as it should); and program *usability* (that it's relatively easy to understand how to use it).

Finding good beta testers is not as hard as you might think. There are lots of companies out there that claim to do it and that will certainly charge you enough to convince you they're doing a good job of it, but my greatest successes in this arena have always involved high school and young college students.

Figure 7-2   The projector "Hello" is using less then half the RAM allocated to it

These people are bright, computer-savvy, and generally willing to pick up a few extra bucks for a couple hours' work. They're also more likely than anyone else to try things with your program you never envisioned, and they are capable of providing you with high-quality and consistent bug reports, provided you use a good bug report form.

It's a good idea, if you're doing a Mac and Windows combination release, to get at least two testers for each platform to beat on your code. You'll also want a profile of their machines so that you know what kind of systems they've got, and you will want to stress to them that reproducibility of an error is key in determining how to solve the condition. Inconsistent errors might not be bugs in your code. They could come from general operating system problems, or confusion on the part of the user.

As for payment, $30 to $50 per program tested and $5 to $10 for each legitimate bug found and reported is a good range for price, variable depending on the complexity of the program and how long it's likely to take to test a lot of possible situations. If you get duplicate error reports from different testers, pay each one the same for the report, since what they've shown you is that the bug reported is consistent, and that's extremely valuable information.

Finding your testers might be a little trickier, but you can start by talking to computer science instructors and seeing if they have any recommendations. I do *not* recommend you stand around outside the local high school and ask students, "Hey, kid, wanna make fifty bucks?"

7

In Figure 7-3, you can see a sample of what a beta tester report form might look like. Not all of the information requested may be needed (for instance, the browser information probably is not an issue if you're not doing a Shockwave release), but this form is a pretty good place to start.

Another thing you might want to do is set up a #field sprite on the Stage that appears in every frame of your program, and that is there just for the beta test. You can put it in a really high-numbered channel—say 500 or so—that's not being used by anything else, and stretch its span so that it appears in every frame of your Score. Set its ink to Reverse in the Sprite tab of the PI; this will make sure the text in it will be visible regardless of the background color. You can then attach this behavior to it:

```
on enterFrame me
   sprite(me.spriteNum).member.text = string ( the frame )
end
```

What this will do is show the frame number in your program as it proceeds along. In this way, if some bizarre error seems to be consistently happening at one location in your program (or if there's a spelling error in some particular text block), your testers can make a note of the frame number where the problem arises. This can go a long way toward helping you figure out where things are going wrong. Just make sure to remove the #field sprite before you distribute the final version!

Also, make sure to listen to what your testers tell you about how easy the program is to use. If the program is impossible to understand, you are not guilty of writing a program bug, but you still have created a program that essentially malfunctions. Sometimes you might not want to make changes for aesthetic reasons, and sometimes you might not be able to make changes because of client insistence; however, it never hurts to have another set of eyes looking over your design.

Finally, don't give your testers very much information on how to use the program or what it's supposed to do. Let them run it with minimal instruction from you and see how they fare with it. If they manage to get it working and seem to be pretty satisfied with its overall design, this means you have created a program that is simple to operate and that doesn't behave in wildly unexpected ways.

And that's a good thing.

Beta tester profile

Name _____

Address _____

Phone _____ SSN _____

Computer profile

Brand _____ Model _____ OS _____

RAM _____ VM/swap _____ CPU type & speed _____

HD space total _____ Space used _____ Space free _____

Networking type _____ Speed _____

System extensions apart from standard suite

```
┌──────────────────────────────────────────────────────────────────┐
│                                                                    │
│                                                                    │
└──────────────────────────────────────────────────────────────────┘
```

Monitor card(s) and version(s) _____

Sound card and version _____

QuickTime version _____

Browser(s) and version(s) _____

Description of error

```
┌──────────────────────────────────────────────────────────────────┐
│                                                                    │
│                                                                    │
└──────────────────────────────────────────────────────────────────┘
```

Severity

System death   System lock   Program lock   Program exit   Annoyance   Aesthetic

Precise steps to follow to reproduce error

```
┌──────────────────────────────────────────────────────────────────┐
│                                                                    │
│                                                                    │
│                                                                    │
└──────────────────────────────────────────────────────────────────┘
```

Steps to recover from error

```
┌──────────────────────────────────────────────────────────────────┐
│                                                                    │
│                                                                    │
│                                                                    │
└──────────────────────────────────────────────────────────────────┘
```

Comments on program's apparent reaction to error

```
┌──────────────────────────────────────────────────────────────────┐
│                                                                    │
│                                                                    │
│                                                                    │
└──────────────────────────────────────────────────────────────────┘
```

Suggestions to fix error/work around

```
┌──────────────────────────────────────────────────────────────────┐
│                                                                    │
│                                                                    │
│                                                                    │
└──────────────────────────────────────────────────────────────────┘
```

General comments

```
┌──────────────────────────────────────────────────────────────────┐
│                                                                    │
│                                                                    │
└──────────────────────────────────────────────────────────────────┘
```

Figure 7-3   One example of a beta test bug report form

1-Minute Drill

- Why shouldn't you beta-test your own programs?
- What should you tell your beta testers about your program before they try it out?

That's a Wrap?

So you've got your program handling different display issues and have passed it through some testing. It seems to be going well, but now you're thinking of all sorts of nice ways you might improve it—or, worse yet, your client is beginning to make "suggestions" regarding enhancements he'd like to see.

It's not a bad thing to want to improve a program, but you have to watch out for something called *scope creep.* This is defined loosely as making so many changes to a program that it no longer resembles in any way what you were originally asked to produce. It's giving your client three times the program she initially paid you for.

Naturally, you'll want a satisfied client, but you've also got to strike a balance between a happy customer and being asked to do more than a fair share of work. After all, you can't get *more* clients if your time is being monopolized by one.

Clients don't generally intentionally start acting this way, but they can begin to ask for more and more improvements to a piece of software that was, under the terms of your initial contract, completed several weeks earlier. This is really something you should probably try to resist, but diplomatically. Two decent replies that tend to work are "That's a great idea for the next version" and the less-blunt "Let's get this one out there first and get folks used to it, and then really start throwing the cool stuff at them for the next release." Both phrases say essentially the same thing—*not gonna put it in this program*—and both imply your client will be coming back to get a second version of the program, which in turn implies repeat business for you.

At some point when you began working on your project, you had a definite goal in mind for it, and once you've reached that goal, you should be willing to

---

- You know how the program is supposed to operate, and so are not likely to do anything that may cause a malfunction.
- Ideally, nothing at all. As little as possible. This is a way to add general usability testing to the various things your beta team is examining.

consider the job finished. If you feel that you're being pressed too hard by a client that's taking advantage of your better nature, you may well have to remind him that he got what he paid for—and more—already, and that while his ideas for enhancements are great, they really constitute a second phase or version two of the program and just aren't covered under the current contract.

This is a little harder to accomplish if you're an in-house programmer at a company, or if you're working on something on your own. In the latter case, there may never be a clear finish date for the program, and in the former case you can't fall back on a contract to delineate task completion.

This is why *logical* conclusions are worth considering as well. If you were asked to write a simple text editor program, but now you're being asked to include image handling and binary file editing, you've gone beyond the logical description of the program you were asked to make. This, again, is the time to start talking about phase two, the argument being that a text editor is something that is already useful and can be released right away, with later enhancements that can be added as modules to the core program. This allows you to spike the current project without having to invoke contractual obligation.

7

A Word About Safety

You should be in the habit of making regular backups of all your program and resource files, ideally at the end of any day you've made changes. That way, if your system crashes, you can recover; or if you make some changes to the program that actually cause it to cease functioning, you can revert to the last good version. I've had to restore from backups I've made for both reasons, and I can't tell you what a relief it is to know I can.

You might also want to regularly place backups of your files in a fireproof safe or a safe deposit box at a bank, to help guard against other possible calamities, and you will *definitely* want to place duplicates of the source and release software into such safe locations once you have a final release.

Some clients ask for source code as well. Go ahead and give it to them, since if what you've made is relatively simple, they'd be able to reproduce it anyway; and if it's complex, they probably don't stand a chance of "figuring out" what you did. Besides, they'd need their own Director programmer on staff to do anything with it anyway, and if they had that, why would they hire you?

It's also not a bad idea to consider project insurance. This is there to reimburse the client should some catastrophic thing happen and you're unable to complete the job. Some clients, particularly governmental agencies, *require* this.

1-Minute Drill

- What is scope creep?

Pack It Up and Ship It Out

Finally, the great day has arrived. Your client has signed off on the program, you've put it through its testing paces, and it is ready for distribution.

Now what?

Before you actually release anything, you *do* need to make sure you're in licensing compliance with Macromedia's requirements. Information on this subject is to be found in the "Made with Macromedia" section of the CD you got with your copy of Director. You can also look for this information at Macromedia's Web site. The requirements are not especially egregious, so don't protest too much about having to include their logo somewhere on your CD's package, or someplace in your program.

Then you can start handling the actual distribution of your product.

For Shockwave files, it's just a question of uploading them to wherever they need to go. From there, anyone who wants to look at the program will.

If you've created something small enough to be downloadable, you just need to compress it and put it online someplace those who need it can get to it.

However, most releases of programs made using Director are pretty large, which means you're probably going to be looking at a CD. I'm going to start from the assumption you've never actually had to burn a CD before, but that you've got the hardware and software you need already in place and have a basic understanding of how to use them.

Before You Even Make the CD...

The first thing you must remember if you are doing a Windows release is to avoid *autorun* at all costs. Autorun CDs load a given program whenever the disc is inserted into a CD-ROM drive. CDs that have autorun programs on them are very common on Windows now, and they are very annoying.

- An effect that happens when a program, through client-requested changes, begins to go way beyond the initial parameters agreed upon for its design.

Autorun simply does not work at all on some systems, sometimes because of system errors and sometimes because the system's owner has specifically *disabled* the autorun feature. Also, autorun can cause some systems to freeze completely, which means every time the user inserts your CD his computer will lock up. Sometimes autorun launches the same program twice, which will cause errors. Sometimes your user will be impatient, so she'll double-click the program after the disc is in the drive, causing several sessions of the program to try to run at once, and all sorts of nasty things will surely ensue.

Clients seem to like autorun and *do* ask for it until you begin pointing out the problems inherent in it. It's an unstable feature and not well implemented on the system level, and I urgently advise you not to do it.

Note

The strongest argument in favor of using autorun is that it's more or less standard now for Windows, but that's not a good enough reason. If everyone else jumped off a bridge....

7

If, however, you *must* do it, it's pretty easy. All you have to do is create a text file called AUTORUN.INF and put it at the topmost level of your CD layout when you make the disc. In that text file, you add a line like this:

```
open=myprogram.exe
```

where *myprogram.exe* is the name of your program. In theory, then, when the CD is inserted into a Windows 95 or later PC, your program will run automatically.

It's also possible to do autorun on the Mac, but the steps involved require performing some special operations with your CD recording software, and you'll want to check the manual that came with your program for information on that. This is something else I don't advise, for two reasons:

- Mac users don't generally get CDs with autorun programs on them, and they will not be expecting yours to do it either. If it does, it'll be reacted to with anything from surprise to mild annoyance to extreme irritation. ("Who does this programmer think she is, telling me which program I want to run when I put in a CD...?")

● If a Mac user does not know the program is running, and does not exit it before trying to eject the CD, the Mac will refuse to let the CD eject. It can take a few moments to figure out why, and it's always annoying when it happens.

Note

There's a philosophical reason to object to autorun as well. In general, autorun assumes your user doesn't know what he wants to do when he puts a disc into his computer, or is too stupid to figure out what she's supposed to do after putting the disc into her computer. If you treat users with a little respect for their intelligence, you can educate them on how to work with their computers a little more efficiently (if it's even *necessary* to tell the user where to find an inserted CD, or what to do with it once it's in the computer), and you avoid the entire mess I described in dealing with potential trouble.

Since we're on the subject of instructions, let me point out something you could call a pet peeve of mine. Many Windows CDs have "instructions" on them that read like this:

1. Insert the CD into your CD-ROM drive.

2. From the Start menu, select Run…

3. Type D:\SETUP.EXE, where D is the letter of your CD-ROM drive.

Were these instructions written by extraterrestrials? Windows is a GUI-driven operating system, which means there are things you can do with a *mouse,* and this has been true for about a decade now. Here's the correct way to write those instructions:

1. Insert the CD into your CD-ROM drive.

2. Open the My Computer icon on your desktop by double-clicking it.

3. Open the CD-ROM drive icon by double-clicking it.

4. Double-click the program called "Setup" to get started.

What's all this "Select run and type this letter, but not if it's that letter" kerfuffle? Just have your users do some clicking. They'll find it a lot easier to understand.

Planning the CD Layout

For Windows, getting the CD ready for distribution isn't especially difficult; you just need to put all the content you want to ship into the CD recorder's layout program, and off you go.

For Mac, it's a little more involved, since you can configure the CD's window to open and display the program, folder, and document icons in a specific way. Thus, it's a good idea to get things set up in a visually pleasing and logical fashion before you begin burning the disc.

Hybrid discs are a little more confusing, but not a lot more. A hybrid CD is one that can work on either Mac or Windows, and as a Director programmer you're likely to be called on one day to make such a disc.

This isn't readily doable on Windows yet, which means your CD recorder will be connected to a Mac and you'll likely be using a product such as Roxio's Toast to create the CD. The newest version of Toast, Titanium 5, has really simplified things for you. All you have to do is gather your Mac and Windows files together on your Mac's hard drive, and then drag those files into Toast's program window. You can choose the type of disc you want to burn from Toast's pop-up menu at the top of that window and, once you have the files laid out as you need them, click the Record button. Figure 7-4 illustrates how the layout might look if you were getting ready to burn such a hybrid CD.

Beyond that, there's not much magic to creating CDs, though I have some suggestions for you:

1. Begin by using CD-RW discs. These discs can be erased and rewritten, and you can use them to do some practice runs to see how things work out. Usually, the first couple of burns you do will have minor errors (at least that's usually the case for me), so using rewritable discs will save you money. Once you've got a good solid disc, you can crank out as many copies of it as you want on nonrewritable media.

2. Never, *ever* write a "session" disc. This leaves the CD in a more or less incomplete state, and some computers can't handle that. Furthermore, if you later write more information to that disc in a different "session," some systems will become confused regarding which session is supposed to be the "current" one. It's not worth the frustration.

3. Avoid really cheap discs. Many of these are translucent and don't read well in a lot of lower-priced CD-ROM drives, which means you could end up

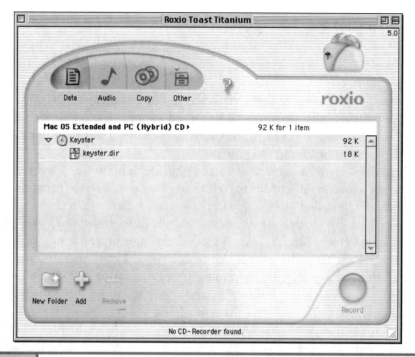

Figure 7-4 What Toast Titanium looks like before burning a hybrid disc

creating a disc that works fine on your machine but fails on the client's—or worse still, the client's boss's.

1-Minute Drill

● What is one danger of using autorun?

● Would you be more likely to release a Shockwave file or a projector on a CD?

● Multiple sessions of your projector might load at once; the autorun might not work at all; the system might freeze.

● Since Shockwave files are designed for Internet distribution but projectors must run from a computer's hard drive, the projector is more likely to be released on CD.

Common Release Troubles

Even a carefully tested program will not always work perfectly in the field, and sometimes it can be very hard to determine what exactly is going wrong when you've got a vague complaint from a user somewhere that something isn't working. If at all possible, you should talk to this user directly over the phone to get firsthand descriptions of what is going wrong, and you should talk to this person while he is sitting at the computer and trying to run your program. That way, if any errors occur, you can get the exact text of the message as it's happening, not a hazy recollection from a week previous.

Some of what follows might seem a little technical for now; some of it is. You don't necessarily need to understand everything here right away. Just know it's here and you can return to it later, after you've had more of a chance to work with Director and have a better overall understanding of how it works.

For Windows, you're likely to hear, occasionally, of problems with files named either IML32.DLL or DIRAPI.DLL, both of which are external program resources used by a projector when it's running your movie. In my experience, these happen most often if you're using MIAWs and do not correctly clear them from memory before closing them out. We'll learn more about the right way to clear MIAWs from memory in Part 4. Odds are, if you are running everything from one Director movie file, you won't see these errors.

Another problem can arise if you have QuickTime video files playing back in a Director movie and you try to exit the program (or close the video's MIAW) before you pause the video's playback. I'm not sure exactly why this happens, but it does seem to, at least to me. One way around this is to add this behavior to any QuickTime movie you place on your Stage:

```
on endSprite me
  sprite(me.spriteNum).movieRate = 0
end
```

This sets the **movieRate** (playback rate) of the QuickTime file to zero, or pause, when the sprite is no longer onscreen.

Note

If you're using MPEG or AVI video, you will want to do the same kind of thing.

This won't work as well with MIAWs, though, because sprites don't necessarily end when the MIAW is closed; that is, no **endSprite** event is necessarily generated for anything when you close a MIAW in Director. To get past that, you probably have to tell your MIAW to go to another, empty frame, which will create the necessary **endSprite** events, before you close it.

You may occasionally hear of Windows kicking up a message saying that a given file is "open with write permission by another user." This happens most often if the end user has accidentally run your program twice, or more accurately, has got two sessions of the same program running at the same time. If you recall, I mentioned this possibility in discussing the dangers of autorun a few pages back. The solution there, of course, is to exit one of the program sessions.

Generally, the troubles you're likely to encounter on Macintosh are nowhere near as nasty. Macs are more stable and better at handling the kinds of rich media that Director displays most, so problems there will be pretty uncommon.

In the most challenging cases, you might end up with complaints regarding Xtras you're using, and dealing with those can be much tougher.

For instance, there's been a long history of difficulty in getting the Print-O-Matic Xtra to work well on Windows with Hewlett-Packard inkjet printers. This isn't really the fault of any one party involved, which makes it even more difficult to get to an easy solution. What used to happen was that the printer would spit out blank pages, even though legitimate data had been sent to it. The solution at the time was to have the user reduce her display color depth to 8 bit and try printing again; apparently producing page after page of 65,000-color graphics proved to be too much for some memory routine somewhere deep in the guts of the Xtra and the printer as they talked to each other.

Finally, you might get occasional physical media errors, such as a damaged CD. That can result in your program working fine, but all of its graphics past a certain point looking like scrambled garbage.

You may also have major problems, on Windows, getting sounds to work. The reasons behind this are myriad and complex, but basically have to do with the fact that on many Windows systems, only one kind of file at a time can have the sound driver for playback. This means if you try to play MP3 sounds after running a digital video file, the MP3 sounds might not work. The solution there is to change the default setting for **the soundKeepDevice**, a Lingo parameter that determines whether your movie file tries to hold onto one sound driver type for the entire time the program is running. The default setting is true, which can help sounds play back a little faster; as mentioned, however, this can cause problems if you have multiple media types on Windows. You'd set up your script to look a little like this:

```
on startMovie

  the soundKeepDevice = FALSE

END startMovie
```

Remote Troubleshooting Suggestions

While it's impossible to account for every problem you might hear of, there are some basic troubleshooting steps I can offer that will help you in most situations. These steps involve a dual approach of eliminating the obvious and trying to narrow the possibilities.

7

1. **Make sure you're dealing with a user who is describing a legitimate problem with your program** This would be a user familiar with computers enough to know how to handle a CD, a mouse, and so on. If you suspect the user is putting the CD into the tray label side down, for instance, the time to suggest he get some local "nerdish" help is now. Often, if you call a computer company for tech support, the very first thing you will be asked is if the computer is plugged in and switched on, and all the cables are connected in their proper locations. They ask this because this initial question tends to weed out somewhere between 20 and 40 percent of all callers.

2. **Ensure that the system is functioning properly** If you're dealing with a computer that's regularly having troubles performing any task at all, there's simply no way to ensure your software will work any better than anything else.

3. **Find out if the system is up to the specs required to run your program** If your program requires 64MB of RAM and someone is trying to run it on a machine that has only 16MB, no one can really be surprised that it's not working. Using the tests I described at the beginning of this

module will also help ensure that the display resolution and color depth are at or beyond the minimum requirements.

4. **Make sure the medium is not damaged**   You'd be amazed at what some people will try to get running in a CD-ROM drive. Discs that have been scraped along sidewalks, discs that have been written on with magic marker, discs that were left in a car and are now warped, discs that are cracked. Water will not damage a CD; in fact, if a CD has fingerprints or dust on it, you can wash it with warm water and a mild dish soap. However, physical damage to the plastic on the shiny side of the disc usually means it's dead.

5. **Try to ensure the error condition is consistent and reproducible**   This is not that different from what you insist on with your beta testers, and for the same reasons. If a user is complaining that your program froze up after his cat laid down on the keyboard, you can sympathize with his plight but you don't really need to feel responsible for the situation.

6. **Try to get a clear description of the steps required to reproduce the error, and see if you can make it happen yourself on your own machine**   You might discover that a very consistent set of actions can be taken that cause the error to recur with complete reliability. Even closely tested software can have these kinds of problems, if the steps required to cause them are involved enough.

7. **Understand that you cannot plan for every contingency**   If your software regularly writes data to a file somewhere, and power is cut while it's writing that data (or it's forced to quit in some other, abnormal way), odds are good that data file will be irretrievably corrupted. Well, dropping the computer out the door of a 747 flying at 50,000 feet will also irretrievably corrupt the data on its drive. Some events take place that, while disastrous, are completely beyond your capability to control or guard against.

With this little checklist in hand and some creative effort and thinking on your part, you should be able to handle many different possible complaints and situations.

It's also a good idea for you to keep a notebook or some other record of problems you've dealt with so that you can track possible troubles in the future and avoid them. You will also want to become a regular reader of some or all of the forums I list in the online resources at http://www.nightwares.com/director_beginners_guide/. There you'll find lots of people running into lots of nasty situations; you might see how they're ultimately resolved, and as you become more experienced yourself with Director, you might occasionally be able to offer solutions you've discovered as well.

1-Minute Drill

● What's a good first question to ask when trying to handle troubleshooting over the phone?

● Why might a Director movie on Windows play sounds for a QuickTime video but not play any other sounds in the program?

Maintaining and Upgrading Your Programs

This can be one of the harder things to manage with Director, since you're quite capable of creating programs that occupy hundreds of megabytes of storage when they're completed. When it comes time to issue a bug fix or maintenance upgrade, e-mailing it as an attachment might be out of the question.

But here Director helps you, since you can create programs that are *modular* in nature. For instance, you can create a simple program file that does nothing but access another program, as you saw with Module 4. Well, imagine such a scenario that involves changing some of the code in the file that is loaded by the main program. If that file is the only thing that's changed, that's all you'd have to send out as an update.

Similarly, you can place a lot of scripts into an external Cast file. Since such Cast files will tend to be small, if you fix bugs in those scripts all you have to do is release the updated Cast file. Users then replace the old Cast file with the new one, and they've quickly got an upgraded, debugged program.

● Whether the CD is physically damaged; whether the computer is having problems in general; whether the computer is up to the minimum system requirements for running the program.

● The QuickTime video has grabbed the sound driver and won't release it to let any other sounds play; this is alleviated by setting **the soundKeepDevice** to false.

You can do similar things with sounds, videos, and so on, creating something that works in gestalt form as a complete and compelling program experience, but that is actually composed of smaller, interchangeable modules that can be improved, replaced, and patched in any combination. In Part 4, we'll get into the finer aspects of this approach to designing programs in Director, since it's probably the very best way to proceed, especially if you are making software that does complex things or that is meant to be scalable to a very high degree.

Naturally, there will be some situations where this modular approach is either impractical or effectively impossible, or where it wouldn't represent any kind of improvement to the overall maintainability of your program. In those situations, you just have to do the best you can with the constraints under which you work. As you become more skilled with Director, and as you pick up more experience writing programs with it, you'll be in a better position to judge which approach will work best in a given situation. One rule you can count on is that there's no such thing as a catch-all approach to doing anything in Director. While that makes it harder sometimes to get started with the program (after all, there are multiple different ways to do just about anything), this flexibility ultimately helps you by allowing you to come up with your own creative, innovative solutions to almost any programming situation you can think of.

Project 7-1: Repurposing Keyster

In the preceding module, you made a MIAW Xtra that displays the ASCII and Director keyCode values for any key pressed. This is handy for Director programmers, but it might be nice for other programmers to have as well. Here we're going to rebuild Keyster a little so that it can work in either a Shockwave environment or as a stand-alone projector, without your having to create special versions of the program for either situation. You will then be able to make the program available to anyone who wants it.

This project will show you

● How to restructure a file intended for one purpose (use within Director) to be used for another (use as a stand-alone program)

● How to do the equivalent for the Shockwave (Web) environment

Step-by-Step

1. Start by working with a copy of your original Keyster Director file (since the one in your Director program Xtras folder is handy and you'll want to keep it around). Add a little prompt text somewhere on your Stage that gives the user a hint what to do, such as "Press any key to see its ASCII and keyCode values." You might need to shift the other text sprites around a little to make this fit.

2. Next, add a *Quit* button. Click the button tool in the Tool Palette, and put a button on your Stage with the word *Quit* in it. Then, select the Behavior tab of the PI and, from the + menu, select New Behavior.... Call it something useful like "quitButton," since that's what it's going to be for.

3. Open this new behavior's script window and enter the following:

```
on beginSprite me

  if the runMode = "plugin" then

    sprite(me.spriteNum).visible = FALSE

  end if


end



on mouseUp me

  if the runMode = "projector" then

    QUIT

  else

    HALT
```

7

```
   end if


end
```

Here we've discovered a new keyword, **the runMode**. This returns one of three possible options and can be used to determine in which situation your movie is running. The three possible returns for **the runMode** are

- **Projector**   Your movie is playing back as a stand-alone program, just like any other program in the world.

- **Author**   Your movie is currently playing back in Director itself.

- **Plugin**   Your movie is playing back in a browser via the Shockwave browser plug-in.

Depending on which circumstance is true, you're going to want your movies to behave differently sometimes. For instance, when a movie is playing back in Shockwave, the **quit** command will have no effect. The movie won't quit, and it won't cause the browser to quit either.

So this little behavior is doing something sneaky with its **beginSprite** function. It's determining if the Director file is playing back as a Shockwave movie and, if it is, it's making the *Quit* button completely invisible. This is not a problem, of course, because the *Quit* button won't even work in Shockwave in the first place. So removing it from the Stage by making it invisible will result in less confusion for anyone who runs it as a Shockwave movie. ("Hey, I'm clicking *quit,* but nothing's happening!")

The second function, a **mouseUp** call, will be activated only if your movie is running either in Director itself or as a projector, since the *Quit* button's invisible in Shockwave and cannot be clicked.

In this script, we test to see whether we're running in author or projector mode. If we're running as a projector, we **quit** the program, but if we're running in author mode, we simply **halt**. This stops playback of the file without actually exiting the Director program itself. This is a very handy way to make it seem as though a program has ended even though it hasn't, without actually kicking out of Director in the process.

Tip

Many Director users of moderate skill will use **halt** all the time rather than **quit**, since calling **halt** in a projector will cause the projector to quit. However, issuing a **halt** command in a projector is not a good idea, because with versions of Director prior to 8.5, **halt** did not call the **stopMovie** handler. This is very important to know, because you will often use **stopMovie** to save progress files, restore settings you changed, and so on. Do not use **halt** in place of **quit**. (This situation was corrected with Director 8.5, by the way; however, if you are using an older version of Director for some reason, this habit can really jump out and bite you.)

4. Now add the following line in your Movie script to your **startMovie** handler:

```
the exitLock = TRUE
```

This prevents the projector from quitting if the user presses CMD-Q on Mac or CTRL-X, ESC, or ALT-F4 on Windows. This is nice to add, since presumably you're trying to show keystrokes when they are pressed, and under normal circumstances those keystrokes would cause your program to quit. By setting **the exitLock** to true, however, we ensure the program will not quit unless it is explicitly told to do so via Lingo. (The standard close buttons on the program's window frame won't work either when **the exitLock** is set to true, which is why we have to provide a *quit* button on the Stage.)

Now you're ready to release Keyster to the world!

5. To set Keyster up as a Shockwave movie, choose File | Publish. Director will compress the movie file as a DCR (Shockwave movie), generate an HTML page automatically that loads the file, and then launch your default Web browser to let you see the movie running more or less as it will if you put it someplace on the Internet. All you have to do if you like the results is upload that HTML page and the DCR that Director made, and you're done.

6. To set Keyster up as a projector, just choose File | Create Projector… and do what you've done with other movies so far through this book, setting it to run in a window and so on.

And that's all there is to it. You've learned that, by testing a few things with Lingo, you assure that your Director movies can be made to automatically handle

7

several different playback situations, and respond appropriately to each, without your having to release several different versions.

Project Summary

Between this module and the preceding one, you've learned a lot about considerations and pitfalls involved in preparing for and releasing programs made using Director. In the next module, the last one for this part, we'll explore further the way in which your Lingo code can affect the behaviors of sprites, and how sprites can tell Lingo how to behave—the true essence of interactivity, which is what makes all computer programs more interesting.

☑ *Mastery Check*

1. Of 8, 16, or 32, which monitor color depth would display the most colors?

_____

_____

2. If you look at **the deskTopRectList** and see [rect(0, 0, 800, 600), rect(800, 0, 1600, 600)], what does this tell you about the display settings for that computer?

_____

_____

3. In terms of computer graphics, what is *dithering?*

_____

_____

4. If your Director program uses MIAW and users report crashes with errors in either IML32.DLL or DIRAPI.DLL, what is a likely cause?

_____

_____

5. If your Director movie plays a lot of MP3 audio and AVI video, and the video sounds don't work, what do you know already about the kind of computer on which the movie is running, and what the likely cause is?

_____

_____

6. What is the difference between **QUIT** and **HALT**?

_____

_____

7

Mastery Check

7. What is a *hybrid* CD?

_____

_____

8. What is an advantage of making modular programs in Director?

_____

_____

Module 8

Integrating Lingo and Sprites

The Goals of this Module

- Learn how sprites can send messages to Director through Lingo
- Learn how Lingo can send messages to sprites
- Learn how sprites can interact with each other
- Learn how all of this will allow your program to interact with the user

In the preceding module, we covered the basic considerations you'll have in preparing a Director movie to be released to the world. In this final module for Part 2, we're going to explore ways in which Lingo and sprites can be made to interact with each other and with users. We'll be doing this module's project as we go through the text, so you may want to skim through this module once first and then sit down with this book and your copy of Director running to take on the full project itself.

Interface

When messages are sent from one section or part of a program to another, this is referred to as communication through an *interface*. This is a pretty technical term in a programming context and is not to be confused with the idea of *user* interface, which is the means by which an end user can make changes in the state of a computer, perhaps by running a program or saving a document file to the hard drive.

When we speak of an interface in terms of programming, we're talking about ways in which the program itself can send and receive messages, either among its own internal tools or among objects we create such as handlers. Without this interface—this ability for a program to talk to itself—there'd be no way at all programs could even be written, or at least not interesting ones. It's this ability to query its own internal state and respond appropriately to those query results that makes a program truly interactive, and that can even allow it to behave in more or less intelligent ways, or at least in ways that involve the program itself making decisions regarding what to do next.

It should come as no surprise, then, that Director supplies us with several ways for sprites and Lingo to interface with each other, and for us to test whether certain conditions are true or not with any given set of sprites. In fact, if you consult the Lingo documentation that came with your copy of Director, you'll find there's a fairly rich collection of sprite-oriented Lingo available to you. Some of this Lingo affects sprite location onscreen; some is used to test whether one sprite is touching another; some is used to send messages to sprites and among sprites.

We're going to be using Lingo from all those categories in this module to create a single-player racquetball game. Our game won't be the most exciting thing in the world, perhaps, but it will work, and it will serve to introduce you pretty effectively to the ways in which a program can be made to be genuinely interactive, perhaps even moderately entertaining. This module will be largely composed of separate related projects.

Project 8-1: Up the Paddle Without a Creek

With this project, we're going to start our racquetball game by creating a "paddle" for the player that moves around a racquetball "court" depending on where the mouse is pointing.

The goals of this project include:

● Learning more about sprites interacting with the user

● Constraining sprites to specific routes of motion and places on the Stage

Step-by-Step

1. To begin, we're going to need to make the paddle sprite onscreen that the player can use to bounce the "ball" off. Start with a new Director movie file and give yourself a Stage size of 512 × 342 or so, selecting this dimension from the size pop-up in the Movie tab of the PI. That's enough room to be interesting, and to let this movie play well in Shockwave too if you decide to put it online sometime.

2. In frame 1 of the Score, place a **go the frame** script, because we don't have much to do here right now except keep our movie on this frame when it's playing.

3. Next, select the filled rectangle tool from the Tool Palette and draw a wide, short rectangle near the bottom of your Stage. It should be about 10 pixels above the bottom of the Stage itself, perhaps five pixels tall, and about 40 wide. You can use the Sprite tab of the PI to set up its dimensions and location precisely. This is our paddle, and it'll run all along the bottom of the Stage.

For this program, you need to shrink your paddle's span so that it occupies only frames 1 and 2 of your Score. I'll show you why later.

Of course, if you click the Play button now nothing will happen; we haven't actually programmed anything into our racquetball game yet, except for the framescript that keeps it sitting there on frame 1.

4. Click the paddle sprite you made and, in the Behavior tab of the PI, select New Behavior... from the plus menu. Name it something meaningful to

8

you, perhaps "paddleScript." Open this new script for editing and type the following:

```
on enterFrame me

  sprite(me.spriteNum).locH = the mouseH

end
```

Again, we've got some new keywords, **locH** and **the mouseH**. **locH** is the horizontal location onscreen of the sprite in question, in this case the paddle sprite to which this behavior is attached. **the mouseH** is the horizontal location of the mouse pointer itself.

If you look at the code, you can probably infer what will happen when you click the Play button now: The paddle will move left and right across the Stage, always keeping itself aligned with where your mouse pointer is located. It won't move up and down, because we have not programmed it to do so; rather, its motion will be *constrained* to the strictly horizontal. Here we've used some Lingo to control where sprites (well, one sprite) appear on the Stage, based on the location of another object entirely (the mouse pointer).

So go ahead and click Play and move your mouse around a little. If you do this for a few moments, you'll notice something wrong right away with the way the paddle moves.

Did you see it? The paddle actually *does* follow your mouse—right off the Stage entirely! It's *really* connected to the location onscreen of your pointer, to the extent that even if your pointer is no longer over the Stage, the paddle is still following it around. That's no good; we want our paddle to remain visible on the screen at all times. (It's probably not strictly necessary to do so, since most players would surely understand what happened if the paddle vanished to the left or right, but for the sake of this program, we're not going to consider that acceptable.)

So what we need to do, then, is figure out whether the paddle has moved beyond the edges of the Stage, and prevent it doing so, or at least put it back onto the Stage if it manages to "sneak away."

5. Reopen the paddle's behavior, because we're going to go ahead and do just that by using a new Lingo keyword, **the stage.drawRect**. This keyword is used to denote the rectangle that the Stage is drawing itself in on your monitor, and we can work with it just as we can with any other rect. It has a left, top, right, and bottom just like any other rect you find in Director. We're also going to be looking at the left and right boundaries of the paddle's rectangle. We'll do all this in an **exitFrame** script we enter below the **enterFrame** one.

Note

Lingo also has another set of keywords, **the stageLeft**, **the stageRight**, **the stageTop**, and **the stageBottom**, which ostensibly behave in the same fashion as **the stage.drawRect** (left/top/right/bottom), but with Director 8.5 those older keywords began malfunctioning—a salient point you will not find listed anywhere in the documentation published by Macromedia. Thus, we are going to make use of **the stage.drawRect** instead.

Here's the code to add:

```
on exitFrame me

 if sprite(me.spriteNum).left < the stage.drawRect.left then

   sprite(me.spriteNum).locH = the stage.drawRect.left

 end if

 if sprite(me.spriteNum).right > the stage.drawRect.right then

   sprite(me.spriteNum).locH = the stage.drawRect.right -
sprite(me.spriteNum).width

 end if

end
```

8

Wowie. What's going on there? Before I answer that question, look over the Lingo and see if you can't guess on your own, drawing on context and what you can assume about the meaning of the keywords **the stage.drawRect.left** and **the stage.drawRect.right**.

Okay, here's the skinny:

if sprite(me.spriteNum).left < the stage.drawRect.left then

Determines whether the left edge of the paddle sprite has gone beyond the left edge of the Stage, by testing to see if the left side of the paddle's location is less than the left side of the Stage. The left edge of the Stage is, of course, the place on your monitor defined by the leftmost border of the Stage's window. The paddle's left edge, similarly, is the location on the screen where the paddle's left border begins. Both values are given as pixel coordinates and are absolute relative to the actual monitor dimensions. So if your Stage's left frame is located ten pixels away from your monitor's left, **the stage.drawRect.left** is 10. If the paddle is then five pixels inside the Stage's frame, its left location is 15. If, however, the paddle has slipped *outside* the leftmost edge of the Stage by five pixels, its left value will be 5, which is less than **the stage.drawRect.left** itself. Therefore, in playing your movie, the preceding test will be true, and the next line of Lingo will execute.

sprite(me.spriteNum).locH = the stage.drawRect.left

We can do this because Tool Palette shapes are understood by Director as being drawn on the Stage from the upper-left corner of the shape. This means that, as far as Director is concerned, the leftmost side of the paddle is the "zero point" where it begins drawing the paddle. So by setting the horizontal location of the paddle to be equal to the left edge of the Stage, we "lock" the paddle's position at that point and don't let it go any farther to the left.

That's it for that **if...then** structure; the following one is a little weird.

if sprite(me.spriteNum).right > the stage.drawRect.right then

This line is predictable enough. What we did for the left edges of the paddle and Stage we're now doing for the right edges, seeing if the right-hand side of the paddle has drifted outside the right frame of the Stage. But the next line might throw you a little.

sprite(me.spriteNum).locH = the stage.drawRect.right –
sprite(me.spriteNum).width

What does this mean? Well, let's break it down a little. The stuff on the left side of the equal sign you already know about, so we'll concentrate on what's on the other side. First off, we have **the stage.drawRect.right**, which is, of course, the pixel coordinate of the right-hand frame of your Stage. Then we have the phrase **sprite(me.spriteNum).width**, which seems to be a way of determining what the width of the paddle sprite is. If you set it up earlier as I suggested in the PI, the sprite's width is 40 pixels, so presumably that's what **sprite(me.spriteNum).width** is calculating.

Ask the Expert

Question   Why are we even bothering to calculate the width of the paddle? Don't we know it already? Can't we just do the code as

sprite(me.spriteNum).locH = the stage.drawRect.right – 40

Answer   Yes, we could, but suppose we want to make this game with skill levels, and reduce the width of the paddle to make it more challenging for advanced players? We'd have to reset that width value somehow, probably by putting it into a variable, to determine where to locate the paddle when it's too far to the right.

Well, it's every bit as easy to simply get the width of the paddle on the fly, and this method helps ensure we won't run into trouble later on by changing some parameters and then forgetting to update our code. By writing the Lingo as we have done, we're making the computer do the work for us, which *is* after all the computer's job.

Question   But why, then, are we *subtracting* that value from the stage.drawRect.right?

Answer   Just now I told you that with rectangular shapes, Director begins "drawing" from the *upper-left* corner of the shape, which it regards as being location zero for the beginning of that shape. Well, in order to find out what location zero is for our paddle relative to its *right* edge, we have to subtract its *width* in pixels from the *location* of its right edge. This gives us the pixel location for the beginning of the drawing point as far as Director is concerned, and that is the value to which we really want to set the paddle's horizontal location.

As you might infer, we would have to do the same thing to adjust its vertical location when we were looking at the *bottom* edge, but in this program that's not an issue.

8

Now, however, when we play the movie something really weird happens to the paddle when the mouse goes past the left or right edges of the Stage: It flickers onscreen. Why?

Look at the sprite's behavior again. You'll see that its location relative to the mouse is being set in an **enterFrame** event, but that it's being moved onto the Stage if the mouse is out of bounds in an **exitFrame** event. Since there is a measurable amount of time between the **enterFrame** and **exitFrame** events taking place, Director is actually updating the sprite's location *twice* each time it refreshes the screen, and this conflict between the mouse's location and the boundaries of the Stage is resulting in the paddle flickering. We'll find out how to fix that in a few moments. First, though, I have to see if you've been paying attention.

1-Minute Drill

- Define **locH, the mouseH, the stage.drawRect.left** and **the stage.drawRect.right**.

- If you wanted to make a sprite move up and down the Stage according to where the mouse cursor was, what Lingo keywords do you think you would use?

6. We can get beyond the blinking we've seen in our paddle by determining if the mouse is outside the boundaries set by the Stage, and not even trying to move the paddle in the first place if it is. Given what you now know about calculating locations from **the stage.drawRect.left**; **the stage.drawRect.right**; the sprite's left, right, and width; and the sprite's **locH** and **the mouseH**, see if you can guess what we'll do next. A hint is that it will be a change in the **enterFrame** event script.

Here's what I did. Was it what you expected?

```
on enterFrame me

  if the mouseH > the stage.drawRect.left and the mouseH < the
```

- The horizontal location of a sprite; the horizontal location of the mouse cursor; the left edge of the Stage; the right edge of the Stage.
- **locV** and **the mouseV**

```
stage.drawRect.right - sprite(me.spriteNum).width then

  sprite(me.spriteNum).locH = the mouseH

 end if


end
```

Here, of course, I'm just seeing whether the mouse is inside the boundaries for the Stage itself. If its horizontal location is more than the left edge of the Stage *and* it is less than the right edge of the Stage (minus the width of the paddle), then I go ahead and move the paddle so that it matches the cursor's horizontal position. Otherwise, I don't move the paddle at all, because the mouse is somewhere outside the left or right border of the Stage. Seems reasonable, right?

Oh, but now when I click Play, the paddle doesn't always go all the way to the left or right edge of the Stage any more! Why do you think that is?

If you answered, "Because the mouse is moving faster than Director can keep up with, so sometimes it 'escapes' the Stage before the paddle has moved all the way to one of the edges" (or something like that), you were right. My mouse pointer is actually going across the screen so fast that Director doesn't "see" its position accurately, and we notice this the most when the pointer is at the extreme boundaries of our racquetball court.

We're going to have to break things down a little more, to ensure that the paddle will go all the way up to the edges of our Stage, even if the mouse moves faster than Director can "see" on a frame event.

7. Our **enterFrame** event script is really starting to look complicated now:

```
on enterFrame me


if the mouseH > (the stage).drawRect.right - sprite(me.spriteNum).width then

    sprite(me.spriteNum).locH = (the stage).drawRect.right -
sprite(me.spriteNum).width

  else if the mouseH < (the stage).drawRect.left then

    sprite(me.spriteNum).locH = (the stage).drawRect.left
```

8

```
    else

       sprite(me.spriteNum).locH = the mouseH

    end if

end
```

All we've really done is get a little more particular in testing whether the mouse is past the left side of the Stage, and then whether it's past the right side.

First, we see if the paddle's right edge is beyond the edge of the Stage. If it isn't, we just move the paddle so that it's connected to the mouse's location. If, however, the paddle's side is outside the right border of the Stage, we instead "park" the paddle right against the Stage's edge.

Then, we do exactly the same thing for the left edge of the Stage.

But if you look at this **enterFrame** event script closely, you might notice something very interesting. Everything that we were doing in the **exitFrame** script is now included right here in the **enterFrame** script! Does this mean we can get rid of the **exitFrame** script entirely now?

Try it and see. Open the paddle script window and remove the **exitFrame** script. Just select the text and delete it. Then run the movie and see what happens.

Note

In any single behavior, the commands you type into an **enterFrame** event handler will always run before anything you type into the **exitFrame** handler for that behavior. It gets messier if you have more than one behavior attached that has **enterFrame** and **exitFrame** scripts, but not by much: The **enterFrame** script in the first behavior (going by the order listed in the Behavior tab of the PI) will run before the **enterFrame** in the second behavior, followed by the **exitFrame** in the first behavior, and finally by the **exitFrame** in the second one.

This exercise might have seemed a little strange. If I knew we wouldn't need the **exitFrame** script after all, why did I put you through the effort of writing it, then rewriting the **enterFrame** script to eliminate the need for the **exitFrame**? Wasn't that a waste of effort?

I don't think so, because you just got a chance to see how to fine-tune a program's reaction to user events. If I'd simply handed the completed **enterFrame** script to you and done some canned explanation of how it worked, would you have had a chance to learn yourself by direct manipulation and observation how and why this is a better way of doing things than where we originally began?

Project Summary

With this beginning to the racquetball game, you have learned:

● How to cause sprites to react intelligently to user decisions, in this case by moving in sync with the mouse.

● How to use Lingo to constrain a sprite such that it can move only in one axis (in this case, horizontally).

● How to use Lingo to constrain a sprite such that it cannot move beyond a given boundary—for this program, the Stage itself.

1-Minute Drill

● If you have written a behavior that has commands that cause a sprite to move, and that conflict with each other in the **enterFrame** and **exitFrame** event scripts, what will happen?

● In any one behavior, which event takes place first, **enterFrame** or **exitFrame**?

8

Project 8-2: Having a Ball

We're just going to keep right on going with the racquetball court and paddle program you made for the first project in this module. Since this is supposed to be a *racquetball* game, we need to have a ball to slap around, don't we?
    The goals of this project include:

● Learning to cause sprites to interact with each other

● Teaching sprites how to move realistically (or somewhat so) across the Stage

---

● The sprite motion will appear to flicker on the Stage.

● **enterFrame** in a behavior always takes place before **exitFrame** in that same behavior.

Step-by-Step

1. Select the filled ellipse tool from the trusty Tool Palette and make a small, ball-shaped sprite on the Stage. Remember, if you SHIFT-drag on the Stage using this tool, your oval will end up being a perfect circle. Make it about 10 pixels wide by ten high, and place it in the center of your Stage for now. Shrink your ball sprite's span so that it occupies only frame 1 of the Score. You don't want it extending into frame 2 along with the paddle sprite. Again, I'll show you why soon.

This is where things will get interesting, because we want to do two different things with the ball. First, we want to get it moving across the screen. Then, we want to make it react appropriately to different conditions *as it is moving*.

For instance, if it's at the top, left, or right edges of the Stage, we want to make it rebound, since those represent the "walls" of our racquetball court. We also want to make it rebound off the paddle. Finally, if it happens to make it all the way to the bottom of the Stage, we want to reset the game, since the player let the ball go past him.

Vector motion—moving a sprite in a straight line but at some particular angle—is surprisingly hard to create and make smooth on a computer. This is because, at least with Director, motion for a sprite can take place only on the minimum level of one pixel at a time, which means that we're more or less constrained to strictly horizontal or vertical motion, or motion in diagonals of 45º, because to produce motion along any other angle, we would have to either move fractional pixels, which is impossible, or do some interesting mathematical tricks to virtually "scale up" the size of the Stage.

We're in luck, because James Newton (who wrote the Advanced Guide for Director 8.5) created a behavior called **Vector Motion**, and it's in your Library Palette right now.

2. Open your Library Palette and choose Animation | Interactive. Find the behavior there called **Vector Motion**—it's probably the very last one in the list—and drag it right on top of your ball sprite. Don't bother setting anything in the parameters dialog box; just click OK to continue. We don't need to set any parameters, because we are going to write another behavior of our own that makes our ball act like a real ball, bouncing to and fro across the screen. We're using James's Vector Motion behavior to actually cause the ball to move, but we'll be determining ourselves in which direction it's going to be moving, and how fast.

3. Click the Behavior tab of the PI and from the plus pop-up menu, select New Behavior…. Name it something useful such as "ballScript." In the script we are about to write, we're going to have to do several things. First, we're going to have to choose a random direction we want the ball to begin moving, and then we need to tell the Vector Motion behavior which direction to move the ball.

As the ball is moving, we'll need to test its location and respond appropriately to what we learn.

You might surmise that we'll put this latter set of tests into an **enterFrame** or **exitFrame** event script, and that's correct. However, we need to get the ball rolling, as it were, and so the first script we'll create is the one that sets the initial parameters for motion. Here it is:

```
on ChooseVector me, fHMultiplier, fVMultiplier


  fHorizDelta = float ( random ( 20, 40 ) ) * fHMultiplier
  fVertDelta = float ( random ( 20, 40 ) ) * fVMultiplier

  fHorizSend = fHorizDelta / 10.0
  fVertSend = fVertDelta / 10.0

  sendSprite ( me.spriteNum, #VectorMotion_SetVector, [fHorizSend, fVertSend]
)

END ChooseVector
```

Homina homina homina. Don't panic. I'm right here.

on ChooseVector me, fHMultiplier, fVMultiplier

This is a behavior handler definition. The word "me" is something you've seen before and might be wondering about, and I'll tell you all about it in Part 4. For now, just remember that that "me" always has to be there when you're doing handlers in a behavior. The other two words, **fHMultiplier** and **fVMultiplier**, are parameters. You remember parameters from Part 1. We've got them there because we're going to be passing parameters to this handler once we're all finished with our ball script. You can guess by the simplified Hungarian Notation prefixes on them that they are floating-point, or decimal, parameters that will be passed.

8

fHorizDelta = float (random (20, 40)) * fHMultiplier

Okay, here we're doing some complicated-looking operations to put a value into some variable called **fHorizDelta**. Let's look at what's happening inside the parentheses first.

random is another Lingo keyword; it returns a randomly selected integer from within a range that we specify. In this case, we are looking for a random number somewhere between 20 and 40, inclusive. Thus, our **random** call might give us 32 the first time, 27 the second time, 40 the third time, and so on, but the random number we get will never be less than 20 nor greater than 40.

I chose this range myself after doing some lengthy experimentation with this project, because otherwise you would have had to do it and it would end up being even more stressful than the first part of this module.

Now that we have the random number, plucked from the range of values from 20 to 40, we pass it through the **float** keyword. This forces the number we get to be a decimal, or floating-point number. In other words, it takes the random number (say 23) and turns it into 23.0.

After that, you can see we're multiplying that number by our passed parameter. The next line does almost exactly the same thing, but with different variables:

fVertDelta = float (random (20, 40)) * fVMultiplier

Again, we're taking a random number from 20 to 40, turning it into a decimal, and multiplying it by a passed parameter. Then, we're putting the result into the variable **fVertDelta**.

?Ask the Expert

Question   Delta as in the airline, or delta as in the thing at the end of a large river?

Answer   *Delta* is a mathematical term that means the difference between two things. We're setting up some variables here that will determine the *offset*, or difference, between sets of horizontal and vertical coordinates. That offset is a delta value, hence my use of the word *delta* in the variable names.

Next, we do some division.

fHorizSend = fHorizDelta / 10.0

This is just to slip the decimal point over by one place in the number we just calculated. If the final result for the variable **fHorizDelta** ended up being 36.0, this operation would convert it to 3.60. That's all. We do the same thing to **fVertDelta**,

fVertSend = fVertDelta / 10.0

plugging the result into another variable. The next line, though, is definitely a little on the odd side:

sendSprite (me.spriteNum, #VectorMotion_SetVector, [fHorizSend, fVertSend])

What the holy cannoli does *that* mean? Well, as you can see, we've taken the variables **fHorizSend** and **fVertSend**, which we just got done calculating, and placed them inside brackets. You recall brackets from the last module. They're special characters in the world of Lingo, denoting a list.

But what about the **#VectorMotion_SetVector** part just before that?

Believe it or not, this and our little list of variables are also parameters, very special parameters we're sending to another piece of code in our Director movie. But where is this code to be found?

Locate the Vector Motion behavior script in your Cast window and double-click it to open it. About two-thirds of the way down in that script, you will see a handler that begins with the line

on VectorMotion_SetVector me, scaledVector, scaleFactor, theLoc

Aha, that's the handler we're invoking, it seems, with some extra parameters attached. (You don't really need to worry about those right now.) But this handler does not begin with a pound sign, so why are we using one in our script?

The reason is that we are invoking this handler using a very special Lingo command, **sendSprite**. This command is used whenever you want to specifically send a command to a given sprite, a command that invokes a specified handler in a behavior attached to that sprite. The general form at for a **sendSprite** call is

sendSprite (spriteNumber, #handlerToRun, parameters)

Here, **spriteNumber** is the number of the channel that the sprite occupies in Director's Score. #**handlerToRun** is the name of the handler you want the sprite to run; it is preceded by the pound sign to indicate that fact. (Macromedia could have set things up so that you didn't have to use the pound sign, but having it there is a good thing really, because it serves as a visual reminder that we are doing some interface messaging to a behavior. The reason this distinction matters will become quite clear to you in Part 4. For now, just accept that it's there and it's a requirement.) Finally, there are **parameters**, if any, that we send with the rest of the sendSprite message.

So now when you look at the line

> **sendSprite (me.spriteNum, #VectorMotion_SetVector,**
> **[fHorizSend,**
> **fVertSend])**

you can infer that we are sending an interface message to this sprite (**me.spriteNum**), telling it to run the handler named **VectorMotion_SetVector**, and passing two variables we calculated in a Director list format (**[fHorizSend, fVertSend]**). In this fashion, you can see that behaviors attached to sprites can talk to each other. This is a great way for us to be able to have our program talk to itself when we want it to, and to get it to do some really interesting things.

1-Minute Drill

- What does **random** do?
- What does **sendSprite** do?

4. We're also going to put in a simple little extra handler to the current behavior that gives us a positive or negative number depending on the value of another number sent into it.

```
on ReturnVectorDirection me, fNumber


  if fNumber > 0.0 then


    return 1.0
```

- Returns a randomly selected integer from the range specified.
- Sends a message to the specified sprite telling it to run a handler in its behavior instances with parameters passed as appropriate.

```
else

  return -1.0

end if


END ReturnVectorDirection
```

This script just takes a parameter passed to it, **fNumber**, and determines if that number is greater than or less than zero. If it's more than zero, we **return** (pass back) the value 1.0; if **fNumber** is less than zero, we **return** −1.0. We'll be making use of this script to ensure that when the ball bounces it continues to head in more or less the same direction it was before. So if it's coming from the lower left and needs to bounce off the top edge of the Stage, the ball will move toward the lower right after the bounce.

5. These scripts are just part of the package. We also need to figure out exactly where on the Stage our ball is, and decide what to do next accordingly. For this reason, we enter the following **exitFrame** event script:

```
on exitFrame me

  lVector = sendSprite ( me.spriteNum, #VectorMotion_GetVector )

  if lVector = [ 0, 0 ] then

    if random ( 2 ) = 1 then

      fHMult = -1.0

    else

      fHMult = 1.0

    end if

    me.ChooseVector( fHMult, 1.0 )

  end if

  if sprite(me.spriteNum).left < the stage.drawRect.left then

    fVMult = me.ReturnVectorDirection( lVector[2] )
    me.ChooseVector( 1.0, fVMult )
```

8

```
  else if sprite(me.spriteNum).right > the stage.drawRect.right then

   fVMult = me.ReturnVectorDirection( lVector[2] )
   me.ChooseVector( -1.0, fVMult )

  else if sprite(me.spriteNum).top < the stage.drawRect.top then

   fHMult = me.ReturnVectorDirection( lVector[1] )
   me.ChooseVector( fHMult, 1.0 )

  else if intersect ( sprite(me.spriteNum).rect, sprite(1).rect ) <> rect (
0, 0, 0, 0 ) then

   fHMult = me.ReturnVectorDirection( lVector[1] )
   me.ChooseVector( fHMult, -1.0 )

  else if sprite(me.spriteNum).bottom > the stage.drawRect.bottom then

   go ( the frame + 1 )

  end if

END exitFrame
```

Okay, take a couple deep breaths. This isn't anywhere near as bad as it looks.

**lVector = sendSprite (me.spriteNum,
#VectorMotion_GetVector)**

You already know, now, what **sendSprite** does. All we're doing here is asking the Vector Motion behavior to run the handler called **VectorMotion_GetVector**. This will **return** another Director list, this one containing a description of the direction in which the ball sprite has been programmed to move. We put that value into the variable named **lVector**.

if lVector = [0, 0] then

We're determining here whether the **lVector** list we just got from the **sendSprite** call is [0, 0]. If it is, this means that the ball sprite has not yet been programmed to move. If that turns out to be the case, the next few lines are executed, which pick a random horizontal direction to get the ball moving and then set up the initial motion parameters for the ball. Here's how it works:

if random (2) = 1 then

fHMult = –1.0

else

fHMult = 1.0

end if

We take a random value for the number 2, which will always be either 1 or 2, and if the value is 1 we set a variable to be negative 1. Otherwise, the value for random (2) was 2, and so we set the variable to be positive 1 instead. (As you can see, the positive or negative number is also a decimal.)

me.ChooseVector(fHMult, 1.0)

Here we make a direct internal call to the **ChooseVector** script we created earlier, and pass along the **fHMult** variable whose value we just randomly set to either –1.0 or 1.0, along with another hard-set value, 1.0. By passing along a random negative or positive number in the first slot, we allow the **ChooseVector** script to cause the ball to tend either left or right across the screen as it begins moving. This is because a *positive* value for the horizontal motion variable will make the ball move more or less rightward, while a *negative* value will make it move more or less leftward. The positive value in the second position causes the vertical motion parameter to be positive, which will make the ball move generally downward. A negative value here would make the ball move upward.

We want the game to start with the ball moving downward, since it will be heading toward the paddle. However we also want to let it move randomly to the left or right, so the game never begins with the ball moving in exactly the same direction every time.

However, everything in the if...then control structure will be skipped if **lVector** is not equal to [0, 0], because in that case the ball is already in motion and we need to figure out where it is and what to do next. That's what the rest of this **exitFrame** event script does.

if sprite(me.spriteNum).left < the stage.drawRect.left then

This you recognize from your paddle script. We're checking to see if the left edge of the ball sprite is at or beyond the left edge of the Stage. If it is, we need to make it bounce.

fVMult = me.ReturnVectorDirection(lVector[2])

This calls the other little utility script we made. We grab the number at position 2 of the **lVector** list, which represents the current *vertical* motion of the ball. We then pass that number to our **ReturnVectorDirection** script, which determines whether the number we send it is more or less than

8

zero, and kicks back a value based on that determination. This number turns into the vertical multiplier we'll send along to our **ChooseVector** script, which will make the ball continue moving in more or less the same vertical direction, but which will reverse its horizontal direction. Thus, if it was moving toward the bottom of the Stage when it hit the left wall, it will continue moving more or less downward, but it will bounce toward the right as well.

```
me.ChooseVector( 1.0, fVMult )
```

This line calls our **ChooseVector** script with a positive number for the horizontal parameter, which will make the ball move rightwards on the Stage, and with our previously calculated number for the vertical modifier, which will allow it to continue moving in the same vertical direction it was going toward before it hit the left "wall."

```
else if sprite(me.spriteNum).right > the stage.drawRect.right
then

fVMult = me.ReturnVectorDirection( lVector[2] )

me.ChooseVector( –1.0, fVMult )
```

This set of lines does exactly the same as those preceding, but for the right edge of the Stage. Note that this time the horizontal modifier is a *negative* number, which will cause the ball to bounce to the left.

```
else if sprite(me.spriteNum).top < the stage.drawRect.top then

fHMult = me.ReturnVectorDirection( lVector[1] )

me.ChooseVector( fHMult, 1.0 )
```

Here again we're doing something similar, this time for the top of the Stage. This time we want the ball to keep moving in more or less the same *horizontal* direction, which is why we determine whether the number in **lVector**'s first position is positive or negative, but we want its *vertical* direction to change so that it will bounce.

```
else if intersect ( sprite(me.spriteNum).rect, sprite(1).rect ) <>
rect ( 0, 0, 0, 0
) then

fHMult = me.ReturnVectorDirection( lVector[1] )
```

me.ChooseVector(fHMult, –1.0)

This one might not look quite as you expected, but we're just using Lingoesque terminology to determine if the ball has actually hit the player's paddle. We do this by testing the **intersect** of the rectangles for the paddle sprite and the ball sprite. The **intersect** test returns the rectangle defined by the area where the two sprites overlap. If the area is defined by rect (0, 0, 0, 0), this means the sprites are not overlapping at all; they're not even touching. If the **intersect** value is anything else, we know that the ball has hit the paddle, and we do another calculation to make it bounce back upward.

else if sprite(me.spriteNum).bottom > the stage.drawRect.bottom then

go (the frame + 1)

end if

This is the final test in our **exitFrame** event script; it determines if the bottom of the ball sprite is at or below the bottom of the Stage. If it is, it's because the player missed the ball, and we need to reset the game. We do this by jumping to frame 2, which is why I had you make the paddle occupy the first two frames of the Score, while the ball occupies only frame 1.

6. Into the framescript for frame 2, enter the following:

```
on exitFrame
  go ( the frame - 1 )
end
```

This will cause your playback head to jump back to frame 1 after it's gone into this second frame. What this does is force a **beginSprite** event to happen all over again with the ball sprite, which will reset its location onscreen and start the next round of racquetball.

7. Now go ahead and click the Play button. If all goes well, your ball sprite should start from the center of the Stage and begin moving more or less downward. If you hit it with the paddle, it should bounce back up, and whenever it hits the left, right, or top edges of the Stage, it should rebound appropriately. If you let it get past you and it goes past the bottom of the Stage, the program should reset and start you over with another ball.

8

Project Summary

With this project, you have learned

- How to make sprites interact with each other in meaningful ways

- How to allow a sprite to determine its own direction of motion, and get it moving in that direction

- How to use the spans of sprites across frames to set and reset parameters for them

1-Minute Drill

- In terms of handlers communicating with each other, what does **return** do?

- What would the following Lingo be testing?
  if sprite(5).right > sprite(7).right then...

Project 8-3: Upping the Ante

After playing racquetball for a while, you might notice that it's not especially riveting. In fact, it gets rather dull. Why? Because the ball always moves at more or less the same speed, which really isn't very challenging.

Well, we can change that. Imagine how interesting the game might be if the speed of the ball increased just a little bit every time it hit a wall. Sure, the game would start out slow, but it would gradually and inexorably get faster, and faster, and faster still.

We're going to modify the ball script just a little bit, using another Director keyword, **puppetTempo**, to increase the speed at which the program operates.

The goals of this project include:

- Learning how to change the apparent speed of animation in Director

- Learning more about how to react to users

Step-by-Step

When referring to how fast a Director movie is set to play back, we use the term *tempo*. By default, Director's tempo is 30, which means that ideally it will play back animations at 30 frames per second. This also means it will try to update the screen 30 times per second, and since the ball moves every time the

---

- It returns the specified value to the handler that called this one.
- Whether the right edge of sprite 5 is beyond the right edge of sprite 7.

screen is updated, you can see that if we increase the tempo, we'll increase how frequently the screen updates. Thus, we can really get that ball flying. The maximum value to which the tempo may be set through the Tempo channel is 999, which theoretically will cause Director to update the screen nearly a thousand times per second. In the real world, of course, that's unlikely to happen. However, by setting the tempo through the **puppetTempo** call, we can take the rate up to a maximum value of 30,000. Naturally, most computers simply won't be able to update the screen thirty thousand times a second, but it's certainly an interesting theoretical maximum, isn't it?

We need to start with a fairly low-key value for the frame rate, and we also need to store it so that we can increase it as the game heats up. For this, we'll define a property variable for the ball script.

1. Add the following lines to your hand-made ball sprite behavior:

```
PROPERTY pnTempo


on beginSprite me

 pnTempo = 20

END beginSprite


on enterFrame me

 puppetTempo pnTempo

END enterFrame
```

The new stuff:

PROPERTY pnTempo

This is declaring the **property** variable **pnTempo**, which you may recall from Part 1 is analogous to declaring a **global** variable. This variable belongs only to this behavior and is something that will persist for as long as the ball sprite remains onscreen.

pnTempo = 20

Here we're just initializing our **pnTempo** variable to 20.

puppetTempo pnTempo

This tells Director to refresh the screen **pnTempo** times every second (or at least to attempt to do so). As you may infer, then, when the ball first appears the number of times Director will refresh the screen will be 20 per second.

So we've got the initial tempo setting; now we just have to set up our script to increase it a little each time the ball hits a wall.

2. In the ball script's **exitFrame** handler, add the following line to each test that determines if the ball has hit the left, top, or right of the Stage:

pnTempo = pnTempo + 1

So, for example, the part of your exitFrame script that tests to see if the ball has hit the left edge or not might now look like this:

if sprite(me.spriteNum).left < the stage.drawRect.left then

pnTempo = pnTempo + 1

fVMult = me.ReturnVectorDirection(lVector[2])

me.ChooseVector(1.0, fVMult)

3. Do something similar for the scripts that determine if the ball has gone past the **stage.drawRect.right** and if it's gone past the **stage.drawRect.top**.

Do not add this to the line that tests to see if the ball has hit the paddle, since you want to give your player a little slack, and don't bother adding it to the part that tests to see if it's gone past the bottom of the Stage, since in that case the game resets anyway.

4. Now click the Play button and try your hand again. As you continue playing, you'll notice that the game gradually increases its speed, until you finally get to the point that you just can't keep up any more, assuming your machine's fast enough.

Note that when the ball finally gets away from you and the game resets, the tempo goes back to its bucolic 20 refreshes per second. This is, of course, because when the playback head jumps to frame 2, which does not contain the ball sprite, and then returns to frame 1, the ball sprite's **beginSprite** event script runs again, setting our **pnTempo** variable back to 20.

Project Summary

With this project, you have seen that you can control the speed at which Director animates sprites on the Stage, thus increasing (or appearing to) the overall performance of the movie. You've also seen that you can get things moving pretty fast!

1-Minute Drill

● What is a property variable?

● In terms of Director, what is tempo?

Taking It Easy

Perhaps our racquetball gets a little too challenging, but we can do the player a couple more favors.

For starters, we might want to set a cap on **pnTempo**, not letting it go past a certain maximum value. That way, the game won't become impossible to keep playing after a while. We can do this by modifying the **enterFrame** event script a little:

```
on enterFrame me


if pnTempo > 60 then

  pnTempo = 60

 end if

 puppetTempo pnTempo


END enterFrame
```

● A variable that belongs to a specific behavior (or parent script) instance.
● The rate at which the screen refreshes, or the rate in frames per second at which a movie plays.

8

This doesn't let the screen refresh rate go beyond 60 times per second regardless of how often the ball has bounced off any walls. This way there is no chance the tempo will be (for instance) 300.

Finally, perhaps we should add a line to the **exitFrame** script that reduces **pnTempo** by 1 each time the user manages to hit the ball with her paddle. That way, the user's interaction with the ball can help her keep the play speed a little more reasonable. You don't have to add that line, of course.

There are other things you can do, such as cause the game speed to be reduced by a larger number each time the ball hits the paddle, but *not* put a cap on the maximum speed itself, or increase that cap to something much higher than 60.

You can even get really clever and have the paddle detect the frame number it's showing in (remember, the paddle spans two frames, while the ball spans only one). Each time the paddle detects it's in frame 2, you can have it reduce its width by one or two pixels. So as the user continues to let the ball get past her, her paddle will slowly shrink until it's perhaps ten pixels wide.

Or, you could even make the paddle width vary depending on the tempo. The faster the game goes, perhaps, the wider the paddle gets—but not by much. After all, you don't want to make it too easy!

Summary

In this module, you learned that it's possible to make really interactive programs with Director, by having Lingo and sprites interact with each other. You also learned a little about handling interfaces to sprite controls and even to another behavior, and you have seen that a little creativity, exploration of your Behavior Library, and a willingness to experiment can yield some pretty rich rewards.

That does it for Part 2. Beginning with the next module, we'll start getting our hands dirty in the guts of the Lingo engine. We'll begin by taking out racquetball game as a basis from which to construct another program entirely.

☑ *Mastery Check*

1. What is the difference between **locH** and the **mouseH**?

_____

_____

2. If you see a Lingo command that reads "puppetTempo 120," what is happening?

_____

_____

3. What is happening here?

```
sendSprite ( 22, #ExecuteReset, 7 )
```

_____

_____

4. Why won't this script work?

```
on beginSprite me
 nSpeed = 15
end

on exitFrame me
 puppetTempo nSpeed
end
```

_____

_____

5. Why won't this script work?

```
PROPERTY pnSpeed

on beginSprite
 pnSpeed = 15
end
```

8

☑ Mastery Check

```
on exitFrame
 puppetTempo pnSpeed
end
```

_____

_____

6. If I have two behaviors attached to a sprite, and the first behavior has an **exitFrame** event script, and the second one has an **enterFrame** event script, which script will execute first?

_____

_____

7. Even though the highest value I can set the tempo to is 30,000, why is it unlikely I'd see anything happening that quickly onscreen?

_____

_____

Part 3

Unlocking the Power of Lingo

Module 9

Understanding the Power of Lists

The Goals of this Module

- Learn what a list is
- Explore some of the applications of lists
- Discover how to apply the power of lists

Beginning with Part 2, you explored some of the fundamentals of getting your programs to be *truly* interactive—to present the user with the ability to affect the state of the program, and to allow the program to respond appropriately to those changes. This is the definition of interactivity, and in this part we'll add several more skills to your growing collection, beginning with list manipulation.

Lists Aren't Just for Shopping

I've alluded to lists a few times now, and in Modules 7 and 8, you even used them a little. So what are lists, and what purpose do they serve?

Put most concisely, a *list* in Director is a collection of information that is indexed and stored in a single data container. This information can be almost anything; any data or variable type that Director itself can handle can also be tucked away into a list and passed around your Lingo like any other variable.

What makes lists particularly unique is the fact they are *indexed*. This means that if you stuff the value of pi into some list someplace at index position 2, it will remain in that position for as long as your program's running and the list variable persists, provided you don't explicitly change the list's contents or sort order. No matter where you are in your code, you will be able to get that value from its index location in the list.

Director permits you to make two different kind of lists: *linear* lists, which we'll be discussing right away, and *property* lists, which we'll cover in the next few pages. The two formats are available because each works better than the other in a given circumstance.

A linear list can be thought of in terms of shopping. Before you go to the store, you might make a note that you need eggs, lettuce, milk, flour, and apples. If you were to put this kind of list into a variable in Director, you might do something like this:

shoppingList = ["eggs", "lettuce", "milk", "flour", "apples"]

That's pretty simple, isn't it? Then, if you wanted to find out what the third item in your list was, you would simply grab that item at its specific index number:

item = shoppingList[3]

In our example, the variable item would contain "milk", because "milk" is the third thing in the **shoppingList** container.

But this list isn't all that well sorted, is it? Director includes a **sort** keyword, though, which allows us to sort lists in alphabetical order. (Numbers come first.) So if we did this to our list:

shoppingList.sort()

it would now look like this:

["apples", "eggs", "flour", "lettuce", "milk"]

Suppose we want to add some more items to our list, items we've just remembered we need. Perhaps we need some grapes, cheese, and eggplant. We can't just set **shoppingList** equal to those items, because if we do, the original contents of **shoppingList** will be gone forever.

You might be thinking of using addition here, something like:

shoppingList = shoppingList + ["grapes", "cheese", "eggplant"]

Clever, but Director doesn't let you get away with that, unfortunately. What we want to do here is *append* the new items we need to the shoppingList, and **append** happens to be exactly the Lingo keyword we use to do that:

shoppingList.append("grapes")

This would append "grapes" to our shopping list variable, putting it at the end, so **shoppingList** now contains

["apples", "eggs", "flour", "lettuce", "milk", "grapes"]

We then do the **append** two more times for "cheese" and "eggplant" and end up with this as our grand result:

["apples", "eggs", "flour", "lettuce", "milk", "grapes", "cheese", "eggplant"]

Oh, but our alphabetical sort is off again. Furthermore, this list is not at all well organized. There are dairy products scattered through it, and frankly getting any item from a list by its index number is not especially convenient.

9

How are you supposed to know, without actually looking at the list, whether "milk" is in index position 5 (or if it's even in the list for this week at all)? That's not a very effective way to handle a list of any appreciable size, and it certainly would not be useful for handling contents that some user has entered him- or herself.

Imagine a 500-item list! Imagine a shopping list that contained things you never even considered adding, such as tofu or baklava!

1-Minute Drill

- What is a list?
- What is one way to add things to a list?

Organizing Lists More Effectively

What we'd really need to make this shopping list of ours considerably easier to sort, modify, add things to, and read would be some kind of way to categorize the list's contents, perhaps by produce type.

You might be thinking, *well, then use different variables.* For dairy, you could do this:

dairyList = ["cheese", "eggs", "milk"]

...and for vegetables you could do:

vegetableList = ["eggplant" , "lettuce"]

...and so on. That's not the worst possible idea, of course, but it's not particularly efficient, and it does not take into account how people may sort things. It also doesn't let you add more categories to the overall shopping list; for instance, there's no variable set for cleaning supplies. If a list is going to really be useful, it will be *expandable,* but it should be *sortable* as well.

- A container that can hold many different kinds of data, including text, numbers, and quite a lot more besides.
- By using the **append** keyword.

This is where *property* lists come into play. In the examples we've done in the book so far, you haven't used these; they add a dimension of sortability to plain linear lists that makes them genuinely powerful tools. (In fact, with a well-designed property list, you can create a rich, searchable database.) Property lists allow you to create lists like our one for shopping, but they allow you to create *index handles in the list itself,* which can give you an additional layer of sorting.

Tip

Actually, you can have essentially an infinite number of layers and categories in a property list.

Property lists ideally use either integer *numbers* for those index handles, or *symbols.* A symbol is a special Lingo creature that consists of a single word preceded by the pound sign:

#thisIsASymbol

You might remember the pound sign from the last module, where it was used in a **sendSprite** call to tell a specific sprite to run a handler. The handler name was preceded by the pound sign, and that does in fact imply a little something about how Director works under the hood, but that's a discussion several parsecs off the main point here.

Symbols are extremely nice things. They are faster for Lingo to process than plain text, but they possess a great strength in that they can be made human readable. This means that if you get into the practice of using symbols instead of numbers to pass information around in your program (wherever feasible), your scripts will be considerably easier to understand.

I said that symbols must be one word. The rules that apply for handler names are the same as those for symbols: No spaces, no punctuation, no special characters except the underscore. Thus

#this_is_a_valid_symbol

but

#this is not

9

That's pretty nice to know, but what's even more fun is that you can convert plain text to a symbol, or a symbol to plain text, by using the **symbol** and **string** keywords, respectively. You probably remember seeing the **string** keyword in Module 6; it's a way to specify that a given chunk of data is supposed to be converted to text, which in Director space is something surrounded by double quotes.

Well, if you pass something through the **symbol** keyword, it surely will be converted to a symbol, at least until Director encounters an illegal character. Here are some examples.

```
put symbol ( "hello" )
-- #hello
put string ( #goodMorning )
-- "goodMorning"
put symbol ( "Hello, world!" )
-- #Hello
```

Aha, in that third example you can see that our original text, "Hello, world!", did not get completely converted to a symbol. Only the first word ended up in the symbol result, with everything past the first illegal character (in this case, the comma) *truncated,* or removed entirely.

And why does any of this bear any relevance to our discussion of property lists? Because, if you remember, property lists can use symbols *as well as* integers to provide index handles, that's why, and those symbols can make our property lists very easy to manage.

1-Minute Drill

● What is a symbol?

● Which of these text strings would be converted (in entirety) to valid symbols using the symbol keyword?
"HiThere"
"Hello, Mrs. Smith"
"wazzup_doc?"
"That's_not_right"

● A special data type used in Director that contains letters, but that is handled as quickly as a number.
● Only the first one; the others will eventually truncate someplace.

Sorting Our Shopping

Let's go back to our **shoppingList** variable for a moment. It got to be pretty involved:

> **["apples", "eggs", "flour", "lettuce", "milk", "grapes", "cheese", "eggplant"]**

Suppose we convert this to a property list instead, and we create a few index handles to sort things a little more effectively. Let's make one each for *produce, dairy,* and *baking*. In order to implement this effectively, we'd set our list to resemble this:

> **shoppingList = [#produce: ["apples", "eggplant", "grapes", "lettuce"],**
> **#dairy: ["cheese", "eggs", "milk"], #baking: ["flour"]]**

What this resembles more than anything else is one larger list that contains several smaller lists, and that's more or less exactly what a property list is. But now we can really get a handle on the things our list contains by referring to specific index type, as opposed to blindly trying to grab something at some index position somewhere and hoping we get it right. If, for instance, we are in the dairy section of the store, we don't really care about anything else in our shopping list at the moment, and we can specifically get just the dairy-related items in our list by accessing the dairy property of our new shopping list:

> **dairyList = shoppingList[#dairy]**

Here we just ask for the stuff in the **#dairy** part of the **shoppingList** variable, telling Director this is what we want not by sending a number to request an index position, but rather by passing the symbol property we set earlier. What **dairyList** will contain, then, is

> **["cheese", "eggs", "milk"]**

…that is, the second minilist we assigned to the dairy property when we created our list.

9

That's pretty useful, but suppose we want to add cleaning products to the shopping list? We don't even have a *category* for that.

Director also gives us several tools to modify property lists. For this specific example, the one we're interested in is **addProp**, which you might infer is a contracted way of saying "add property."

The syntax for using **addProp** is this:

listName.addProp (propertyToAdd, valueToAdd)

Of course, our **propertyToAdd**, being a symbol, will have to be one word, but that's not too hard to figure out. What about that **valueToAdd** thing, though?

If you look at **shoppingList** so far, you'll see that each property is associated with another list of items, so perhaps we need to do the same thing when we use **addProp** to insert a new property. But we don't necessarily know what kind of cleaning products we're going to add yet, so we need to add an empty list as a sort of placeholder.

Director lets us get away with that, and so we can do something like this:

shoppingList.addProp (#cleaning_supplies, [])

Was it really that easy? Well, since **shoppingList** now looks like this:

[#produce: ["apples", "eggplant", "grapes", "lettuce"], #dairy: ["cheese", "eggs", "milk"], #baking: ["flour"], #cleaning_supplies: []]

clearly it was.

1-Minute Drill

● What is one way to add a new property to a property list?

● What is happening here?
myList.addProp(#thirdCategory, "green")

● With the addProp keyword.

● The value "green" is being added to the variable myList, with a property index of #thirdCategory.

Care and Feeding of Properties

Now that we've added another index property to our property list, we've got to plug some stuff into it. Perhaps we need some dish soap. How in the world are we supposed to add dish soap to the cleaning supplies part of our shopping list?

If we try to **append** that to our **shoppingList** variable now

shoppingList.append("dish soap")

the results will not be what we want at all. Director will give us a script error saying, "Handler not found in object." That's not an especially helpful message; what is really happening here is we're trying to use **append**, which works for *linear* lists, to tack a new value onto a *property* list, which is a no-no.

What we need to do, then, is first get the contents of the cleaning supplies index, and then append dish soap to *that*. There's a long way to do this and a short way, and for clarity I'll use the long way first.

```
lCleaning = shoppingList[#cleaning_supplies]
lCleaning.append ( "dish soap" )
shoppingList[#cleaning_supplies] = lCleaning
```

In the first line, we just grab the list contained in the cleaning supplies index location and put it into a temporary variable. You've seen that before. In the second line, we **append** the dish soap item to that list, something else you've seen already.

9

Tip

If the list is empty, "dish soap" becomes its sole entry. Otherwise, "dish soap" is added to the end of the list.

Finally, we put our modified temporary list back into the main shopping list variable at the cleaning supplies index location.

But that's three lines of Lingo, which could also be rendered thus:

shoppingList[#cleaning_supplies].append ("dish soap")

This one line of Lingo does exactly the same thing as the three I gave you earlier. I took you through the long way first, though, so that you could have a feel for the steps being taken. You can use either method in your own code, but I'd recommend by starting with the long way first, since it will probably help reduce possible confusion.

All the preceding line does is **append** "dish soap" to the list contained at index location **#cleaning_supplies** of the variable **shoppingList**, packing the commands into one line instead of letting them spread over three. This condensed method is one of the side effects of using dot-syntax notation.

Getting Some Dimension

You don't actually need to create a property list with just one tier of nested lists. You can actually increase the depth of a property list indefinitely, by adding lists into lists into lists. For instance, our shopping list so far is just stuff you might find at any market, but suppose you also want to do some shopping at the mall. You may have a second list, then, like this:

```
mallShopping = [ #clothes: [ "jacket", "pants" ], #gifts: [ "executive desk
set", "anniversary clock", "fine china" ], #entertainment: [ "books", "DVDs" ] ]
```

You could combine this and your grocery list into a meta-shopping list like this:

```
metaShopping = [ #mallShopping: [ #clothes: [ "jacket", "pants" ], #gifts: [
"executive desk set", "anniversary clock", "fine china" ],
#entertainment: [ "books",
"DVDs" ] ], #groceryShopping: [ #produce: [ "apples", "eggplant", "grapes",
"lettuce" ], #dairy: [ "cheese", "eggs", "milk" ], #baking: [ "flour" ],
#cleaning_supplies: [ "dish soap" ] ] ]
```

To grab shopping targets, you just add another level to your property index commands:

```
lClothing = metaShopping[#mallShopping][#clothes]
```

This would put the list ["**jacket**", "**pants**"] into the **lClothing** variable, retrieved from the **#clothes** index location contained in the **#mallShopping** index location of the **metaShopping** list variable.

And, of course, if you wanted to simply get one specific index item within a list in a list like this, you could do it as well:

secondProduceItem = metaShopping[#groceryShopping][#produce][2]

That would retrieve the item "eggplant", which is the second index item contained in the **#produce** index section of the **#groceryShopping** index section of the **metaShopping** list variable.

Hopefully, this hasn't thrown you. You don't need to fully comprehend everything I just went over; however, I do *hope* you do, and at the very least I hope you can see that lists—particularly property lists—are extremely flexible and powerful means of organizing, storing, sorting, and accessing all manner of information.

List Caution

There's one thing you need to know about lists that is not adequately covered in the Director documentation, and that is that any list you create is a sort of master catch-all in your Lingo scripts.

What this means practically I'll have to illustrate by example. Fire up Director and do this in the Message window:

```
firstList = [ "hi", "bye" ]
secondList = firstList
secondList.append ( "aloha" )
```

Now if you look at the contents of **secondList**, you will expect to see this:

["hi", "bye", "aloha"]

...which is, after all, what you told Director to do. You might then also assume that **firstList** will still be

["hi", "bye"]

But if you actually look at the contents of **firstList** now, you'll see that it *also* contains

["hi", "bye", "aloha"]

What happened here? Director didn't just change the value for **secondList**; it also changed **firstList**. This is because of a peculiarity in the way Director works with lists, essentially using one as the master or template, and subsequently pointing *back to* that original whenever a copy of the list is modified. In order to bypass this little pitfall, you need to *duplicate* the original list using the Lingo keyword **duplicate**:

```
firstList = [ "hi", "bye" ]
secondList = firstList.duplicate()
secondList.append ( "aloha" )
```

Note that in the second line I've added the **duplicate** command, which takes a copy of the **firstList** variable and plugs it into **secondList**, rather than simply making **secondList** *point* to **firstList**.

This is a potentially unpleasant thing, because if you're using some kind of master list as an index and you've got it in a global variable, and you want to make some changes to it in one handler as a specifically local modification (that is, you don't want to change the global list itself, but rather you want to temporarily alter some of its content in just one handler), you'll be in for a world of trouble if you don't use the **duplicate** command to get that global list into your local variable.

Note

Users of languages such as C++ and anything derived from C in general will not find this unusual at all, since arrays (which behave like Director's lists) also act in this fashion; however, if you're relatively new to programming or are not used to this kind of behavior with arrays or lists, this can be a very nasty little surprise the first time it happens to you.

Put another way, unless you specifically duplicate a list when you put its value into another variable, any changes you make to the list in either variable will affect the list in both variables.

Ouch!

1-Minute Drill

● What does duplicate do? Why is it important to remember to use it?

● How many property index items can you nest into a property list?

Project 9-1: Putting Lists to Work

Now that we've gotten a taste of lists, it's time to put our new understanding to use. In the last module, we made a simple racquetball game. I want you to make a copy of that Director file and open it now, because we're going to turn racquetball into "breakout," and we're going to use lists to help us along.

The goals of this project are to

● Give a working knowledge of lists by using them to make a program more interesting.

● Illustrate how to enhance an existing program by adding new functionality to it.

Step-by-Step

1. First, we need to add some bricks to our Stage, but before that, we need to make room for them. Grab your existing paddle and ball sprites and move them down in your Score so that the paddle is in channel 42, and the ball is in 43.

2. Before you go farther, open the ball sprite behavior you made in the last module and change this line in the exitFrame script:

```
else if intersect ( sprite(me.spriteNum).rect, sprite(1).rect ) <>
rect ( 0, 0, 0, 0 )
then
```

so that it reads as

```
else if intersect ( sprite(me.spriteNum).rect, sprite(42).rect )
<> rect ( 0, 0, 0, 0 )
then
```

9

● It duplicates the contents of a list into another variable. If you don't use it, any time you alter the list contained in one variable, you may be altering the original list as well.

● As many as you want to.

Note that I changed **sprite(1).rect** to **sprite(42).rect**. I did this because the paddle sprite is now in channel 42; in the racquetball game, it was in channel 1. If you don't remember to make this change, the ball will float right through the paddle instead of bouncing off it.

3. Now that you've got some room for bricks, start making them. We're going to have a total of 40 bricks in this game, ten each in four rows, near the top of the Stage. All you really have to do, though, is use the rectangle tool to make one brick sprite, and then copy and paste it nine times into the Score to make the top "row" of ten bricks. Make sure your brick sprite spans only two frames, like the paddle sprite; then just copy and paste it into the next nine channels.

   We're going to be using Lingo to actually position the bricks across the screen, so you don't need to worry about their *horizontal* positions or their width. I made mine 15 pixels high; you may want to do the same.

4. Next, select all ten brick sprites you just made by dragging across them either in the Score or on the Stage, and then copy and paste them into the next ten Score channels. Then, shift the entire second row of bricks down the Stage so that they occupy a discrete space below the first ten bricks. Repeat this process two more times so that your Stage resembles the illustration in Figure 9-1. Make sure to give them a nice even vertical spacing as you position them.

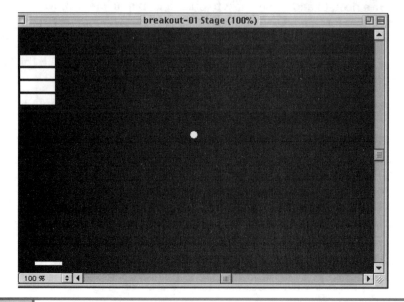

Figure 9-1 The four rectangles in the upper-left quadrant of my Stage represent a total of forty sprites, ten in each row, stacked atop each other

5. After you've done that, open a new Movie script window. We're going to create a property list that assigns color values and widths for each row of bricks. We'll then access that property list when the game is playing to put the bricks in their initial positions onscreen.

We don't have to actually make that property list by hand, though; we can use a **repeat with...** loop to do most of the work for us. Here's what I entered in my script:

```
GLOBAL glBrickList



on prepareMovie

  InitBrickList()

END prepareMovie


on InitBrickList

  glBrickList = [:]
  repeat with nBrick = 1 to 40

    if nBrick <= 10 then

      glBrickList.addProp( nBrick, [random ( 16, 35 ), 44] )

    else if nBrick <= 20 then

      glBrickList.addProp( nBrick, [random ( 72, 83 ), 46] )

    else if nBrick <= 30 then

      glBrickList.addProp( nBrick, [random ( 144, 159 ), 48] )
```

9

```
    else

      glBrickList.addProp( nBrick, [random ( 204, 214 ), 50] )

    end if

  end repeat


END InitBrickList
```

This is actually a pretty simple script given what it does. For starters, I declare a global variable, **glBrickList**. Then, just as the movie starts playing, I call the **InitBrickList** handler, which does the actual loading of my brick property list.

Tip

You'll note I'm doing that call from a **prepareMovie** script, which is invoked in Director *before* **startMovie**. Why this matters is that **startMovie** is called *after* **beginSprite**, if you have a behavior attached to a sprite in frame 1 of your Score, while **prepareMovie** is called before the **beginSprite** script. I have to get my brick property list initialized before any brick sprites actually appear on the Stage, because I will be using that property list to get the bricks set up for play. Thus, I must initialize my brick property list from a call within a **prepareMovie** script rather than the more typical **startMovie**.

Here's the breakdown of the **InitBrickList** script:

glBrickList = [:]

This is important; it clears out any previous contents that might have been in the brick list variable. I use a *colon* between the brackets to tell Director that this is an empty *property* list I'm setting up here. Not using that colon would give me a *linear* list instead, which would result in my **addProp** calls, used in the repeat loop, giving me a script error.

repeat with nBrick = 1 to 40

I plan to use only 40 bricks, so I need to fill my property list with only enough information to create 40 bricks on the Stage. Thus, my repeat loop will terminate after 40 iterations.

if nBrick <= 10 then

glBrickList.addProp(nBrick, [random (16, 35), 44])

If the value for my brick counter, **nBrick**, is less than or equal to 10, I know I'm creating list content for the *first* row of bricks that will appear on the screen (since there are ten bricks in each row). What I then do is add a property index to my brick list, only this time I give it an *integer* for its index handle rather than an actual symbol. I do this because each brick sprite already knows what its number is (that's the sprite number itself), and so when it comes time to make the brick sprite behavior, I can simply use that knowledge to grab the correct entry in my property list.

As you can infer, I'm putting a list into that index location containing two values: a randomly selected number from within a specific range, and another integer.

The random number will be used to set the color of the brick sprite when it appears on the screen; the second value is the width that brick will have. We choose the color value from a range to help ensure that each row of bricks will have randomly selected colors of more or less the same shade.

Note

I arrived at the values for the colors by looking at the index positions of color chips available to me in the foreground color selector of the Tool palette. You can do something similar with your own copy of Director, of course, if you don't like the colors I've chosen.

The next pair of lines,

else if nBrick <= 20 then

glBrickList.addProp(nBrick, [random (72, 83), 46])

does something similar for the *second* row of bricks, choosing a different random number from a different range and assigning a slightly higher value to the width of the brick.

The code proceeds to do the same kind of operation for the third and fourth rows of bricks as well, after which we're done and the repeat loop exits.

What we get from this is a property list containing 40 sets of nested lists, each of which contains two numbers: an integer representing the color we want any given brick to have, and another integer representing the width in pixels the brick is to hold onscreen.

9

6. That's only half of the work, though; we now need to create a brick behavior script that reads those values in the property list, and that causes its associated sprite to take on the attributes we've assigned.

Select all your brick sprites at once in the Score, and in the Behavior tab in the PI choose New Behavior... from the Plus pop-up menu. This will simultaneously create a new, single behavior script and set things up such that it will automatically be attached to all 40 brick sprites when we're done entering it.

Here's the script I'd like you to key in for the brick behavior:

```
GLOBAL glBrickList

PROPERTY plThisBrick



on beginSprite me

  me.SetTheBrick()

END beginSprite



on SetTheBrick me

  plThisBrick = glBrickList[(me.spriteNum)]

  if me.spriteNum <= 10 then

    nHorizReference = (me.spriteNum) - 1

  else if me.spriteNum <= 20 then

    nHorizReference = (me.spriteNum) - 11

  else if me.spriteNum <= 30 then

    nHorizReference = (me.spriteNum) - 21

  else
```

```
    nHorizReference = (me.spriteNum) - 31

 end if

 nWidth = plThisBrick[2]
 nHOffset = ( 52 - nWidth ) / 2

 sprite(me.spriteNum).foreColor = plThisBrick[1]
 sprite(me.spriteNum).locH = ( 51 * nHorizReference ) + nHOffset
 sprite(me.spriteNum).width = nWidth


END SetTheBrick
```

Some of this, again, you recognize. For instance, you see we're getting a reference to our global brick property list, and that we've also declared a property variable for this behavior, **plThisBrick**. Then, in **beginSprite**, we make a call to the **SetTheBrick** handler we create immediately following. Here's what's happening in that handler.

plThisBrick = glBrickList[(me.spriteNum)]

We're getting a list of values here, the list we made in the **InitBrickList** script, contained at a given index position in the main brick property list. We know which index number to get the list from because, as mentioned before, each sprite knows already which channel number it's occupying. Therefore, the line for sprite 5 would get the little list in index position 5 of the **glBrickList** variable. That list, again, contains two numbers, the first of which represents the brick's color, the second, its width.

if me.spriteNum <= 10 then

nHorizReference = (me.spriteNum) – 1

Here we're setting a local variable, **nHorizReference**, to be one less than the current sprite number if the current sprite number is less than or equal to 10. I'll show you why in just a few moments.

else if me.spriteNum <= 20 then

nHorizReference = (me.spriteNum) – 11

In the case of the current sprite number being between 11 and 20, we set **nHorizReference** to be equal to the sprite number minus eleven. We do similar things for sprites in the range of 21 through 30 and 31 through 40, subtracting 21 and 31, respectively. Again, I'll show you why soon.

nWidth = plThisBrick[2]

9

Here we get the integer in position 2 of the little list we read from the big global property list, and put that number into a local variable called **nWidth**, because this number represents the width our brick is going to be.

nHOffset = (52 – nWidth) / 2

Here we make a new variable, **nHOffset**, equal to the value of 52 minus the width of our brick, divided by 2. We do this because we're going to space the bricks apart onscreen horizontally, giving each one a little room to the left and right so that the player can see the individual dividing lines between the bricks. This gives our wall a more "brickish" appearance.

However, though we know that there's going to be a 52-pixel-wide zone for each brick to occupy, we also know that each brick is not going to be exactly 50 pixels wide, and we want each brick to appear centered in the 52-pixel space it will fit into on the screen. In order to do that, we have to figure out how far to *offset* each brick within that 52-pixel space.

Suppose, for instance, the brick is 46 pixels wide, and it's supposed to be centered in a space that is 52 pixels wide. There's a 6-pixel difference there, so if we set the brick's location to be equal to the left edge of the zone it was to occupy, there'd be a noticeable gap to the right. Thus, what we do is take the width of the region it's supposed to fill (52), and subtract the brick's width from that region, giving us 6. We then divide 6 by 2, which gives us 3, meaning that in order for this brick to appear centered in a 52-pixel space, it must be shifted over by 3 pixels. This will give us 3 pixels of space on the left side of the brick, and another 3 pixels on the right side.

All this work just to center a brick! No wonder masons are well paid!

sprite(me.spriteNum).foreColor = plThisBrick[1]

Here we're setting the **foreColor**, or foreground color, of our brick sprite to the randomly selected value we prepared in the **InitBrickList** handler in the movie script.

sprite(me.spriteNum).locH = (51 * nHorizReference) + nHOffset

Now we set the brick's location onscreen, using the variable **nHorizReference** we set near the top of this handler and multiplying it by 51, then adding our little pixel offset value, **nHOffset**, to the final result.

This is why I did some testing and subtraction with the **nHorizReference** variable. If I just set its value to be equal to the current sprite's number, by the time I got to the second row of bricks I'd be off the Stage entirely. What

I want, of course, is for each row of bricks to begin at the left edge of the Stage, which would put the **locH** of the first brick in each row at zero, or 0 pixels over from the left Stage edge. But the second brick needs to be at least 51 pixels farther to the right, and the third needs to be 51 past that, and so on. By using numbers from 0 to 9 for my horizontal reference, I'm able to correctly place each successive brick in the row I've defined (since 51 times 0 is 0, the first brick in each row will always start at the leftmost edge). That's why I needed to test which sprite number was running this behavior in a particular case, and subtract either 1, 11, 21, or 31 from that sprite's number to get my horizontal offset reference.

Sprites 1 to 10 will have horizontal offset references equal to 0 through 9, respectively, because the reference would be the sprite's number minus 1. Sprites 11 to 20 will *also* have offsets equal to 0 through 9, though, because in that case the offset number would be calculated as the sprite number minus 11. So 21 through 30, then, would be the sprite number minus 21 for the horizontal offset reference, and of course 31 through 40 would get the sprite number minus 31 for the horizontal offset.

Note

I know that seeing all this described here in a completed state makes it look like I just popped this carefully crafted Lingo out of my skull as you see it now, like some kind of latter-day Kronos. In fact, I tinkered with just the preceding location code for a half hour before I got it looking like I really wanted it. Remember: 99.44 percent perspiration.

sprite(me.spriteNum).width = nWidth

Finally, we set the width of the brick sprite to the number we prepared in the **InitBrickList** handler. That represents the main bulk of work for the brick initialization; in code, at least, our wall has been built. If you click the Play button now, you should see a Stage that looks a little like the one in Figure 9-2.

Of course, you'll also see, if you run your game now, that the ball still behaves as before in the racquetball program. *Exactly* as before. It sails blithely through the bricks as though they didn't exist, which is not the way a "breakout" program is supposed to operate.

This is because we have not created a *collision detection* script for our bricks yet, so as far as the ball is concerned, it's not actually hitting anything at all when it moves into a brick.

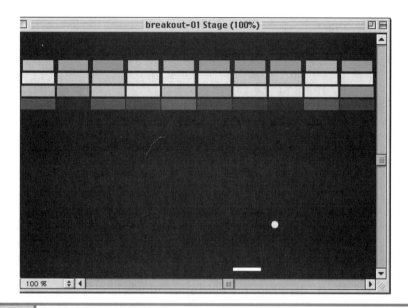

Figure 9-2 This is the wall that Lingo built

7. To start our brick collision detection, we need to create a frame event script for the brick behavior. I recommend using an **enterFrame** script here, since that will make Director appear to react a little more quickly to the ball hitting the wall than an **exitFrame** script would.

For the first version of our code, we'll borrow a little from our paddle's script, testing for an intersect. We'll also make use of **sendSprite** to get information from the ball regarding its direction of travel, since we want the ball to rebound off the bricks in a way very much like the way it rebounds off the walls of the court.

Here's the **enterFrame** script so far.

```
on enterFrame me

  if intersect ( sprite(me.spriteNum).rect, sprite(43).rect ) <> rect ( 0,
0, 0, 0 ) then

    lVector = sendSprite ( 43, #VectorMotion_GetVector )

    if sprite(43).top <= sprite(me.spriteNum).bottom then
```

```
     fHMult = sendSprite ( 43, #ReturnVectorDirection, lVector[1] )
     sendSprite ( 43, #ChooseVector, fHMult, 1.0 )

  else if sprite(43).right >= sprite(me.spriteNum).left then

     fVMult = sendSprite ( 43, #ReturnVectorDirection, lVector[2] )
     sendSprite ( 43, #ChooseVector, -1.0, fVMult )

  else if sprite(43).left <= sprite(me.spriteNum).right then

     fVMult = sendSprite ( 43, #ReturnVectorDirection, lVector[2] )
     sendSprite ( 43, #ChooseVector, 1.0, fVMult )

  else if sprite(43).bottom >= sprite(me.spriteNum).top then

     fHMult = sendSprite ( 43, #ReturnVectorDirection, lVector[1] )
     sendSprite ( 43, #ChooseVector, fHMult, -1.0 )

  end if

 end if


END enterFrame
```

Shoot, a lot of that was practically copy and paste from the ball script!

Well, okay, maybe not, but let's look at some of the beginning lines and you'll see there are some strong similarities.

if intersect (sprite(me.spriteNum).rect, sprite(43).rect) <>
rect (0, 0, 0, 0)
then

This you surely recognize from our paddle script; it's a close cousin. In this case, we're testing to see if sprite 43 (the ball) is intersecting the current sprite (any given brick) at this time. If it is, the script continues to execute at the next line.

lVector = sendSprite (43, #VectorMotion_GetVector)

This is almost identical to the routine the ball itself uses to determine which direction it's moving across the screen at the moment it's supposed to bounce off either the paddle or one of the walls. The ball's script, you remember, looked like this:

lVector = sendSprite (me.spriteNum, #VectorMotion_GetVector)

...because the ball was talking to a different behavior attached to itself. We've only had to modify it for our brick behavior to send the call to sprite 43 explicitly.

Tip

We get the value for **lVector** right away because now that we've detected a collision of some type, we know that no matter what happens next we're going to be sending the ball off in some direction or other, and we need the **lVector** variable to help us in calculating it.

if sprite(43).top <= sprite(me.spriteNum).bottom then

Here we're seeing if the location of the top of the ball sprite is less than the location of the bottom of the brick sprite. If it is, that means that the ball has hit the bottom edge of the brick. We then do exactly the same kind of calculation that's done for the ball whenever it is supposed to bounce off the top edge of the Stage, but we do it with some more **sendSprite** calls.

fHMult = sendSprite (43, #ReturnVectorDirection, lVector[1])

In the ball's script, this line is rendered as

fHMult = me.ReturnVectorDirection(lVector[1])

By doing a **sendSprite** call instead, we're recycling the **ReturnVectorDirection** handler. We don't have to enter a duplicate of it here in our brick script, since it's already in the ball script, and we can get right to it by using **sendSprite**. We're pretty darned clever, aren't we?

sendSprite (43, #ChooseVector, fHMult, 1.0)

Here we're recycling again; in the ball's script this line is written as

me.ChooseVector(fHMult, 1.0)

Again, since the script is already in place in the ball's behavior, we can get it to execute with **sendSprite**.

The next few tests in our **enterFrame** script simply do the same things, testing to see if the ball has hit the left, right, or top edge of a brick, respectively. If any of these events turns out to be the case, we just calculate our rebounds exactly as we did for the ball running into the right or left edges of the Stage, or into the paddle.

8. Now if you click Play, the ball should bounce off any brick it hits, and in fact when you play your movie, that's what happens.

Uh-oh. Now we've gone too far the other direction. Before, the ball ignored the bricks and just flew over them. Now, it hits a brick and rebounds, but *the brick does not disappear.* That's also not how "breakout" is supposed to work.

We need to set up the bricks so that they are removed from the screen as the ball hits them, and the best way to do that is to physically relocate the brick somewhere way, way outside the Stage's window onscreen. That way, there's no chance for the ball to hit the brick, since the brick isn't even there.

Note

You might think another way to do this would be to simply set the **visible** of the brick to false, but this won't work as expected. Even though the brick is not visible, it will still be occupying a "virtual" space on the Stage. What this means in practical terms is that the ball will continue bouncing off the invisible bricks!

Well, of course, we can move any hit brick, this time using another Lingo keyword, **loc**. That's short for location, and the general syntax is

loc (horizontalCoordinate, verticalCoordinate)

...*always* in pixels. So all we have to do when a brick gets run into is make it disappear by doing something like this:

sprite(me.spriteNum).loc = point (5000, 5000)

We put that line toward the end of the **enterFrame** script, just *before* the final **end if**, so the modified code looks like this:

9

```
on enterFrame me

  if intersect ( sprite(me.spriteNum).rect, sprite(43).rect ) <> rect ( 0,
0, 0, 0 ) then

    lVector = sendSprite ( 43, #VectorMotion_GetVector )

    if sprite(43).top <= sprite(me.spriteNum).bottom then

      fHMult = sendSprite ( 43, #ReturnVectorDirection, lVector[1] )
      sendSprite ( 43, #ChooseVector, fHMult, 1.0 )

    else if sprite(43).right >= sprite(me.spriteNum).left then
```

```
      fVMult = sendSprite ( 43, #ReturnVectorDirection, lVector[2] )
      sendSprite ( 43, #ChooseVector, -1.0, fVMult )

   else if sprite(43).left <= sprite(me.spriteNum).right then

      fVMult = sendSprite ( 43, #ReturnVectorDirection, lVector[2] )
      sendSprite ( 43, #ChooseVector, 1.0, fVMult )

   else if sprite(43).bottom >= sprite(me.spriteNum).top then

      fHMult = sendSprite ( 43, #ReturnVectorDirection, lVector[1] )
      sendSprite ( 43, #ChooseVector, fHMult, -1.0 )

   end if

   sprite(me.spriteNum).loc = point ( 5000, 5000 )

  end if

END enterFrame
```

Take care not to put that line *above* the next to last **end if**, or it won't run unless the ball hits the top edge of a brick. Also, don't put it *after* the *last* **end if**, or that line will run with the very first **enterFrame** for each brick— and they'll all disappear before the ball hits any of them!

Ask the Expert

Question   Why don't we put the relocation code at the top of the enterFrame script, once we've realized the ball hit the brick?

Answer   You can do that if you want to. However, there's always a chance that somehow, somewhere, the Stage's image will be refreshed before the actual collision calculation takes place between the ball and the brick. It's not likely, but it's not impossible.

And if that happens you'll get a script error, because suddenly the brick that used to be there won't be, it won't be in contact with the ball sprite any more, and the entire thing will just fall right over.

Besides, even if putting the brick relocation command is technically valid, it's disruptive of the implicit logic flow of the program. A human reading that code would wonder how and why you're doing collision detection on a brick shape you just moved several thousand pixels offscreen.

Now try clicking Play and seeing what happens. This game has definitely become more interesting—the ball hits bricks, and sure enough, it bounces off them just as you expect. Until, that is, it gets through the wall and tries to bounce off the top edges of the bricks. That doesn't work! It plows right through them, instead of bouncing up and down between the topmost row of bricks and the top of the Stage. If you've ever played a "breakout" game, you know that's not right. In fact, a lot of the fun of "breakout" games is getting the ball up behind the wall of bricks and watching it bounce along, clearing blocks out of the way as it goes, without your having to try to catch it with the paddle.

Another problem is that the ball pretty much always seems to rebound from any brick as though it hit the brick's bottom, even if it looks more as if it hit one of the edges.

The reason for this is really not very obvious, so don't feel too badly if you don't see it. It all has to do with the way the intersection code is running.

1-Minute Drill

- What is being defined by this term?
  point (37, 124)

- Would a sprite located at point (–500, –300) be visible on the Stage? Why or why not?

9. In our collision detection, the first thing we're checking is whether the top edge of the ball is at or above the bottom edge of a brick. If it is, we assume the ball has hit the bottom of a brick and give it a downward-pointing rebound command, which sounds reasonable. The problem there is that if the ball happens to be behind the wall and hits the top edge of a brick, the top of the ball is *still* above the bottom of the brick, and so our code mistakenly sends another downward-pointing rebound order.

What we need to do, then, is try to figure out whether the ball is above or below a brick when it hits it.

- A pixel coordinate 37 pixels to the left of the Stage's border and 124 pixels below the top of the Stage.
- Not unless it was a very large sprite, because that coordinate position is about half a monitor's width to the left of and another half a monitor width above the top-left corner of the Stage.

You'll remember the **locH** testing we did for our paddle; we can do something similar with our ball now. If the ball hits a brick and its vertical location onscreen (**locV**) is a number *greater than* the **locV** of that brick, the ball is *beneath* the brick and has hit it from below, because the higher a vertical coordinate is on the Stage, the lower on the Stage a sprite appears to be. Therefore, we rebound the ball downward.

Similarly, if the **locV** of the ball is a *lower* number than the **locV** of the brick, the ball has hit it from *above*. In this case, we rebound the ball upward.

But there's still the question of bouncing to the left and right, which doesn't seem to work very well. This is because our collision test looks at vertical position first, determining if the top edge of the ball is somewhere above the bottom edge of the brick and, if so, doing a vertical rebound. Well, if the ball has hit either the right or left side of a brick, its top edge is *by definition* higher than the bottom edge of that brick.

This is where we begin looking at the actual rectangle of intersection defined by the ball colliding with the brick. We do this to see if the intersection rectangle is tall and thin or short and wide. If it's short and wide, the ball has hit either the top or bottom edge of a brick; if it's tall and thin, it's because the ball has hit one of the brick's sides.

So if the ball and brick intersection rectangle is taller than it is wide, we want to do a rebound to the left or right. If the intersection rectangle is wider than it is tall, we want to do a rebound up or down. Therefore, the first question we need to answer is what the *shape* of the intersection rectangle is. If we determine we need to do some kind of vertical rebound, we then determine if the ball was above or below the brick; if we need a horizontal rebound, we then determine if the ball was to the left or right of the brick.

That's why our **enterFrame** script should now look something like this:

```
on enterFrame me


  rIntersect = intersect ( sprite(me.spriteNum).rect, sprite(43).rect )

  if rIntersect <> rect ( 0, 0, 0, 0 ) then
```

```
   nRectHeight = abs ( rIntersect.top - rIntersect.bottom )
   nRectWidth = abs ( rIntersect.left - rIntersect.right )

   lVector = sendSprite ( 43, #VectorMotion_GetVector )

   if nRectHeight > nRectWidth then

     if sprite(43).locH < sprite(me.spriteNum).locH then

       fVMult = sendSprite ( 43, #ReturnVectorDirection, lVector[2] )
       sendSprite ( 43, #ChooseVector, -1.0, fVMult )

     else

       fVMult = sendSprite ( 43, #ReturnVectorDirection, lVector[2] )
       sendSprite ( 43, #ChooseVector, 1.0, fVMult )

     end if

   else

     if sprite(43).locV < sprite(me.spriteNum).locV then

       fHMult = sendSprite ( 43, #ReturnVectorDirection, lVector[1] )
       sendSprite ( 43, #ChooseVector, fHMult, -1.0 )

     else

       fHMult = sendSprite ( 43, #ReturnVectorDirection, lVector[1] )
       sendSprite ( 43, #ChooseVector, fHMult, 1.0 )

     end if

   end if

   sprite(me.spriteNum).loc = point ( 5000, 5000 )

 end if

END enterFrame
```

Oh joy, more keywords.

**rIntersect = intersect (sprite(me.spriteNum).rect,
sprite(43).rect)**

Here we're simply taking the **intersect** rectangle of the ball sprite and the current brick sprite and putting it into a variable, **rIntersect**.

if rIntersect <> rect (0, 0, 0, 0) then

…then the ball is intersecting this brick, and we need to figure out which edge it hit.

nRectHeight = abs (rIntersect.top – rIntersect.bottom)

Here, **abs** is not as in what Arnold Schwarzenegger has in abundance. In this context, **abs** means *absolute value,* a fancy way of saying "the difference between two numbers." The advantage of using absolute value here is that absolute values are always positive, even if you've subtracted a larger number from a smaller one.

Ask the Expert

Question   Oh man, this is why I stopped paying attention in math class. How can this possibly work?

Answer   Just think of things in terms of how far apart two numbers are, regardless of what those numbers may actually be.

For instance $10 - 2$ is 8, and $2 - 10$ is –8. However, in terms of absolute value, $10 - 2$ is 8, and $2 - 10$ is *also* 8, because the difference between 2 and 10 is always 8, no matter which "direction" the subtraction operation is taking. The numbers 2 and 10 are 8 places apart from each other no matter how you look at it.

This is why it is the *absolute* value: it's the absolute difference between two numbers, not the result of a subtraction operation. And that's why we take the absolute value here: We don't care whether the top coordinate of the intersection rectangle is a larger number than the bottom coordinate; we just want to know how "far apart" these numbers are in absolute terms. This gives us the actual height of the intersection rectangle no matter where its top and bottom edges are.

nRectWidth = abs (rIntersect.left – rIntersect.right)

Here we get the same kind of value for the width of the intersection rectangle.

if nRectHeight > nRectWidth then

…then our intersection rectangle is *taller* than it is *wide.* This means that the ball must have hit either the left or right edge of the brick.

if sprite(43).locH < sprite(me.spriteNum).locH then

If the horizontal location of the ball is less than the horizontal location of the brick, then the ball is somewhere on the left side of the brick. Therefore, we execute code to make it bounce off to the left, using the Lingo you've already seen. Else, the ball's **locH** is more than the brick's **locH**, and so the ball is someplace to the right of the brick, and we rebound it rightward.

Then we pop out with another **else**. We do this because we now know that the intersection rectangle is *wider* than it is *tall* (it must be, if it's not taller than it is wide; if the brick were square, this line of Lingo would also execute, by the way), which means that the ball hit either the top or bottom side of the brick. We then do some **locV** testing to determine if we want the ball to rebound up or down.

Now our "breakout" game is really taking shape. If you run it now, you'll see that it behaves exactly as we expect, with the ball bouncing off the edges of the screen, off the bricks in the correct direction, and so on. Hard to imagine that this was state of the art for computer games just a couple of decades ago, but there it is.

9

1-Minute Drill

● What would be the result of the following mathematical operations?
  10 – 7
  4 – 16
  abs (12 – 24)
  4 – (abs (4 – 8))

● 3, –12, 12, and 0

Project Summary

In this module, you collected and applied a *lot* of information. You learned about lists, which are chunks of data that can be formatted, changed, and accessed in myriad ways, and with which you can do some pretty amazing things. You also learned that it's possible to perform some reasonably sophisticated collision detection to see if one sprite is bumping into another, to the point of discovering some pitfalls in basic routines and learning how to get past those pitfalls.

By comparison, the next module should be a cakewalk, since all we're going to be doing is exploring different ways to handle external files, such as video or sound, text, and so on.

Meanwhile, have a nice cup of tea. You've earned it.

☑ *Mastery Check*

No questions this time; just some things for you to ponder.

1. The "breakout" game never resets. If you clear off all the bricks, the ball just bounces around on the screen as it did for the racquetball game in Module 8. It would be nice to do some Lingo that determines if the player has cleared the screen, and then lets her choose to play again or quit the game.
There are many approaches to take to that. I've got one way to do it online; before you download that file and look over its Lingo, though, try it yourself and see if your solution was the same as mine.
I'll give you two hints. I set a global variable, and I used another Lingo keyword, **count**. (Look it up in the *Lingo Dictionary!*)

_____

_____

2. Suppose you wanted to allow the bricks in each row to be given random widths within a specific range, say no more than 50 pixels wide but no less than 30. What part of the "breakout" game might you modify to make that happen, and in what way?
This is another one where the answer is online. Again, try it yourself before you look at my code, though.

_____

_____

3. Conceptually, the differences between our "breakout" game and a "space invaders" style game are pretty small. After all, the invaders can be thought of as little more than bricks that move, and that shoot back. The paddle isn't that different from a little mobile rocket launcher that fires a ball-like missile each time you click or press a button.
How hard do you think it would be to revise this game to turn it into an invader shooting match? How do you think you'd go about doing that?

_____

_____

9

✓ Mastery Check

4. There are quite a few commands you can use to create, manipulate, and handle lists, so when you've got a little extra time why not look over your Lingo documentation and see what else you can discover? Lists are spectacularly powerful tools to have at your disposal, and if you understand them well, you can do some genuinely incredible things with Director.

Module 10

External Files

The Goals of this Module

- Learn how to handle external text-based files
- Learn how to pull files into your Director Cast on-the-fly
- Learn the procedures necessary for finding and loading external video, sound, and Flash files

So far, we've mostly been working with *internal* files in Director—either single Movie files, or #text or #field elements you've made internally, and so on. In this module, we'll begin exploring the wide variety of media types you can import or otherwise use in Director, giving you an opportunity to vastly increase the potential richness of the user experience for those who run your programs.

It's All Just Ones and Zeros

By now, you've become used to the idea that files, stored on a computer, are really little more than collections of data or instructions of some kind that either tell the computer how to behave (as with system files) or tell the program that opened the file how to behave (as with your own Director movies when you're running them in Director itself). And the files themselves exist on disk as nothing but binary information, which is a collection of ones and zeros, laid down magnetically on the hard drive.

Fortunately for us, computers understand how to write out those ones and zeros so that they create document files that make sense, such as a letter to someone, an image file, and so on—documents that, when opened using a program that can understand how to interpret their contents, become humanly comprehensible items of information.

You saw in Module 2 that it's possible to get Director to access an HTML file from the Internet, and that your Director movie understood the file well enough to display it onscreen. You might be interested to know that HTML files are nothing more than plain text, with some formatting instructions embedded in them. This implies that Director can read and understand text files that have been created in other programs entirely—and that's exactly the case, as it turns out.

Just as HTML is text with some hidden formatting instructions, there's a file type that most word processors can create, called Rich Text Format (RTF), that behaves a lot like HTML. It, too, contains hidden formatting instructions, but RTF files are meant mostly for use in desktop publishing applications, not for general use on the Internet. As it happens, RTF is another file type that Director can read and understand, just as it does with HTML.

There's a third kind of text file that Director handles with ease, and that is the plain-vanilla American Standard Code for Information Interchange (ASCII) text file. These files are generally not formatted with any special font instructions; they're raw data, containing nothing but straightforward text characters, spaces, and so on. Some e-mail programs use ASCII-formatted text to transmit information. Programs such as Notepad or SimpleText write ASCII text files.

Tip

In Windows, ASCII text filenames generally end with a .txt extension.

You can easily confirm all the above by importing some HTML, RTF, and ASCII files into Director, but that's not all that interesting compared to giving the end user the ability to do exactly the same.

File not Found

You've worked with programs and documents enough now to realize that it's not sufficient for a program to simply try to automatically load some random file every time it's run. After all, different people configure their computers differently, place their files in different folders on the drive, and give their files different names. How would any program know which file to try to load when it runs? Such a scheme would be doomed.

This is why programs have a File | Open command. Selecting File | Open in a program opens a dialog box asking you to locate the file you want to open. Once you've done so, the program proceeds, and your file is opened, usually in a document window, ready for you to peruse, edit, save, rename, and so on. Director is no exception; if you're working on a movie and want to open another, you can do so with File | Open…just as you can with any other program.

I'm sure you can think of situations in which you'd want to have that ability in your own Director movies, running as projectors, and since I've alluded to FileIO previously, perhaps you're guessing that ability exists. You're guessing correctly.

10

FileIO is an Xtra provided with Director by Macromedia. Originally, it was used to write plain-text (ASCII) files to disk and to read those files off of disk, in the days before Director was capable of importing or saving such files on its own. Over the years, Director's abilities in these areas have expanded, but you still need FileIO to get information, such as where the file is located or where the user wants a file saved, and there are still plenty of times when FileIO is the best way to go about saving any manner of external data.

The chief purpose of FileIO is to permit you to program Director to locate any desired file, open it, read its contents, save any changes made to the file, and close it again. FileIO is also designed to allow you to create new documents on-the-fly, documents that never existed before you constructed them.

Ask the Expert

Question How can giving one of my Director-made programs the ability to read or write different files help me, as a programmer?

Answer Being able to do so greatly increases your ability to let the user make her own decisions, turning your projectors into things that look, act, and feel just like any other program—custom-written to suit the needs of your client.

For example, on one project I wrote a program that was very little more than a gigantic, user-selectable database of images and text content. This program let the user choose images and titles from a library that had been preselected by the client, thus constructing presentation "slideshows" that used only approved images and text content on the screen, and that could at the same time be assembled quickly and with relative ease.

Since the images and titles already existed in my Director Cast, I didn't really have to keep track of anything much more than the actual items the user had chosen for display. I did this internally using a property list, and then let the user save that property list (as text) to a file on disk, so she could pick up where she left off later, or show the presentation to someone else, or whatever.

Naturally, I did not have one single premanufactured text element to save to disk; I created the text on-the-fly and saved it out using FileIO. The client went away happy with the program, and so we have another Director success story—in this case, one that made use of external data files in much the same way as any other program, to store information, retain changes, and so on.

Note

The *IO* in FileIO is short for *input and output*, which is what FileIO does. It allows you to perform file input and output operations from and to the hard drive.

If you're looking through your Lingo manuals for information on FileIO, don't bother. This particular Xtra has never been especially well documented by Macromedia, in spite of the fact that it's one of the more important Xtras available. In fact, the documentation for FileIO is nowhere to be found except online. I've added a link to the page you need in the online resource site for this text at **www.nightwares.com/director_beginners_guide/** in the section named "FileIO." You won't need the full text of that document to proceed here; just know that it's available to you when the time comes for you to go looking for it.

Opening a Dialog Box

10

There are two basic steps to working with FileIO:

1. Open a dialog box that asks the user to locate a file to open or choose a place to save a file.

2. Read information from or write information to that file once the user has told you where it is.

So, logically, we'll start with the dialog box you use in FileIO to open files.

Begin, as always, with a new Director file. You can use the same Stage size you used for the racquetball and breakout games, if you want. Place a button on the Stage someplace and label it **Open file...** Then, create a new behavior in the PI for that sprite. Into the behavior, type the following code:

```
on mouseUp me


  oFileObject = new ( xtra "fileio" )
  oFileObject.displayOpen()


END mouseUp
```

You probably don't recognize anything in either of these lines, but you can infer their meaning. In the first line, **oFileObject = new (xtra "fileio")**, we're creating an *instance* of the FileIO Xtra, using the **new** keyword, and putting that instance into a variable called **oFileObject**. The letter *o* at the beginning of this variable's name indicates that we are in fact using a *code object* in this script. We'll be making extensive use of objects in Part 4; this is a sort of preview.

The second line, **oFileObject.displayOpen()**, sends a command, **displayOpen()**, to the code object instance we have in the **oFileObject** variable. To demonstrate what the **displayOpen()**command does, click the Play button in your movie, and then click the Open file... button you just programmed. Once you've seen it in action, click the Cancel button; there's no real point in doing anything else just yet.

As you've just seen, the premanufactured commands in the FileIO Xtra permit you to create a system-standard Open File dialog box. This is just like any other Open File dialog box you see on your computer, and all of its controls behave in exactly the same fashion. What's more, the dialog box you get on a Mac will be a Mac-style box, and the one you get on Windows will be a Windows-style one. In other words, you're presenting users with the controls they have already seen and know how to use. With *two lines of code*!

Getting Something Back

You just saw an example of how to get a dialog box out of FileIO; however, you're not interested in simply putting a dialog box onscreen. We need to figure

Ask the Expert

Question   How am I supposed to know what I can do with FileIO? Or, for that matter, with *any* Xtra? Xtras' commands aren't covered in the Lingo documentation that came with my copy of Director.

Answer   The first line of defense is to consult the documentation included with the Xtra, of course; however, that's not always feasible. For this reason, a well-designed Xtra that has commands you can access built into it will also have a special **interface** call you can make to it.
   For FileIO, as an example, type this into the Message window:

```
put interface ( xtra "fileio" )
```

   This is a terse list of the commands—all the commands—you can send to FileIO, brief descriptions of how to format those commands so the Xtra will understand them, and the kind of information that is returned from those commands.
   But those really are crib notes. The best way to find out what you can do with an Xtra is to consult that Xtra's documentation, even if it is a little hard to find sometimes.

out what file the user has chosen, since that's the reason we're asking her to choose a file in the first place. This is where **displayOpen()** becomes truly useful, because it returns a string when it's done running (that is, after the user has clicked either Open or Cancel in the dialog box). That string contains the full path to the file.
   What this means is you get, from the **displayOpen()** command, an exact description of the location of the file the user has chosen—that, or you get an empty string, which means the user has clicked the Cancel button rather than the Open button.
   Here's an example that applies this, going back to the movie we just made:

```
on mouseUp me

  oFileObject = new ( xtra "fileio" )
  sFile = oFileObject.displayOpen()

  If voidP (sFile) or sFile = "" then
```

10

```
    ALERT "You didn't pick a file."

  else

    ALERT "The file you chose was" && sFile

  end if


END mouseUp
```

As you see, we haven't really changed much here. With the line

```
sFile = oFileObject.DisplayOpen()
```

we take the result of the **displayOpen**() call and put it into a text variable, **sFile**, and then we test **sFile** to see first whether its contents are void (via the **voidP**() test) and then whether its contents are an empty string. We do this because if the user clicks Cancel on Windows, FileIO will return nothing, leaving the file string variable void; whereas on a Mac, it returns an empty string. If our variable turns out to be void or empty, we put up an **ALERT** telling the user that no file was chosen; otherwise, we put an **ALERT** that describes the actual location and name of the file.

Naturally, this is not the most practical code in the universe. While we've proved that we can get the user to choose a file, and we can even determine if she has decided not to pick one, we're not accomplishing anything at all by kicking up an alert telling her what file she picked. She already knows that; she was there, after all. What we need to do is take that information and do something useful with it.

1-Minute Drill

● What does **displayOpen**() do?

Opening Files

Everything up to this point has been simple *preparation* for opening a file; we're looking for the file to get and, assuming the user has not clicked Cancel, we

---

● Opens a standard system Open File dialog box.

Ask the Expert

Question   I see that the variable sFile contains backslashes (or colons, because I'm on a Mac instead of Windows). What are those characters doing there? I don't see them in any of the filenames in my computer's desktop.

Answer   Backslashes are *directory delimiters* on Windows; colons are directory delimiters on Mac. Directory delimiters serve to indicate where the names of folders begin, just as quotation marks delimit places in text where you're quoting someone.

In other words, any time you see a backslash on Windows or a colon on a Mac, you know that the name immediately preceding it is the name of a folder.

By the way, you'll find that it's impossible to use a backslash in any filename on Windows; if you try to name some folder or document on your computer's desktop with backslash characters, Windows will tell you that you can't do that. The Mac, similarly, won't let you use colons in filenames, but instead of giving you an alert message telling you not to do that any more, it just automatically changes the colons to hyphens. I prefer that more; I'd rather just have the forbidden character silently modified than have the computer yell at me.

This is one of the fun little things you have to take into account if you're making Director movies that are intended to run on both platforms and you want to do anything with pathnames other than simply use them to get file locations.

10

now know exactly where on the drive the file is located. Wonderful. Now we need to actually open the file, and then read its contents into memory, and for that we use a couple more commands in the FileIO suite.

Here's the modified behavior. Note I removed the insipid alerts and replaced them with things more useful.

```
on mouseUp me


  oFileObject = new ( xtra "fileio" )
```

```
    sFile = oFileObject.displayOpen()

    If voidP (sFile) or sFile = "" then

      oFileObject = 0

    else

      oFileObject.openFile ( sFile, 0 )
      sFileContents = oFileObject.readFile()
      oFileObject.closeFile()
      oFileObject = 0
      put sFileContents

    end if


END mouseUp
```

Hmm, these are some interesting commands, aren't they? First is what we do if sFile is empty:

```
oFileObject = 0
```

We do this to clear the Xtra's instance from memory. This is not strictly necessary in the case of a local variable such as this, but it's a very good habit to be in when you're dealing with code objects. We'll need to be in this habit for Part 4 anyway.

Next is this line, if **sFile** happens to be something other than empty:

```
oFileObject.openFile ( sFile, 1 )
```

This almost makes sense, doesn't it? **OpenFile**() seems like a perfectly reasonable command to send. **sFile** is, of course, the file target we just got from the **displayOpen**() command. But what's with that number 1 at the end?

There are three different *modes* in which FileIO can be made to open any particular file: It can open it in *read/write* mode, in *read-only* mode, and in *write-only* mode. When a file is opened in read/write mode, you can issue commands to FileIO that will cause it to read the information in the file and to write new information to the file. In other words, you can both look at a file's contents and make changes to those contents. If you open a file in read-only mode, all you can do is look at the file. You can't tell FileIO to make changes to what the file contains. Finally, if a file is opened in write-only mode, you can't read what's in the file at all; you can only make alterations to the contents.

These three different ways of opening files with FileIO are represented by 0, 1, and 2, respectively; that is, if you send an **openFile()** command to FileIO that includes 0 for the open state, you will be able to both read from and write to the file; if you open it with a 1, you will only be able to read from the file; and if you open it with a 2, you will only be able to write to the file. In this example, I sent along a 1, which means that FileIO opens the specified file with read permission only.

The next line does make sense:

```
sFileContents = oFileObject.readFile()
```

We're sending a **readFile()** command to the FileIO object, and even though that's not a Lingo keyword, its meaning is perfectly clear. It's reading the contents of the file, and putting that file's contents into a variable.

The next line also makes sense:

```
oFileObject.closeFile()
```

Now that we've read the file, we close it again.

?—Ask the Expert

Question   What difference does it make whether I open a file for read, write, or both? Why not just open it for read/write all the time?

Answer   You could, but there are circumstances where you might not want to. For instance, you might want a user to be able to look at a file (such as a system file), but not make any changes to it (since that could crash the system). You might also want to open a file read-only if you're accessing something from a networked location.

Both Macintosh and Windows strictly forbid files to be open with write permission by multiple users; you can use read-only, then, to handle databases that are stored on a central server on a client's network, as an example.

Note

This is an important command. If a computer detects that a file has been opened but not yet closed, it won't let anything else happen with that file. That means the user won't be able to move it to a different location on his drive, or delete it, or perhaps open it with any other programs. So always, always, *always* close a file after you are done with it, and I mean *immediately* after you are done with it.

The next line, just like before, is used to clear the file object from memory:

```
oFileObject = 0
```

The final line puts the variable we just created and filled with the data in the file we opened into the Message window:

```
put sFileContents
```

This is pretty simple code, and you might be thinking *it can't be that easy*. You're right. Try playing around with this movie for a while and you'll see why. You aren't limited to opening text files; you can also open *program* files as though they were text files. You can do the same, in fact, for pretty much *any* file on your computer.

Now that is not really a good thing, at least not for most end users. You don't want them poking into files that perhaps they should not even have open (such as system files), and you surely will be using FileIO in a way that supports other Lingo code you've written and that is actually looking for a specific kind of file, such as an ASCII or HTML file. So, you don't want your end users to just be able to see and open any old file they feel like. That'll make your program malfunction.

1-Minute Drill

- What do the numbers 0, 1, and 2 mean in the context of the **openFile()** command?

- What does **readFile()** do?

- Open the file with read/write permission, read-only permission, and write-only permission, respectively.
- Reads the contents of the specified file into a variable or other container.

Filtering the Files

Let's suppose you want your users to open just plain-vanilla ASCII files. Nothing else. Simply text. You don't want users to even see any other files in the FileIO dialog box; only the kind of file you're looking for.

For this, FileIO includes another command, **setFilterMask**, which creates a *filter* that prevents any file from being seen in the dialog box except for the type you specify. By default, FileIO lets you see everything; however, we can use **setFilterMask** to restrict the user to just the kinds of file we want.

Here's the modified behavior:

```
on mouseUp me

  oFileObject = new ( xtra "fileio" )

  if the platform contains "mac" then

    oFileObject.setFilterMask ( "TEXT" )

  else

    oFileObject.setFilterMask ( "Text files,*.txt" )

  end if

  sFile = oFileObject.displayOpen()

  If voidP (sFile) or sFile = "" then

    oFileObject = 0

  else

    oFileObject.openFile ( sFile, 1 )
    sFileContents = oFileObject.readFile()
    oFileObject.closeFile()
    oFileObject = 0
    put sFileContents
```

10

```
    end if

END mouseUp
```

The part that interests us is near the top:

```
if the platform contains "mac" then
```

the platform is a Director keyword that tells us what kind of computer the movie is running on. You can find out what the full return is for **the platform** for your system by entering the command **put the platform** in the Message window. Here's what I get:

```
put the platform
-- "Macintosh,PowerPC"
```

Yes, that's right. I'm on an iBook, which is a Mac, and it's got a G3 processor, which puts it in the PowerMac category. If you're on Windows, the likely return for the platform will be

```
"Windows,32"
```

meaning you're using the 32-bit version of Windows. (Everything from Win95 up is 32-bit. Windows 3.1 and earlier were 16-bit versions, and in the days that Director ran on Windows 3.1, the return for the platform was "Windows,16". This was, of course, right before the dinosaurs went extinct and I had to walk to school 50 miles uphill both ways in roaring blizzards in the dead of summer, you young punks.)

We then use the word **contains** to determine if just a few letters of the platform name exist in **the platform** itself, because we don't need to know if it's a PowerMac, 32-bit Windows, or anything else; we just need to know if it's a Mac or Windows system in general.

```
oFileObject.setFilterMask ( "TEXT" )
```

We do this if **the platform** contains "mac". This tells FileIO that the only kind of files we want showing in its Open File dialog box are text files, or files that have been marked by the Mac system as being text-only.

Ask the Expert

Question   How am I supposed to know what kinds of things to put into the setFilterMask() call? I guess on Windows it's kind of obvious, but what are common types I'd see on a Mac?

Answer   This can be pretty hard, because it's not always easy to determine—*particularly* on a Mac—how to filter for file types. You can use programs such as ResEdit to find out what the file type is for given documents on the Mac, but there are also pretty common types you'll probably be using more often than others.

Here's a list of the types you'll probably use most often. Note the file types for Mac are case-sensitive.

● **Text**   .txt for Windows, TEXT for Mac

● **HTML page**   .htm for Windows, TEXT for Mac (remember, HTML files are really just specially formatted text)

● **RTF word processor file**   .rtf for Windows, TEXT for Mac (Again!)

● **JPEG image**   .jpg for Windows, JPEG for Mac

● **GIF image**   .gif for Windows, GIFf for Mac

● **WAV sound**   .wav for Windows, WAVE for Mac

● **AIFF sound**   .aif for Windows, AIFF for Mac

● **QuickTime file**   .mov for Windows, MooV for Mac

If you want to let the user select more than one type of file, you need to make some changes to the **setFilterMask**() call. For instance, suppose you want the user to pick an image file, either a GIF or a JPEG. For Mac, your **setFilterMask**() would then look like this:

```
oFileObject.setFilterMask( "GIFfJPEG" )
```

10

> Note the lack of spaces. For Windows, it would be the following:
>
> ```
> oFileObject.setFilterMask( "GIF Files,*.gif, JPEG files,*.jpg" )
> ```
>
> You can have up to 16 characters in the **setFilterMask()** string on Mac, and up to 255 characters for Windows.

Otherwise, we're on a Windows system, so we use the following:

```
oFileObject.setFilterMask ( "Text files,*.txt" )
```

When the FileIO dialog box opens on Windows, it will be looking only for files with the .txt extension, meaning that all it will be displaying is plain-text files, as with the Mac version (which of course looks quite a bit different because of the differences between the two operating systems).

Now we've got a dialog box that only lets the user see text files, so we can be reasonably sure she's not going to open a program by mistake, or get into something the computer itself needs to continue operating. The rest of your code behaves exactly as before, opening the file (if one was selected), getting its contents, and so on.

1-Minute Drill

● What does **setFilterMask()** do?

● What are some common file types on Mac that you would put into the **setFilterMask()** string?

● What are those same file types for Windows?

Project 10-1: Making Ourselves Useful

Now we get to start having a little more fun. We're going to revisit the idea of a text editor from Module 2, and we're going to turn it into something that allows

---

● Constrains the dialog called by **displayOpen()** to display only files of the specified type.
● TEXT, GIFf, JPEG, and MooV
● .txt, .gif, .jpg, and .mov

us to open external files, change them, and then save the changes. (We're starting our project midmodule, which is becoming a bit of a trend for us.)
   The following are the goals of this project:

● To give you practical knowledge of working with FileIO

● To expand your Director movie's ability to interact with a user's system

Step-by-Step

1. Make a couple of alterations to your Open file... button's script:

```
on mouseUp me

  oFileObject = new ( xtra "fileio" )

  if the platform contains "mac" then

    oFileObject.setFilterMask ( "TEXT" )

  else

    oFileObject.setFilterMask ( "Text files,*.txt" )

  end if

  sFile = oFileObject.displayOpen()

  If voidP (sFile) or sFile = "" then

    oFileObject = 0

  else

    oFileObject.openFile ( sFile, 1 )
    sFileContents = oFileObject.readFile()
    oFileObject.closeFile()
    oFileObject = 0
    sendSprite ( 2, #ReceiveFileData, sFile, sFileContents )

  end if

END mouseUp
```

10

The line of most interest to us is

sendSprite (2, #ReceiveFileData, sFile, sFileContents)

Here we're making a **sendSprite** call—you remember those—and running a handler called **ReceiveFileData**, which passes along the path to the file we've opened as well as its contents.

Of course, there's no sprite 2 yet, so if you run your movie now, you won't see anything happen. This is because, naturally, there's no behavior on the nonexistent sprite 2 to receive your command.

2. You can probably guess what to do next. Create a #text member (not a #field member) in channel 2 and use the Text tab in the PI to set its **Framing** type to **scrolling**. Also check the Editable checkbox. This will let the end user type things into the #text member, as was the case with our proto-editor in Module 2.

3. Now it's time to create the behavior for this sprite. Here's the code:

```
PROPERTY psFilePath



on beginSprite me

  psFilePath = "No file opened"
  sprite(me.spriteNum).member.text = ""


END beginSprite



on ReceiveFileData me, sFile, sContents

  psFilePath = sFile
  sprite(me.spriteNum).member.text = sContents


END ReceiveFileData
```

Probably a lot of this isn't a surprise to you by now. We start by declaring a property variable for this behavior, **psFilePath**. We then assign it an initial value (indicating no file has been opened), and set the scrolling #text window to empty as well.

Then, in the **ReceiveFileData** handler, we put the full path to the file that was sent by our Open file... button script into the **psFilePath** variable. (We'll be needing this in a few moments.) We then put the actual contents of the file that was opened into the editor's text window. Now it's ready for the user to make any changes, or just read the contents, or whatever.

4. Of course, this text editor isn't all that handy; there's no provision to save anything. What's the point of making changes? So we'll go ahead and make a Save button, too.

Here's the code for that button:

```
on mouseUp me


  sFileName = sendSprite ( 2, #ReturnFileName )

  if sFileName <> "No file opened" then

    sTextToSave = sendSprite ( 2, #ReturnFileContents )

    oFileObject = new ( xtra "fileio" )
    oFileObject.openFile ( sFileName, 2 )
    oFileObject.delete()
    oFileObject.closeFile()
    oFileObject = 0

    oFileObject = new ( xtra "fileio" )
    oFileObject.createFile ( sFileName )
    oFileObject.openFile ( sFileName, 2 )
    oFileObject.writeString ( sTextToSave )
    oFileObject.closeFile()
    oFileObject = 0

  end if


END mouseUp
```

10

The first few lines probably make a lot of sense to you.

> **sFileName = sendSprite (2, #ReturnFileName)**

Even though we haven't yet written this handler in our #text sprite's behavior, you can infer exactly what this will do. It returns the name of the file that's been opened for editing, and that's why, of course, we stored that filename in a property variable.

> **if sFileName <> "No file opened" then**

...then the user hasn't mistakenly clicked the Save button before even opening a file to begin with. So we get the actual text we need to save:

> **sTextToSave = sendSprite (2, #ReturnFileContents)**

Another handler we haven't written yet, but again, you can surely infer what it's going to look like when we do make it. And this is where it gets a little strange.

> **oFileObject = new (xtra "fileio")**

> **oFileObject.openFile (sFileName, 2)**

These two lines seem reasonable enough. We're creating a new instance of the FileIO object in memory, and then we're opening the file the user wants saved with write permission. But then we do something odd:

> **oFileObject.delete()**

Now if we're supposed to be *saving* a file, why on Earth would we send a **delete** command?

The answer is a little surprising. FileIO is not perfect, at least not entirely. When you make changes to a file via FileIO, the entire file is not necessarily entirely overwritten with the new material. Let me explain that.

Suppose your file originally contained the following text:

> **"This is my sample text file."**

Suppose you then open it for editing, and remove the word *sample*, so the edited text now reads:

> **"This is my text file."**

Happy with the look, you click the Save button, expecting FileIO to simply be able to do a **writeString** call to update your document. Well, if you then open the file again, you will *not* see

"This is my text file."

…but instead will see the following:

"This is my text file.xt file."

What happened there? The new text you wanted saved was *shorter* than the text contained in the original file, so FileIO only wrote out the string to the end of the new text. It left the rest of the original text file untouched.

This has been a particular gotcha of the FileIO Xtra for years, since Director was at version 5. I'm not sure why Macromedia never fixed this, because it's rather frustrating to deal with if you've never been warned about it by some kind soul who doesn't want *you* tearing your hair out either.

This little glitch is why we delete the original file before we write out the new one in our Save button code. Unless we do this, there's always a chance that fragments of the older file will end up getting left behind in the update!

Note

You must open a file with read/write or write-only permission to delete it. You can't delete a file if you've opened it with read-only access.

After deleting the old file, we close it, reset our file object variable, and then create a new instance of FileIO. However, the file we wanted to save changes to isn't there any more, which means we now have to re-create it:

oFileObject.createFile (sFileName)

That part done, we open the file with write permission a second time and then write the new text data to it:

oFileObject.writeString (sTextToSave)

After doing this, we can close the file and zero the file object reference once more, because the changes the user made have now been successfully written.

5. Now we just need to go back to our #text window's behavior and add the two handlers we invoke in our Save button:

```
on ReturnFileName me
```

10

```
      return psFilePath

END ReturnFileName



on ReturnFileContents me

   return sprite(me.spriteNum).member.text


END ReturnFileContents
```

These two handlers allow our Save button to retrieve the name of the file it needs to write changes to and the actual changes themselves, respectively.

Try it out now. Click the Play button, open a file, make some changes, and click Save. Then, open the file again in some other text editor just to prove it worked.

1-Minute Drill

● Why should you delete an edited file with FileIO before you save the changes to it?

Adding a Safety

One characteristic of text editors is that they don't let you open a second file if you haven't made changes to the first, at least not without asking.

We're going to use another Macromedia Xtra, MUI, to help us here. MUI, short for *Macromedia User Interface*, allows us to create custom dialog boxes that can include all kinds of controls, information, widgets, and so on. We're not going to be doing anything especially complicated here; in fact, we're going to use a pretty standard MUI call that simply puts up a dialog box that allows the user to confirm, refuse, or cancel an action.

But before we do that, we have to know whether the user has even made any changes to the file, and the easiest way to do that is by seeing if the user has pressed any keys.

● To make sure extra content from the older file doesn't end up in the new one.

6. Make some changes to your #text sprite's behavior so that it now looks like this:

```
PROPERTY psFilePath, pbFileChanged




on beginSprite me

  psFilePath = "No file opened"
  sprite(me.spriteNum).member.text = ""
  pbFileChanged = FALSE


END beginSprite




on keyDown me

  pbFileChanged = TRUE
  pass

END keyDown




on ReceiveFileData me, sFile, sContents

  psFilePath = sFile
  sprite(me.spriteNum).member.text = sContents
  pbFileChanged = FALSE


END ReceiveFileData
```

10

```
on ReturnFileName me

  return psFilePath

END ReturnFileName



on ReturnFileContents me

  return sprite(me.spriteNum).member.text

END ReturnFileContents



on ReturnChangeState me

  return pbFileChanged

END ReturnChangeState



on ChangesSaved me

  pbFileChanged = FALSE

END ChangesSaved
```

All we've done at the beginning is declare another property, **pbFileChanged**, and set it initially to be false. But we've also added a new event handler, **on**

keyDown. As you might well guess, this handler is executed each time a key is pressed as the user types in the #text member. When that occurs, we set **pbFileChanged** to true, because odds are pretty good that the user has chosen to make changes if he's typing on the keyboard.

We also add the command **pass** after setting the change variable to true. If we don't do that, Director will trap the keystroke itself, which will keep anything from happening in the #text sprite. That is, Director will "grab" the keystroke and not send it along to the text editor window—which rather defeats the purpose of having a text editor. By including the **pass** command, we ensure that the keystroke will in fact go on through to the #text sprite.

We then add two more custom handlers. The first is **ReturnChangeState**, which passes the **pbFileChanged** variable to anything that asks for it. The second simply tells this behavior that the file has been saved and it can stop thinking there have been changes (until a key is pressed again).

Ask the Expert

Question   What if the user just presses the arrow keys, but doesn't actually enter or delete any text? Will the program think the file has changed?

Answer   Yes, it will. One way around that would be to put a copy of the text file's contents into memory someplace, and to compare what's currently in the #text member with the contents of the original variable. If they don't match, we know the file has been edited.

This would also allow us to put in a Revert button, which would permit the user to restore the file to its original state before he made any changes, without also having to close the program.

We could even set things up so this variable is updated every time the user clicks Save, permitting the editor to undo only the most recent unsaved changes.

I'll leave it to you to put that in place if you want. For this module, what we've got going now is plenty.

10

7. Now that we've added these few extra functions to the #text sprite's behavior, we have to modify our Open file... and Save buttons to make use of them, and to ask the user for more information if there have been changes made, but she's chosen to open a different file.

First the easy part, the Save button:

```
on mouseUp me


  sFileName = sendSprite ( 2, #ReturnFileName )

  if sFileName <> "No file opened" then

    sTextToSave = sendSprite ( 2, #ReturnFileContents )

    oFileObject = new ( xtra "fileio" )

    oFileObject.openFile ( sFileName, 2 )
    oFileObject.delete()
    oFileObject.closeFile()
    oFileObject = 0

    oFileObject = new ( xtra "fileio" )

    oFileObject.createFile ( sFileName )
    oFileObject.openFile ( sFileName, 2 )
    oFileObject.writeString ( sTextToSave )
    oFileObject.closeFile()
    oFileObject = 0

    sendSprite ( 2, #ChangesSaved )

  end if


END mouseUp
```

Did you see what I did? I added this line:

sendSprite (2, #ChangesSaved)

This, of course, tells the #text sprite's behavior that the file has been saved since the last time it was changed.

8. Now for the greater challenge, which is getting the Open file... button to ask the user a question if there have been unsaved changes made, but the user is trying to open a different file. We're going to use MUI for this.

Going into a lot of detail on using MUI is well beyond the scope of this book, but there are some fairly simple functions we can use, such as the one I've added here. You can consult the online resources for more documentation on MUI; I've included a link to the documentation at **www.nightwares.com/ director_beginners_guide/** in the section titled "MUI." It's another Xtra, like FileIO, that has no documentation available anyplace but from Macromedia's site.

Here's what I've done to the Open file... button behavior:

```
on mouseUp me


  if sendSprite ( 2, #ReturnChangeState ) = TRUE then

    nDialogReply = me.AskForFeedback( "Save changes?", "Do you want
to save changes to this file before opening another one?" )

    if nDialogReply = 1 then

      sendSprite ( 3, #mouseUp )

    else if nDialogReply = 3 then

      exit

    end if

  end if

  oFileObject = new ( xtra "fileio" )

  if the platform contains "mac" then

    oFileObject.setFilterMask ( "TEXT" )

  else

    oFileObject.setFilterMask ( "Text files,*.txt" )

  end if

  sFile = oFileObject.displayOpen()
```

10

```
   If voidP (sFile) or sFile = "" then

      oFileObject = 0

   else

      oFileObject.openFile ( sFile, 1 )
      sFileContents = oFileObject.readFile()
      oFileObject.closeFile()
      oFileObject = 0

      sendSprite ( 2, #ReceiveFileData, sFile, sFileContents )

   end if


END mouseUp



on AskForFeedback me, sDialogTitle, sDialogText

   oDialogObject = new ( xtra "mui" )

   lDialogProperties  = [:]

   lDialogProperties.addProp ( #buttons, #YesNoCancel )
   lDialogProperties.addProp ( #title, sDialogTitle )
   lDialogProperties.addProp ( #message, sDialogText )
   lDialogProperties.addProp ( #icon, #question )

   nResult = ALERT ( oDialogObject, lDialogProperties )

   return nResult

END AskForFeedback
```

Wow, that's a lot of Lingo, isn't it? Here's the new stuff I added to **mouseUp**:

if sendSprite (2, #ReturnChangeState) = TRUE then

...then the #text sprite thinks the user has made changes to the text in the window, and we need to ask the user a question before we proceed:

nDialogReply = me.AskForFeedback("Save changes?", "Do you want to save changes to this file before opening another one?")

Here we're sending a call to another handler in this behavior and passing a couple of parameters to that handler in the process, and then we're taking the response the handler returns and putting it into a variable, **nDialogReply**. We then test **nDialogReply** below. The variable can have the value of 1, 2, or 3, for reasons I will cover in just a few moments.

if nDialogReply = 1 then

  sendSprite (3, #mouseUp)

If the **nDialogReply** variable has the value of 1, we tell sprite 3 to behave as though it was just clicked. What's sprite 3? Our Save button. So what we're telling sprite 3 to do with this command is to save the file in the #text sprite.

Tip

You can use sendSprite to activate all kinds of event commands, not just **mouseUp**. In this way, you can make sprites behave as though they have been clicked, typed into, and so on. This is a very handy way to add a lot of internal interactivity to your programs.

  else if nDialogReply = 3 then

  exit

If the value of **nDialogReply** is 3, we exit this entire handler completely, not executing any further code at all.

But what if the reply is 2? We don't have a test for it, which means that if **nDialogReply** has a value of 2, we just continue with the rest of this behavior's **mouseUp** code, which means we open a new file *without* saving changes to the current one.

Now let's go over the **AskForFeedback** handler.

  oDialogObject = new (xtra "mui")

Here we're invoking another Xtra, in this case the MUI Xtra previously mentioned.

  lDialogProperties = [:]

You can infer from the brackets and colon that **lDialogProperties** is going to be a property list.

  lDialogProperties.addProp (#buttons, #YesNoCancel)

Here we're adding a new property index to the list we're creating, one named #buttons and possessing the value #YesNoCancel. At this point, the **lDialogProperties** variable contains this:

[#buttons: #YesNoCancel]

We then continue adding to the list.

lDialogProperties.addProp (#title, sDialogTitle)

We're adding another property to the list, this time the title text we passed into this handler as a parameter. So now **lDialogProperties** looks like this:

[#buttons: #YesNoCancel, #title: "Save changes?"]

We proceed in this fashion, adding more elements to the property list.

lDialogProperties.addProp (#message, sDialogText)

The next property we add is given the index property #message, and contains the question text we sent to this handler as a parameter when we first called it.

lDialogProperties.addProp (#icon, #question)

Here we're adding a property called #icon, with the value #question. What this will do is, when our dialog box appears onscreen, place a standard "question" style graphic in one corner of it. This is to give the dialog box a nice system-type appearance.

nResult = ALERT (oDialogObject, lDialogProperties)

Now we're passing the dialog box object itself, along with our formatted property list, into a standard **ALERT** call. What this does is open the dialog box for us, complete with a system beep and the question icon we added, having the title we gave it (if the title for the dialog box is visible), and asking the user the question we passed along.

What this also gives us, though, is a row of three buttons in the dialog box, Yes, No, and Cancel. So this dialog box is asking the user if she wants to save the changes she made to the current text file, and allowing her to choose Yes, to *save* the changes and then open another file, No, to *discard* the changes and then open another file, and Cancel, which stops the text editor from opening another file at all.

Well, not yet. First we have to find out what the user clicked, which is why we put the result of this custom **ALERT** dialog box into the variable **nResult**. **nResult**, as you see, is what gets passed back to the **mouseUp** event handler, plugged into the variable **nDialogReply**, and that's how **nDialogReply** gets its 1, 2, or 3 value; the Yes button in our dialog has a value of 1, No has a value of 2, and Cancel has a value of 3!

This is why we send the Save button a **mouseUp** if **nDialogReply** is 1; the user has clicked Yes in response to our question about saving changes. This is also why we *exit* the **mouseUp** call entirely if **nDialogReply** is 3; the user has clicked Cancel and we skip opening a new file altogether. And it's why we just proceed and open another file *without* saving changes to the current one if the value of **nDialogReply** is 2, because the user has clicked No, meaning he wants to discard changes in the current file.

1-Minute Drill

● What is MUI?

● What are the three buttons created in a #YesNoCancel MUI dialog object, and what values do they return?

9. Before you make a projector out of this file, you need to make one special preparation. You've made use of the FileIO and MUI Xtras, which are not part of the standard collection of Xtras that Director adds to your projector when you create it. You need to specifically tell Director that you want it to include FileIO and MUI when it creates a projector out of this movie. If you don't do so, your users will get script errors when they do anything that might require FileIO or MUI.

Also note that, since our movie uses both FileIO and MUI, there's no way we'll get it to work in Shockwave. This has to be an installed desktop program.

Here's how to tell Director to add FileIO and MUI when it makes the projector. It's pretty easy.

● Choose Modify | Movie | Xtras.

● In the dialog box that appears, click Add.

● Select the FileIO Xtra from the scrolling list that opens, and then click OK. This will add FileIO to the list of items in the Movie Xtras dialog box.

● Click Add again and select the item named Mui Dialog, and then click OK.

10

● Macromedia User Interface, an Xtra that lets you create custom dialog boxes.

● Yes, No, and Cancel; 1, 2, and 3.

● Click OK again to dismiss the Movie Xtras dialog box.

That's it. Now when you make your projector, Director will automatically add the FileIO and MUI Xtras to it, so they'll be there and ready to use when your program is running.

10. Go ahead now and create a projector, and then try out your custom-built text editor. Pretty exciting, isn't it?

Project Summary

With this Project, you've had a real taste of some tools you can use to make Director display dialog boxes asking the user for more feedback, and how to respond meaningfully to the information you get from the user.

You've also learned how you can get paths to different external files from your user, and how to read files from and save files to those locations.

Other External Files

As I hinted earlier, you can use FileIO to get other files' locations off the user's hard drive. Why this is interesting is simply that if the file is a format Director supports, you can import that file on-the-fly and display it in a projector, just as if you had included it in the Cast yourself.

As an example, consider using FileIO to get the location of an HTML document from the user's drive. You might then want to put that HTML file on the screen. Here's a simple way to do it. Start with another blank Director file and make another Open file... button on the Stage. Here's the code to enter; it'll look pretty familiar:

```
on mouseUp me

  oFileObject = new ( xtra "fileio" )

  if the platform contains "mac" then

    oFileObject.setFilterMask ( "TEXT" )

  else

    oFileObject.setFilterMask ( "HTML files,*.htm" )
```

```
  end if

 sFile = oFileObject.displayOpen()

 If voidP (sFile) or sFile = "" then

   oFileObject = 0

 else

   sendSprite ( 2, #ReceiveExternalFile, sFile )

 end if


END mouseUp
```

Note the changed lines here:

oFileObject.setFilterMask ("HTML files,*.htm")

This is for Windows, and restricts the kinds of files that can be opened to HTML files only. I don't change the **setFilterMask** call for Mac, because HTML files are really text anyway.

sendSprite (2, #ReceiveExternalFile, sFile)

I just pass along the *path* to the external file to the behavior in sprite 2 this time. I don't use FileIO to open the file or read its contents, because I don't have to. I just need to know where the file is actually located.

Here's the behavior to attach to your #text sprite in channel 2:

10

```
on ReceiveExternalFile me, sFile


  sprite(me.spriteNum).member.fileName = sFile
  sprite(me.spriteNum).member.boxType = #scroll

  nTargetWidth = abs ( (the stage).drawRect.left - (the
stage).drawRect.right ) - 25
  nTargetHeight = abs ( (the stage).drawRect.top - (the
stage).drawRect.bottom ) - 40

  sprite(me.spriteNum).member.width = nTargetWidth
```

```
      sprite(me.spriteNum).member.height = nTargetHeight


END ReceiveExternalFile
```

This is considerably simplified compared to what we were doing with FileIO before, but that's because we're not editing anything here. We're just looking at HTML contents.

There are several new Lingo keywords here:

sprite(me.spriteNum).member.fileName = sFile

fileName is a keyword that allows any specified Cast member's media to be replaced by the item contained in **fileName**. **fileName** itself must be a valid path to some file location or other, and the file media *does* have to be a type that Director recognizes. If these two things are not the case, you won't see any changes happen onscreen, and you could end up with script errors.

What's nice about this, though, is that with the **fileName** command, and some creative use of FileIO, you can allow users (or your code, on its own) to import all kinds of media and materials from a user's hard drive. In this way, you can actively alter the content of a Director movie *while it is running as a projector on a different machine entirely*. Think of the possibilities there. You could add custom graphics, text content, sounds, video, even Flash files... without having to build a custom Director movie every time.

Note

We're going to be using this **fileName** keyword pretty extensively in Part 4 for one of the projects I've got in mind for you, so pay attention now.

sprite(me.spriteNum).member.boxType = #scroll

We do this so the sprite's #text member will be a scrolling type window. If we don't do this, whenever we put a new HTML file into the sprite's member with **fileName**, the text window will forget its scroll bars, and that could prevent the user being able to see everything in the HTML document she chose to open.

nTargetWidth = abs ((the stage).drawRect.left - (the stage). drawRect.right) - 25
nTargetHeight = abs ((the stage).drawRect.top - (the stage). drawRect.bottom) - 40

You remember **abs** from the last Module, and **(the Stage).drawRect** from the last couple of them. Here we're getting the width and height of the Stage, and then subtracting 25 and 50 from those values, respectively. We then put those numbers we've calculated into a pair of variables, **nTargetWidth** and **nTargetHeight**:

sprite(me.spriteNum).member.width = nTargetWidth

sprite(me.spriteNum).member.height = nTargetHeight

Aha, here's what we're doing with those values. We're setting the width and height of the #text sprite's member, so it will correctly occupy a fixed space on the Stage. We subtracted 25 from the width of the Stage to make room for the scroll bars, and we subtracted 50 from the height to allow for the fact that this #text sprite does not appear right at the top of the Stage.

So when this handler is called by our Open file... button, it does the following things:

- It loads the HTML file the user chose into the member that belongs to the sprite to which this behavior is attached, using the **fileName** command.

- It makes sure that the member has scroll bars.

- It makes sure that the member is sized in such a way that it doesn't go past the right or bottom edges of the Stage.

The HTML file the user chose is then displayed in the #text sprite on the Stage, just as though we'd put it there ourselves instead of letting her pick her own HTML file to open.

You would use a similar procedure if you wanted to display an image file, though of course you couldn't make it scroll. However, you *could* create a behavior that resized the *sprite* to fill the Stage appropriately, or you could create a behavior that lets the user drag the image around on the Stage instead. (In fact, I have a file online that does exactly this; it looks a lot like the text editor, and you might enjoy exploring its code a little. I used the Draggable behavior from the Behavior Library.) Again, we will be looking at commands that enable us to do exactly this kind of thing in Part 4.

You could get Flash or video files to load and play in this fashion, as well.

Finally, you could get the location of a sound file off the user's drive, and then play it using the **puppetSound** command. All you really need to make it happen is some kind of placeholder in the member's slot to get started, and a willingness to experiment a little.

10

Ask the Expert

Question I tried to open an HTML file that has a lot of images in it, and some tables and so on, but the images and tables don't appear in the #text sprite. Why not?

Answer The HTML rendering capabilities built into #text members are pretty basic. They don't allow embedded content (such as JPEGs, Flash files, video, or even Shockwave files) to be shown on the Stage, and they have very limited table- and special text-formatting abilities. Also, you won't get CSS (cascading style sheets) or frames to display at all.

For that reason, if you're planning to make extensive use of HTML files for content in Director, you might want to consider finding an Xtra that lets you display Web pages in a native browser window, or if you have control over the kinds of files that will be loaded, keep them simple.

Put another way, #text members are not little Web browsers built into Director, more's the pity.

As you can see, the combination of FileIO and the **fileName** keyword vastly expands the possibilities open to you with Director.

And you thought it was just for making animation with a little scripting on the side!

Summary

This was another heavy module. You learned how to use FileIO to locate files on a user's system, how to open those files and save changes to them, and how to create a useful dialog box with MUI. You also learned that you can import and display files into your Director movies on-the-fly. Not bad, not bad at all. In the next module, we'll be exploring Internet operations, which will increase the possibilities for your users, since they won't have to just settle for files on their own computers. By the time we're done there, you'll be able to write programs that let users get files from the other side of the planet.

☑ *Mastery Check*

1. What does **displayOpen()** do?

_____

_____

2. What is happening with this command?
   openFile(sExternalFile, 1)

_____

_____

3. What does this command do?
   oDialog = new (xtra "mui")

_____

_____

4. What is wrong with this command?
   oFileObject.setFilterMask("Text files, TEXT")

_____

_____

5. Why don't images appear in HTML files you've imported into a Director
   Cast member?

_____

_____

6. If you save a changed file using FileIO, and don't delete the old file first,
   what might happen?

_____

_____

10

☑ Mastery Check

7. If you've created a projector from a movie that uses FileIO and users report that when they click the Open file... button they get a script error, what is the likely cause?

_____

_____

8. Why should you not open some files with write permission?

_____

_____

Module 11

The Internet Revisited

The Goals of this Module

- Learn how to handle basic Internet operations in Director
- Learn how to retrieve and download files
- Learn how to properly handle hyperlinks
- Learn how to integrate files into your Director movies

With Module 10, you learned a little of how to attach external media files and other resources to your Director movies just as though they'd been there from the beginning. The restriction was that those files had to be locally available—they had to already be present on the user's computer. With this module, you'll remove that restriction by adding the ability to get external resources right off the Internet.

Distributed Information

The first thing to understand about the Internet is that, while there are protocols and conventions in use with which you may be unfamiliar, there's little real difference in the way files are stored on Net machines compared to how they're stored on your own desktop system. The data is still all ones and zeros. The only major differences are these:

● Security on Net machines can substantially restrict the folders (directories) you may access on them.

● Usually you must specify some kind of network prefix (such as http://) to gain access to Internet machines.

Discussion of Internet communication protocols and security (in any depth) is considerably beyond the scope of this text. However, fortunately, you don't really need to know that much about such topics to be able to get basic Internet operations in place in your Director movies.

In this module, we are most interested in the operations that can handle Web page content and that can retrieve remote files, such as other Director-readable media that may be online someplace.

Web Content

You already explored some of the possibilities in retrieving HTML pages with **getNetText** in a #text member. Well, it might not surprise you much to know that your Director movies can be made to react to *hyperlinks* in #text members as well.

Note

A hyperlink is represented in an HTML page, usually, by text that is blue in color and underlined. It's the part of the HTML page you click to get someplace else in your browser.

Now we're returning to the idea of an online information pool, and I'm going to show you how you can intelligently handle hyperlinks in your Director movies (provided the HTML page you're using in the movie has been designed with a few limitations in mind).

Start, as always, with a new Director movie and place a #text member on the Stage. Give it the following behavior:

```
PROPERTY pnWebRetrieve, psServerPrefix




on beginSprite me


 clearCache
 pnWebRetrieve = 0
 psServerPrefix = "http://www.nightwares.com/director_beginners_guide/11/"
 sTarget = "index.htm"
 pnWebRetrieve = getNetText ( psServerPrefix & sTarget )


END beginSprite me




on exitFrame me


 if pnWebRetrieve <> 0 then
```

11

```
cursor 4

if netDone( pnWebRetrieve ) then

  sprite(me.spriteNum).member.html = netTextResult ( pnWebRetrieve )
  sprite(me.spriteNum).member.media = sprite(me.spriteNum).member.media
  pnWebRetrieve = 0
  cursor -1

end if

end if


END exitFrame
```

Some of this you've seen before, way back in Part 1. Some of this will be new to you.

clearCache

This clears Director's cache of previously downloaded pages. I've added it here because almost everyone runs into trouble when doing a **getNetText** operation that happens to include pages that have changeable content.

What happens is that Director stores a *cache* of Web pages it's previously downloaded, so if you try to do a **getNetText** operation on a page you've already seen, it'll pull that page from its cache. This is to save time, because loading a page from the local cache is quicker than going out to the Net and retrieving it all over again.

However, if you're editing your HTML content live in something like Dreamweaver or Netscape Composer and comparing it to the visual and programming results in a Director movie, you will *not* see the changes you've made reflected in your **getNetText** operations, because the old page will still be in Director's cache, and that will be what gets displayed after the **getNetText** call.

Thus, to get around that problem, we issue a **clearCache** command that takes place every time you click the Play button, ensuring that the page being displayed is, in fact, the most current version.

Every Director programmer—and I mean *every one*—runs into hitches with **getNetText** and the download cache, forgetting to do a **clearCache** at the right place and mistakenly getting the wrong data. Some programmers work on the problem for hours, believing perhaps it's a problem with their server or Internet connection. I might have just saved you half a day's future frustration.

pnWebRetrieve = 0

This will be our Internet operation ID.
psServerPrefix = "http://www.nightwares.com/director_beginners_guide/11/"
This is the server address to a location I have online containing the content we're going to retrieve. We hard-set the prefix for reasons that will become apparent shortly.

sTarget = "index.htm"

This is an initial page target.

pnWebRetrieve = getNetText (psServerPrefix & sTarget)

This initiates a **getNetText** operation, telling Director to begin loading the specific page named in **sTarget** from the location we gave it earlier in psServerPrefix.

We then go on to the frame event script:

if pnWebRetrieve <> 0 then
cursor 4

If there's some kind of Web retrieve operation going on, we turn the cursor into an hourglass (Windows) or watch (Mac) to let the user know that something is happening:

```
if netDone( pnWebRetrieve ) then
 sprite(me.spriteNum).member.html = netTextResult (
pnWebRetrieve )
 sprite(me.spriteNum).member.media =
sprite(me.spriteNum).member.media
pnWebRetrieve = 0
cursor -1
end if
```

If the Net operation is finished, we plug the HTML we just got into our #text member and reset the cursor to the system default (usually an arrow). We also set the Net retrieve ID to 0 so Director doesn't continue thinking we're trying to download anything. (After all, we got it already.)

11

I want you to notice this line especially:

sprite(me.spriteNum).member.media =
sprite(me.spriteNum).member.media

This is a *workaround* to a bug in Director that's been present since version 7. If you dynamically alter the HTML of a #text member, its hyperlinks *will not function* unless you set the media of the member equal to itself. Though I can't tell you for certain why this happens, I suspect it has to do with needing to "remind" Director of what a given #text member's contents are, especially if there are interactive elements (such as clickable hyperlinks) involved. Think of it as the Cast member equivalent of an **updateStage** call.

If you click the Play button now (and you're online), in a few moments, the index.htm page I prepared for this module should appear in your #text sprite. If you're not online, your computer should do a dial-up connection, after which you'll see the index.htm page.

1-Minute Drill

● What does **clearCache** do?

● Why is it important to remember to send a **clearCache** call?

Aren't Programs Supposed to Be Interactive?

As you can see, there's a hyperlink in the HTML file we've retrieved, but when you click it, nothing happens. In order to change that, we need to create an event script for those times when the user clicks a link. Predictably, this event script is called **on hyperLinkClicked**, and it goes into your #text sprite's behavior:

```
on hyperLinkClicked me, sLink

 if sLink starts "http" or sLink starts "ftp" then
```

● It purges Director's cache of any files it may have downloaded from the Net.
● Cached files will be displayed preferentially in Director, so if the files' contents have changed, you won't see the updates. **clearCache** purges those old files.

```
  goToNetPage ( sLink )

else

  pnWebRetrieve = getNetText ( psServerPrefix & sLink )

end if


END hyperLinkClicked
```

There's not a whole lot you can't guess here beyond the handler definition itself.

on hyperLinkClicked me, sLink

sLink is the link text that is passed when the user clicks a hyperlink. It's not the word or phrase in the link itself; rather, it is the name of the thing that's supposed to be loaded. So, if you have a link to a Web server, say http://www.foobar.com/, the blue text points to that server, and the name of the server itself will be sent along in the **sLink** parameter.

if sLink starts "http" or sLink starts "ftp" then

Maybe you didn't expect this. We're checking to see if the link that was clicked is to another server entirely, either a Web server (HTTP) or a server from which you can download files (FTP). In either case, we need to do a **goToNetPage** call, because we can't handle the information that might be on an FTP server, and since we don't know how the HTML might be formatted on someone else's server (it might not show up correctly in Director), we can't try to get that into our #text sprite. Thus, we load any outside servers or FTP locations in a browser, not into our #text member.

That's what **goToNetPage** does: It causes the user's browser to load and access the Web page or server that you specify.

else
pnWebRetrieve = getNetText (psServerPrefix & sLink)

Otherwise, the link is to another page next to the current one we're looking at, so we just grab it right off the current location (defined, remember, in **psServerPrefix**), and after a few moments, it's there in our #text sprite.

Now that you've added the **hyperLinkClicked** event handler, try clicking Play again, and then clicking the blue text. You should see a second page, and

11

when you click the link in there, you should find yourself at Macromedia's Web site.

1-Minute Drill

- What is **on hyperLinkClicked**?
- What does **goToNetPage** do?

Are You Being Served?

Of course, you don't necessarily want people loading information just from my server. There are two ways you can get server addresses:

- You can let users type them in.

- You can determine what the server address currently is if your movie is running as a Shockwave file.

The first option is pretty easy; just put an editable #text or #field member onscreen and let users type in the location they want, just as you would with a regular Web browser.

Note

If you use the first option, you'll want to make sure the user has typed in the correct information, that it's in an acceptable format, and so on, which can get rather tricky. At the very least, you should confirm that the text starts with http://.

The second option is even *easier*.
Here's the modified code:

```
on beginSprite me


    clearCache
    pnWebRetrieve = 0
```

- An event handler specific to #text sprites that lets Director behave, somewhat, like a Web browser.
- It causes Director to load a specified file or site in a Web browser.

```
if the runMode = "plugin" then

  psServerPrefix = the moviePath

else

  psServerPrefix = "http://www.nightwares.com/director_beginners_guide/11/"

end if

sTarget = "index.htm"
pnWebRetrieve = getNetText ( psServerPrefix & sTarget )


END beginSprite me
```

Do you see what I did there? I determined whether or not the movie is running as a Shockwave file (**the runMode** would then be "plugin") and, if it is, I did this:

psServerPrefix = the moviePath

the moviePath, as you've no doubt guessed, is the location from which the Director movie is currently playing. This means that the Internet location that contains the movie is now assumed to be the basic server path.

Try this in your Message window to find out more about **the moviePath**:

```
put the moviePath
```

When I do, here's what I see:

```
-- Welcome to Director --
put the moviePath
-- "nightbook ii:Documents:Dir. 8.5 Beginner's Guide:code:56211-code:"
```

That's exactly correct. The movie into which I entered that command is located precisely where Director just told me it is.

Of course, your response will be different, because your computer is set up differently, and naturally **the moviePath** will also be different for any Director movie that is playing as a Shockwave file.

This is a nice way to build in some "piracy" security for Shockwave movies. You can do something like this, for instance:

```
on startMovie

if the runMode = "plugin" and not ( the moviePath starts
"http://www.nightwares.com" ) then

 ALERT "Stop stealing other people's Shockwave files, you naughty person."
 HALT

end if


END startMovie
```

All you really need to know is that, in this line:

> **if the runMode = "plugin" and not (the moviePath starts
> "http://www .nightwares.com") then**

if **the runMode** is "plugin," then it's a Shockwave movie. If **the moviePath** does not start with the specified server address, someone someplace has copied the Shockwave file to a different server, and is trying to run it from there, perhaps even foisting it off as his own work. A naughty person indeed.

You could, of course, be a little more benevolent by putting up a #text or #field sprite which is ordinarily empty but, if the server address doesn't match, might contain text such as "The *official* version of this Shockwave movie can be found at…" with your server name. That way, the file still runs, but the end user realizes she's not seeing the file running from its original creator's site.

Tip

By default, Director now includes the network Xtras you're likely to need when it creates projectors; if you choose Modify | Movie | Xtras in any movie you make, you should see them listed in the dialog box as InetURL, NetFile, and NetLingo. If those Xtras are not present (if, for instance, you removed them), any time you try to do anything with browsers or the Internet, your users will get script errors. (Prior versions of Director didn't always include these Xtras, which resulted in a lot of frustration.)

1-Minute Drill

● What is the **moviePath**?

Pages Are Just Part of the Story

So now you've seen how to get Web pages to load in your Director movies, and even how to make them act a little like Web pages by responding to clicks on hyperlinks, but that's not all the fun you can have with online resources.

You'll recall in the last module that I illustrated different ways for you to handle external files that were located on the user's system. As you've probably guessed, getting those files from the Internet isn't much different.

Let's do a quick sample now. Create a new Director movie and put a rectangular shape from the Tool Palette on the Stage. It's just a placeholder, so don't worry too much about making it look beautiful.

Now attach this behavior to the shape:

```
on beginSprite me

  clearCache

  if the runMode = "plugin" then

   sServerPrefix = the moviePath

  else

   sServerPrefix = "http://www.nightwares.com/director_beginners_guide/11/"

  end if

  sTarget = "happy-happy.jpg"

  sprite(me.spriteNum).member.fileName = ( sServerPrefix & sTarget )
  sprite(me.spriteNum).member.regPoint = point ( 0, 0 )
  rImageRect = sprite(me.spriteNum).member.rect
  sprite(me.spriteNum).loc = point ( 5, 5 )
  sprite(me.spriteNum).width = rImageRect.width
  sprite(me.spriteNum).height = rImageRect.height
```

11

● The location on a given computer where the Director file is residing.

```
END beginSprite me
```

Wow, it really doesn't get much easier than that, does it? You've seen most of the Lingo keywords here already, and even with the ones that are new, you probably see what's happening.

The behavior starts by substituting the rectangle you attached it to for an image file retrieved remotely—off of a completely different computer in another part of the world—and putting it on the Stage for you.

Where it gets funny is after the image **fileName** has been set:

sprite(me.spriteNum).member.regPoint = point (0, 0)

regPoint is the *registration point* that bitmaps have; it's the coordinate that Director uses to indicate to itself the horizontal and vertical coordinates of any given sprite as it appears on the Stage.

By default, bitmaps have the **regPoint** set to the center of the image, which means that a 32×32-pixel image would have its **regPoint** set to be point (16, 16)—the image's center.

The problem is that the shape members we draw using the Tool Palette (including #text and #field sprites and all the button items) have their **regPoint** set to be point (0, 0), which means that if we substitute just any old bitmap for one of the rectangle shapes on the Stage, the bitmap's position will not be correctly shown.

The simplest way to alleviate this is to automatically set the **regPoint** of any bitmap we're going to exchange for a shape sprite to be point (0, 0), which matches that of the shape being replaced.

The rest of the Lingo is some variation or other of keywords and commands you've seen several times by now.

What's more, this will work in Shockwave movies and in projectors (provided the projector's user is online or has Net access).

1-Minute Drill

● What is a **regPoint**?

● Why is **regPoint** pertinent with regard to switching sprite graphics?

● The point that Director uses to set alignment on a given sprite.

● If the new image's **regPoint** doesn't match that of the old one, the new image will not appear to be placed or centered correctly on the Stage.

Ask the Expert

Question   I've been practicing with these different Net operations, and sometimes it doesn't seem like a file is downloaded, even though I know it exists. Why?

Answer   Check the case of the filenames. In general, Internet servers are very particular beasts, and they expect the upper- and lowercase states of files to be correct. So, if you're trying to access a file at http://www.foobar.com/someplace/Page3.htm but you've issued a command asking for http://www.foobar.com/someplace/page3.htm, you probably won't get anything at all.

Another Way of Getting Files

But wait, there's more! Make another new Director movie and place a button on the Stage named "Get image." Add this behavior to it:

```
PROPERTY pnNetRetrieve, psFileTarget



on beginSprite me

  clearCache
  pnNetRetrieve = 0
  psFileTarget = ""


END beginSprite




on mouseUp me

  sServerPrefix = "http://www.nightwares.com/director_beginners_guide/11/"
  psFileTarget = "happy-happy.jpg"
  pnNetRetrieve = downloadNetThing ( ( sServerPrefix & psFileTarget ), ( the
moviePath & psFileTarget ) )


END mouseUp me
```

11

```
on exitFrame me

 if pnNetRetrieve <> 0 then

  cursor 4

  if netDone ( pnNetRetrieve ) then
   sendSprite ( 2, #ReceiveImage, ( the moviePath & psFileTarget ) )
   pnNetRetrieve = 0
   cursor -1

  end if

 end if


END exitFrame
```

The only line in this entire behavior that's new to you by now is

**pnNetRetrieve = downloadNetThing ((sServerPrefix & psFileTarget),
(the moviePath & psFileTarget))**

Given what you already know about Director, you can probably guess
what **downLoadNetThing** does. If your answer is, "It downloads a file off the
Internet, Warren; I'm not a total chowderhead," then you win. Your prize is a
warm feeling of satisfaction that comes from having a healthy understanding
of something.

The syntax for **downLoadNetThing** is as follows:

downLoadNetThing (sourceLocation, destinationLocation)

Both location paths have to include the filename. As you see from the preceding
line, you can set an Internet operation ID to the **downLoadNetThing** call,
which lets you know when the operation is completed.

Tip

downLoadNetThing is actually a file copy operation. This means you don't
necessarily have to be retrieving files off the Internet to make it work; you can
also use this command to copy files from one location to another on any given
computer. Don't do this with program files on a Macintosh, though, because
some resources the program needs to operate won't be copied. To make a really
good copy of a file, you need to use an Xtra. We'll be getting into that in Part 4.

We're not totally done with our code yet; there's still that **sendSprite** call.

Put a shape on the Stage (make sure it's a filled shape, since we're going to be setting the **regPoint**, and you can't do that with one of the unfilled shapes) and attach this behavior to it:

```
on ReceiveImage me, sLocation


 sprite(me.spriteNum).member.fileName = sLocation
 sprite(me.spriteNum).member.regPoint = point ( 0, 0 )
 rImageRect = sprite(me.spriteNum).member.rect
 sprite(me.spriteNum).loc = point ( 5, 5 )
 sprite(me.spriteNum).width = rImageRect.width
 sprite(me.spriteNum).height = rImageRect.height


END ReceiveImage
```

You've seen this behavior before. You know exactly what it's going to do. The difference here is that with our earlier file, the **fileName** was being set to some item on the Net, whereas with this movie, the file is first being downloaded and then the **fileName** is being set to the local file.

If you are planning a Shockwave release for your movie, you'll want to use the former method, because **downLoadNetThing** does not work in Shockwave. If, however, you're doing a desktop install, this latter method will be the one you want to go with.

Ask the Expert

Question What kinds of files can I get from the Net?

Answer Any kind of file that Director can normally recognize should also be retrievable from the Internet and includable in your movies with the **fileName** keyword.

Furthermore, theoretically, you can download anything you want with **downLoadNetThing**, even if you can't actually use it in Director.

For instance, you could create a program that retrieves an installer from some server someplace, and then, once that installer has been saved to the local system, you could run it using the **open** command in Lingo.

Why? Because once the image has been retrieved locally and the **fileName** has been set, all you have to do is **saveMovie** (this would be a movie file loaded as an external resource, *a la* our proto-text editor from Module 4) and that image will be what's displayed from that point on.

1-Minute Drill

● What does **downLoadNetThing** do?

● Why should you avoid using **downLoadNetThing** in Shockwave movies?

Getting Net-Happy

Hopefully, your head's now full of interesting ideas you can pursue with this knowledge. Imagine, as I mentioned in Part 1, distributing a program that retrieves information as necessary off the Internet in order to ensure that it's always up to date. This program could reside on the local system any particular user has, and just access anything it needs whenever it needs it (perhaps monthly, to check for updates).

Better still, imagine a program that doesn't even have to fully reside on the end user's machine.

In this fashion, it's possible to distribute installed desktop software that has the innate ability to retrieve updates to media files, text, and even entire sections of itself with the click of a button. The only thing that could be easier would be software that is smart enough to know the updates are there to begin with.

That's not theoretically impossible; I leave it to you as an exercise of thought to imagine ways in which this would be done. There are lots of possible approaches:

● Your program could simply automatically check for and retrieve updates once a month (check **the systemDate**() in your Lingo manual for some tips on date and time).

● It retrieves a given file from a remote location and saves it to a different location.
● It won't work at all in Shockwave.

- Your program could look for some kind of version-tracking file online (perhaps a text file) whenever it loads and, if it finds one, retrieve the items listed in that version file.

- Your program could load a small Director movie from the Internet that contains nothing but update information.

What? Load Director movies off the Internet? Of course; that's what Shockwave files are, after all: Director movies that have been compressed and "protected" (made uneditable), playing back in a browser off the Net.

Why would you be surprised to know Director can gain direct access to those movies?

Here's something to try. Start with a new Director file and type this into the Message window:

```
goToNetMovie
"http://www.nightwares.com/director_beginners_guide/11/moviepath-sample.dir"
```

After a few moments, look at that! You got something that probably looks pretty familiar: A Director movie that contains the code and Net content we went over earlier in this module. Not bad at all!

Now try this:

```
goToNetMovie
"http://www.nightwares.com/director_beginners_guide/11/filename-sample.dir"
```

Interesting, no? Everything's running from the Net, including the Director movies themselves, and they're all loading their external resources correctly, exactly as if they were residing on your hard drive.

There are lots of further Internet accessibility options that Director gives you; for instance, you can use **postNetText** to send formatted information to a CGI script on a server someplace, just like many online Web page forms do, and then respond appropriately based on the feedback you get from the CGI. In fact, with the Shockwave Multiuser package, you can even send and receive e-mail in Director. These communication tricks, however, are considerably more complicated than I can cover here.

Besides, I think you've got enough to explore and try out now!

11

Ask the Expert

Question   What happens if someone out there tries to run a Shockwave file by using a goToNetMovie call in Director? Will they be able to save it on their hard drive?

Answer   This is a security-conscious question, and the bad news is that yes, any Director user can retrieve a Shockwave file in this fashion.

The good news is that when a Shockwave file is made, its internal resources are (for the most part) removed.

The media that is used by the file—sounds, images, and so on—might still be obtainable, but the Lingo code in the Shockwave file is gone.

Question   So how do I protect files that I put online?

Answer   You have to adopt a sort of disconnected feeling from the digital materials you produce—all of them. Over the last several decades, numerous copy-protection schemes have been tried, and all of them (as far as I know) have been defeated in one way or another.

Essentially, the cardinal rule of digital data is that it's all open to piracy, if the pirate is committed enough to stealing your work. While some protection might be in order, there's simply no sense in losing sleep over the issue. Besides, some of the steepest copy-protection and antipiracy schemes also have the effect of scaring off legitimate users.

It's an irony that while we strive to make computers easier to use all the time, we also don't want to make it *too* easy to get information we want protected. It's a fine line.

That's it for Part 3. In the fourth and final parts of this book, we're going to explore the mysteries and pitfalls of that most mysterious of programming methods, the object-oriented approach. But we're also going to have the most fun we've had so far.

Project 11-1: A Simple Web Browser

While you can't use Director to easily read super-wowie Web sites full of fun interactive animations, heavy frames, or lots of scripting, you can use it to create a sort of browser of your own if you want, and I've done that for this project, using the various skills we covered in this module to do it.

Note

You can, in fact, use Director to read most Web sites, but it is pretty difficult because you have to be able to parse HTML content to display things correctly, and that is no mean feat. Creating an online set of files that are custom-built to work best with your Director movie is much simpler than trying to make your Director movie handle anything the Internet cares to throw at it.

The goals of this project are to

● Introduce you to combined Internet operations in Director.

● Give you some pointers on how you can do some interesting things of your own.

Step-by-Step

1. This module's project is going to be really easy. Just make a Director movie that does this:

```
on startMovie


goToNetMovie
"http://www.nightwares.com/director_beginners_guide//11/menagerie/menagerie.
dir"


END startMovie
```

2. Save this file with a name like **loader.dir**.

3. Run the file from Director first, and save the movie you get locally.

4. Explore it to see what I did and how I did it; then, try doing something like it yourself. (This is a perfect opportunity for you to use the Debugger. Place some breakpoints in the menagerie movie and see what's happening while it's happening!)

5. Make a projector out of your loader movie and run it on different systems. Make sure the Internet Xtras are included in the projector you make.

11

6. Publish your loader movie as a Shockwave file, upload it to a server someplace, and try running it.

Project Summary

As you can see, Director is capable of working so extensively with networked files that it's sometimes not easy to tell what parts of a Director movie are actually resident in that movie's Cast, and what parts might be originally located on some machine in a different time zone—or even a different nation.

This silly little browser isn't much until you consider the fact that Director can actually retrieve any recognizable media type, including digital video, sound, Flash, and even other Director movies; suddenly, your quasirestricted browser begins to much more closely resemble a proprietary or custom-designed application. And when you start talking in those terms, clients begin to drool, because they all have brand consciousness. (For instance, you could pitch an idea that a client's site is only readable with a custom browser, which contains the client's logo most prominently, and that can also be used to track information regarding what's visited on her Web site. Instant demographics!)

☑ Mastery Check

1. What is a hyperlink?

_____

_____

2. How do you make Director respond appropriately to a hyperlink?

_____

_____

3. What does **downLoadNetThing** do?

_____

_____

4. I've just made a Director movie I want to put online, and I use this call:
downLoadNetThing (remoteFileLocation, localFileLocation)
What's wrong here?

_____

_____

5. If I make a projector that has a **goToNetPage** call in it and users tell me
they get script errors when they click the button that makes that call,
what's the likely reason?

_____

_____

6. What does **goToNetMovie** do?

_____

_____

11

Part 4

Object Oriented Programming

Module 12

The Fundamentals of OOP

The Goals of this Module

- Learn the basics of OOP
- Learn how and why OOP can be a better method for writing programs
- Learn how and why OOP is not *always* the best way to go
- Learn how OOP and databases are a perfect match

So far you've been working on a more or less single level with Director, taking care of all your programming needs in one movie. Imagine the possibilities if you could take several different movies and have them intercommunicate. You could have one movie that handles text editing, another that shows images, and perhaps a third that downloads files from the Internet—all functioning as one coherent package, but each responsible for doing only one part of the task. Imagine further the ability to have multiple copies of the text editor running at the same time, each one handling its own text file independently of the others. That's the concept behind object-oriented programming, or OOP.

The Black Box and the Pizza Shop

OOP breaks the world of programming into modules that behave as *black boxes*, and this doesn't mean airplane flight recorders.

A black box, in programming terminology, is any object that receives something as input, does something to that thing it's received, and spits out a result. What's going on inside the black box is anyone's guess, but that's okay, because you don't need to know what's happening inside to work with it.

As an example, consider your VCR or DVD player. You have (at least) a basic understanding of its operation: put some media in and watch a movie. However, you might not know all the details of how, precisely, that media yields up its information and has it transformed into patterns of light and shadow you interpret on your TV screen as being representations of real-world objects, such as buildings, people, or trees.

Furthermore, you don't *need* to know. You do not have to have a degree in engineering to make a DVD player work, and you certainly don't have to have an intimate understanding of helical-scan recording and playback, sync pulses, or the methods of encoding information magnetically to pop in a tape. All you really need to understand is a few simple interface controls in order to get all of this fabulously complicated technology to work for you.

This is a lot like what object-oriented programming principles do in the programmer's world. They allow code objects to be produced that do rather complicated things with any data they have been passed, and then to return some kind of result; then they're done.

What's even more useful, though, about OOP code is that you can have multiple instances of the same code object in memory, each of which is responsible for performing related but discrete functions.

Think of pizza delivery. You call up the local pizza shop and ask them to create an *instance* of the object called pizza, medium sized, thick crust. You further instruct the shop to put green peppers, tomatoes, and mushrooms on this pizza thing. You then inform them of the location you wish to have the pizza result delivered.

It would be mad to assert that this pizza shop had come into being the moment you made contact with it, and it would be equally crazy to think that the pizza you just ordered will be exactly the same kind of pizza that everyone else wants. Therefore, the pizza shop is both *persistent* (it exists whether or not you're calling it at any given moment) and capable of receiving parameters to modify its behavior (the pizza you ordered can be different from the pizzas ordered by others; in fact, there's a wide range of different possible pizzas that can be ordered).

How OOP Is Related to Other Kinds of Programming

The pizza shop example is analogous to the way object code works, like the VCR or DVD example. Since you've had some practical programming experience by now, you might think that it makes more sense to just write a handler that makes your pizza for you, and forget about all the fuss. You'd be correct, of course, because in this case a pizza is not especially complicated. It would probably take longer, in fact, to create the pizza-producing code object than it would to simply write a handler that did the pizza for you.

But consider expanding the pizza shop idea a little. Imagine a shop that still has the same phone number, but that also bakes lasagna, makes spaghetti, and produces sandwiches (both hot and cold) of various types. Suddenly, you are no longer looking at a simple pizza every time you call the shop; you're looking at different types of possible food results entirely.

That would get a little more difficult to write as a single handler; you'd be happier breaking it into discrete handlers, one of which describes the kind of food, one of which handles just the pizzas, one for the lasagna, and so on. So much for your nice, simple little pizza shop!

That's why you'd want to put this kind of code into an object. You would then have everything wrapped up into a neat little package and you'd still be able to work with it as though it were a very simple black box.

12

But even there you might argue the pizza shop isn't all that complicated. However, I could counter with a shop that remembers the orders you've made recently and gives you a chance to do a "speed order," where you simply call without saying anything and hang up, and the shop immediately cranks out a duplicate of the last food item you ordered; further, this shop could intelligently interpret your gustatory needs and not send you a food object that's larger than you can actually handle at one sitting. Pretty soon, the pizza shop becomes very complex and large, and might continue to expand considerably before we're through. In fact, your single pizza shop handler might now look a lot more like its own, complete program.

At some point or another, you probably would have begun to wilt and see the wisdom of *encapsulating* the entire mess into its own code object, and you might even recognize now that (in some cases, at least) a program is effectively nothing more nor less than a collection of object modules that communicate with some master control element, almost like a large company with department managers reporting to the CEO—little programs, in other words, operating inside a big metaprogram.

The one downside of OOP from this point of view is that someone has to *write* the code objects, and if that someone is you, then yes, by golly, you do have to worry about what goes on inside them after all.

How OOP Isn't Like Other Programming Methods

It's important to understand that object-oriented design is not wildly at variance from the way you might think of programs now. You still use basically the same Lingo you've been using so far. There are very few special conditions to consider. And this is true for other object-oriented languages, such as Java, C++, Perl, Python, and even JavaScript.

How OOP is different is in the arena of *encapsulation*. Encapsulation, in this context, means that individual code objects do not talk to each other, and do not directly share information with each other. No variables get passed directly between objects, and no two instances of the same code object work on the same information at once. There is a high degree of compartmentalization and division of labor here, and when you are dealing with complex data or complex operations, that's a good thing.

However, it is possible to get "OOP happy," and that's something to watch out for. You do not need to instantiate a code object, for instance, to install system menus in your Director movies; the **installMenu** command works fine on its own without a lot of help from you.

Note

If you're going to do a lot of dynamic menu changing and updating, the foregoing sentence might not be true.

You also do not necessarily need OOP to place a sprite on the Stage, if all it's ever going to do is put text on the screen (and not even text that changes, at that). You don't really need OOP to test single keystrokes or to respond to a mouse click. Breaking down your program to that degree is highly counterproductive, because you will waste more time and effort trying to get your individual objects to communicate with each other than if you simply remove OOP from the picture at that level of detail. That's really applying a level of granularity you don't need, and that you do not want.

Put another way, if you really got into it, you could see that *every* possible event that can be responded to in your code could be handled by an object dedicated to just that event. But then you'd spend a month creating a text editor, as opposed to 30 minutes.

Understanding the risk of overcomplexifying is very important in Director, which is meant to give you a more or less comprehensible, manipulable representation of elements in your program. I have two real-world examples of the dangers of this kind of overcomplexification that I want to share with you.

I once knew of a Director programmer who needed to cause a shape to animate across the Stage at a variable speed, along a curvilinear path, its overall velocity dependent on some parameters that were set by the user. There are two approaches (basically) that you can take to this challenge:

- Create *code* that causes the sprite to move across the screen, including testing to see if it moves long a curved path when necessary, and at the correct speed as defined by the input received from the user (that is, have it all happen by program control, without a single frame of Director's Score being used to actually set the sprite's location onscreen).

- Do the animation live on the Stage and make a **puppetTempo** call to change its speed (that is, use the Score entirely to set the sprite's location, and just alter the tempo of the movie as needed).

12

This individual unfortunately fell prey to the overcomplexification trap and opted for solution 1. Solution 1 took about a work-week to create, 39 hours of which could have been spared if our programmer had instead opted for the second solution.

The second example comes from Lingo seminars that some relative newcomers to Director attend. There always seems to be someone teaching at those seminars who makes mention of "one-frame Director movies," which results in a flurry of messages being posted to Director groups soon afterward from these poor attendees, all of whom want to know how to make a one-frame movie, as though it's some kind of Ultimate Goal for Director programmers.

Let me dispel a myth here. It is quite possible to make a one-frame movie in Director that does absolutely everything you could accomplish across dozens or even hundreds of frames' worth of Score. In fact, if you're really feeling masochistic, you can do it without even using *one* frame, causing everything to happen first in code objects and then creating sprites on-the-fly.

You are *insane* if you seriously want to attempt something like that.

What those seminar instructors never tell you is the following:

- Most of the time, a one-frame movie doesn't try to show a lot of animation or heavy tricks relating to items changing on the Stage; it's about as complicated in those terms as a standard system dialog box, though it might be doing some really fantastic programming stunts in that dialog box mode.

- The effort of creating really complicated one-frame movies is not worth the result, generally, since such movies can be *extremely* hard to maintain or upgrade if things change. Suppose, for instance, you animate a graphic in your one-framer, but your client wants a different graphic put in instead. One that is not the same size or shape. You have to rewrite your animation code now, don't you? Wouldn't it have been easier just to make an animation in the Score?

Director has a Score for a *reason*. It has tools that allow you to manipulate sprites for a purpose. Do not spurn these tools. They provide you with extremely handy and relatively intuitive means of creating and presenting quite complicated programs. There is no inherent inferiority in creating multiple-frame, multiple-channel movies, and anyone who boasts that all he ever writes are one-frame Director movies is *very probably a bad programmer*, simply because he refuses to make use of the full range of tools available to him. I would never hire him, because his movies would almost certainly be incomprehensible to and unmaintainable by anyone except himself. Anyone who preferentially chooses a harder path is probably several K short of a megabyte, if you follow.

We can extrapolate from this a formula with two dimensions. The maintainability of any program decreases as its complexity increases; however, that increase in complexity often represents an expansion of flexibility in the program itself. Thus, a balance must be struck in the interest of resolving these conflicting truths.

In short, the essence of being a good programmer is knowing when increasing complexity is necessary (to increase flexibility) and using it only when that increase represents a greater advantage than the inherent disadvantage (harder maintainability) that comes with the increase in complexity.

This is a kind of striving for what's called *elegance*, which can be defined in this context as something that behaves in a really powerful or interesting way, but that is also quite simple to understand, operate, and maintain. The Pythagorean theorem is elegant; the epicyclic addenda to the Ptolemaic astronomical model are not. (Epicycles were used to explain why planets appear to wobble a little as they move across the sky over time, and bolted on to the belief that Earth was at the center of the solar system. The idea was that, as the planets orbit Earth, they move in little circles of their own, called epicycles. In truth, the planets appear to wobble a little because, as Earth moves in its orbit around the sun, the perspective from which we view the planets changes enough that they appear to have *retrograde* or backward motion from time to time. Epicycles were introduced to prop up an untenable model of the universe, which had the effect of making that model inelegant relative to the simpler Copernican heliocentric model.)

The greatest thing about OOP, though, is that it is *conceptually portable*. If you grasp its fundamentals as they pertain to Lingo, you will already be well on your way to being able to work in other programming languages entirely. OOP skills are not like language-specific skills in that sense; they can be taken anyplace, almost completely independent even of the program language's syntax.

12

Alley OOP

So now that you've had a little background on OOP, let's go ahead and jump in. You're going to be working with a special Director script type, the *parent* script. You haven't seen these before, probably.

A parent script is the chief container for OOP code in Director. It's where you put the handlers that you invent to make your OOP module work.

We'll start simply with this. Create a new movie script and give it the name "pizzaShop" (yes, we're going to follow that concept), then enter the following code:

```
on new me


  return me


END new
```

If you paid attention to Director's syntax highlighting, then you've noticed that every word you just entered is a Lingo keyword.

Now, *before you do anything else*, change the script type to **Parent** using the Type pop-up menu from the Script tab of the PI. This is very important. If you don't transform your pizzaShop script from a movie script to a parent in this fashion, you won't be able to create an object out of it.

Let's look at the code we entered.

on new me

This is an event handler that is called when the parent script is instantiated. *Instantiation* is the creation in memory of a code object. Every code object must be instantiated in some fashion.

me is a keyword that refers to the object's location in memory. What this means is that when the object is instantiated, it is given a memory address where it lives. **me** is, in essence, the location of that address.

If that's not especially helpful, think of Director as being the landlord in a block of apartments, and of code objects as being like tenants. Instantiating an object is a little like telling the landlord that a new tenant is moving in, and the

me reference is the number of the apartment that the tenant occupies. When someone wants to find a particular tenant, she asks the landlord what the apartment number is. Similarly, if you want to talk to an instance of a code object, you tell Director to refer to it by its memory location.

Note

You don't actually have to use **me** for the object reference. You can use another term instead if you want, such as **thisScript**, as long as it is the *first* thing after any handler definition in any object script. **me** is used by convention, though, so it's best to use that as your object reference.

Thus, when **me** is used within any object script, it is always referring to the location in memory that is occupied by that script's instance. And since instantiating a script causes an instance of it to be pulled into memory, we have to know how to get a handle on where it's located. That's where the second line comes in:

return me

You know what **return** does. In this case, it's passing the variable **me**, which, as you now know, is the object's memory reference. Thus, when the pizzaShop script is instantiated, it will tell the thing calling it where it's located. I'll explain what that means in a moment.

1-Minute Drill

● What does **me** represent?

Making an Instance

12

Now that you have the absolute bare bones of your pizzaShop script, do the following in the Message window:

```
-- Welcome to Director --
oShop = new ( script "pizzaShop" )
```

● The location in memory occupied by a particular instance of a code object.

```
put oShop
-- <offspring "pizzaShop" 2 12d82a08>
```

This first line might well look fairly familiar to you:

oShop = new (script "pizzaShop")

This looks a lot like the way you gained access to the FileIO Xtra in Module 10, doesn't it? There's a reason for that, of course; when you used FileIO, you were instantiating and making use of an external code object. The concepts and means for handling Xtras are exactly the same as they are for handling parent scripts.

The next line tells Director to put out the thing it stuck into **oShop** when you sent the **new** command that instantiated the script:

-- <offspring "pizzaShop" 2 12d82a08>

Holy cow, what's that? It's the memory reference that was created with **the on new me** event handler in your pizzaShop parent script. As you can see, it's visually somewhat messy, which is why you put it into a variable (**oShop**). It's simpler to handle that variable than it is to try to deal with the computerese version of it you see here.

I mentioned that working with a parent script is very much like working with an Xtra. I'll prove it now. Do this in the Message window:

```
oFile = new ( xtra "fileio" )
put oFile
-- <Xtra child "fileio" 2 12d8314c>
```

The results, as you see, are very similar to what you got for **oShop**. This is because of the way Director has been designed. There's meant to be as little difference as possible between code objects you make through parent scripts and code objects you access as Xtras.

Adding an Employee

Before you go further, you need to zero your two variables (**oShop** and **oFile**), because any variable you enter in the Message window is global in scope, and you've got to set the objects you instantiated here back to 0 or you'll end up with problems later in your program. Just do this in the Message window:

```
oShop = 0
oFile = 0
```

That closes the objects and clears them from memory.

Note

Improperly cleared objects can result in situations where the current object, if it's of the same type as the one that was not correctly purged before, can encounter *dirty* bits of memory that contain information that's been left over. That can definitely cause your program to malfunction, and sometimes in truly bizarre ways.

It's not enough to say your pizza shop is open for business. You have to allow it to take messages from other things, after all. To do that, you need to create some kind of handler that can be called in the pizzaShop object, which will receive input.

Modify your pizzaShop parent script to look like this:

```
PROPERTY pyType, pySize, plAddOns


on new me


 pyType = #none
 pySize = #none
 plAddOns = []
 return me


END new




on TakeAnOrder me, sFoodType, sSize, lExtras
```

12

```
pyType = symbol ( sFoodType )
pySize = symbol ( sSize )
plAddOns = lExtras


END TakeAnOrder
```

First, we've added some property variables here, which have the letter *y* as prefixes. These indicate the variables are to be symbols. We also have a list in there. We instantiate the properties to #none, and empty the list.

Then, we've created another handler:

on TakeAnOrder me, sFoodType, sSize, lExtras

This accepts the parameters **sFoodType**, **sSize**, and **lExtras** and puts them into the property variables we instantiate in our new handler.

Note

The type and size parameters are being converted to symbol format for the two property variables.

Now you are ready to send a command to your script object. First, set a breakpoint next to the line **pyType = symbol (sFoodType)** so you can step through the **TakeAnOrder** handler and see your parameters being plugged into the properties. Then, do this in the Message window:

```
oShop = new ( script "pizzaShop" )
oShop.TakeAnOrder ( "Pizza", "Medium", ["pepperoni", "sausage"] )
```

Your pizzaShop object has just been given a command to take an order for a medium pizza with pepperoni and sausage. You might see that this syntax is very, very reminiscent of the way in which you sent commands to FileIO in Module 10.

In the Debugger, you can see that the parameters you've passed as strings are being converted to symbols and stored in their respective property variables, and you can see that you now have a list property containing the toppings you ordered as well.

After you've stepped through, go ahead and zero your **oShop** variable reference, because we need to add a little more to it than it currently has. Right now, while your pizza shop is happy to take orders, it's not particularly good at delivering. So we'll add a delivery handler to it, right under the **TakeAnOrder** handler:

```
on Deliver me


 lDeliveryList = [:]
 lDeliveryList.addProp ( #kind, pyType )
 lDeliveryList.addProp ( #size, pySize )
 lDeliveryList.addProp ( #extras, plAddOns )
 return lDeliveryList


END Deliver
```

This isn't anything you haven't seen already. We're just taking the properties that were set in the **TakeAnOrder** handler and returning them as a formatted property list.

Now you can have some fun with this, even if it's just in the Message window:

```
oShop = new ( script "pizzaShop" )
oShop.TakeAnOrder ( "Pizza", "Large", ["mushrooms", "black olives"] )
lDelivery = oShop.Deliver()
put lDelivery
-- [#kind: #Pizza, #size: #large, #extras: ["mushrooms", "black olives"]]
```

So what? So this:

```
oShop2 = new ( script "pizzaShop" )
oShop2.TakeAnOrder ( "Pizza", "Medium", ["anchovies", "pineapple"] )
lDelivery2 = oShop2.Deliver()
put lDelivery2
-- [#kind: #Pizza, #size: #medium, #extras: ["anchovies", "pineapple"]]
```

Do you see what's happened here? You've created two completely different pizza orders from exactly the same pizzaShop object script. The orders have gone to the same basic parent template, but they obviously occupy two discrete addresses in memory (a good thing, too, since you probably would not want to get the second order confused with the first).

What this means in practical terms is that you can have any number of references you want to the pizzaShop object, and that each reference will have its own specific set of parameters that the pizzaShop object stores and remembers. You've created a code object that acts as a kind of internal memory-cum-miniature program.

In fact, once you've made the order to the shop, you don't even have to remake it if you want another copy of it someplace. Suppose, for instance, you liked the first delivery order you placed but want it delivered someplace else:

```
lDeliver3 = oShop.Deliver()
put lDeliver3
-- [#kind: #Pizza, #size: #large, #extras: ["mushrooms", "black olives"]]
```

Since you're accessing the same shop object you made the first time (**oShop**), the properties you set for that initial call have been retained. They're now available anywhere, as many times as you want, as many places as you want.

1-Minute Drill

● What is encapsulation?

● What is the general method for instantiating a code object?

Closing the Shop

At the end of the day, you're going to want your pizza shop to close. This means, in object-oriented programming, removing the object's instance from memory. The best way to do that is to first set all of your object's internal variables to *null* or zero values, and then to clear the shop's reference itself.

● The quality of OOP design that causes objects to remain discrete and not share information readily.
● **object = new (script "scriptName")**

To do this, you must add a destruct routine to your object, one that may be called by you at any time. Here's the code to add:

```
on Destruct me


  pyType = 0
  pySize = 0
  plAddOns = 0


END Destruct
```

This is pretty straightforward, of course. It's important to remember to do this, though, because, as previously mentioned, if you do not properly clear all the variables in an object before you actually remove that object's reference, some really unpredictable and strange things can happen in your programs.

After you destruct the object, you'd set the variable containing it to zero as well.

However, if you try it now with the objects you instantiated earlier:

```
oShop.Destruct()
```

you get a script error, "Handler not found in object." That's right. Even though you entered more code into the parent script for the pizza shop, the older objects you created came into existence *before* that code was added. You need to set their values to zero and reinstantiate them before you can send them the **Destruct** call.

Once you've done all that, though, you can see that things are working smoothly:

```
oShop = new ( script "pizzaShop" )
put oShop
-- <offspring "pizzaShop" 2 12dbfc7c>
oShop.TakeAnOrder ( "Pizza", "Large", ["mushrooms", "black olives"] )
lDelivery = oShop.Deliver()
oShop.Destruct()
oShop = 0
put oShop
-- 0
put lDelivery
-- [#kind: #Pizza, #size: #large, #extras: ["mushrooms", "black olives"]]
```

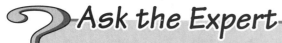

Ask the Expert

Question   Why can't I just auto-destruct the object? I mean, at the end of the Destruct handler, why can't I just enter me = 0, and use that to purge the object?

Answer   That's a clever idea, but it won't work. The variable that had been containing the object will still think the object is there, and if you mistakenly try to use it again, you'll get script errors.

Question   Well then, why don't I put the object variable in a global reference, and then set the global variable to 0 as the last item in my Destruct call?

Answer   You really are thinking today, aren't you? That won't work either, though; in general, it's neither safe nor particularly good OOP design to make objects self-destruct like that. It's also possible for very low-level code errors to occur. External destruct and clear calls are simply the safest, most reliable way to go here.

And there it is. You've successfully instantiated an object, which persists in memory for as long as you need it to, and correctly allowed its contents to be destructed and the object itself removed from memory.

That's it, really. That's the basic procedure for OOP. Everything else is commentary.

1-Minute Drill

● Why are **Destruct** calls necessary?

Project 12-1: Doing Something Useful

Now that we have the pizza shop, let's have a little fun with it. All this symbolic manipulation of code is interesting, of course, but it's not a whole lot of thrill without something happening onscreen.

● To properly remove an object's contents from memory, so the object itself can be cleared.

The goals of this project are to do the following:

● Illustrate how to integrate code objects in memory with manipulable objects on the Stage.

● Provide additional experience in working with code objects.

● Illustrate how a resident code object can be turned into a useful database that remembers set parameters.

Step-by-Step

Many programmers are not terribly well inclined graphically, and the most sainted of them are aware of this fact. Nevertheless, there are many times when you need to have graphics in place to illustrate or provide interface, so, at the least, you use *placeholders*. If we were making a pizza shop program for a client, we'd likely take this approach, creating example graphics and interface elements that would serve as proof of concept until our high-priced graphics expert was able to generate the required images.

1. Fire up Director's Paint window and create some bitmap graphics that roughly resemble basic small, medium, and large cheese pizzas, and some (separate) topping items as well, such as pepperoni, mushrooms, and so on. They don't have to be gorgeous. They just have to be.

2. Create a Stage control cluster that looks a little like the one in Figure 12-1.

At the top of the control cluster I've added a scrolling #field list with the sizes Small, Medium, Large, and Jumbo. I named it pizzaSize in the Cast.

Underneath is a series of checkboxes, named (respectively) pepperoniCheckbox, olivesCheckbox, sausageCheckbox, mushroomCheckbox, and peppersCheckbox.

Then I have an Order button, named (unsurprisingly) orderButton. Finally, my scrolling #field order list is named orderList. Right now it's empty because, of course, there are no orders.

3. To begin preparing to write behaviors, we're going to place the basic pizza sprites on the Stage. We're going to put the (ahem) cheesy crust down first, and then the images for the various toppings.

We only need to put down the smallest crust bitmap, since we'll switch it out as the size orders change.

We'll also set the ink for those sprites to Matte in the Sprite tab of the PI, because otherwise they'll all have white rectangles around them.

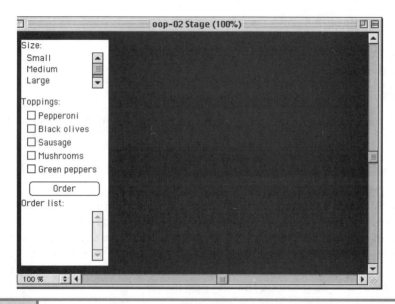

Figure 12-1 The basic controls for my pizza shop

Now my Stage looks like the image in Figure 12-2.

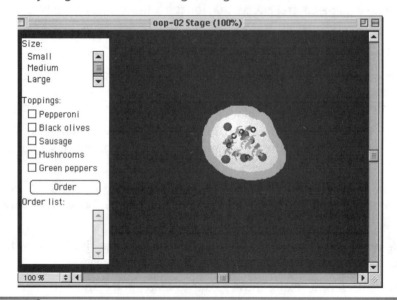

Figure 12-2 What the pizza shop looks like before any code has been entered

4. Time to start programming. Let's begin with the scrolling list for crust size:

```
PROPERTY pnLine


on beginSprite me

 pnLine = 1

END beginSprite



on enterFrame me

 sprite(me.spriteNum).member.line[pnLine].hilite()

END enterFrame



on mouseUp me


 pnLine = the mouseLine
 sendAllSprites ( #SetLocationOnPizza )


END mouseUp



on ReturnPizzaSize me


 sSize = sprite(me.spriteNum).member.text.line[pnLine]
```

```
return sSize


END ReturnPizzaSize
```

Not a whole lot going on there that's especially complicated. We start in **beginSprite** by setting a variable, **pnLine**, equal to 1. Why becomes apparent when we look at the next handler, our **enterFrame** script:

sprite(me.spriteNum).member.line[pnLine].hilite()

Here we're setting the **hilite** of a specific line in the Cast member associated with this sprite. What that does is reverse the colors on that specified line, sort of like what happens when you drag across some text in a word processor, and more or less exactly what it looks like when you select an item from a system control menu. This is to indicate which pizza size has been chosen.

Next we have a **mouseUp** handler with only two lines of Lingo in it:

pnLine = the mouseLine

This sets our line indicator variable to match the number of the line that was just clicked. So if you click line 3, the value of **pnLine** would be set to 3, and line 3 of the scrolling size list ("Large") would have its **hilite** set.

sendAllSprites (#SetLocationOnPizza)

Hmm, it appears we're sending a command to the other sprites on the Stage, but there are two things to note here: We haven't actually entered the **SetLocationOnPizza** handler yet, and we're using **sendAllSprites** this time, instead of **sendSprite**, as you've seen before. The difference, as you can guess, is that **sendSprite** targets one specific sprite, while **sendAllSprites** shoots the same command to all of them.

Finally, we have a custom handler, **ReturnPizzaSize**, which is also only two lines long:

sSize = sprite(me.spriteNum).member.text.line[pnLine]

This gets the size of the pizza, as determined by looking at the line that's been clicked and has its **hilite** set, that line coming from the text of the #field associated with this sprite. So, **sSize** can only be Small, Medium, Large, or Jumbo.

Ask the Expert

Question   What happens if I do a **sendAllSprites** call but not all of my sprites have that handler? Will I get a "handler not found" script error?

Answer   Given what you know about Director, you'd think so, but in this particular case, that does not happen. In fact, if you do a simple **sendSprite** call to a sprite that does not have the handler you invoke, you *also* will not get an error.

This is really a good thing. There will be times when you want to do a **sendAllSprites** call because it's just plain going to be faster than trying to target individual sprites (as with a repeat loop); the folks at Macromedia thoughtfully designed Director in such a way that you don't get script errors in this particular case.

Of course, that does mean you need to be sure the handler you want to execute has in fact been attached to a given sprite, but that's the tradeoff you make for no "handler not defined" errors.

```
return sSize
```

This, of course, passes the size we just determined back to whatever piece of code called this handler in the first place. Since we haven't written the rest of the behaviors yet, it remains uncalled, at least for now.

5. Now we can write the code for the checkboxes that let us pick the toppings. The same behavior can be attached to all five sprites, because it's very simple:

```
on ReturnCheckedStatus me


  bChecked = sprite(me.spriteNum).member.hilite
  return bChecked


END ReturnCheckedStatus
```

12

The **hilite** referred to here is not the same kind of **hilite** we used in the last script. In this case, **hilite** is referring to whether a given checkbox has been clicked or not.

Note

The same state would be true for radio buttons. If a radio button is selected, its **hilite** is true; otherwise, the **hilite** is false.

Again, this handler is obviously returning a variable that indicates whether its associated sprite has been clicked, but we don't yet have a handler out there that's calling it. We will, though.

6. From the topping controls, we move on to the pizza crust sprite on our Stage. To that, attach this behavior:

```
on exitFrame me


  sCrustSprite = sendSprite ( 2, #ReturnPizzaSize )
  sprite(me.spriteNum).member = member(sCrustSprite).number


END exitFrame
```

Now we see where the **ReturnPizzaSize** handler is being referenced; it's being called from here in our pizza crust behavior. Clearly, then, the variable **sCrustSprite** will contain either Small, Medium, Large, or Jumbo—which just happen to be the names I gave to the four different crust graphics I drew in my Paint window.

sprite(me.spriteNum).member = member(sCrustSprite).number

And here, of course, we update the crust sprite on the Stage so it visually matches the size that was selected in the scrolling Size list. Thus, we have a small, medium, large, or jumbo crust, depending on which line has been hilited in the scrolling size #field sprite over in channel 2.

7. Now we create our topping behavior. This, too, can be attached to all five topping sprites on the Stage, since we're using a little math to determine something:

```
on enterFrame me

  bVisible = sendSprite ( (me.spriteNum - 8), #ReturnCheckedStatus )

  if sprite(me.spriteNum).visible = FALSE and bVisible = TRUE then
```

```
  me.SetLocationOnPizza()

 end if

 sprite(me.spriteNum).visible = bVisible


END enterFrame



on SetLocationOnPizza me

 nMaxHorizOffset = sprite(10).width - sprite(me.spriteNum).width - 20
 nMaxVertOffset = sprite(10).height - sprite(me.spriteNum).height - 20

 nLocHBase = sprite(10).left + 20 + ( sprite(me.spriteNum).width / 2 )
 nLocVBase = sprite(10).top + 20 + ( sprite(me.spriteNum).height / 2 )

 nLocHOffset = nLocHBase + nMaxHorizOffset
 nLocVOffset = nLocVBase + nMaxVertOffset

 nLocH = random ( nLocHBase, nLocHOffset )
 nLocV = random ( nLocVBase, nLocVOffset )

 sprite(me.spriteNum).loc = point ( nLocH, nLocV )


END SetLocationOnPizza
```

This one is more complicated than the others, because it's actually setting the locations of the toppings such that they appear to spread out over the crust rather than being clustered in its center. (Sometimes they end up spilling off the edges of the crust a little, in fact, if you've made a round-crust pizza instead of one of the square ones.) But that's later; first we have the **enterFrame** handler:

> **bVisible = sendSprite ((me.spriteNum - 8),**
> **#ReturnCheckedStatus)**

Aha, here's that call to the **ReturnCheckedStatus** handler we attached to the five checkboxes. Note especially the place where I subtract 8 from the current sprite number. Why do I do that? Because the Pepperoni checkbox is in channel 3, and the pepperoni sprite graphic is located in channel 11; the Black olives checkbox is in channel 4, while the olives sprite is located

12

in channel 12; and so on. Thus, each topping *graphic* is located eight channels above the *checkbox* that indicates whether it's been selected or not.

This line, then, is asking whether or not the checkbox associated with this topping sprite has been marked. If not, **bVisible** is false; otherwise, it's true.

> **if sprite(me.spriteNum).visible = FALSE and bVisible = TRUE then**

…then the user has *just* clicked that checkbox. We know this because the topping sprite is currently not visible, which means that the last time the screen updated, the topping had not been selected. Now, with this particular **enterFrame** event, this topping has been chosen but the sprite is not yet visible. So then we do the next line:

> **me.SetLocationOnPizza()**

This calls the second handler in this behavior (which is also called whenever a line is clicked in the size scrolling #field), the handler responsible for putting the topping graphic in a random location on the pizza's crust.

> **sprite(me.spriteNum).visible = bVisible**

Here we set the topping graphic to match the checkbox associated with it. If the checkbox is not marked, the topping graphic sprite isn't visible; otherwise, it will be.

Then we get into the placement handler, **SetLocationOnPizza**. In the first two lines, we are determining the maximum range, horizontally and vertically, we can offset the toppings before they are definitely off the edge of the pizza:

> **nMaxHorizOffset = sprite(10).width - sprite(me.spriteNum).width - 20**
>
> **nMaxVertOffset = sprite(10).height - sprite(me.spriteNum).height - 20**

Sprite 10 is the pizza crust. Obviously, we can't go beyond the right or bottom edges there or the toppings will end up all over the counter. We then subtract from the dimensions of the pizza those of the current topping graphic, because if we just went with the pizza dimensions, the topping would overshoot the crust's sprite.

The toppings will go beyond the edges of the pizza crust because the topping images have *dimension*; they are rectangles, rather than simply being points in space. As rectangles, they have both width and height.

If we simply picked a random point somewhere in the pizza crust and put the topping at that point, odds would be decent that some or most of the topping would not appear to be on the pizza. So we have to pick a point in the pizza that also accounts for the dimensions of the topping we're going to place.

I've subtracted 20 from both values to keep the topping even closer to being inside the right and bottom edges of the pizza.

Then, we determine the range for the left and top edges of the pizza, using the same logic:

> **nLocHBase = sprite(10).left + 20 + (sprite(me.spriteNum).width / 2)**
>
> **nLocVBase = sprite(10).top + 20 + (sprite(me.spriteNum).height / 2)**

These values represent the minimum horizontal and vertical locations we're going to use to determine the location of the pizza toppings. We start with the left and top edges of the crust, adding 20 to reduce spillage, and then we take the dimensions of the topping graphic, divide those values by 2, and add them to the top and left offsets.

Why? You'll remember I mentioned in Module 11 that Director uses something called **regPoint** to determine the horizontal and vertical coordinates of any sprite on the Stage. You'll remember, further, that I told you this point is set to the *center* of a bitmap by default. Thus, our toppings have mathematical centers (as defined by Director) halfway between their width and height values.

Take a look at Figure 12-3, which is a screenshot of Director's Paint window, in which you'll see my pepperoni graphic and some dotted lines. Those dotted lines represent the **regPoint** of the pepperoni graphic, the point at which Director considers the graphic to be centered and with which it aligns it on the Stage.

As you can see, the **regPoint** is not anywhere near the top or left of the graphic. If I take the leftmost edge of the crust, then, and assume that I can start placing the pepperoni from that point on to hit the pizza, Director will occasionally set things up visually such that only half the pepperoni appears over the crust. In order to get around that, we calculate the offset of the **regPoint** by determining what half the height and width of the bitmap graphic are. This allows us to offset the graphics' locations relative to each other in such a way that they'll overlap like we want them to.

12

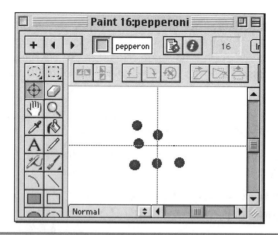

Figure 12-3 The pepperoni graphic and its regPoint as Director sees them

nLocHOffset = nLocHBase + nMaxHorizOffset

nLocVOffset = nLocVBase + nMaxVertOffset

Here we're calculating the farthest horizontal and vertical offsets we can use based on our maximum crust edge values, added to the minimum values for the topping sprite location. This, along with the horizontal and vertical base

Ask the Expert

Question   So why not just set the regPoint to point (0, 0) like we did before? Wouldn't that be easier?

Answer   Not really. In Module 11, that worked because we weren't *dynamically* setting a sprite's location based on a rectangular area it could occupy at random; we had a definite start coordinate where we wanted it to exist.

Since, in this case, I want my sprite to appear over a somewhat broad area, no matter where the **regPoint** is set, I'm going to have to do some boundary calculation. This method is as good as any other for that, and has the added advantage of not requiring you to reset the member **regPoint**.

ranges, gives us a rough rectangle of space into which we can put the toppings and still be reasonably sure they'll mostly end up on the pizza.

> **nLocH = random (nLocHBase, nLocHOffset)**

> **nLocV = random (nLocVBase, nLocVOffset)**

Here we choose random horizontal and vertical coordinates from within our calculated ranges.

> **sprite(me.spriteNum).loc = point (nLocH, nLocV)**

...and finally, here we put the topping onto the pizza.

8. Now that you've entered all that code, go ahead and click Play, and then choose different crust size and topping combinations. (You might notice that if you size the crust down, sometimes the toppings end up outside the pizza; this is irritating but not a show stopper.)

Great. So we have the pizza-making facility. On to handling the order processing.

Scalability

You'll recall I mentioned in Part 1 that a key factor in writing good programs is that they have to be scalable, and we've got a scalability issue right now with the pizzaShop parent script.

You saw earlier, in experimenting with the pizzaShop object, that you can instantiate it into as many variables as you want, and that you can then use those variables to place discrete orders. This sounds like a golden way to forge ahead with the program because you can make as many pizza orders as you want, right?

Wrong. Director does not allow you to actually define new variables on-the-fly like that. This means that you won't be able to make an infinite number of pizzas at one time using such a method. You cannot, any old time someone wants another pizza, create a whole new variable that contains just that one pizza order.

Look at it this way. Suppose you have an order variable:

> **oOrder = new (script "pizzaShop")**

That's terrific. That's also the end. You can't then do

> **oOrder2 = new (script "pizzaShop")**

12

when someone else places an order, because you can't just define variables out of something that didn't used to exist.

So, with the way the pizzaShop code works now, the following are your options:

● Set a maximum number of orders that can be placed.

● Try to use the **Deliver** call to place the pizza ordered into some kind of expandable container, probably a list.

Well, if you're going to make this program scalable, you should pick the second option, but not exactly as stated. Rather than store the delivery *outside* of the pizzaShop object, you keep a record of it *within the object itself*.

9. Modify your pizza shop parent script a little:

```
PROPERTY pyType, pySize, plAddOns, plMasterOrderList


on new me


  pyType = #none
  pySize = #none
  plAddOns = []
  plMasterOrderList = [:]

  return me


END new



on TakeAnOrder me, sOrderName, sFoodType, sSize, lExtras


  pyType = symbol ( sFoodType )
  pySize = symbol ( sSize )
  plAddOns = lExtras

  lPizza = me.Bake()
```

```
yOrder = symbol ( sOrderName )

plMasterOrderList.addProp( yOrder, lPizza )


END TakeAnOrder




on Bake me


 lPizzaList = [:]
 lPizzaList.addProp ( #kind, pyType )
 lPizzaList.addProp ( #size, pySize )
 lPizzaList.addProp ( #extras, plAddOns )
 return lPizzaList


END Bake




on Deliver me, sOrder


 yReference = symbol ( sOrder )
 lPizzaContents = plMasterOrderList[yReference]

 return lPizzaContents


END Deliver




on Destruct me

 pyType = 0
 pySize = 0
 plAddOns = 0
```

```
plMasterOrderList = 0


END Destruct
```

Here the most interesting alteration is that I've renamed the **Deliver** handler; it's now called **Bake**, because all it does is bake the pizza. I've then created a *new* set of commands that I have named **Deliver**. Let's check out the differences.

At the top, you can see I've added a new list, **plMasterOrderList**. We'll be using this throughout the duration of the pizzaShop object's life to store records of the orders sent to the shop.

There are changes to be seen in the **TakeAnOrder** handler, too:

on TakeAnOrder me, sOrderName, sFoodType, sSize, lExtras

Do you see the extra parameter here? **sOrderName** is used a little later in this very call; it's passed in whenever an order is placed. We'll get to that momentarily. Then there are some additional lines:

lPizza = me.Bake()

This is a call to the old **Deliver** handler, which has been renamed **Bake**. It still gets a list of the pizza parameters.

yOrder = symbol (sOrderName)

Here we take the **sOrderName** parameter and convert it to a symbol. We do this for the benefit of the next line of code.

plMasterOrderList.addProp(yOrder, lPizza)

Here we add an index to the master order list, which is the name of the order we received. That index then references the pizza itself, as created in the **Bake** handler.

Now on to the new **Deliver** handler:

on Deliver me, sOrder

Again, there's a string parameter being passed.

yReference = symbol (sOrder)

Here that string is converted to a symbol.

lPizzaContents = plMasterOrderList[yReference]

And here that symbol is being used to get a list from an index location in our master order container. That list, of course, is the pizza made then the **TakeAnOrder** command was issued.

return lPizzaContents

Here we're returning the pizza description to the calling handler. We'll get to that next.

Note

In the **Destruct** routine, I've added a line that clears the **plMasterOrderList** variable. You'll want to do the same.

10. Now that we have the shop, let's go ahead and get it working. First create this behavior for your **Order** button:

```
on mouseUp me

 sendSprite ( 9, #OrderPizza )

END mouseUp
```

11. You're surely guessing now that a lot of work is going to be happening in that scrolling order list (sprite 9). You're right; here's the behavior:

```
PROPERTY poPizzaShop, pnLine



on beginSprite me

 poPizzaShop = new ( script "pizzaShop" )
 sprite(me.spriteNum).member.text = ""
 pnLine = 1
```

12

```
END beginSprite


on endSprite me

 poPizzaShop.Destruct()
 poPizzaShop = 0

END endSprite


on enterFrame me

 sprite(me.spriteNum).member.line[pnLine].hilite()

END enterFrame


on OrderPizza me

 sSize = sendSprite ( 2, #ReturnPizzaSize )
 lToppings = []
 repeat with nSprite = 3 to 7
  if sprite(nSprite).member.hilite = TRUE then
   lToppings.append ( sprite(nSprite).member.text )
  end if
 end repeat
```

```
  sType = "Pizza"

  sOrders = sprite(me.spriteNum).member.text
  nCurrent = the number of lines in sOrders
  sOrder = "Order_" & string ( nCurrent )
  put sOrder & RETURN after sOrders
  sprite(me.spriteNum).member.text = sOrders

  poPizzaShop.TakeAnOrder ( sOrder, sType, sSize, lToppings )

  me.mouseUp( nCurrent )


END OrderPizza



on mouseUp me, nLine

  if voidP ( nLine ) then

   pnLine = the mouseLine

  else

   pnLine = nLine

  end if

  sPizza = sprite(me.spriteNum).member.text.line[pnLine]

  lPizza = poPizzaShop.Deliver( sPizza )

  me.DisplayOrderedPizza( lPizza )


END mouseUp



on DisplayOrderedPizza me, lPizza

  ySize = lPizza[#size]
```

12

```
sSize = string ( ySize )
lToppings = lPizza[#extras]

repeat with nSprite = 3 to 7

  sTopping = sprite(nSprite).member.text

  if lToppings.getOne ( sTopping ) > 0 then

    sprite(nSprite).member.hilite = TRUE

  else

    sprite(nSprite).member.hilite = FALSE

  end if

end repeat

sSizes = sprite(2).member.text
nAllLines = the number of lines in sSizes

repeat with nLine = 1 to nAllLines

  if sSizes.line[nLine] = sSize then

    exit repeat

  end if

end repeat

sendSprite ( 2, #mouseUp, nLine )

END DisplayOrderedPizza
```

Now, now, don't look at me like that. This isn't nearly as scary as it seems. In fact, with the exception of the **voidP** and **getOne** keywords, *there isn't a single piece of Lingo in here you have not seen and used before.*

We'll start with the **beginSprite** handler, which does absolutely nothing but instantiate the pizzaShop parent and put it into the object property variable **poPizzaShop**. It also sets the value of another variable, **pnLine**, to 1.

Then we have the **endSprite** handler, which sends the **Destruct** command to the object code in the **poPizzaShop** variable, and then sets **poPizzaShop** to 0. This totally dereferences everything in the **poPizzaShop** object, allowing it to be properly removed from memory.

From there we go to an **enterFrame** handler that looks and acts exactly like the handler you created for the Size scrolling list.

Then we get to the **OrderPizza** handler, which you'll recall is called from the Order button.

> **sSize = sendSprite (2, #ReturnPizzaSize)**

This is no mystery. The pizza graphic sprite behavior does exactly the same thing to figure out what size crust graphic to display on the Stage.

> **lToppings = []**

You know enough now to understand that we're setting a list to empty here.

> **repeat with nSprite = 3 to 7**
>
> **if sprite(nSprite).member.hilite = TRUE then**
>
> **lToppings.append (sprite(nSprite).member.text)**
>
> **end if**
>
> **end repeat**

Here we're just checking to see whether or not the various toppings have been selected. We look at our checkboxes and, if any given checkbox has been marked, put the text entered for that checkbox into our **lToppings** list.

Tip

Another way to follow this code is to set a breakpoint at the beginning of the **OrderPizza** handler and step through all of these operations, watching as the Lingo does its job.

> **sType = "Pizza"**

This is setting the type of food being ordered.

> **sOrders = sprite(me.spriteNum).member.text**

Here we're getting the current text in the Orders scrolling #field, and putting that into another variable.

nCurrent = the number of lines in sOrders

This tells us how many lines there are in that text. The number of lines represents the current order number we want to place.

sOrder = "Order_" & string (nCurrent)

Now we create a name for the order we're going to put into the scrolling #field (and that we're going to send to the pizza shop). If there are two lines already in the scrolling field, **nCurrent** will have a value of 3, and **sOrder**'s variable will be "Order_3".

put sOrder & RETURN after sOrders

sprite(me.spriteNum).member.text = sOrders

Now we put that order, followed by a RETURN character, into the **sOrders** variable. We then put the entire variable back into the scrolling #field, so the user sees that the current order has been added.

poPizzaShop.TakeAnOrder (sOrder, sType, sSize, lToppings)

With everything we need to know in place, we tell the pizza shop to take an order. The pizza shop then takes over from there, baking the pizza and putting a new reference to its location into its master order list. It takes the variable **sOrder** and converts that to a symbol, which is then used as a master index to determine what pizza is associated with that order.

Finally, we have this call:

me.mouseUp(nCurrent)

Remember from Module 10 that you can send sprites **mouseUp** commands to make them react as though they've been clicked. Here we're doing that to the current sprite itself, and what's more, we're passing a parameter to that call: The line we determined is the one associated with the current pizza order. So if the pizza we just ordered is located in line 3 of our scrolling order #field, its name will be "Order_3", and the variable **nCurrent** we pass in the **mouseUp** call here will also be 3.

What do we do with that variable? Why did we pass it? The answer is to be found in the **mouseUp** handler:

on mouseUp me, nLine

There's the **mouseUp**, and the **nLine** parameter.

> **if voidP (nLine) then**

This is an interesting keyword. **voidP** is a test you can perform on a variable to see if it has been given any value at all.

For instance, into the Message window, type the following:

```
put nVoidTest
```

The result will be **<Void>**, meaning that no value at all has been put into **nVoidTest**. Therefore, its value is void. Not zero, not ""—void.

voidP simply determines whether or not the variable it's testing has a value of **<Void>**. If it does, then it returns true, because the variable has not been given a value. Otherwise, the variable *does* have a value in it, so **voidP** returns false.

To explore further, try this in the Message window:

```
put voidP ( nVoidTest )
```

You get the result 1, or true. Now do this:

```
nVoidTest = 500
put voidP ( nVoidTest )
```

This time you'll get 0, or false, because you put a value into the **nVoidTest** variable, which means it's no longer void.

So the purpose of the code

> **if voidP (nLine) then**

is to determine whether **nLine** has a value here or not. If the **mouseUp** event has been called by an actual click on the scrolling #field, **nLine** will in fact be void. However, if we've called this **mouseUp** function and explicitly passed a value to it (as with our **OrderPizza** handler), the **voidP** test will be false.

If nLine is void, we do this line of Lingo:

> **pnLine = the mouseLine**

12

That is, we set the **pnLine** variable value equal to the line number the user clicked. This is the same functionality the Size scrolling #field had. If, however, **nLine** is not void, we do this instead:

pnLine = nLine

This has the effect of setting the line selected to be equal to the value we passed along from the **OrderPizza** call. Why? So the rest of this handler can function.

sPizza = sprite(me.spriteNum).member.text.line[pnLine]

Here we get the name of the order we have stored in this scrolling #field. The name is entered on line **pnLine** of this #field, which (again) is either a line the user clicked or a line we told this **mouseUp** handler to *think* was clicked.

lPizza = poPizzaShop.Deliver(sPizza)

Aha! This is why we do it. We take the name of the order we just got and send that as a parameter to our pizza shop object, which then responds by sending back a list. That list contains the size and toppings on the pizza associated with the order name we just clicked (or pretended to click), as referenced from the pizza shop's master order list.

Then we have one more line in the **mouseUp** call:

me.DisplayOrderedPizza(lPizza)

Without further delay, let's examine that **DisplayOrderedPizza** handler:

ySize = lPizza[#size]

sSize = string (ySize)

Here we are retrieving the entry for the pizza's size for this order, and converting that entry to a string.

lToppings = lPizza[#extras]

Here, of course, we're getting the list of toppings for that pizza.

repeat with nSprite = 3 to 7

Here we revisit our topping checkboxes.

sTopping = sprite(nSprite).member.text

We start by getting the name of the topping for any particular topping checkbox.

if lToppings.getOne (sTopping) > 0 then

Here we determine if, *anywhere* in the **lToppings** list, there is an entry for the specific topping we're seeking. We use the **getOne** call to do that, with a basic syntax of

list.getOne (itemToFind)

If **itemToFind** is anywhere in the list, **getOne** will return a value greater than 0 (which, in fact, is the location in the list you can find **itemToFind**). Thus, we're testing to see if the topping associated with a given checkbox is in the topping list, and if it is, we execute the next line:

sprite(nSprite).member.hilite = TRUE

This just sets the checkbox to its selected state on the Stage. If, however, the topping is not in the list, we do the other line:

sprite(nSprite).member.hilite = FALSE

which unchecks the checkbox. We then end the repeat and move on in the handler.

sSizes = sprite(2).member.text

Here we get the sizes available in the scrolling size #field for the pizza.

nAllLines = the number of lines in sSizes

This is, of course, the number of lines in that list.

repeat with nLine = 1 to nAllLines

if sSizes.line[nLine] = sSize then

exit repeat

end if

end repeat

All we're doing here is determining which line in the size list matches the size of the pizza for this order. Once we find that line, we kick right out of the repeat, because we don't need any more information than that. We then have one line left:

sendSprite (2, #mouseUp, nLine)

Aha! We've taken that value and sent it to sprite 2, our scrolling size #field, in a **mouseUp** call.

12

12. This implies you will have to modify the **mouseUp** handler in the behavior for sprite 2; in fact, it should look like this once you're done:

```
on mouseUp me, nLine

  if voidP ( nLine ) then

    pnLine = the mouseLine

  else

    pnLine = nLine

  end if

  sendAllSprites ( #SetLocationOnPizza )

END mouseUp
```

In other words, the changes you need to make to the **mouseUp** handler for the scrolling size #field are fundamentally the same as for this order scrolling #field, and for the same reason, really: to allow our code to tell those items to behave as though they were clicked, when in fact they were not.

13. Hey, guess what? You're done! Your pizza shop is ready to take orders! So go ahead and click Play, and then place a few pizza orders. As you click around, you'll see that the program correctly remembers what different pizza orders were made, and when you go back to review those orders, it reconstructs (more or less) the pizza as it had been requested before.

What's more, the pizza shop is now truly scalable. I promise you that you'll get tired of ordering pizzas before the program runs out of memory to store the orders you've made. We're not talking about a couple dozen pizzas here; in fact, you could place *thousands* of orders in one single application session for this program, and not run out of memory.

Project Summary

With this whopping project, you've seen the following:

● How to create a memory-resident code object

- How to interact with that object

- How to cause that object to interact with other sprites and code in Director

- How to generate a simple database using Lingo

I hope you've also got an idea now that Director can be used for a lot more than simply making games or advertising pieces; in fact, you can make a pretty sophisticated data handling program with it, if that's what suits you.

Interface Revisited

I mentioned in Part 3 that it's a good idea to make some kind of interface instructions available to other programmers, and so that's the final thing I want you to do with your pizza shop.

Into the pizzaShop parent script, enter the following handler:

```
on Interface me


 sInterface = "-- Pizza shop methods" & RETURN &\
"-- object = new ( script 'pizzaShop' ): Instantiate the pizza
shop" & RETURN &\
"-- object.TakeAnOrder( string orderName, string foodType,
string size, [toppings] ):" & RETURN &\
"--     Take order named orderName for type foodType of size
with toppings as a list" & RETURN &\
"-- object.Deliver( string order ): Return a formatted list
describing the food associated with order" & RETURN &\
"-- object.Destruct(): Zero all internal variables prefatory
to object purge."

 return sInterface


END Interface
```

12

All this does is construct a multiple-line text string in a variable, **sInterface**, and kick it back out when the **Interface** call is sent. You can test it in your Message window.

```
test = new ( script "pizzaShop" )
put test.Interface()
-- "-- Pizza shop methods
-- object = new ( script 'pizzaShop' ): Instantiate the pizza shop
-- object.TakeAnOrder( string orderName, string foodType, string
size, [toppings] ):
--     Take order named orderName for type foodType of size with
toppings as a list
-- object.Deliver( string order ): Return a formatted list
describing the food associated with order
-- object.Destruct(): Zero all internal variables prefatory
to object purge."
```

That way, if other programmers want to use your pizza shop, they have an idea how to get it working.

Note

Interface calls are useful for *you* as well, particularly if you're creating a very complex object. Get into the habit early of making **Interface** returns for any object you create!

Heck, that's all there is to this OOP thing!

Summary

What you have learned here is twofold. For starters, you got a taste (so to speak) of some of the power inherent in OOP design; but you also just got your first real experience in programming and using a database. (What did you think that master order list in the pizza shop object was?) You also got a positive practical example of how a correctly formatted property list can be used to do some fairly cool things.

In the next module, we'll explore OOP design as it's implemented in Director on the sprite level.

☑ *Mastery Check*

1. What is a code object?

_____

_____

2. What does **me** represent?

_____

_____

3. What is instantiation?

_____

_____

4. What should you always do before clearing a code object's variable?

_____

_____

5. What does encapsulation mean?

_____

_____

6. For exploration: You see that I created a food type variable, but all we ever did was set it to pizza. Consider what might be necessary to modify your program so that it can handle sandwiches, spaghetti, and so on.

_____

_____

12

Module 13

Behaviors Are OOP Too

The Goals of this Module

- Learn more about the nature of object-oriented code through sprite behaviors

- Learn more methods to allow code objects to communicate

- Discover more about the recyclability of OOP code

- Discover more about the value of encapsulation

Now that you've had a look at the way parent scripts can become objects, you're probably aware that behaviors—those handy little bits of code you've been using since Module 1—are also code objects. In this module, we're going to explore the encapsulated nature of behaviors further, and in the process, we're going to make a pretty useful piece of software.

You've Been Object Oriented All Along

As the introductory paragraph states for this module, behaviors are object-oriented code themselves. This means you've been working within an object-oriented framework since your first project in Director. You probably realized (or at least suspected) this was the case once you were introduced to parent scripts, which use the **me** keyword, just as sprite behaviors do. Thus, you've had a pretty good chance to see how straightforward object-oriented code can be, and you might even wonder why it's worth discussing at any length. Well, that's probably because you weren't programming before there was such a thing as OOP, so you don't really have the perspective necessary to appreciate what a great leap forward it is.

That's as may be. Now that you know the true nature of sprite behaviors, we're going to start using that knowledge to real advantage.

You saw an example in the last module of how five different sprites can each have the same behavior attached to them, and that those behaviors are encapsulated at the sprite level. The pepperoni behavior did not get confused, for instance, and think it was handling data for the mushroom sprite.

Well, just as behaviors can retain information specific to the sprite they happen to be associated with, they can also retain discrete properties (including databases). In fact, pretty much everything you can do in a parent script can also be done in a sprite behavior—plus a little more. You can prove to yourself that behaviors are discrete, encapsulated critters by making a really simple one:

```
on beginSprite me

 put me


END beginSprite
```

Attach it to a few sprites in the same frame and then click Play. You'll see that the two identical behaviors, in fact, hold two quite different memory addresses. Although they are the same code, they are not the same *instances*.

Behavior Instantiation, Destruction, and Messaging Hierarchy

That's a scary sounding header, but you're well versed enough by now to know you can handle anything I might throw at you.

Behavior instantiation, as you've realized by now, does not use the same kind of syntax as parent object instantiation. Gone is the **new (script "blaBlaBla")** syntax; instead, it is handled automatically for you, and in fact, it's not even a piece of code you need to enter.

You might think instantiation takes place in **beginSprite**, and that's a reasonable assumption to make, but it's not correct. After all, we've seen sprites that accept **sendSprite** calls even when they don't have a **beginSprite** handler attached; in fact, there's no **return me** you have to code in either. Thus, you can infer (and you'd be correct) that Director handles the instantiation for you where behaviors

Ask the Expert

Question What can I do in behaviors that can't be done in parent scripts?

Answer Behaviors are much more sprite-oriented; it's easier to handle mouse, frame, and keyboard interactions with behaviors on a per-sprite basis than with parent objects.

There are situations in which parent scripts are likely to be desirable; for instance, if you really *are* creating a large database, you'll probably want to encapsulate it and all of its data-reading and -writing controls into a parent script behavior. However, especially for handling sprite-level manipulation and response to user commands, behaviors are quite well suited to meet your needs.

13

are concerned. It associates the behaviors—or collection of them—automatically with their sprites, so you don't have to worry about keeping track of them on your own.

Similarly, Director does the behavior destruction for you as well. This is also convenient, because you don't have to explicitly zero any of the behaviors on your own.

However, you can also get into a little bit of trouble here because of the hierarchy Director uses to instantiate and destruct the sprite behaviors that might exist in any given frame. This is actually pertinent to a larger discussion regarding messaging hierarchy as it occurs in the Lingo engine, so we're going to discuss it here.

Let's begin with a definite example. Create two new sprites in the same frame on the Stage, and to the first sprite, in channel 1, attach this behavior:

```
on beginSprite me

 bAreYouLoaded = sendSprite ( 2, #ReturnLoaded )

 if bAreYouLoaded = TRUE then

  put "Sprite 2 is loaded."

 else

  put "Sprite 2 is NOT loaded"

 end if


END beginSprite
```

Pretty simple, right? Now—without adding any behavior to sprite 2—click Play. What happens? You get the "not loaded" message, and you get it every time. This occurs because **bAreYouLoaded** returns <Void>, which is treated in this context as meaning the same thing as false.

Tip

If you really wanted to test the void status, you would use **voidP**, as we did in the last module.

Now go ahead and attach this behavior to sprite 2:

```
on ReturnLoaded me

 return TRUE

END ReturnLoaded
```

This is, of course, the behavior that's supposed to send an answer to the question asked by sprite 1. Now that you have these behaviors, go ahead and click Play again.

Did the results surprise you? You still get the message saying sprite 2 isn't loaded, and it won't matter how often you click Play, because the message will not change. This is because sprite 1's behavior is actually instantiated *before* that of sprite 2. Thus, sprite 1's code is asking its question before sprite 2's code can even get itself loaded into memory.

Unfortunately, there is no easy way to get around this; if you are relying on **beginSprite** to be able to create some kind of internal list of sprites that are active in a given frame, and are expecting these sprites to intercommunicate with all the others, you might want to consider a *bottom-up* approach.

For example, take sprite 1 as it exists now and put it in channel 3. Then click Play. The results change, of course, because now sprite 2 has in fact been loaded; sprite 3 is asking its question after the instantiation of 2.

It's easy to forget that the topmost sprites in the Score are going to have their behaviors instantiated before the lower ones, because Director does a fine job of displaying all of them at once when they appear in a given frame. That is, we don't see them draw themselves one atop the other when Director enters any given frame, so it can sometimes be hard to remember that, as far as the *system* is concerned, that's actually precisely what is happening. Sprite 1 comes into existence immediately before 2, which comes into existence immediately before 3, and so on.

The same is true, by the way, for **endSprite** events. Sprite 1 is cleared from memory before 2 is.

This also means we should talk about messaging hierarchy, or the order in which Director handles events that occur. The program does not treat every event equally; that is, a mouse click or keypress is not noticed at the same time on all levels of code.

13

For instance, suppose you wanted to check the keys being pressed by the user as she types text into a field, and make sure she didn't use the "\" character for some reason. You might think to attach this behavior to an editable #field or #text member:

```
on keyDown me

  if the key = "\" then

    BEEP

  end if

END keyDown
```

But if you ran your movie, none of your keystrokes would get through to the editable #field, because they're all being intercepted by Lingo, and not explicitly passed down the event hierarchy. You'd need to revise your code a little:

```
on keyDown me

  if the key = "\" then

    BEEP

  else

    pass

  end if

END keyDown
```

Here we still beep and trap the forbidden key, but we also **pass** everything else, since everything else is permissible.

Director in general behaves like this. Another example is with mouse click interactions. If a sprite in channel 20 has a **mouseUp** script attached to it, and it's on top of a sprite in channel 5, which also has a **mouseUp** script, only the one for sprite 20 will execute. Channel 5 will behave as though it never was clicked. This is true, by the way, even if you explicitly **pass** the mouse event. Mouse clicks do not pass like key events do, at least not on the sprite level when the sprite in question has a behavior attached to it.

There are also hierarchies that are followed for event scripts. For instance, we saw in Module 9 that **beginSprite** calls in frame 1 took place before **startMovie**, and in fact, the Director documentation does speak of

Ask the Expert

Question   So if I do want to pass mouse clicks down a stack of sprites, how do I do that?

Answer   Attach a behavior to each sprite that tests for the intersect of sprites beneath it and deliberately sends a **mouseUp** event, perhaps something like this:

```
on mouseUp me

 nSprite = (me.spriteNum) - 1
 rMyRect = sprite(me.spriteNum).rect
 rPseudoRect = rect ( the mouseH, the mouseV, the mouseH + 1, the mouseV + 1
)

 repeat with nTest = nSprite down to 1

  rTestRect = sprite(nSprite).rect

  if intersect ( rMyRect, rTestRect ) <> rect ( 0, 0, 0, 0 ) then

   if intersect ( rTestRect, rPseudoRect ) <> rect ( 0, 0, 0, 0 ) then

    sendSprite ( nSprite, #mouseUp )
    exit repeat

   end if

  end if

 end repeat

END mouseUp
```

Aren't you glad you asked? All this actually does is determine whether the user's click happened inside the boundary of a sprite, which happens to be beneath the current one; if so, a **mouseUp** is passed to that hidden sprite.

13

hierarchies in general. For the Director 8 and 8.5 printed material, the relevant page is 190 of the *Using Director* book. Here's the basic flow of messages that occurs when a movie first runs:

● **prepareMovie**

● **beginSprite** (If there is a sprite in frame 1! If not, this is skipped. It always begins with the lowest-numbered sprite.)

● **prepareFrame** (Again, if there is anything in frame 1, and again, starting from the lowest-numbered sprite.)

● **startMovie**

So, as you can see here, **startMovie** has a rather unfortunate name! Frame events follow this flow:

● **beginSprite** (If new sprites begin in this frame; the lowest-numbered sprite always goes first, as you know.)

● **stepFrame** (This allows parent scripts to handle frame events.)

● **prepareFrame** (Again, lowest-numbered sprite first.)

● **enterFrame** (Right after an **enterFrame**, Director reacts to key and mouse events.)

● **exitFrame**

● **endSprite** (Which happens when a sprite is no longer being displayed, lowest-numbered sprite first, of course.)

Ask the Expert

Question   So why is it called startMovie?

Answer   Legacy. Many, many movies were written in Director long before there was anything like a **beginSprite** call, or even a **prepareMovie** call. Back then, **startMovie** was it, the first moment in a Director movie's life.

So, in the interest of not breaking older Lingo, **startMovie** has never been renamed. Besides, what would you call it? **movieLoaded**? **movieReadyToPlay**?

Finally, you get these two events when a movie stops playing:

- **exitFrame**

- **stopMovie**

Why this matters is simply that you can use this knowledge to do some nice things with code, particularly with **prepareFrame**. You can, for instance, cause a sprite to resize *before* it becomes visible on the Stage, so there's no visual jump effect when it first appears. But it's also important to know this stuff for reasons of variable handling and general movie interaction (again, as we saw in Module 9).

As for mouse clicks and keypresses in general, they are not handled by sprite behaviors first necessarily. If you have activated a key or mouse script for the movie, it'll be detected by that before it reaches anything on the Stage; that is, mouse and key scripts for movies are handled before sprite mouse and key scripts.

As an example, try this in your sprite click test movie:

```
on startMovie

 the mouseUpScript = "PutMessage"

END startMovie



on PutMessage

 put "movie got the click"

END PutMessage
```

No matter where you click, you'll see that the **PutMessage** handler runs before anything else. The same is true for keypresses; you can set **the keyDownScript** in a similar fashion.

You will also see that the mouse click is passed to anything else; you can *block* it by including a **dontPassEvent** call in your **PutMessage** handler. This will completely block all mouse clicks anywhere in your movie. (And, again, the **dontPassEvent** block applies to keypress actions, as well.)

13

Note

You can do the same for the **mouseDownScript** and the **keyUpScript**, which can give you some nice movie-level interaction detection if you need it.

Now that you have a better idea regarding how Director shoots messages around inside itself, let's get on with our project for this module. I think you're really going to like it.

1-Minute Drill

● Place the following events in their correct order as Director responds to them: **startMovie**, **enterFrame**, **beginSprite**, **stopMovie**, **exitFrame**

Project 13-1: Out of Sorts

We're going to make a program in this module that we'll keep working with and refining for the rest of this book, and it's a program that many people can see the usefulness of almost immediately.

The goals of this project include the following:

● Gaining a working knowledge of the object-oriented nature of sprite behaviors

● Understanding how to use behaviors to set specific parameters for any sprite

● Putting these understandings to use in a real-world program made using Director

Step-by-Step

1. You might want to connect to the Internet before you go any further, because I've put a Director movie online for you to download. It's the bare-bones template for the movie we're going to make. You don't *have* to take this step, but if you don't, you'll need to make some graphics of your own, specifically those for folders and a Trash icon.

To get to the file, fire up Director and enter the following in the Message window:

```
goToNetMovie ("http://www.nightwares.com/Director_beginners_
guide/13/tk.dir" )
```

● **beginSprite**, **enterFrame** (assuming a sprite in frame 1), **startMovie**, **exitFrame**, **stopMovie**

Once the movie has loaded, save it someplace on your own system. It is simply a bunch of sprites and some Cast members, with just a **go the frame** script for code. You're going to be programming the rest.

If you don't want to retrieve the bare-bones movie from the Net, set up your Stage so that it resembles the one shown in Figure 13-1.

What we have here is the basic set of interface controls for a really, really useful little program that, when it's done, will let you preview images on your hard drive and sort them into different folders.

This concept is not unique, and you can probably see the value of it. Suppose you have lots of pictures that have been sent to you by your far-flung family, and you want to try to catalog them in some fashion or another. Or perhaps you have a collection of clip art that you want to sort. Or maybe you're downloading, ahem, adult materials and want to categorize the images. It doesn't really matter what you might need such a tool for; the fact is that pretty much every computer user, at some point in his or her interaction with the machine, wishes for a program that makes it easier to sort images.

Of course, the fact that a lot of images are given really arcane names by their creators or distributors, such as media-0003-20010910.jpg, doesn't help you in any way at all. The name has no meaning to you, a real-world person.

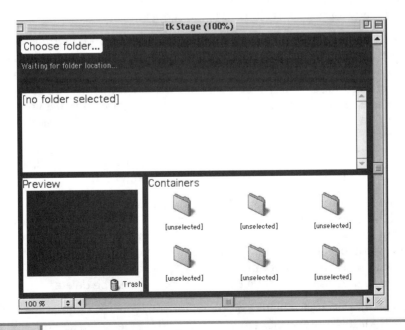

Figure 13-1   The basic Stage setup for our new project

13

So how can you easily know what's in the image, and then put it someplace that makes sense to you?

You need some kind of media processing program to even see what the image is; and you then need a way to drop the image someplace you want it. Well, there are *image cataloging* programs that let you see thumbnails of images, but most of them don't let you *move* an image you're previewing anyplace. You need to get to your computer's desktop to do that. And those few that *do* let you assign target folders for moving images into generally want you to have to select items from menus or go through multiple series of mouse clicks *for every image you want to move.*

Wouldn't it be a lot more convenient to simply be able to preview an image and drag and drop it into a container without having to switch programs, press keys, or do anything else? Of course it would, and that's what we're going to build.

2. Before you go on, locate the FileXtra3 Xtra on your Director installer CD. It should be inside a folder called Xtra Partners. If you can't locate it, you'll need to download it from the programmer's site at **www.kblab.net/xtras/**. You must have the FileXtra external code object to proceed.

Once you have FileXtra3, drop it into the Xtras folder alongside your main Director 8.5 program. Next time you run Director, FileXtra3 will be available and ready for you to use in your Lingo scripts.

FileXtra is an extremely handy, platform-independent Xtra written by Kent Kersten. Kent decided some time ago to make FileXtra freely available to anyone who wanted to use it, and over the years has added some really spectacular functionality to it. There are lots of commands you can use in the latest version; if you've looked at the documentation that came with the Xtra, you'll have a real sense for the kind of extensibility it adds to your Director movies.

You should also note that FileXtra is *not* Shockwave-safe; after all, it's capable of doing some pretty powerful things to a user's system.

3. Now let's consider the goals for our program. We want the user to be able to tell the program to get a list of image files from any particular folder. We then want the program to be able to display little thumbnails of those images. We also want to let the user move those images into other category folders without having to leave our program to do it. And we also want to let the user move a file to the Trash or Recycle Bin, from which it may be deleted.

If you look at the file blank I prepared for you, you can see that the bare tools for this functionality are all in place. This at least makes your task a little easier. But none of the code has been written yet, so while the sprites and Cast are all there, you're going to have to do some programming on your own.

In looking at the layout itself, we want to start by choosing the folder that contains the images to be sorted. You *could* have the user select a folder with FileIO, but Kent's FileXtra utility allows you to put up a dialog box that prompts the user to select a specific *folder*, rather than files *in* the folder. So we're going to use FileXtra for that.

Additionally, we want the user to be able to move images around on her drive, and that is another function built into FileXtra; so we'll use it for that, too.

Because we're going to be using FileXtra in two different contexts, it makes the most sense to instantiate it as a global object, rather than as a property associated with any specific sprite. In this way, any control that needs to use the Xtra can simply grab it, and do so without having to create its own instance.

4. We need a movie script to handle FileXtra and the other things we have to do here, so open a new movie script window and enter the following:

```
GLOBAL goFileXtraObject



on startMovie

  if not ( objectP ( goFileXtraObject ) ) then

   goFileXtraObject = new ( xtra "filextra3" )

  end if

  member("info").text = "Waiting for folder location..."


END startMovie



on stopMovie

  goFileXtraObject = 0


END stopMovie
```

As you can see, we start by declaring a global object container, **goFileXtraObject**. In our **startMovie**, we do the following with it:

if not (objectP (goFileXtraObject)) then

objectP is a test like **voidP**. What we're doing here is determining whether the FileXtra Xtra has been loaded into the variable object container we've made for it. If it has been loaded, **objectP** will return true. Otherwise, it'll be false, so we go ahead and instantiate the Xtra as an object with the next line of code:

goFileXtraObject = new (xtra "filextra3")

Tip

If Kent has released a version 4 of FileXtra by the time you're reading this and you have downloaded it from his Web site, the Xtra name will probably be FileXtra4 rather than FileXtra3, as used here, so look over his documentation if you get an "Xtra not found" script error.

Then we put some prompt text into the "info" #field we have on the Stage, to prompt the user that he's expected to do something.

Finally, in the **stopMovie** handler, we zero the FileXtra object reference, since it's always good programming practice to do so.

1-Minute Drill

● What do **objectP** and **voidP** do?

5. Now that we have the basic FileXtra object instantiated, we need to do something about letting the user choose a folder to browse. This is where the Choose folder... button comes into play. Attach this behavior to it:

```
GLOBAL goFileXtraObject



on mouseUp me


 member("info").text = "Select the folder containing the files you
want to
organize..."
```

● They determine, respectively, whether a given variable contains an object instance, and whether a given variable has had any value set in it yet.

```
updateStage

sTarget = goFileXtraObject.fx_FolderSelectDialog( "" )

if sTarget <> "" then

 LoadFiles( sTarget )

end if


END mouseUp
```

The first few lines are hardly mysterious. We reference the global object we instantiated in our **startMovie** handler, and then, on **mouseUp**, put some prompt text into the "info" #field on the Stage.

Note

updateStage is there to force Director to refresh the screen. If we didn't do the **updateStage** here, the prompt text would not appear when the Folder Selection dialog box became visible.

Next, we have this rather funny-looking line:

sTarget = goFileXtraObject.fx_FolderSelectDialog("")

This really isn't that different, though, from what you've done so far both with Xtras like FileIO and with your own handmade code objects. This sends the command **fx_FolderSelectDialog** to the FileXtra object container, and places the results of that command into the variable **sTarget**. That might remind you of the way you got the path to a text file back in Module 10, and the principle is the same.

Note

We also pass an empty string to the FileXtra object as a parameter to the **fx_FolderSelectDialog** command, because this particular command is expecting something. On Mac, it's expecting a start target location, but on Windows, it's expecting a *title* for the Folder Selection dialog box. Since we don't really know where to start looking, and since there's no real reason to put in a title, and *especially* since the content being expected by the **fx_FolderSelectDialog** command is different on Mac than it is on Windows, we simply pass "" to it.

13

Next, we test to see if **sTarget** is empty. If it is, the user has clicked the Cancel button in the dialog box. Otherwise, the user picked a folder, and we're ready to start processing the list of files in that folder, looking for images.

Or are we? If you try running the program now, you'll get a "handler not defined" error for **LoadFiles**. You can guess what that means.

6. We need to make the **LoadFiles()** handler in our movie script, and it's a real doozy:

```
on LoadFiles sPath


  lFileList = goFileXtraObject.fx_FolderToList( sPath )
  lFileList.sort()
  nAllFiles = lFileList.count()
  sMasterList = ""

  member("info").text = "There are" && string ( nAllFiles ) && "files in
  folder" && sPath & "."
  updateStage

  repeat with nFile = 1 to nAllFiles

   sFileName = lFileList[nFile]
   sFullPath = sPath & sFileName

   sFileType = goFileXtraObject.fx_FileGetType( sFullPath )

   if sFileType starts "JPEG" or sFileType = ".jpeg" or sFileType = ".jpe" or
  sFileType = ".jpg" or sFileType starts "GIF" or sFileType = ".gif" or
  sFileType starts "BMP" or sFileType = ".bmp" or sFileType starts "PNG" or
  sFileType = ".png" or sFileType starts "TIFF" or sFileType = ".tiff" or
  sFileType = ".tif" or sFileType starts "PICT" or sFileType = ".pict" or
  sFileType = ".pic" then

    put sFileName & RETURN after sMasterList

   end if

  end repeat

  delete the last line of sMasterList

  if sMasterList <> "" then

   nFilesRecognized = the number of lines in sMasterList

  else

   nFilesRecognized = "None"

  end if

  member("info").text = "There are" && string ( nAllFiles ) && "files in
```

```
folder" && sPath & "." && string ( nFilesRecognized ) && "were of a
recognizable type."

  sendSprite ( 11, #ReceiveListAndPath, sMasterList, sPath )


END LoadFiles
```

Actually, this is another one that only *looks* complicated, largely because of all those **sFileType** tests. We start by issuing this command to our FileXtra object, using the parameter **sPath** as passed in from the Choose folder… button behavior:

lFileList = goFileXtraObject.fx_FolderToList(sPath)

This tells FileXtra to get all the files contained in the folder located at **sPath**, and put those files' names into a list container, **lFileList**. You may recall that we did something like this internally with Lingo back in Module 3. This method uses FileXtra rather than internal Lingo calls, and also has the advantage of working much faster.

What we end up with, then, is a list containing the names of all the files in the folder the user chose.

lFileList.sort()

This sorts the file list, so we present the user with a nice end result. This is necessary because Windows defaults its sort order in any folder, when a list view is asked for, based on the time when a file was created or added to the folder. So, by sorting our list, we convert it to alphabetical order, with numbers first.

nAllFiles = lFileList.count()

Here we're just getting the number of files that are contained in our **lFileList** variable. We'll need that information in a few moments.

sMasterList = ""

This will eventually be the sorted final output from this handler.

member("info").text = "There are" && string (nAllFiles) && "files in folder" && sPath & "."

updateStage

Here we're just telling the user how many files total were found in the folder she picked.

13

Then we go into our repeat loop, counting from 1 to the total number of files in the folder the user chose.

sFileName = lFileList[nFile]

This is simply getting the name of the file located in position **nFile** of **lFileList**, and putting it into the container **sFileName**.

sFullPath = sPath & sFileName

This is the full path to the file we're looking at right now, meaning we're pointing to this one specific file inside the folder the user picked.

sFileType = goFileXtraObject.fx_FileGetType(sFullPath)

Here, again, we're placing a call to Kent's FileXtra. Now we're asking it to tell us what *type* of file it is that we're looking at.

We do this because we only want to process and handle *image* files. So we need to determine whether a given file is in fact an image file or is something else, such as a Web page document, word processor file, and so on.

if sFileType starts "JPEG" or sFileType = ".jpeg" or sFileType = ".jpe" or sFileType = ".jpg" or sFileType starts "GIF" or sFileType = ".gif" or sFileType starts "BMP" or sFileType = ".bmp" or sFileType starts "PNG" or sFileType = ".png" or sFileType starts "TIFF" or sFileType = ".tiff" or sFileType = ".tif" or sFileType starts "PICT" or sFileType = ".pict" or sFileType = ".pic" then

Ouch. Now that we got **sFileType** from FileXtra, here we're testing it to see if it's of a known image type that we can handle. We are testing for file types that are recognizable on either Mac or Windows.

Let's look at one possible return for **sFileType**; perhaps that will make it more clear. Suppose the file in question is a JPEG resident on a Mac. If it is, **sFileType** will be "JPEG", which means that it's a kind we recognize.

If the file, on the other hand, is sitting on a Windows system, it will have, as its extension, either .jpeg, .jpe, or .jpg. Whichever extension it has, this will be passed along as the **sFileType** variable. So, no matter what kind we get here, we know that we're looking at a JPEG file, and that is one of the types we can recognize. We continue testing for other types in a similar fashion, including GIFs, bitmaps, PNGs, TIFFs, and PICTs. All of these image types we recognize and can handle properly in our program, so if a given file is any of these types, we do the next line of Lingo:

put sFileName & RETURN after sMasterList

In other words, if the file is a type we recognize, we add it to our output list, followed by a RETURN character.

Then we're done testing this file, and eventually we're done with the repeat loop, since we've come to the end of the list. So, we go on to the following line:

delete the last line of sMasterList

Hmm, that seems odd. If we delete the last line of the list of files we recognize, won't we be short one filename?

Actually no, because as you saw from our repeat loop, we put the filename *and* a RETURN character into the list. This means that the last line of the list will *always* be an empty line, because we always put a RETURN after each filename. (That's so our final image list looks like a list, one filename per line, rather than something all run together into one single line of text.)

if sMasterList <> "" then

nFilesRecognized = the number of lines in sMasterList

else

nFilesRecognized = "None"

end if

Here we just see if there's anything in **sMasterList** (which, you'll remember, we set to empty before we began this repeat loop). If so, we get **the number of lines** in the variable and put them into **nFilesRecognized**. Otherwise, we didn't recognize any, so we put "None" into **nFilesRecognized** instead.

Note

I cheated a little here; **nFilesRecognized** implies the variable should contain an *integer*, but you can see that I might also put text into it. In general, that's not a hot plan, but we can get away with it just this once.

member("info").text = "There are" && string (nAllFiles) && "files in folder" && sPath & "." && string (nFilesRecognized) && "were of a recognizable type."

Here we tell the user how many files were actually in the folder she selected and, of those files, how many were of an image type we could understand. We're going to ignore the files we can't recognize, because there's no ready way for us to know exactly what to do with them anyway.

13

Our LoadFiles handler then concludes with:

sendSprite (11, #ReceiveListAndPath, sMasterList, sPath)

Aha, another **sendSprite**, passing along the file list we just made, as well as the folder path from which it comes, this time to sprite 11, which happens to be the large scrolling #field that dominates the middle of the Stage. Another behavior that's not entered yet, this will tell our program to display the file list we just finished processing.

7. So on to the behavior for sprite 11, the scrolling #field sprite:

```
PROPERTY psFilePath, psFileList



on beginSprite me

 psFileList = "[no folder selected]"
 sprite(me.spriteNum).member.text = psFileList
 psFilePath = ""


END beginSprite



on ReceiveListAndPath me, sMasterList, sPath

 psFilePath = sPath
 psFileList = sMasterList
 sprite(me.spriteNum).member.text = psFileList


END ReceiveListAndPath
```

Here we start by preparing some initial property variables, **psFileList** and **psFilePath**. Here we also put some text into the #field to indicate that, when the program first loads, no folder has been chosen yet.

Then we have the actual **ReceiveListAndPath** handler, which takes the parameters we've passed from **LoadFiles** in our movie script and plugs them into a folder path and master list variable, respectively. We then put the file list into our #field.

Now you're ready to see the basic program in action. Click Play, and then click the Choose folder… button and select a folder somewhere on your drive that contains images. If all goes well, your movie will load the files it recognizes into your scrolling #field, and you'll end up with something that looks more or less like Figure 13-2.

That's the first part for this program. Now that the program recognizes image files and loads their names into a list from any folder the user chooses, we need to go on to the image processing part of the code. After all, seeing a list of files in this movie is no more useful than seeing a list of them on your computer's desktop. Your users will want to get a thumbnail view of any file in the list.

8. In this movie, sprite 30 is the black rectangular shape in the lower-left corner of the Stage. This shape is a placeholder; we're going to use it to display a thumbnail preview of any image the user clicks in the scrolling #field. To do that, we have to resize the sprite, because most images are going to be pretty big. Bigger, in fact, than the Stage we're using for our movie. Furthermore, the resized sprite will have to be *proportional*. If the full-sized image is higher than it is wide, its thumbnail will have to maintain the same proportions.

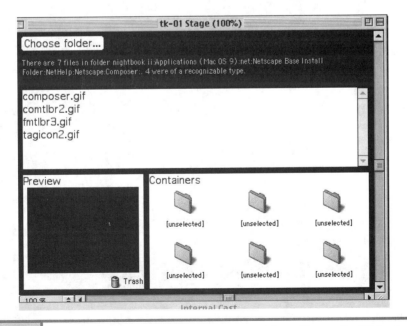

Figure 13-2   The movie has successfully recognized four files in the folder I picked

13

This is why the behavior that we attach to sprite 30 has some more fun math in it. We're defining a handler that isn't yet being called; all it does is calculate the correct thumbnail dimensions:

```
on ReceivePreview me


  member(50).regPoint = point ( 0, 0 )
  sprite(me.spriteNum).member = member(50)
  rBaseRect = member(50).rect

  fCurrentWidth = float ( rBaseRect.width )
  fCurrentHeight = float ( rBaseRect.height )

  if fCurrentWidth > 160.0 or fCurrentHeight > 120.0 then

   if rBaseRect.width > rBaseRect.height then

    fTargetWidth = 160.0
    fPercentResize = fTargetWidth / fCurrentWidth
    fTargetHeight = fCurrentHeight * fPercentResize

   else

    fTargetHeight = 120.0
    fPercentResize = fTargetHeight / fCurrentHeight
    fTargetWidth = fCurrentWidth * fPercentResize

   end if

  else

   fTargetWidth = fCurrentWidth
   fTargetHeight = fCurrentHeight

  end if

  sprite(me.spriteNum).width = integer ( fTargetWidth )
  sprite(me.spriteNum).height = integer ( fTargetHeight )


end
```

We start by setting the **regPoint** of Cast member 50 to the upper-left corner of the image, because we'll soon be using member 50 as the temporary Cast member into which we'll pull the images the user clicks. We do this so the member will align correctly when we execute the next line, which switches out the rectangle with the image in Cast position 50. From there, we go on to get the rectangular dimensions of the image itself, and then it gets a little intense.

fCurrentWidth = float (rBaseRect.width)

fCurrentHeight = float (rBaseRect.height)

These are floating-point values, decimals that store the width and height of the image as it appears full-size.

if fCurrentWidth > 160.0 or fCurrentHeight > 120.0 then

…then the image is wider than our maximum desired thumbnail value (160 pixels) or higher than our desired max of 120, and we need to figure out how to proportionally resize it.

if rBaseRect.width > rBaseRect.height then

…then the image is wider than it is high, and we start our resize operation by figuring out how much of a reduction it is to take it from its current width down to 160 pixels:

fTargetWidth = 160.0

fPercentResize = fTargetWidth / fCurrentWidth

This gives us a number less than one, which represents the percentage reduction we've calculated. We then multiply the current height of the image by that value in order to shrink it vertically to the same proportion we used to reduce its width:

fTargetHeight = fCurrentHeight * fPercentResize

Otherwise, the image is higher than it is wide, so we need to do similar calculations to first reduce its height to 120 pixels and then determine what percentage that was and reduce its width by the same amount:

fTargetHeight = 120.0

fPercentResize = fTargetHeight / fCurrentHeight

fTargetWidth = fCurrentWidth * fPercentResize

However, if the current width and height are not outside of our desired boundaries, we don't want to resize the image at all, because it's already small enough:

else

fTargetWidth = fCurrentWidth

fTargetHeight = fCurrentHeight

13

That done, we set the sprite's dimensions onscreen to the values we calculated (passing them through an **integer** filter in the process, since the dimensions are in pixels, which can only be whole-number values).

9. Now we just need to get an actual image into Cast position 50. Start by creating another placeholder Cast member. A shape is fine for this; it doesn't matter. Put it in Cast position 50 by dragging it there.

╀ *Tip*

Now you see why having your Cast view set to thumbnail rather than list can be useful.

10. Modify your scrolling #field behavior to include the right commands to make the image work by adding a **mouseUp** handler:

```
on mouseUp me

  nLine = the mouseLine

  if psFileList.line[nLine] = "[no folder selected]" then

    exit

  end if

  sprite(me.spriteNum).member.line[nLine].hilite()
  sFileName = psFileList.line[nLine]

  member(50).fileName = ( psFilePath & sFileName )
  sendSprite ( 30, #ReceivePreview )


END mouseUp
```

This contains commands you've seen before. In fact, it's *all* Lingo you've seen before. It just determines which line the user clicked, then loads that image file into Cast member 50. If the text list is simply [no folder selected], then we know the user hasn't yet chosen any folder with images in it, so we kick out.

11. Try it. Click Play and browse some images. If it's working correctly, you should see something like Figure 13-3.

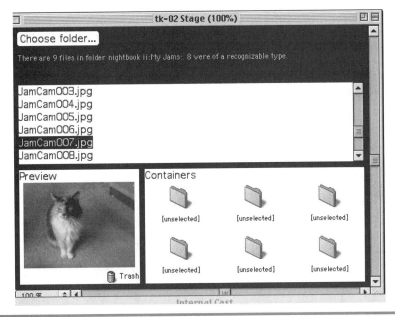

Figure 13-3   The thumbnail is loading correctly; the image I chose from the scrolling list was originally 640×480 pixels in size

1-Minute Drill

● What is the difference between integer and float?

● If you want to convert a floating-point number to an integer, how do you do it in Lingo?

12. Now we need to do something about those folders. They're supposed to allow us to sort images into different containers, and we still haven't activated the Trash icon either.

The folder scripts will have to interact with the image thumbnail, by the way, to let the user know whether the drag action he's attempting is allowable. For instance, if a container folder has not yet had a "real" folder on the user's system associated with it, we have to forbid the drag. (How can you drag an image into no location? That's practically a Zen riddle, isn't it?)

13

● An integer number has no decimal; a float is a floating-point, or decimal, number.
● **intResult = integer (floatNumber)**

Our folders will also interact with the label #field sprites that exist in the channels above them, so the user can have a visual reminder of what each container folder is associated with on his machine.

Let's do the folder behavior first. This same behavior can be attached to all six folder sprites.

```
GLOBAL goFileXtraObject


on mouseEnter me

  sprite(me.spriteNum).member = member("activeFolder")

END mouseEnter



on mouseWithin me

  sprite(me.spriteNum).member = member("activeFolder")

end



on mouseLeave me

  sprite(me.spriteNum).member = member("inactiveFolder")

END mouseLeave



on mouseUp me

  sPath = sendSprite ( (me.spriteNum) + 1, #ReturnPath )

  if sPath = "" or ( the doubleClick ) then

    sBackupPath = sPath
    sPath = ChooseFolderPath()

    if sPath = "" then
```

```
   sPath = sBackupPath

  end if

  sendSprite ( (me.spriteNum) + 1, #AcceptPath, sPath )

 end if


END mouseUp



on CheckFileDrop me

 rPseudoRect = rect ( the mouseH, the mouseV, the mouseH + 1, the mouseV + 1
)

 if intersect ( sprite(me.spriteNum).rect, rPseudoRect ) <> rect ( 0, 0, 0,
0 ) then

  sTarget = sendSprite ( (me.spriteNum) + 1, #ReturnPath )

  if sTarget <> "" then

   lOriginal = sendSprite ( 11, #ReturnItemToMove )
   sSourceLoc = lOriginal[1] & lOriginal[2]
   sDestLoc = sTarget & lOriginal[2]

   bWorked = goFileXtraObject.fx_FileMove( sSourceLoc, sDestLoc )

   if bWorked then

    member("info").text = "The file has been moved to" && sTarget & "."
    sendSprite ( 30, #FileMoved )

   else

    member("info").text = "An error occurred while trying to move the file
to the container folder. Please ensure the source and destination items are
not read-only and that there's room on the destination volume."
    sendSprite ( 30, #ReturnImage )

   end if

  end if

 else

  sendSprite ( 30, #ReturnImage )

 end if

END CheckFileDrop
```

13

Oh man, this is a little hairy, isn't it? The **mouseEnter**, **mouseWithin**, and **mouseLeave** events just switch out the folder sprites to give the user the feeling that the program is paying attention; where it gets a little sticky is with **mouseUp**.

sPath = sendSprite ((me.spriteNum) + 1, #ReturnPath)

This is a call to the sprite right above any one folder, or the #field sprites that appear with each folder. Those sprites don't yet have behaviors on them, though. What it's asking for is a text variable.

if sPath = "" or (the doubleClick) then

Here we're seeing if **sPath** is empty. If it is, it's because this folder sprite doesn't yet have a folder on the hard drive associated with it. But we also check for **the doubleClick**. We do this because the user may have already assigned a folder target to this sprite, and may want to pick a different one. He can do that by double-clicking, which will cause the folder selection dialog box to come up.

sBackupPath = sPath

If the user already assigned a path to this folder and has double-clicked, we put the current path into a backup variable. That way, if the user clicks Cancel in the Folder Selection dialog box, we can still have this container associated with its original folder on the drive.

sPath = ChooseFolderPath()

This is a call to a movie script handler that doesn't exist yet. It gets the folder path the user wants to associate with this folder sprite and puts it into the **sPath** variable.

if sPath = "" then

sPath = sBackupPath

end if

If the user clicked Cancel, **sPath** will be empty. We then restore the old path, which might or might not *also* be empty. Presumably, the behavior being called in the next line of Lingo will be smart enough to know what to do with an empty path.

sendSprite ((me.spriteNum) + 1, #AcceptPath, sPath)

That's the **mouseUp** portion; now on to the custom behavior **CheckFileDrop**. The purpose of that behavior is to determine if the thumbnail image is over any given folder when it's released (as you can surmise, we're going to make the thumbnail draggable soon).

rPseudoRect = rect (the mouseH, the mouseV, the mouseH + 1, the mouseV + 1)

We have to make a pseudorectangle of the point in space that the mouse is over so we can do our intersect test, which, as you recall, determines if one rectangle is touching another. We make our pseudorectangle only one pixel wide and one pixel high.

In this case, we're determining if the mouse happens to be occupying a location in space over a given folder.

if intersect (sprite(me.spriteNum).rect, rPseudoRect) <> rect (0, 0, 0, 0) then

…then the mouse is over this behavior's folder sprite, so we see whether or not there's a folder on the hard drive already associated with this sprite.

sTarget = sendSprite ((me.spriteNum) + 1, #ReturnPath)

We have to do it this way because behaviors do not pass mouse events. If it were possible for lower-level sprites to get mouse events even when an upper-level sprite has a mouse behavior attached to it, this extra math would not be necessary.

if sTarget <> "" then

lOriginal = sendSprite (11, #ReturnItemToMove)

Here we're asking our scrolling #field something, specifically the original path and name of the item the user selected by clicking it. Again, this is a behavior we haven't written yet.

sSourceLoc = lOriginal[1] & lOriginal[2]

We construct the source path and filename using items 1 and 2 from the list returned by sprite 11's behavior.

sDestLoc = sTarget & lOriginal[2]

We then construct the target path and filename based on which folder on the drive this sprite is associated with.

13

bWorked = goFileXtraObject.fx_FileMove(sSourceLoc, sDestLoc)

We then make another call to our trusty FileXtra object, telling it to move a file from one location to another, and return the success of the result. If the file was moved successfully, this will return true; otherwise, it will be false. Whether it worked or not, we should tell the user what happened.

if bWorked then

member("info").text = "The file has been moved to" && sTarget & "."

sendSprite (30, #FileMoved)

else

member("info").text = "An error occurred while trying to move the file to the container folder. Please ensure the source and destination items are not read-only and that there's room on the destination volume."

sendSprite (30, #ReturnImage)

end if

We're also sending some calls to our image sprite behavior, more calls that don't yet exist.

Finally, if the path associated with this folder is empty, we need to tell sprite 30 to put the image back where it came from on the screen.

sendSprite (30, #ReturnImage)

1-Minute Drill

● What does **the doubleClick** do?

● Why do you think we have to create a pseudorectangle to determine if the mouse is located over some other sprite?

13. Going in the order of new handlers as entered in our folder behavior, we'll start by making the one for the label #field sprites that are associated with each folder.

```
PROPERTY psMyPath
```

● It returns true if the user has double-clicked the mouse; otherwise, it returns false.
● Because you can't test the intersect on a rectangle that has no width or height, and because there's no ready way otherwise to see if the mouse is within any other sprite apart from the topmost one, since **mouseUp** doesn't pass.

```
on beginSprite me

 sprite(me.spriteNum).member.text = "[unselected]"
 psMyPath = ""

END beginSprite



on ReturnPath me

 return psMyPath

END ReturnPath



on AcceptPath me, sPath

 sDelimSave = the itemDelimiter
 if the platform contains "mac" then
  the itemDelimiter = ":"
 else
  the itemDelimiter = "\"
 end if
 psMyPath = sPath
 if psMyPath = "" then
  me.beginSprite()
 else
```

```
  if the last char of sPath = the itemDelimiter then

    delete the last char of sPath

  end if

  sprite(me.spriteNum).member.text = the last item of sPath

 end if

 the itemDelimiter = sDelimSave


END AcceptPath
```

This starts with the predictable instantiation routines. In fact, all of it makes sense except for some of the stuff in **AcceptPath**.

> **sDelimSave = the itemDelimiter**

the itemDelimiter is a special character that Lingo uses to count the items in a line of text. By default, it's a comma. So the text "first, second, third" would contain, according to Lingo, three items. You could then tell Director to get an item at a specific location in a text string, a lot like you can with list access:

```
sVar = "first, second, third"
put sVar.item[3]
-- " third"
```

Note the extra space at the beginning of the result. Director returns everything contained in a specific item as defined by **the itemDelimiter**.

Here we're putting the current **itemDelimiter** into a backup variable. We do this because it's not unusual to want to use the **itemDelimiter** a lot in code, and it never hurts to put the master one into some kind of backup from which it's restored when you're done with whatever it is you're doing with your own **itemDelimiter**. In that way, your Lingo, if it's being used by someone else, will not interfere with whatever operations that user's code might be performing with the **itemDelimiter**.

> **if the platform contains "mac" then**
>
> **the itemDelimiter = ":"**
>
> **else**

> **the itemDelimiter = "\"**
>
> **end if**

If we're on a Mac, we now set **the itemDelimiter** to be the same as the directory delimiter, which you'll recall is how you can tell, in any given path to a file, where the folder names begin and end. Otherwise, we do the same for the Windows directory delimiter. We do this because we want to get the last item from the variable **sPath**; this is the actual name of the folder the user chooses in the folder selection dialog box. It's also the text we want to put into our label #field sprites, so the user can see which folder on her drive is being pointed to by any one folder in our program.

> **psMyPath = sPath**

Now we plug the chosen path into our internal property variable.

> **if psMyPath = "" then**
>
> **me.beginSprite()**

We do this if the user has clicked Cancel in the folder selection dialog box, so we reset everything to empty and put the [unselected] label back into the #field. Otherwise, we need to determine if the last character in the **sPath** variable is the current **itemDelimiter**, or Director will assume the last item is an empty string. For instance:

```
sVar = "one, two,"
put the last item of sVar
-- ""
```

Oops, we don't want that. To prevent it from happening, we need to see if the last character in any string is the **itemDelimiter**; if it is, we need to remove that last character so Director knows where the *real* last item is.

> **if the last char of sPath = the itemDelimiter then**
>
> **delete the last char of sPath**
>
> **end if**

Then we just plug the last item into our #field, since that's the name of the folder the user picked from her hard drive:

> **sprite(me.spriteNum).member.text = the last item of sPath**

Finally, we restore **the itemDelimiter** to its original state:

> **the itemDelimiter = sDelimSave**

13

14. The next handler to create is **ChooseFolderPath**, which needs to be in the movie script. This is called by the folder sprite if there's no path currently associated with it, or if the user has double-clicked a folder that already has a path. This one is actually not too bad:

```
on ChooseFolderPath


 member("info").text = "Select the container folder you want to
associate..."
 updateStage
 sTarget = goFileXtraObject.fx_FolderSelectDialog( "" )
 member("info").text = " "
 return sTarget


END ChooseFolderPath
```

I don't think I need to tell you much about this one, since it's a lot like the basic code you used earlier to get the master folder list containing the images we're sorting.

15. Next in our self-imposed to-do list is the **ReturnItemToMove** behavior for sprite 11, our scrolling #field:

```
on ReturnItemToMove me


 sFileName = psFileList.line[pnItem]
 lOriginal = [ psFilePath, sFileName ]

 return lOriginal


END ReturnItemToMove
```

Uh-oh, we have a property variable here, **pnLine**, which hasn't been declared or set to a value. That'll cause a script error.

But not to worry. **pnItem** is actually the line that the user clicks in the scrolling #field sprite onscreen, so all you have to do is declare **pnItem** at the top of the scrolling #field behavior, then set its value to 1 in **beginSprite**, and remember to plug **the mouseLine** into it with your **mouseUp** script in the scrolling #field (changing the line **nLine = the mouseLine**) thus:

   pnLine = the mouseLine

From there, the handler gets the name of the file on the line the user clicked, and returns it, along with the master folder path, in a simple list container variable. That's the list variable that gets processed by the **CheckFileDrop** handler in the folder behavior to determine what the *name* is of the item to be moved, and the *location* from which it's being moved.

1-Minute Drill

● What is the **itemDelimiter**?

16. Finally, we need to add some more code to the image thumbnail behavior in sprite channel 30, to make it draggable and to let it send commands to the folders whenever the user releases the mouse button. We also need to add the **ReturnImage** and **FileMoved** handlers to that behavior.

Here's the modified code for making the thumbnail draggable. Enter all of it before the **ReceivePreview** handler in sprite 30's behavior:

```
PROPERTY ppOriginalLoc



on beginSprite me

 ppOriginalLoc = sprite(me.spriteNum).loc

END beginSprite



on mouseDown me

 if sprite(me.spriteNum).member <> member("rectangle") then

  repeat while the stillDown

   sprite(me.spriteNum).loc = the mouseLoc
   updateStage
```

13

● A special character Director uses to count the number of items in any text string. By default, it's a comma.

```
    end repeat

   end if


END mouseDown




on mouseUp me


  if sprite(me.spriteNum).member <> member("rectangle") then

    sendAllSprites ( #CheckFileDrop )

   end if


END mouseUp




on ReturnImage me


 sprite(me.spriteNum).loc = ppOriginalLoc


END ReturnImage




on FileMoved me


 me.ReturnImage()

 sprite(me.spriteNum).member = member("rectangle")
 sprite(me.spriteNum).width = 160
 sprite(me.spriteNum).height = 120
```

```
sendSprite ( 11, #ItemMoved )


END FileMoved
```

Some of this is just maintenance, such as getting the original location onscreen of the rectangle sprite in the **beginSprite** handler; some of it, though, is fairly interactive, starting with the **mouseDown** handler:

if sprite(me.spriteNum).member <> member("rectangle") then

…then the user has clicked an image thumbnail, so we make the sprite draggable. Otherwise, the user has clicked the black rectangle, which means there's no image to drag.

repeat while the stillDown

the stillDown returns true if the mouse button remains down. So, as long as the user holds the mouse button down, she's dragging the image someplace.

sprite(me.spriteNum).loc = the mouseLoc

updateStage

Here we move the image so it appears to be moving along with the mouse. This is, of course, to let the user have some visual feedback that we know she's doing the dragging, and to let her see which folder icon the image is being dragged to. We have to do an **updateStage**, by the way, to force Director to refresh the screen while the drag is happening. This is because we're moving the image along with the mouse pointer in a repeat loop, which ordinarily causes screen updates to stop happening.

Then, in the **mouseUp** handler, we first see if the event has happened in our black rectangle sprite. If it has not, it's happened in an image, and we send all the sprites on the Stage the command to determine if the mouse is over an active folder. That's the **CheckFileDrop** handler we put into the folder sprites' behavior.

Then we move on to **ReturnImage**, which simply causes the thumbnail image preview to return to its original location in the Preview rectangle space on the Stage. We do that when the user has not actually released the image over a sprite that will cause the image's file to be moved to a different location on the drive.

Finally, we have **FileMoved**, which is sent from the folder behavior once an image has been moved from one location to another. This restores sprite 30's graphic to the black rectangle, and sets its dimensions to 160×120 pixels.

13

But it also sends a new command to the scrolling #field, **ItemMoved**. We need to do this in order to tell the #field behavior to remove the image filename from its display list, since that file is no longer in the master folder; it has been moved to one of the containers.

```
on ItemMoved me

  delete line pnItem of psFileList

  if psFileList = "" then

    psFileList = "[no files in folder]"

  end if

  sprite(me.spriteNum).member.text = psFileList

  me.mouseUp ( pnItem )


END ItemMoved
```

Most of this is just fine, too, but there are a couple of worrisome parts that imply we need to change some other elements of code for this behavior. First is this line:

> **psFileList = "[no files in folder]"**

Well, if we put that line into our #field and the user ends up clicking it, we'll get a script error someplace, because there won't be a file on her drive named [no files in folder]. So, we need to change the **mouseUp** line that reads

> **if psFileList.line[nLine] = "[no folder selected]" then**

and allow it to test for another condition:

> **if psFileList.line[nLine] = "[no folder selected]" or**
> **psFileList.line[nLine] = "[no files in folder]" then**

But we also have the line at the end of **ItemMoved**:

> **me.mouseUp (pnItem)**

which, as you can guess from your experiences in Module 12, means we're going to have to change the beginning of the **mouseUp** handler in this behavior to allow for the passed parameter. This simply moves the highlight in the scrolling list to the next line, which, if it's an image, will cause a thumbnail to load. This makes the program a little more interactive and user-friendly, even if it *is* somewhat programmer-hostile.

17. The first few lines of **mouseUp** in the thumbnail image's behavior should now be as follows:

```
on mouseUp me, nLine

 if voidP ( nLine ) then

  pnItem = the mouseLine

 else

  pnItem = nLine

 end if
```

18. We're almost finished now. We just need to add the behavior to the Trash sprite. It's going to look an awful lot like the one for the folder icons, but it doesn't need all the testing, since it simply moves an image directly to the system's Trash or Recycle Bin:

```
GLOBAL goFileXtraObject


on mouseEnter me

 sprite(me.spriteNum).member = member("trashActive")

END mouseEnter


on mouseWithin me

 sprite(me.spriteNum).member = member("trashActive")
```

```
end


on mouseLeave me

 sprite(me.spriteNum).member = member("trashInactive")

END mouseLeave


on CheckFileDrop me

 rPseudoRect = rect ( the mouseH, the mouseV, the mouseH + 1, the mouseV + 1
)

 if intersect ( sprite(me.spriteNum).rect, rPseudoRect ) <> rect ( 0, 0, 0,
0 ) then

  lOriginal = sendSprite ( 11, #ReturnItemToMove )
  sSourceLoc = lOriginal[1] & lOriginal[2]

  bWorked = goFileXtraObject.fx_FileRecycle( sSourceLoc )

  if bWorked then

   if the platform contains "mac" then

    member("info").text = "The file has been moved to the Trash."

   else

    member("info").text = "The file has been moved to the Recycle Bin."

   end if

   sendSprite ( 30, #FileMoved )

  else

   if the platform contains "mac" then

    member("info").text = "An error occurred while trying to move the file
to the Trash. Please ensure the source item is not read-only."

   else
```

```
    member("info").text = "An error occurred while trying to move the file
to the Recycle Bin. Please ensure the source item is not read-only."

   end if

   sendSprite ( 30, #ReturnImage )

  end if

 else

  sendSprite ( 30, #ReturnImage )

 end if

END CheckFileDrop
```

The differences here are pretty minor. We're switching out Trash graphics on **mouseEnter**, **mouseWithin**, and **mouseLeave**; we're issuing a **FileRecycle** call to our FileXtra object; and, of course, we're giving some system-specific feedback when the operation completes successfully (or doesn't). But apart from those differences, this **CheckFileDrop** call is a lot like the ones the folders used.

Note we're also not asking whether there's a path associated with this particular icon, because we know there is; it's either the Trash (on Mac) or Recycle Bin (on Windows). We also don't bother with a folder selection dialog box on **mouseUp** here, since there's no folder to select for our Trash icon.

Guess what? We're done. Our image thumbnail and catalog program is ready for action! So go ahead and click Play, and then try it out yourself. Associate some folders with the container sprites, get yourself a master list, and start sorting!

Project Summary

With this monster, module-long project, you have

● Learned a little about an Xtra (FileXtra3) that permits you to do some really nice interaction with both the user and her computer

● Learned how to allow the natural object-oriented nature of sprite behaviors to work with you as you encapsulate specific operations

● Learned how to use Director's native image handling to produce a little program that does quite a lot

13

Before You Make That Projector...

You've just done something pretty powerful. You've created a Director movie that's got some genuine use to you and others, and you've done it all with a combination of judicious OOP code, file manipulation with a great Xtra product, and some planning and foresight. But you're not quite ready to roll it into a projector yet.

First, remember that when you get a thumbnail, you're setting the filename of Cast member 50 to that image. Well, you need to remove that bitmap from Cast 50 and replace it with a slug graphic, such as a shape, before you create a projector and begin giving copies of your program to all of your friends. Otherwise, the projector will want to know where the image file is that's supposed to be occupying member position 50 whenever it runs on someone else's machine.

The other thing you need to do is add some media support Xtras to the movie's Xtras list, or else it won't be able to handle most of the images users are likely to want to sort. So, select Modify | Movie | Xtras and add the following items to the current list in the Movie Xtras dialog box:

- Animated GIF Asset

- BMP Agent

- FileXtra3

- GIF Agent

- JPEG Agent

- PICT Agent

- PNG Import Export

- TIFF Import Export

Once you've done that, you're ready to rock and roll. Create your projector and try it out!

I named mine ThumbKnows, because I like the sound of that name. You can name yours anything you want, of course. It's your program, after all.

There are ways you can pretty up the interface for this program, too, to make it a little more friendly to users. I've done that myself; to see the changes I made, fire up Director and enter the following in the Message window:

```
goToNetMovie
http://www.nightwares.com/Director_beginners_guide/13/thumbknows.dir
```

Some of the Lingo you'll see contains keywords that will be new to you; some scripts hold more handlers for deciding how folders should behave; some involve changing the cursor's appearance on the screen; some involve changing the thumbnail's appearance; and some involve adding keyboard interaction as well. Get the file and check out the comments in the scripts for more information.

Summary

You got a whopping lot of code under your belt this time, and you've had some in-depth experience now with sending messages back and forth in code objects. You've seen that it's possible to really encapsulate pieces of your program code into logical divisions that handle their own tasks reliably, and that can be made to interact with each other whenever it's necessary to do so, but only in ways that don't cause problems for your program or for your program's user.

You've also learned that Director is a lot more than simply a program that lets you make games or animations; in fact, you can do some definitely useful things with it.

I suppose you might be wondering how any of this is relevant to designing games, if that is in fact what you have in mind for your future with Director. I'd reply that it's all relevant, because if you have a good working knowledge of how to create databases, put sprites on the screen, control their locations on the Stage, redimension them dynamically as needed, and interact with both the user and his system intelligently, you clearly have the technical expertise you need to create the next greatest thing since Tetris. After all, if you don't know how to control sprites or get them to communicate with each other, how can you make opponents for your users to face that actually shoot back? Or, more succinctly, a good game designer must first be a good software engineer.

In the next module, the penultimate one in this book, you'll expand this program further by creating a MIAW object that lets users batch rename files in folders, and another MIAW object that creates an HTML page containing an image thumbnail index that can be seen in any browser.

If you want to explore further, fire up Director and enter the following in the Message window:

```
goToNetMovie
http://www.nightwares.com/Director_beginners_guide/13/thumbknows.dir
```

13

Look through the more or less completed version I have online there. There are comments throughout the code, and you can use the Debugger to step through things you don't quite understand (as well as learn some more nifty tricks and a few Lingo keywords).

✔ Mastery Check

1. Place the following events in their correct order as Director responds to them:

   startMovie, enterFrame, beginSprite, stopMovie, exitFrame

2. If you want to determine whether a variable has been given a value, what keyword would you use?

   _____

   _____

3. How would you do the same thing for an object?

   _____

   _____

4. If you perform a math operation and get only integer numbers, what is one way you could force Director to work with decimals?

   _____

   _____

5. What happens when you pass a decimal number through the integer keyword?

   _____

   _____

6. How can you tell if a user has double-clicked an item in your Director movies?

   _____

   _____

Module 14

Movies in a Window (MIAW) as OOP Code

The Goals of this Module

- Learn the basics of working with Movies in a Window (MIAWs)
- Learn how to communicate with MIAWs
- Learn how to make modularity and encapsulation in MIAWs work to your advantage

Now you have a very good working knowledge of Director; so good, in fact, that you've been able to create a complete program that does something of genuine value, the kind of software that people go online to find and download, and are even willing to pay for. Our guided tour through Director's innards is almost complete. In this module, we'll discuss using external Director files to expand the capabilities of an already quite capable program by creating two satellite movies that can function either on their own as stand-alone programs or as extensions to the one you've already made.

MIAWs: Better than *Cats*

After the last monster module, you might be thinking you have a pretty good program going, and you're right. You might also think you have a good grasp of Director, and you're right about that, too. But before you go for the pebble in my hand, I have just a little more to tell you.

You may recall from Part 2 that you can take any stand-alone Director movie you make and drop it into Director's Xtras folder, and then select it from the Xtras menu in the Director program. The file you made will then appear on the screen, ready for you to use in your programming environment. I referred to this (in Module 6, when we made the *Keyster* program) as a MIAW Xtra, and by now, it'll be no surprise to you that your movies can call MIAWs on their own.

Why would you want to do this? There are actually multiple reasons; for instance, you might have an "info" window that you want to pop up from time to time to offer assistance or commentary on a program; or you might want to create a kind of navigation or control panel, perhaps containing a clickable table of contents; or you might want to ask the user for some more information about some choice without having to leave a primary program screen. Of course, those are just *some* examples; as you become more familiar with the concept of MIAWs, you will probably find yourself using them for lots of applications that I've not listed here, things no one has really thought of before. In that sense, a MIAW is a lot like the other subtle, powerful tools you've worked with so far, such as lists and object code. While the applications I've mentioned for each of these types of tool are all quite legitimate, there are literally hundreds, or perhaps even thousands, of other uses to which they can all be applied.

The beauty of doing this stuff in Director is that the engine itself takes care of a lot of the low-level work for you. If you wanted to create even a simple dialog box in a lower-level language, you'd have to write the code to define what buttons you wanted, where you wanted them, what their dimensions were to be, the fonts to use, and so on and so on, and even then you'd have to run it multiple times and tweak the code to finesse the look and feel. With Director, you write maybe three dozen lines of Lingo (assuming you're using the MUI Xtra) and test-fire the dialog box live; odds are you'll have to rework it only once, and you've spent 30 minutes doing what would take a day in other languages to get done.

So yes, Lingo can be abstruse, and it can be hard to learn how to think in terms of programming, but you're still getting a lot of help from the folks at Macromedia.

With this module, we'll explore more the idea of creating custom Director movies that let us do some useful things with image files, as we did in the last one. We're going to be building largely on the code we've already written, so you don't have to learn a whole lot of new things, but you're also going to be introduced to some keywords specific to MIAWs.

A MIAW is simply any given Director movie that has been loaded by another movie in a simultaneous session. To clarify, the second movie is not being loaded by the first via a **go to movie** call; it is loaded and running *at the same time* as the first, in a separate window that you can largely control the looks of, as an enhancement or extension of your main Director movie. It's taking the concept of a MIAW Xtra and extending it into the user environment, by creating something that can be accessed and used while your main movie is running in a projector.

Often, the main movie is referred to as the *parent* movie, while the second file being called as a MIAW is referred to as the *child* movie, or a child MIAW. This is reminiscent, of course, of parent scripts, which is probably how this nomenclature came to be.

14

Note

MIAWs do not work in Shockwave. Don't plan on making Shockwave files that use MIAW! There's not even a simple way to get two Shockwave movies to communicate with each other under normal circumstances, let alone have a parent movie call a child MIAW.

MIAWs were introduced with version 4 of Director, and at first it didn't seem to catch on, probably because most Director programmers were not used to the idea of thinking in these terms yet. Now it's hard for me personally to imagine how I'd be able to get anything done without MIAWs.

1-Minute Drill

● What is a MIAW?

● What are some uses for MIAWs?

Project 14-1: Getting Started with Renaming

We'll get rolling on this right away. We're going to add a function to the thumbnail sorting movie that lets it rename an entire folder full of images at one go, but we're not going to make any substantial changes to the thumbnail movie itself—because we're going to do it all in a MIAW instead.

The goals of this project are to do the following:

● Allow you to see how to make further use of an Xtra to perform more utility operations.

● Give you an opportunity to learn how to use MIAWs as additional or satellite objects within a program.

● Illustrate how MIAWs may be thought of as object-oriented artifacts, like parent scripts or sprite behaviors.

● A Director movie running in a window while another movie is playing.
● Information windows, control panels, pop-ups, dialog boxes, and more.

Step-by-Step

1. First, if you have not already done so, retrieve the "final" version of thumbknows.dir from the Web site I pointed you to in the last module. We're going to use it as the basis from which to build. Just save it to disk someplace.

2. Create a new Director file, with a Stage size of about 200 × 300, and save it alongside the one you downloaded. Name your new Director movie **renamer.dir**.

3. Put a **go the frame** script into frame 1 and save your movie.

4. Open the main thumbknows.dir file, because you're about to learn how easy it can be to load a MIAW.

There are two basic ways to load a MIAW; there's the one-liner, which simply requires one line of Lingo, and then there's the long way around, which sets some parameters before loading the MIAW. We'll do the one-liner first.

With the thumbknows.dir file open, enter the following in the Message window:

```
open window "renamer"
```

You should see something a little like Figure 14-1.

Ask the Expert

Question   Why don't I have to type "renamer.dir" instead?

Answer   Director automatically assumes, if you are using a **play movie**, **go to movie**, or **open window** call, that you are looking for some kind of Director file. However, when you "protect" a file, its extension is changed from .dir to .dxr. So, if you specified the extension as .dir, but were trying to open a file with a .dxr extension, you'd have problems. The folks at Macromedia made it easier for us by setting up Director so you don't have to enter the filename extension at all.

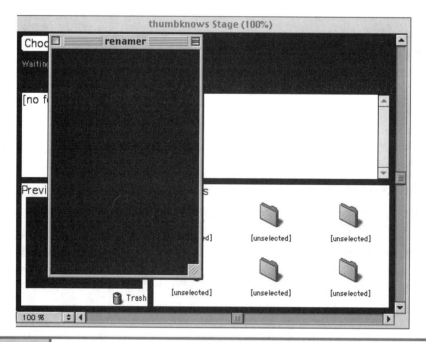

Figure 14-1   The quick and easy method of opening a MIAW also has its flaws

There. You just opened a MIAW. That's pretty easy, isn't it? But if you look carefully at the renamer child window, you'll see some problems with it. For starters, it has the word *renamer* as the title, which (while it is in fact the name of the movie) is not especially pleasing aesthetically. Also, there's a resize box on the lower right, meaning the MIAW could be resized up or down by anyone, even though there's no reason to let this happen.

That's why the one-liner isn't going to be adequate to meet our needs. And that's why we have some nice keywords to make use of with MIAWs— keywords that let us set things such as the title of the window, what kind of frame it has, and even its location as it appears on the monitor.

5. In general, setting up a MIAW is a lot like talking to other object code, as with Xtras or parent scripts. That makes the job a little easier. And you do perform some instantiation and destruction, so really the ideas here aren't going to be new, just some of the code.

Start by clicking the close box on the renamer MIAW, and then place a new button on your thumbnail movie's Stage. Label the button **Batch rename...**, and then attach this behavior to it:

```
PROPERTY pwMyFloater




on beginSprite me


 pwMyFloater = window ( "Batch rename" )
 pwMyFloater.fileName = "renamer"
 pwMyFloater.windowType = 4
 rBaseRect = pwMyFloater.sourceRect
 rBaseRect = rBaseRect + rect ( 30, 50, 30, 50 )
 pwMyFloater.rect = rBaseRect


END beginSprite



on mouseUp me


 open pwMyFloater


END mouseUp



on endSprite me


 close pwMyFloater
 forget pwMyFloater


END endSprite
```

14

First, you see that the property variable **pwMyFloater** has a *w* in it, which I use to indicate that the variable is meant to contain a *window*.

Then, in the **beginSprite** handler, we set up the parameters we want the window to have:

pwMyFloater = window ("Batch rename")

This serves two purposes. One, it give the window-to-be a name by which it may be referenced in Lingo. Two, it gives the window-to-be a *title* that will appear in the window's frame, so instead of *renamer*, you'll see the words *Batch rename*. Nice!

pwMyFloater.fileName = "renamer"

You can probably guess what this does. It sets the name of the file for the up-and-coming window to our renamer.dir movie.

pwMyFloater.windowType = 4

windowType defines the kind of *frame* the window will have. Multiple types of frame are available:

- **0** a window that is moveable and resizable, but that doesn't have a zoom box (that's the thing you click in many window frames to cause the window to expand to fill the entire screen);

- **1** A modal dialog box, which has a solid border around it, can't be dragged, and has no close or zoom controls; these are often used for alerts, since you can't do anything outside the window until it's been closed.

- **2** A plain rectangle without even a title bar, zoom controls, or anything else, but that can be put into the background, unlike type 1.

Ask the Expert

Question   What if the movie I want to open isn't in the same folder? Can I use pathnames?

Answer   Yes, you can. You can use any standard navigation commands. In fact, you could even try it with **goToNetMovie** if you wanted to.

● **3**   Exactly like 2, but has a drop-shadow-like appearance to its right and lower edges.

● **4**   A moveable window with a title bar, but that has no zoom or resize controls.

● **5**   Also modal like 1, but has a title bar and can be dragged around.

● **8**   A standard system document window such as you might see in a word processor file.

● **12**   A window with a title bar and zoom controls, but no resize control.

● **16**   A rounded-corner window (these are very common on Macs for control panels, and have a title bar and close box, but no zoom or resize controls).

● **49**   A floating palette frame, which gives you a window of the kind the PI uses.

Note

Modal means that, until you've finished with the thing in question (usually a dialog box), you are stuck in a single mode of operation. Windows that let you do things outside of them, as with a word processor document window, are referred to as *modeless*.

Figure 14-2 shows you what these window types resemble on Macintosh; on Windows, of course, you'll have different results, the window frames being set to their closest counterparts for that operating system. In general, the functionality and modality of the window types will remain the same across systems, but it never hurts to test a little when you're in doubt.

rBaseRect = pwMyFloater.sourceRect

This determines what the "real" dimensions of the window are to be, by getting the size of the Stage as you set it in the renamer.dir file. So, if you set your Stage to be 200 pixels wide by 300 tall, the value of **rBaseRect** will be **rect (0, 0, 200, 300)**.

rBaseRect = rBaseRect + rect (30, 50, 30, 50)

This provides us with a rectangular offset. It's necessary because the rectangle defined above for **rBaseRect** defines a space in the top-left corner of the monitor. This becomes significant in the last line of our **beginSprite** call:

pwMyFloater.rect = rBaseRect

14

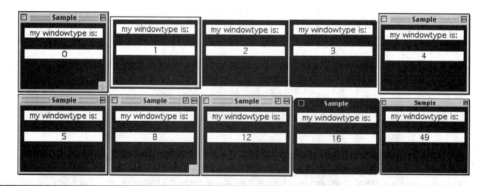

Figure 14-2 The various windowTypes available in Director, as they appear on a Macintosh. Each window's Stage size is 160 × 120; note the differences in the frame boundaries

This is a lot like the kind of command you'd use to set the dimensions of a sprite on the Stage, and it has a similar effect for MIAWs. This sets the dimensions onscreen of the window-to-be, and as you can see, we've offset those dimensions so they'll be 30 pixels from the left of the screen, and 50 from the top. This gives us a nice offset on the computer monitor, keeping us clear of system menus (on Mac) and allowing the window to have room to draw its title bar and so on, so the user can see what its name is, and so it can be "grabbed" and dragged around on the screen.

This done, we've set up the basic parameters for our child MIAW. We've set up a frame type, given it a nice title, and prepared it to open in a desirable location on the screen. The line in the **mouseUp** handler that actually opens the MIAW is almost anticlimactic:

open pwMyFloater

This, predictably, opens the MIAW with the dimensions and other parameters we set.

Then we just have some cleanup in **endSprite** to do:

close pwMyFloater

This, of course, closes the window. It has the same effect as the user clicking its close box in its window frame.

forget pwMyFloater

This acts like the **destruct** call you send to a parent script object, clearing the window's file, location, and so on from memory.

6. Hey, you're ready to go! Click Play, click the Batch rename… button, and check out your MIAW. You can drag it around, close it, reopen it, do whatever you want with it, really. And the controls on it are of a more limited type, which is really what we want here. We want the user to be able to minimize, move, or close the window, but that's it. So, now you're ready to start entering some code into the MIAW file itself, and turn it into an actual utility that can be used with your main thumbknows.dir file.

1-Minute Drill

● When you're loading an external Director movie from a projector, why would you not want to include the movie file's extension?

● What is a quick way to open a MIAW?

Forget about the Parent Movie

The way to begin turning renamer.dir into a utility MIAW file is effectively the same as it would be for making any new, stand-alone Director movie. You don't need to worry about this MIAW having to do special things to talk to its parent; all you have to do is forge ahead with this MIAW as though you were getting ready to make a self-contained utility.

The purpose of this movie will be to let the user point to a folder containing a large group of files, and then have them all renamed at once, following a pattern. This pattern will include integers for numbering the files and some parameters for date and time (to ensure we don't mistakenly overwrite files), and will allow the user to enter some characters to use as a prefix for the filenames.

For instance, suppose your user has just sorted a whole lot of digital camera files, some of which are of her vacation at the beach, some of which are of her best friend Carolyn's bridal shower, and some of which are of her pet hamster Sparky. She'll probably want to rename all the files, because most digital cameras give files default names such as photo-0001.jpg, photo-0002.jpg, and so on. The idea of having these images indexed sort of like that is not a bad one, but since she wants to have some text associated with her pictures, and since she'll probably want to renumber them in a different sequence, she'll have a lot of use for a batch rename function that can do the tedious work for her.

So, she'd use this renamer to point to the folder containing the beach pictures first, and perhaps enter "beach" as the filename prefix. Then, she'd tell

---

● When a movie is protected, its file extension is changed, so the code referring to it will not work any more.
● **open window filename**

the renamer to go ahead and do its thing, which it would, renaming all the files in the folder with the parameter she entered. Then, she'd do the same thing for the shower, perhaps starting with the prefix Carolyn. Finally, she'd do the same for Sparky.

We're going to do the same kind of folder choosing and file type processing in this movie that we did for thumbknows.dir, so you can handle some of the Lingo by copy and paste, and, for the most part, I won't have to do a lot of explaining of the rationale. We are going to have to test for file type, though, because it's possible that the user might point to a folder containing things other than image files (as well as the image files to be renamed), and we do not want to just blindly assume that any given file on the drive is meant to have some other name attached to it.

7. Get your renamer's Stage looking a little like the one in Figure 14-3, with an editable #field for entering a prefix, a button to get everything started, and an info window prompting the user on what to do.

8. We'll begin by attaching a behavior to the Choose folder... button:

```
GLOBAL goFileXtraObject



on mouseUp me


member("info").text = "Select the folder containing the files
you want to rename..."
 updateStage

 sTarget = goFileXtraObject.fx_FolderSelectDialog( "" )

 if sTarget <> "" then

   RenameFiles( sTarget )

 end if


END mouseUp
```

| **Figure 14-3** | The basic Stage for the renamer.dir movie |

Looks familiar, doesn't it? That's intentional, of course. The only line here that's different from the one in the Choose folder… button in thumbknows.dir is

RenameFiles(sTarget)

Ask the Expert

Question   Okay, wait a minute. In this handler, I'm also putting some text into an "info" #field. Won't that make the text go into the "info" #field I have in the thumbknows.dir movie?

Answer   No. By default, a MIAW will assume such commands are referring to its own set of Cast member resources, so, since you have an "info" #field in your renamer.dir movie, all the commands that refer to it in this MIAW will affect only the #field in this movie. Similarly, the commands in thumbknows.dir will only affect the "info" #field in that movie.

14

9. So, let's go ahead and see what **RenameFiles** should look like. This is to be a handler in the renamer movie's movie script:

```
on RenameFiles sPath


 lFileList = goFileXtraObject.fx_FolderToList( sPath )
 lFileList.sort()
 nAllFiles = lFileList.count()

 member("info").text = "There are" && string ( nAllFiles ) &&
"files in folder" && sPath & "."
 updateStage

 sYear = string ( (the systemDate).year )
 sMonth = string ( (the systemDate).month )
 sDay = string ( (the systemDate).day )

 delete char 1 to 2 of sYear

 if the number of chars in sMonth < 2 then

  put "0" before sMonth

 end if

 if the number of chars in sDay < 2 then

  put "0" before sDay

 end if

 sAbsoluteDay = sYear & sMonth & sDay

 member("info").text = "There are" && string ( nAllFiles ) &&
"files in folder" && sPath & ". Now renaming the files."
 updateStage

 nFilesRenamed = 0
 nFilePrefix = 0

 repeat with nFile = 1 to nAllFiles

  sFileName = lFileList[nFile]
  sOrigName = sPath & sFileName

  member("info").text = "There are" && string ( nAllFiles ) &&
"files in folder" && sPath & ". Now renaming the files.
 File number" && string ( nFile ) & ", originally" &&
```

```
sFileName & ", is being renamed."
  updateStage

  sFileType = goFileXtraObject.fx_FileGetType( sOrigName )

  if sFileType starts "JPEG" or sFileType = ".jpeg" or sFileType =
".jpe" or
sFileType = ".jpg" then

    sExtension = ".jpg"
    nFilePrefix = nFilePrefix + 1

  else if sFileType starts "BMP" or sFileType = ".bmp" then

    sExtension = ".bmp"
    nFilePrefix = nFilePrefix + 1

  else if sFileType starts "TIFF" or sFileType = ".tiff" or
sFileType = ".tif" then

    sExtension = ".tif"
    nFilePrefix = nFilePrefix + 1

  else if sFileType starts "GIF" or sFileType = ".gif" then

    sExtension = ".gif"
    nFilePrefix = nFilePrefix + 1

  else if sFileType starts "PICT" or sFileType = ".pict" or
sFileType = ".pic" then

    sExtension = ".pic"
    nFilePrefix = nFilePrefix + 1

  else if sFileType starts "PNG" or sFileType = ".png" then

    sExtension = ".png"
    nFilePrefix = nFilePrefix + 1

  else

    next repeat

  end if

  sIntPrefixString = string ( nFilePrefix )

  repeat while the number of chars in sIntPrefixString < 6
```

```
  put "0" before sIntPrefixString

end repeat

sTime = string ( (the systemDate).seconds )

repeat while the number of chars in sTime < 5

 put "0" before sTime

end repeat

sPrepend = member("prefixField").text
sConstructedName = sPrepend & sIntPrefixString & "-"
sRealTime = sAbsoluteDay & sTime
sFinalPreName = sConstructedName & sRealTime
sNewName = sPath & sFinalPreName & sExtension
nRename = goFileXtraObject.fx_FileRename( sOrigName, sNewName )
nFilesRenamed = nFilesRenamed + nRename

end repeat

member("info").text = string ( nFilesRenamed ) && "items of"
&& string ( nFilePrefix ) & ", that were recognizable, from
a total of" && string ( nAllFiles ) && "in folder" &&
sPath & ", were renamed."
```

```
END RenameFiles
```

Yow! Well, some of this is quite a lot like what you've seen before, but some of it's rather new.

Let's start by looking over the Lingo that involves the call to **the systemDate**.

sYear = string ((the systemDate).year)

the systemDate is a Lingo keyword that returns the current date (according to the user's computer clock) in a consistently formatted way. In this sense, it's very different from **the date**, which gives the date in the way the local convention dictates.

For example, if today's date is June 20, in the United States, you'd call it 6/20. However, in many parts of Europe, it would be 20.6. **the date** returns the correct date, but in the way the user's local tradition indicates. Thus, trying to figure out how to display something as simple as the month could be really tricky.

That's why Macromedia introduced **the systemDate**, which always returns in the following format:

date (year, month, day)

So, by getting **(the systemDate).year**, we're asking for just the year, nothing else, and then passing it through a **string** filter (since it pops out as an integer).

We then do the same kind of thing for **(the systemDate).month** and **(the systemDate).day**, ultimately telling us our location on the Gregorian calendar.

delete char 1 to 2 of sYear

We delete the "20" in the year. This will make our batch renamer non-Y3K-compliant, but if you're still around in the year 3000, you'll probably have other things on your mind than reworking this little bit of Lingo.

if the number of chars in sMonth < 2 then

  put "0" before sMonth

end if

This is just so June will be represented by "06" rather than "6". We do the same thing for the day.

sAbsoluteDay = sYear & sMonth & sDay

Here we construct a string made up of the year, month, and day in which the targeted files have been renamed. Again, if it's June 20, the **sAbsoluteDay** will be "020620."

The next part of this handler that you might have trouble with begins in the repeat loop, with the series of **if...then** tests; here's the first one:

if sFileType starts "JPEG" or sFileType = ".jpeg" or sFileType = ".jpe" or
sFileType = ".jpg" then

  sExtension = ".jpg"

  nFilePrefix = nFilePrefix + 1

This is a somewhat more involved way of determining the file type of any given item in the folder the user chose, and determining if it's a kind we can recognize. In this code, we have to break it down into specific types, though,

14

so we can set two variables. The first, **sExtension**, will contain a system-standard file extension for the image (so .jpeg will become .jpg, as an example). The second, **nFilePrefix**, is a number we originally set to 0 before we started this repeat loop. It's used as the actual counter of the file that we're renaming, and will be added to the final filename that we're constructing with our code.

Note

At the end of this lengthy **if**...**then** test, we have a **next repeat**, because if we make it that far through our file-type testing, the file is of a kind we do not recognize, and so we kick out of the rest of this repeat loop and jump ahead one. That way, we don't end up renaming *all* the files in any given folder, but just the image types we can *recognize* as such.

Finally, we do some interesting things to **nFilePrefix**:

sIntPrefixString = string (nFilePrefix)

repeat while the number of chars in sIntPrefixString < 6

put "0" before sIntPrefixString

end repeat

We're just testing to see what the file number is and, if it's below an arbitrary number, we're bolting extra zeroes onto the front of it again. This is to give the filenames a nice ordered appearance the next time they're looked at in a list view. Note that this code will work with any integer number up to six places, which is 999,999—and if you're trying to index a folder containing one million or more recognizable images, well, heaven help you.

Then we make another call to **the systemDate**:

sTime = string ((the systemDate).seconds)

This is actually *undocumented*—something you will not find in your Director 8.5 Lingo documentation. **(the systemDate).seconds** is the time, in seconds, since midnight on any particular day. So, if it was one minute after midnight, **(the systemDate).seconds** would be 60.

repeat while the number of chars in sTime < 5

put "0" before sTime

end repeat

Here, again, we're adding extra zeroes to the time in seconds since midnight, to give the file list an ordered appearance.

Note

There can never be more than five digits in **(the systemDate).seconds**, because 24 hours is 86,400 seconds.

We're adding the seconds value just to be a little extra safe. For instance, suppose your user has renamed an entire folder of files, but then finds three more images she forgot to add. Well, in renaming them a second time around, by using this seconds value, we're almost guaranteed not to accidentally rename one of the new files so that its name is the same as one of the older ones, since **(the systemDate).seconds** changes over 86,000 times a day. We put the year, month, and day into the file to ensure that files renamed at the same time on a *different* day also do not overwrite older images. In other words, we're trying to be extra careful with our users' data here.

Now we construct the name of the file based on everything we just calculated, plus one extra parameter:

> **sPrepend = member("prefixField").text**

This is the text the user typed into our editable #field onscreen. Obviously, you'll want to name yours **"prefixField"**. That, or change the reference in your code.

> **sConstructedName = sPrepend & sIntPrefixString & "-"**

This combines the text the user typed with the file index number we determined earlier.

> **sRealTime = sAbsoluteDay & sTime**

This is the year, month, day, and time in seconds, all added together into one string.

> **sFinalPreName = sConstructedName & sRealTime**

This is the "final" name prefix, sans the file extension.

> **sNewName = sPath & sFinalPreName & sExtension**

And here we add the path to the folder the user chose before the "final" name we constructed, and then we put the file's extension onto the end.

14

nRename = goFileXtraObject.fx_FileRename(sOrigName, sNewName)

Here we make a call to the FileXtra object, telling it to rename the original file to the new one. If it works, this function returns 1; otherwise, it returns 0.

nFilesRenamed = nFilesRenamed + nRename

Here we're just keeping count of all the files we've successfully renamed so we can tell the user, once we're done, how we did. That's what we put into the "info" window at the end of this handler.

10. That's not quite all for this movie script; you also need to declare the FileXtra object as a global object and instantiate it in your **startMovie** handler, but that's a copy and paste from the movie script for the thumbknows.dir movie.

11. Now there's the question of that prefix #field. We don't want the user to just type in anything, because there are some keystrokes that won't work, characters we can't use in filenames, such as \ on Windows, : on Mac, and so on. So, we need to attach a behavior to that editable #field that filters the input for acceptable characters only. Here it is:

```
on keyDown me


  if the key = RETURN \
or the key = ENTER \
or the key = " " \
or the key = "\" \
or the key = "|" \
or the key = "/" \
or the key = "?" \
or the key = "." \
or the key = ":" \
or the key = TAB \
or the key = "*" \
or the key = "&" \
or the key = "<" \
or the key = ">" then

    BEEP
    member("warning").text = "You can't use the" && the key && "key in your
prefix name."
    dontPassEvent

  else if the number of chars in sprite(me.spriteNum).member.text > 9 then

    if the keyCode <> 123 and the keyCode <> 124 and the keyCode <> 51 and the
keyCode <> 117 then

      BEEP
      member("warning").text = "You can't enter more than 10 characters for
your prefix."
```

```
   dontPassEvent
  else
    pass
  end if
 else
  member("warning").text = " "
  pass
  end if

END keyDown
```

You can see that this behavior is activated whenever there's a keystroke meant to be entered in the editable #field. You can also see that I've made use of the Lingo \ continuation character at the top to make my **if…then** test a little more human-readable.

For starters, we block either the RETURN or the ENTER keys, since neither is useful in a filename anyway. Every other key I've specifically listed in this handler is a no-no key on one or more systems, and we're renaming files in such a way that they will be usable on any modern computer, whether it's running Windows, Macintosh, or some flavor of UNIX, including Linux. (The *movie* might be limited to Mac or Windows, but the image files themselves have to be 100 percent portable.)

From there, you can see we make use of another #field member, called "warning." You'll want to add that to your Stage so the user can see the caution you send when an illegal key is pressed.

Then, you can see I'm counting the strokes, and that I don't let the user get past 10 characters. Why? Because our constructed filenames, without the text but with the extensions, are 21 characters long, and Macintosh won't let filenames go past 31 characters. Again, since we're trying to give our images portable names that can work on any modern machine, we can't let the total name length go past 31 characters. This means the user's stuck with only 10 characters for a prefix, but such is the price of truly portable code with results that will work anywhere.

You also see we're testing for **the keyCode**. This is to disallow all keys other than the left and right arrows, the BACKSPACE key, and the DELETE key, when the number of characters in the #field has gone past the limit we set. So, the user can edit the text in the #field but can't add any more characters unless

14

some have been removed. Otherwise, everything's fine and we pass the keystroke to the #field.

12. That's it. The renamer is finished and ready to go. Go ahead and click Play and rename some files; see what the movie does.

13. Close this movie and play the modified thumbknows.dir movie. Click the Batch rename... button and note that your child MIAW behaves just like a floating extension of your main image-sorting program.

Note, by the way, that this batch renamer will rename all the image files in a given folder according to the name/number scheme we've created here, so you might want to make sure you're pointing the program to files you actually want renamed!

Project Summary

With this project, you have seen the following:

● How rapidly you can extend your Director movies by using MIAWs

● How MIAWs can behave as object-oriented code capsules

● How a MIAW can behave as either a stand-alone program or as an extension to another Director movie

1-Minute Drill

● What is the **systemDate**?

● What is an undocumented feature of the **systemDate**?

Project 14-2: One More Utility MIAW...

Not bad, you're thinking, *but we still have the issue of files with names that are not very descriptive.* That's right; and furthermore, you won't necessarily want to force others to use some kind of image sorter to see what's what in all of those graphics files. So, some kind of "contact sheet" is in order here, and fortunately we're going to be able to make one rather easily. That's what we'll be doing with this project.

● The year, month, and day returned in an absolutely consistent format regardless of a computer's regional settings for displaying year, month, and day.

● **(the systemDate).seconds**

The goals of this project include the following:

● Illustrating further the concept of using MIAWs to extend a Director movie's capabilities

● Demonstrating how Director movies can be programmed to generate results that can be used in other programs entirely (in this case, a Web browser)

This movie will have the same characteristics as the renamer; ultimately, it'll work as a MIAW. This movie will ask the user to locate a folder of files to be indexed in an HTML page, which can then be opened in any Web browser. The images, distributed with the index HTML page, will let anyone with Netscape, Internet Explorer, or any other graphical browser see what all the images are. We're also going to add some code that lets the user click an image's thumbnail to get the full-screen view, and we're going to let the user set a base size for the thumbnails themselves (small, medium, or large).

Fortunately, we don't have to actually resize the images and save them to disk in a smaller format. It's possible, via HTML, to cause a full-sized image to display in a reduced view; thus, the images loaded as thumbnails in the browser window will actually be miniaturized from the real files on disk. In this way, the index page will act a lot like the thumbnail code does in thumbknows.dir itself.

Step-by-Step

1. I'm going to go easy on you again, because your indexer movie is going to have to write some preformatted HTML code in order to make an index page. Rather than put you through the process involved in preparing such HTML content, I've created another blank file that has the worst of the work done already. To get to the file, fire up Director and enter the following in the Message window:

```
goToNetMovie http://www.nightwares.com/director_beginners_guide/14/ix.dir
```

2. When you've retrieved the movie, save it as **indexer.dir** alongside the other two movies you've made.

3. Now add a Create index... button to your thumbknows.dir Stage.

4. To that button, attach a behavior that's essentially the same as the one you used for the Batch rename... button, but change the window's name to **Create index...**.

Make sure the **fileName** setting points to "indexer" instead of "renamer."

14

Tip

You can copy and paste the code from the Batch rename... button and make those two changes, since it's an *encapsulated* behavior. Clever, eh?

---

5. Open the indexer.dir file you retrieved from the Internet. For starters, attach a behavior to the "Choose folder..." button like the one you used for the button in the renamer movie earlier in this module. This time, however, instead of calling a handler named **RenameFiles**, call one named **GenerateCatalogs**.

   Now hold on to your hat, because things get a little wild.

6. Create a new movie script in the indexer movie, and add the following handlers to it:

```
GLOBAL goFileXtraObject, gnThumbRow



on startMovie

  if not ( objectP ( goFileXtraObject ) ) then

    goFileXtraObject = new ( xtra "filextra3" )

  end if

  member(50).media = member("rectangle").media
  member(50).name = "slug"
  member("info").text = "Waiting for folder location..."
  gnThumbRow = 7


END startMovie



on stopMovie
```

```
member(50).media = member("rectangle").media
member(50).name = "slug"


END stopMovie
```

Note we're switching out a graphic in member position 50, like we did in the revised thumbknows.dir movie, and for the same reasons. We're going to be using member 50 as our slug import Cast member, to get the dimensions of images and make thumbnails.

Also note the presence of a variable, **gnThumbRow**, that's initially set to 7. We'll get to this soon. It's the variable that lets the user choose the size for the thumbnails, but it also lets us know something rather important about how to lay out the HTML file as we're creating its content out of *nothing at all*.

Finally, note we've added a **stopMovie** to this one, which switches out the placeholder slug again (just to be on the safe side).

7. Now you're ready to enter the **GenerateCatalogs** handler into your indexer movie script, and it's a little on the scary side at first:

```
on GenerateCatalogs sPath


 lFileList = goFileXtraObject.fx_FolderToList( sPath )
 lFileList.sort()
 nAllFiles = lFileList.count()

 member("info").text = "There are" && string ( nAllFiles ) && "files in
folder" && sPath & "."
 updateStage

 lFilesToIndex = []
 lThisRow = [:]

 repeat with nFile = 1 to nAllFiles

  sFileName = lFileList[nFile]
  sOrigName = sPath & sFileName

  member("info").text = "There are" && string ( nAllFiles ) && "files in
folder" && sPath & ". Preprocessing file" && string ( nFile ) && "..."
  updateStage

  sFileType = goFileXtraObject.fx_FileGetType( sOrigName )

  if sFileType starts "JPEG" or sFileType = ".jpeg" or sFileType = ".jpe" or
sFileType = ".jpg" or sFileType starts "BMP" or sFileType = ".bmp" or
```

14

```
sFileType starts "TIFF" or sFileType = ".tiff" or sFileType = ".tif" or
sFileType starts "GIF" or sFileType = ".gif" or sFileType starts "PICT" or
sFileType = ".pict" or sFileType = ".pic" or sFileType starts "PNG" or
sFileType = ".png" then

    member(50).fileName = sOrigName

    nWidth = member(50).width
    nHeight = member(50).height

    lThisRow.addProp( sFileName, [nWidth, nHeight] )

  else

  next repeat

  end if

  if lThisRow.count() >= gnThumbRow then

  lFilesToIndex.append ( lThisRow )
  lThisRow = [:]

  end if

end repeat

lFilesToIndex.append ( lThisRow )

SetFileDimensions( sPath, lFilesToIndex )


END GenerateCatalogs
```

Actually, if you look this code over closely, you'll see it's not that different from the **LoadFiles** handler in thumbknows.dir; in fact, you could almost copy and paste to get started. But there are some lines you need to pay attention to.

lFilesToIndex = []

lThisRow = [:]

This pair of lists, a linear and a property list, will contain the names of each of the files we want indexed, as well as their current dimensions in pixels as they exist on the user's hard drive.

Then things are rather conventional for a while until we find a file we recognize:

member(50).fileName = sOrigName

nWidth = member(50).width

nHeight = member(50).height

You've seen this. We're simply putting the image file into Cast member 50's slot, and then getting its width and height.

lThisRow.addProp(sFileName, [nWidth, nHeight])

Here we are creating a property list entry for the image in member 50. The entry uses the actual file's name for the property index, and then has as its value a minilist containing the width and height of the image. So, if the image was named cats-miaw.jpg, and had a dimension of 320 × 175 pixels, its entry in the list would be

["cats-miaw.jpg": [320, 175]]

Note

We don't convert filenames to symbols here, because we haven't actually preprocessed any of the image names (necessarily). This means the names could contain all kinds of characters we can't use for symbols, such as spaces, punctuation, and more; in fact, the filename extension would be truncated with a symbol conversion. We are not requiring the user, in other words, to have batch-renamed any files before we make this index.

Then, once we're out of the **if…then** test, but before we exit the repeat loop, you see this:

if lThisRow.count() >= gnThumbRow then

lFilesToIndex.append (lThisRow)

lThisRow = [:]

end if

Clearly, we do not want the total number of files and their associated dimensions we have inside the **lThisRow** container to exceed the number set in **gnThumbRow**. If that turns out to be the case, we **append** the **lThisRow** property list to the **lFilesToIndex** linear list, and then reset **lThisRow** so it's empty again.

We do this because the variable **gnThumbRow** is actually the maximum number of thumbnails we want to create in any row on the HTML page we're making. If **gnThumbRow** is 7, we only want seven images per row,

14

and so when the count of images for **lThisRow** gets past 7, we add the current row list to the **lFilesToIndex** list, and then clear out **lThisRow** so we can start fresh, adding up to seven more files again before we go through this append-and-purge cycle once more.

What this will give us, when we're done, is a *linear* list containing a collection of *property* lists in series. Each property list represents a row of images; the entire list represents all the data we need to write to disk as HTML parameters. So, if **lFilesToIndex** contains four groups of seven-item property lists, we'll end up with four rows of images in the HTML page, each row comprised of seven thumbnails.

After we're out of the repeat loop, we do a final append:

> **lFilesToIndex.append (lThisRow)**

We do this to make sure any stragglers from the last cycle get attached to our overall representative list.

We then call another handler, passing along both the folder path and the **lFilesToIndex** container list. As you may infer from its name, in this handler (entered in the movie script), we'll be recalculating the image sizes so they'll appear as thumbnails in the HTML page.

8. We now add a handler named **SetFileDimensions** to the indexer's movie script:

```
on SetFileDimensions sPath, lFilesToIndex


  member("info").text = "Now calculating thumbnail image sizes..."
  updateStage

  if gnThumbRow = 7 then

   nMaxWidth = 80
   nMaxHeight = 60

  else if gnThumbRow = 5 then

   nMaxWidth = 120
   nMaxHeight = 90

  else

   nMaxWidth = 160
   nMaxHeight = 120
```

```
end if

nAllFiles = lFilesToIndex.count()

repeat with nRowEntry = 1 to nAllFiles

 lCurrentRow = lFilesToIndex[nRowEntry]
 nImagesInRow = lCurrentRow.count()

 repeat with nImage = 1 to nImagesInRow

  lImageDims = lCurrentRow[nImage]
  nCurrentWidth = lImageDims[1]
  nCurrentHeight = lImageDims[2]

  if nCurrentWidth > nMaxWidth or nCurrentHeight > nMaxHeight then

   if nCurrentWidth > nCurrentHeight then

    fTargetWidth = float ( nMaxWidth )
    fPercentResize = fTargetWidth / float ( nCurrentWidth )
    fTargetHeight = float ( nCurrentHeight ) * fPercentResize

   else

    fTargetHeight = float ( nMaxHeight )
    fPercentResize = fTargetHeight / float ( nCurrentHeight )
    fTargetWidth = float ( nCurrentWidth ) * fPercentResize

   end if

  else

   fTargetWidth = nCurrentWidth
   fTargetHeight = nCurrentHeight

  end if

  lImageDims[1] = integer ( fTargetWidth )
  lImageDims[2] = integer ( fTargetHeight )
  lCurrentRow[nImage] = lImageDims

 end repeat

 lFilesToIndex[nRowEntry] = lCurrentRow

end repeat
```

14

```
GenerateHTML( sPath, lFilesToIndex )


END SetFileDimensions
```

Here again, you see that mysterious **gnThumbRow** variable, this time being used to determine what some values are for **nMaxWidth** and **nMaxHeight**. Given their dimensions and names, you'd be quite correct if you were to assume that they represent the maximum-size values we want the thumbnails to have. There's a range there because you can fit seven images at 80 × 60 pixels into a row on an HTML page and still have it fit into a browser running at 640 × 480; but you can only fit five images across at 120 × 90 pixels, and, finally, you can only fit four images across at 160 × 120. So, that's how we arrive at our thumbnail sizes: by determining how many images across we're going to display, which also happens to be the number of property indices we plugged into each **lThisRow** list as we made the main **lFilesToIndex** list. Coincidence? Surely not!

We then move on to some nested repeat loops. First, we start by getting the number of lists we have stored in the **lFilesToIndex** list. We then get into each of those specific lists that are nested inside **lFilesToIndex**, because we need to get the width and height entries for each of the images contained there.

Once we have the width and height values, we recalculate them proportionally in a way very reminiscent of what we did for the preview image in thumbknows.dir.

After doing that, we put those recalculated values back into their proper places for each image, and then plug the modified image index values back into the larger container that holds them. Finally, we put that larger container back into its proper place in the main **lFilesToIndex** list.

From there, we make a call to a handler that's intended to actually generate the HTML for us, passing along, again, **lFilesToIndex** and **sPath** as parameters.

This handler is the one that makes use of the HTML template #field members I added to the ix.dir file you retrieved from the Net. These #field members contain the raw HTML tags and other data necessary to make a Web file that browsers can read, and, overall, I think it's easier on you to just hand you that information rather than ask you to reverse-engineer a Web page, or explain to you how I got that content or what any of it means.

Note

If you're already experienced at writing HTML on your own, feel free to modify the tags I've provided so that you get something you like.

9. Here's the **GenerateHTML** movie script handler for the indexer movie; this writes out the HTML necessary to create a Web page full of image thumbnails:

```
on GenerateHTML sPath, lFilesToIndex

  member("info").text = "Now creating HTML text to write to hard drive..."
  updateStage

  sHeader = member("pageHeader").text
  sHREF = member("hrefTag").text
  sSrc = member("srcTag").text
  sBrdHt = member("borderHtTag").text
  sWdth = member("widthTag").text
  sEndLine = member("endLine").text
  sLineBrk = "<br>"
  sFileClose = member("fileClose").text

  sHTMLContent = sHeader

  nAllFiles = lFilesToIndex.count()

  repeat with nRowEntry = 1 to nAllFiles

   lCurrentRow = lFilesToIndex[nRowEntry]
   nImagesInRow = lCurrentRow.count()

   repeat with nImage = 1 to nImagesInRow

    lImageDims = lCurrentRow[nImage]
    nTargetWidth = lImageDims[1]
    nTargetHeight = lImageDims[2]
    sFileName = lCurrentRow.getPropAt ( nImage )

    put sHREF & sFileName & sSrc & sFileName & sBrdHt & nTargetHeight & sWdth
& nTargetWidth & sEndLine after sHTMLContent

   end repeat

   put sLineBrk after sHTMLContent

  end repeat

  put sFileClose after sHTMLContent

  oHTMLWrite = new ( xtra "fileio" )
  oHTMLWrite.createFile ( sPath & "index.htm" )
  oHTMLWrite.openFile ( sPath & "index.htm", 2 )
  oHTMLWrite.writeString ( sHTMLContent )
```

14

```
oHTMLWrite.closeFile()
oHTMLWrite = 0

if the platform contains "mac" then

  sFileType = goFileXtraObject.fx_FileGetType( browserName() )
  delete sFileType.char[1..4]
  put "TEXT" before sFileType
  goFileXtraObject.fx_FileSetType( ( sPath & "index.htm" ), sFileType )

end if

BEEP

member("info").text = "HTML index successfully written to" && sPath & "."

END GenerateHTML
```

We start here by plugging the #field text into some variables. We'll be stringing those together along with the filenames and thumbnail sizes later on in this handler. That's how we end up putting together browser-comprehensible HTML.

Once again, we traverse our image lists, getting the values for width and height. Note, too, the following line:

sFileName = lCurrentRow.getPropAt (nImage)

What do you think that command does? Well, you know what **addProp** does for property lists; it adds an index property and value. Given the name of this keyword, **getPropAt**, you can infer that we're retrieving the name of the index property itself that we set back when we were getting the original names and dimensions of all of these image files. In other words, the property index entry for each image is the image's filename itself, and by using **getPropAt** for the specific item we're currently reading, we can recover that image's name.

I *told* you lists are terrific!

Anyway, we cycle through our lists in this fashion, attaching a "**
" whenever we come to the end of a row of images (that's what's in the **sLineBrk variable) to break the row into another line in the Web page and, when we're completely done going through our lists, finish it off by attaching some HTML footer and page close tags from another variable. What's left? Just some FileIO calls that create an index.htm document, open it with write access, and then write out the HTML we just made.

Finally, we do something nice for Mac users by setting up the HTML file so that it'll automatically be recognized by whatever their default browser is:

sFileType = goFileXtraObject.fx_FileGetType(browserName())

browserName(), by default, reports the path and name of the browser the user chooses. What we're doing here is finding out what "tag" this browser puts onto HTML files that it considers readable.

delete sFileType.char[1..4]

In this case, **sFileType** will always begin *APPL*, because those are the first four characters that Macintosh uses to distinguish a program. The *last* four characters are the actual tag we want to attach to the index.htm file.

Note

This is generally called the *creator* tag.

put "TEXT" before sFileType

On a Mac, all regular Web pages are type "TEXT". We put that before the creator tag, because that's the file type.

goFileXtraObject.fx_FileSetType((sPath & "index.htm"), sFileType)

Now we've set the index.htm file type to something a Mac can recognize as being a Web page, intended to be opened in the user's default browser. So, when the user double-clicks the index.htm file he just made on his Mac, it'll load in whatever his favorite browser is, just like it will on Windows.

We then beep and let the user know we're done, because we are. That's it for the movie scripts.

10. You're almost ready. You still need to attach a behavior to the three size radio buttons on the Stage, but doing so is cake compared to this other stuff. This can be attached to all three sprites:

```
GLOBAL gnThumbRow



on enterFrame me
```

```
if voidP ( gnThumbRow ) then

  gnThumbRow = 7

end if

if sprite(me.spriteNum).member.name = ( string ( gnThumbRow ) && "button" )
then

  sprite(me.spriteNum).member.hilite = 1

else

  sprite(me.spriteNum).member.hilite = 0

end if

END enterFrame


on mouseUp me

  gnThumbRow = value ( sprite(me.spriteNum).member.name.word[1] )

END mouseUp
```

We test **gnThumbRow** for **voidP** on **enterFrame** because, remember, **enterFrame** on sprites in frame 1 runs *before* **startMovie**, which is where we traditionally put the **gnThumbRow** initializer.

After that, it's just a question of seeing if the value for **gnThumbRow** matches the first word of the sprite's member name, which, as you can see by looking in the Cast, is either 7, 5, or 4, and determining based on that whether this particular radio button sprite has its **hilite** set, or shown to be clicked.

Then, on **mouseUp**, we get the first word of the sprite's member name, convert it to a number by passing it through the **value** filter, and plug it into the **gnThumbRow** variable. And that's how the user chooses a size of small, medium, or large for his thumbnails.

11. What a lot of work! But go ahead and click Play now and try making an index someplace. Then, close this file and open the thumbknows.dir movie. Play that and try running the batch-rename and index-generating MIAWs. As you can see, they work just fine on their own, as stand-alone movies, and as plug-in modules for your main image-sorting utility.

Oh, but it's *not* an image-sorting utility any more. It's *also* a file batch-renaming utility, *and* a thumbnail-index generator! And, as you can see from the screenshot in Figure 4, it actually works!

Project Summary

With this second project in this module, you've learned the following:

● How to have several MIAWs available in your Director movies at once

● How to use different MIAWs for different purposes to extend the basic capabilities of a program without substantially altering the basic program itself

● How to program Director movies to create files that can be used in different programs entirely

More Xtras

Before you roll a projector out of the updated sorting, renaming, and cataloging movie, make sure to add the FileIO Xtra to the list for the thumbknows.dir movie file. Then, you can choose to create a projector out of just the ThumbKnows movie, and as long as your indexer and renamer movies are in the same folder when it runs, you've got a nice little utility package you can show off, or give to friends, or use for your own needs.

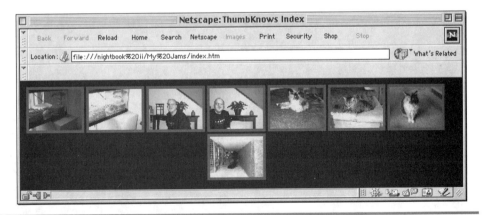

Figure 14-4   This is either a sample of an index page made using the ThumbKnows indexer MIAW or the FBI's Ten Most Wanted list

14

You can also make projectors out of just the renamer and indexer movies (taking care to add the correct Xtras in each case), because they're both quite capable of functioning on their own.

Mac users, note: ThumbKnows uses quite a lot of RAM, so set its memory allocation to 40960, or 40MB. To do that, click once on the projector's icon in the Finder, and then choose File | Get info | Memory. Into the Preferred Size field, type **40960**, and then close the dialog box.

Summary

With this module, you've learned how to use MIAW files to extend the functionality of any Director movie you've made, turning it into something that goes beyond what your original vision for it might have been. In the next module, the last one in this book, we'll discuss getting MIAWs to talk to each other, since it's the ability to share information that makes them even more powerful.

☑ Mastery Check

1. What is a MIAW?

_____

_____

2. What's a quick way to open a MIAW?

_____

_____

3. What's a disadvantage of using the quick way to open a MIAW?

_____

_____

4. If you have two Cast members with the same names, but one is in a parent movie and the other is in a MIAW, will you have trouble when you write Lingo that refers to that Cast member's name? In other words, will Director become confused about which Cast member you mean?

_____

_____

5. What is **windowType**?

_____

_____

6. What is **sourceRect**?

_____

_____

7. What is the maximum value that might be returned by (**the systemDate**). **seconds**? How do you know that?

_____

_____

14

Module 15

Communication
with MIAWs

The Goals of this Module

- Understand the basics of communication among MIAWs
- Learn how to use communication among MIAWs to extend your programs

Having worked through Module 14, you've had lots of experience working with encapsulation in MIAWs, seeing their power as you work with them as individual extensions to programs. However, they can also communicate, which means you can share information among MIAWs much as you would with any other kind of code object. This can help us to expand our thumbnail program even more.

Not Just Stand-Alone

In the last module, you saw that MIAWs can extend your Director programs considerably, allowing conceptually related ideas to be clustered into satellite controls that don't seriously affect the performance of your main program. In fact, you saw that these MIAWs would work quite well as stand-alone modules in their own right, and perhaps you even packaged them that way by making extra projectors of them.

But a MIAW doesn't do a lot of good if all it does is sit there on the screen awaiting input, aloof in its own little universe. It might as well be its own projector if that's all you want to do with it.

The *real* usefulness of MIAWs lies in the fact that they can communicate with each other and with their parent movies, allowing you to pass information to the MIAW that you want only it to handle, freeing your main movie up to do other things.

In this last module, we're going to do exactly that, enhancing our thumbnail program even further.

Zoom!

Having thumbnails—even the generously sized ones we've created—is not always enough when you're trying to sort images. Sometimes, you want to see that image in a full-screen mode before you can decide whether it belongs in the Trash, in the prewedding album, or in the post-wedding album.

Naturally, it would be very convenient to simply be able to enlarge the thumbnail to its full-screen size somehow, letting you get a look at it in all of its unshrunken glory. However, you don't want to do that on your main list, thumbnail, and folder interface, because doing so would force you to resize the Stage every time the user wanted to see the full-sized view (or set up the image so it's scrollable), and then all the controls you've so carefully created would no longer be available. Imagine the headaches you'd invite by trying to do all of that reprogramming!

Of *course* MIAW is the way to go here. We just need to get the image to open in its "regular" size in a MIAW, and to do that, we need to use **tell**, a Director keyword that causes one movie to talk to another. You can talk to any MIAW by using **tell** in conjunction with its variable container or window instance. The general grammar is as follows:

tell target

   doCommands

end tell

target is, of course, the object containing your window; however, MIAWs can also do this with the Stage by using the command **tell the stage**. In other words, MIAWs can send commands *to* the Stage, as well as receive them.

doCommands can be any kind of Lingo you want executed. This can be a **go to frame** command, a command to run a handler, or even a call to **sendSprite** or **sendAllSprites**. Essentially, any command you can do in Lingo can be done in **tell** as well, the difference being that it is not the parent movie or source of the **tell** command that executes the code; rather, the *target* specified in **tell** performs the functions.

As an example, create a Director movie named *main*, and give it this movie script:

```
on startMovie

  wChild = ( window "Child" )
  wChild.fileName = "child"
  open wChild

  sMovie1 = the movieName

  tell wChild

    sMovie2 = the movieName

  end tell

  put "Main movie is" && sMovie1
  put "Child movie is" && sMovie2


END startMovie
```

15

Naturally, I'll need you to make a movie named "child" as well; you can give it a simple **go the frame** script. Then, run your main movie and note the feedback in the Message window.

Do you see that, even though you issued identical commands in your **startMovie** script, you got different results? This occurs because the second variable was set by a **tell** command; it was feedback from the child movie that we plugged into the second variable, not from the parent.

Your child movie could also have issued a **tell** command to the parent movie by using a call such as the following:

```
tell the stage
  put "Hello from the child movie" && the movieName
end tell
```

Not a very interesting message, to be sure, but it would be coming from the *child* MIAW, not the parent movie, and that kind of command passing allows us to make our full-screen preview for our thumbnails.

Ask the Expert

Question   In the Lingo documentation, I see a reference to tell window. How come we aren't doing that here?

Answer   tell window is only necessary if you need to specify that the thing you're addressing is a window. In our previous example, **wChild** is already specified as being a window in the code we made to set it up.

Instances where you might use **tell window** instead of just **tell** would include cases where you were referring to windows by *name*, not by object or variable container. Ideally, you won't be doing that, because it implies your MIAWs are somehow not being stored in variables when they're being opened. While you can technically do things that way with Lingo, it's a little on the sloppy side.

Project 15-1: Hammer Your Thumb Again

The goals of this project are the following:

- Illustrating how to cause MIAWs to communicate with each other
- Illustrating how to load external media on demand in a given Director movie

Step-by-Step

1. To me, the most intuitive means of getting a full-screen image is to simply double-click the thumbnail, so we'll start there. You probably recall that **the doubleClick** tests to determine whether something's been double-clicked. So, we're going to add some code to the **mouseUp** handler for the thumbnail sprite we're using in the thumbknows.dir movie; here's the revised edition:

```
if sprite(me.spriteNum).member <> member("rectangle") then

  if the doubleClick then

    cursor -1

    lParams = sendSprite ( 11, #ReturnItemToMove )
    sFile = lParams[1] & lParams[2]

    rImageRect = sprite(me.spriteNum).member.rect
    rBaseRect = rImageRect + rect ( 10, 40, 10, 40 )
    pwMyFloater.rect = rBaseRect

    tell pwMyFloater

      ReceiveFilePath( sFile )

    end tell

    open pwMyFloater

  else

    -- Restore the cursor to the open hand

    cursor 260
```

```
    sendAllSprites ( #CheckFileDrop )

  end if

end if
```

Note

Don't forget to declare **pwMyFloater** as a property at the top of your thumbnail behavior!

First, we do a **cursor -1** to reset the mouse pointer to the system default; then, we ask the scrolling #field behavior to tell us the path to the file and the filename itself. (We don't do any of this, however, if the sprite happens to be the rectangle placeholder; if it is, there's no reason to open a preview.)

We also get the original size of the image and set the **rect** of a window, **pwMyFloater**, to that size, plus some offset, to allow the full-screen graphic to appear in a floating window that is just exactly the size of the image. If we didn't do that, the window in which it appeared would likely be either too large or too small. In this way, we're assured of always having the window be an exact fit.

We then construct the path and filename into a complete variable and pass it along in a **ReceiveFilePath** call we make to the window stored in **pwMyFloater**.

2. The window floater is a property variable for this behavior, but it hasn't been set up. You're probably guessing by now that it'll be prepared in **beginSprite** for the thumbnail, just like the other floaters were, and you're right:

```
pwMyFloater = window ( "Image" )
pwMyFloater.fileName = "fullsize"
pwMyFloater.windowType = 4
```

These addenda to the **beginSprite** script for the thumbnail tell you already that you need to make a new Director movie called "fullsize" alongside your main ThumbKnows movie. This is the movie that will accept the name of the image you pass to it with the **tell** call, and that will then open, giving the user a full-sized preview of any image she double-clicks.

3. Creating the movie is *really* simple. Just start a new Director movie and put a rectangle shape into Cast member 1, also placing it on the Stage in channel 1.

4. Put a **go the frame** script into script channel 1 of your new "fullsize" movie.

5. Do this for the "fullsize" movie script:

```
on ReceiveFilePath sPath


  member(1).fileName = sPath
  member(1).regPoint =  point ( 0, 0 )
  rImageRect = member(1).rect
  sprite(1).loc = point ( 0, 0 )
  sprite(1).width = rImageRect.width
  sprite(1).height = rImageRect.height
  sprite(1).member = member(1)


END ReceiveFilePath
```

As you can see, the only thing that's happening is the rectangle in Cast position 1 is being switched for the line passed to this movie in the **ReceiveFilePath** call. We then set up the sprite so it has the same visual dimensions of the member, and place the member on the Stage with its registration point set to 0, 0 and its horizontal and vertical coordinates to the same values (locking it in the upper-left corner of the Stage itself).

6. That's all. Save the movie, alongside the main thumbknows file, under the name **"fullsize"** and then run thumbknows, double-clicking thumbnails whenever you want to see a full-screen view.

1-Minute Drill

● What does **tell** do?

● When a **tell** command is issued, which movie runs the code: the movie issuing the **tell** command or the movie receiving the **tell** command?

Keyboarding About Again

As nice as the double-clicking is, we can add to it by allowing the user to press RETURN or ENTER to get an image to load right off the scrolling list, by getting the name of the item selected and passing it along to the thumbnail behavior.

You've done similar things by now, so think for a few moments about how you'd do it, before you see the lines I added to the basic key handlers for the scrolling #field.

● It causes the object specified in the **tell** call to execute the commands sent along.
● The movie receiving the **tell** command always runs the code sent by the **tell** command.

7. This is what I put into the **KeyPress** routine of the scrolling #field (sprite 11) in the ThumbKnows movie, right after I did the up and down arrow testing, before I calculated the line offset and **scrollTop** information:

```
else if the key = RETURN or the key = ENTER then

  if psFileList.line[pnItem] = "[no folder selected]" or
psFileList.line[pnItem] = "[no files in folder]" then

    exit

  else

    sendSprite ( 30, #mouseUp, 1 )

  end if
```

As you can see, it's pretty simple. If the line selected happens to be an indicator that there's nothing to see at all, we exit. Otherwise, we just send a **mouseUp** to sprite 30 (the thumbnail), passing a 1 as the parameter.

8. Of course, the current **mouseUp** for the image thumbnail has no receiving variable for the one we're passing, so naturally we need to alter it just a little further:

```
on mouseUp me, bDblClick

  sprite(me.spriteNum).blend = 100

  if voidP ( bDblClick ) then

    bDblClick = 0

  end if

  if sprite(me.spriteNum).member <> member("rectangle") then

    if the doubleClick or bDblClick then
```

...the rest of the code is as it was before. Here we're just seeing whether or not a mock double-click is sent. If so, we know this is a command to load the image specified by the **hilite**-marked line in the #field sprite. Otherwise, it's either a simple mouseUp or an actual user-generated double-click. Either way, we do what we need to do.

Project Summary

With this project, you've seen that communication between MIAWs can allow you to not simply open one, but also cause it to perform various functions based on what your parent movie needs—and, in fact, allow you to (once again) enhance the functionality of a preexisting movie without substantially modifying its code.

Project 15-2: One More Idea

Many thumbnail and sorting programs allow the user to run a "slideshow" of images from a given folder. I think our program can do this, too, with just a little more MIAW intercommunication.

The goals of this project include the following:

● Enhancing further the functionality of the thumbnail program

● Illustrating again how MIAWs function as code objects and can expand a program and user experience

Step-by-Step

For starters, you'd need another floating control window, this one a simple slideshow control panel that allows the user to choose delay lengths, determine whether the slideshow should loop (that is, run forever), and decide whether the images from the selected folder run in random order or the order given them by their filenames on disk.

Then, once the folder was chosen and those options set, you'd just need another movie that took commands from the control floater, ran as a full-screen movie, and loaded images whenever it was required to do so.

1. Add a button that opens the slideshow floater from the main ThumbKnows movie, and set it up like the others we've made. I won't go into too much detail here because I believe you're ready to do something like that on your own; start with the behavior you made for the Create index... button.

2. Create a basic slideshow control panel movie similar to the renamer and indexer ones. This will include some controls for looping the slideshow, delaying between slides, and determining whether or not the slides load in random order. It will also have a Choose folder... button that allows the user to pick the folder containing the images she wants played in the slideshow.

3. The basic slideshow playback script is simple enough that I was able to enter it into the Choose folder... button I put onto the floating MIAW slideshow control panel's Stage. This is the behavior I attached to that button:

```
GLOBAL goFileXtraObject, gnDelay

PROPERTY plSlideList, plDisplayList, pwMySlideWindow, psFolderPath, pnTicks



on beginSprite me

  pnTicks = 0
  plSlideList = []
  plDisplayList = []
  psFolderPath = ""

  pwMySlideWindow = window ( "Slideshow" )
  pwMySlideWindow.fileName = "slide"
  pwMySlideWindow.windowType = 2
  pwMySlideWindow.rect = the deskTopRectList[1]


END beginSprite



on endSprite me

  pwMySlideWindow.close()
  pwMySlideWindow.forget()
  pnTicks = 0
  plSlideList = []
  plDisplayList = []
  psFolderPath = ""

END endSprite



on mouseUp me

  member("info").text = "Select the folder containing the files you want to
run as a slideshow..."
  updateStage

  sTarget = goFileXtraObject.fx_FolderSelectDialog( "" )
```

```
  if sTarget <> "" then

    plSlideList = GetSlides( sTarget )

  end if

  if plSlideList.count > 1 then

    psFolderPath = plSlideList[1]
    deleteAt ( plSlideList, 1 )

    me.PrepareShow()

  end if

END mouseUp



on PrepareShow me

  plDisplayList = []

  if member("random").hilite = 1 then

    repeat while plSlideList.count > 0

      nRandomFile = random ( plSlideList.count() )
      sFile = plSlideList[nRandomFile]
      plDisplayList.append ( sFile )
      deleteAt ( plSlideList, nRandomFile )

    end repeat

    plSlideList = duplicate ( plDisplayList )

  else

    plDisplayList = duplicate ( plSlideList )

  end if

  pwMySlideWindow.open()
  me.UpdateSlide()

  pnTicks = the ticks

END PrepareShow
```

15

```
on UpdateSlide me

  if plDisplayList <> [] then

    sFile = plDisplayList[1]
    deleteAt ( plDisplayList, 1 )
    sPath = psFolderPath & sFile

    tell pwMySlideWindow

      ReceiveImagePath ( sPath )

    end tell

  else

    if member("loop").hilite = 1 then

      me.PrepareShow()

    else

      pwMySlideWindow.close()
      pnTicks = 0

    end if

  end if

END UpdateSlide
```

You can make some inferences there, starting with **beginSprite**:

> **pnTicks = 0**
>
> **plSlideList = []**
>
> **plDisplayList = []**
>
> **psFolderPath = ""**

Here we're setting some properties to initial empty or zero states. We'll be using these properties later, of course.

> **pwMySlideWindow = window ("Slideshow")**
>
> **pwMySlideWindow.fileName = "slide"**
>
> **pwMySlideWindow.windowType = 2**
>
> **pwMySlideWindow.rect = the deskTopRectList[1]**

Here we're setting things up for our slideshow, referencing a movie named "slide" (you know what that means—you'll be making that movie soon), setting its window frame so it will be a plain box, and setting its dimensions to fill the entire monitor. All of these are commands you've seen and used before, of course.

Then, in **endSprite**, we just undo everything, zeroing all the variables and values again, closing and forgetting the window, and so on. We do this partly to avoid dirty RAM and partly to prevent the possibility of the slideshow window still existing in memory someplace even after the user has closed its control panel—which would definitely slow down the rest of the program!

Then, in the **mouseUp** handler, we kick up another folder selection dialog box and pass the result to a handler you know very well by now, having used it already in this program.

Note

Make sure to enter a **GetSlides** handler into your slideshow control panel movie script, or you will get a script error. You can copy and paste out of one of the other movie scripts; all you want to do is get a list of the image files contained in a given folder on the user's system.

This time, though, the handler returns its results in the form of a list, the very first item in that list being the location containing the image files.

In order for this to happen, we simply cause the **GetSlides** handler to add the path to the folder in the list it's going to return—the very path sent by the folder selection code—before adding any image files to that list.

4. We then continue with the slide file processing:

   psFolderPath = plSlideList[1]

   deleteAt (plSlideList, 1)

   me.PrepareShow()

5. In **PrepareShow**, we determine whether or not we're doing a random playback by referring to the **hilite** of a member called **random**. This is actually a *checkbox* on the Stage, and since all we're doing is seeing whether or not it's been checked, you don't even need to add a behavior to it. (Clicking a checkbox automatically changes it to checked or unchecked, without any code at all.)

6. Create a checkbox on the Stage (if you haven't already) labeled **Random playback**, and name it **random** in your Cast.

15

7. Back to our code. If we are going for random playback, we do this:

```
repeat while plSlideList.count > 0

  nRandomFile = random ( plSlideList.count() )

  sFile = plSlideList[nRandomFile]

  plDisplayList.append ( sFile )

  deleteAt ( plSlideList, nRandomFile )

end repeat

plSlideList = duplicate ( plDisplayList )
```

We go through this repeat loop, grabbing slides from random positions in the main slide list and plugging them into the display list, until the main slide list is empty. We then put the display list back *into* the main slide list in case the user has decided to loop the show, because later on we're going to have to go through the same procedure again.

If the user has not selected random playback, we just put the main list right into the display list.

Then we open the slide window, issue an **UpdateSlide** command, and set a timer variable:

```
pnTicks = the ticks
```

ticks are 1/60 of a second, counted from the moment the program begins running, and we're storing **the ticks** in a variable that we're going to use later.

UpdateSlide is the last handler in this button. We start by determining if the slide play list is not empty. If that's the case, we get the next slide in the list and then delete it (so each time we do this, the list's contents are reduced by one). We then send a command to the slideshow window, **ReceiveImagePath**— and you can probably guess exactly what this command does.

If, however, **plDisplayList** is empty, we then determine if the user has set this slideshow to loop indefinitely. This, predictably enough, just tests the **hilite** of another checkbox, this one called **loop**. If **loop** is checked, we go through **PrepareShow** again. Otherwise, since we're at the end of the slide list, and since the user doesn't want to play the show again, we close the slideshow window and zero out the **pnTicks** variable.

Where **pnTicks** really comes into play is in the **enterFrame** script. First, we determine whether or not **pnTicks** is 0. If it is, then there is not a slideshow going on right now, so we just kick out. Otherwise, we do some math:

```
nTarget = gnDelay * 60
if pnTicks + nTarget <= the ticks then
  me.UpdateSlide()
  pnTicks = the ticks
end if
```

8. What's **gnDelay**? It's the amount of time, in seconds, the user has chosen to make a slide stay onscreen. Since **ticks** are 1/60 of a second, we take that time delay in seconds and multiply it by 60, then add that to the time since the slide first appeared. If the delay time has elapsed, the current value for **the ticks** will be greater than this number, so we call **UpdateSlide** and then set **pnTicks** to the current time for another round of delay counting.

   How we arrive at the delay time I leave as an exercise to you, but I'll give you the hint that I used a mechanism very similar conceptually to the one I used in determining thumbnail dimensions for the index MIAW we made in the last module, including radio buttons and behaviors that set a global variable based on the name of the member that has been clicked.

9. Finally, we wrap it up with the slideshow movie file, which is almost a duplicate of the full-sized preview except for these changes. Start with another new Director movie and name it **slide**.

10. Place an image placeholder sprite in frame 1, and put a **go the frame** script into the script channel of frame 1.

11. Attach the following behavior to the image sprite on the Stage:

```
on mouseDown me


  (the activeWindow).close()


END mouseDown
```

   This is to let the user close the slideshow window (which fills the main monitor) by clicking the image being displayed. As you may infer, **the activeWindow** refers to the one in the foreground, in this case the slideshow window itself.

12. Make this handler in the movie script to accept the actual images. This will look a lot like the thumbnail resizer, so I won't have to explain it to you; it's there because it's always possible for an image to be *larger* than the current monitor's display size; if that happens to be the case, our slideshow program will scale the image down so it fills the monitor as much as possible.

15

```
on ReceiveImagePath sPath


  sprite(1).member.fileName = sPath
  sprite(1).member.regPoint =  point ( 0, 0 )
  rImageRect = sprite(1).member.rect
  rDisplayRect = (the activeWindow).rect

  nScreenWidth = rDisplayRect.width
  nScreenHeight = rDisplayRect.height

  nWidth = rImageRect.width
  nHeight = rImageRect.height

  nMidHPoint = nScreenWidth / 2
  nMidVPoint = nScreenHeight / 2

  if nWidth > nScreenWidth or nHeight > nScreenHeight then

    if nWidth > nHeight then

      fTargetWidth = float ( nScreenWidth )
      fPercentResize = float ( fTargetWidth / nWidth )
      fTargetHeight = float ( nHeight ) * fPercentResize

    else

      fTargetHeight = float ( nScreenHeight )
      fPercentResize = fTargetHeight / float ( nHeight )
      fTargetWidth = float ( nWidth ) * fPercentResize

    end if

    nWidth = integer ( fTargetWidth )
    nHeight = integer ( fTargetHeight )

  end if

nImageHMid = nWidth / 2
nImageVMid = nHeight / 2

nLocH = nMidHPoint - nImageHMid
nLocV = nMidVPoint - nImageVMid

sprite(1).loc = point ( nLocH, nLocV )
sprite(1).width = nWidth
```

```
sprite(1).height = nHeight
sprite(1).member = member(1)

END ReceiveImagePath
```

1-Minute Drill

● What is **the ticks**?

● What are the values, in seconds, defined by the following?
30 ticks
120 ticks
3600 ticks

Finesse

How you actually lay out the slideshow floater, get it to open in the first place, and so on are your decisions to make. You might want to look at the fully functional version I put online at **www.nightwares.com/Director_beginners_guide/ 15/tk.sit.hqx**. This is a compressed file that contains all the Director source movies, ready for you to open, look through, and so on—and, of course, it's ready to run as well.

Note

If this file doesn't correctly decompress for you, go to **www.aladdinsys.com/** and download StuffIt Expander from there. It's a free utility module you can use to uncompress many different kinds of files.

You might look over what I have there and feel like making changes, such as adding some extra graphics or changing colors or fonts—in fact, you might feel like rebuilding everything from the ground up to improve the look and feel. You might want to add the "breakout" game, for instance, just for the heck of it, or you might want to change the batch renamer in such a way that it doesn't limit you to ten characters (this is only safe if you know your images are always going to be on either Windows or some version of Linux or UNIX). Or, you might want to experiment with setting up different colors for the backgrounds and links in the HTML indexer, or even use your own HTML programming skills to improve the overall look and feel of the indexed page, perhaps by using tables to center the images.

● The time, in 1/60-second intervals, since any given Director program or movie began running.
● 1/2 second; 2 seconds; 60 seconds (1 minute)

Project Summary

With this final project, you've seen how you can expand your Director movies quite a ways, using a combination of behaviors, MIAWs, and so on—in fact, good general object-oriented approaches to programming. You've learned that Director is much more than simply an animation engine with some scripting; that it is much more than simply a way to create interactive cartoons or advertisements. You've seen that it's a powerful tool that can be used to create interesting and useful programs of many different kinds.

What Next?

What you do with these movies is nowhere nearly as important as the fact that you now have the tools and knowledge at your disposal to actually do the things you conceive. By a judicious application of your own creative skills, your technical knowledge, and the spark of imagination that is uniquely yours, you are now ready to truly enter a world that is limited by very few things indeed, a world wherein you are free to explore, experiment, and enhance your skills enormously.

Go to Macromedia seminars, read other books on Director, and learn more about Flash (it's really a worthy ally to the Director programmer). Frequent the user lists and discussion groups. Learn from others, and let others gain from your experience. And always remember that if you can conceive it, you likely can conceive a way to achieve it, using Director, Xtras, MIAWs, parent objects, and all the other tools available to you.

And, most importantly, welcome to the community of Director programmers! I'll be seeing you!

☑ *Mastery Check*

1. What does **tell** do, and which movie runs the commands issued in **tell**?

_____

_____

2. What is **the ticks**?

_____

_____

3. Explore MIAWs a little further by trying to open the same Director movie more than once at the same time as a MIAW from within the same parent movie, and from two different parent movies. What do you discover, and why do you think it's true?

_____

_____

15

Appendix

Answers to Mastery Checks

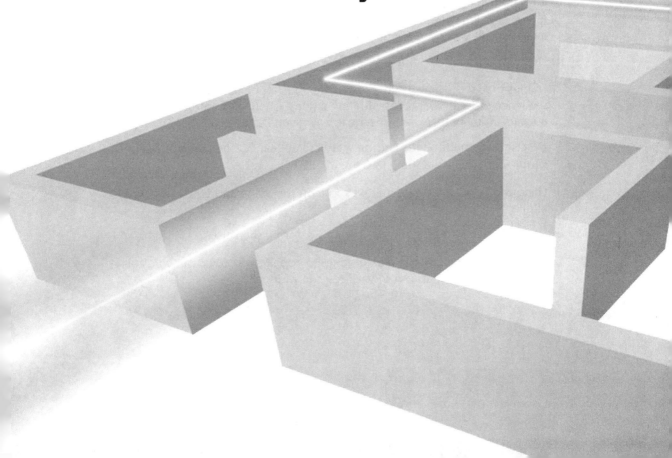

Module 1: Director's "Physical" Tools

1. Do movies created in Director work on Macintosh only, Windows only, or both?

They theoretically work on either platform, provided they are not projectors.

2. Define projector and movie, and describe their differences.

A projector is the stand-alone version of a program made in Director; it can run on any computer that supports it. A movie is the file you create in Director, from which projectors are made. While projectors are usually self-contained, movies either need the Director program, the Shockwave plugin, or a projector to run.

3. Define the Stage, the Score, and the Cast, and describe their purposes in creating programs.

The Stage is a virtual control canvas for assembling images, graphics, text, animation, and other program elements. The Score is a linear model for illustrating the stack order in which items lie on top of each other onscreen, and the order in time in which they appear. The Cast is a catch-all storage container for any media items you might want to use in your Score or on the Stage.

4. Define frames and channels, and describe their uses.

Frames model the flow of time in a Score and can be used to control the sequence order of events (as with animation). Channels control what sprite appears atop another on the Stage in any given frame.

5. Describe one method for getting words to appear on the Director Stage. (This is not the same thing as using ALERT!)

Using the Text tool, create a #text sprite on the Stage and type some words into it.

6. Name at least two Lingo keywords and describe their use.

ALERT to cause alert-style dialog boxes to appear; **put** to cause words or variable contents to appear in the Message window.

7. Describe the basic steps required to create a simple standalone program in Director.

Save the movie you want to convert to a projector; then choose File I Create Projector.... Add the movie to the list of files to make into a projector, then click the Create... button.

Module 2: The Library Palette

1. Define the Library Palette.

A window containing premanufactured behaviors that are available for use in Director movies.

2. What is a way to get a behavior from the Library Palette into your Director movie?

Drag it from the Library Palette onto the sprite in your Score that you want to attach it to. Or, drag it directly into your Cast window.

3. How do you change the contents of your Library Palette?

Copy the given Library Palette file from the Libs folder on your hard drive to another location, make changes to that file, and then replace the original with the changed version. Or, you can save an external Director movie cast file with the name you want it to have and place it directly into the "Libs" folder.

4. Why are Library Palette behaviors often not enough to create a complete Director program?

Library Palette behaviors are generally not intended to handle really complex functions; mostly they are there to help you make interesting things happen.

Module 3: Code Tools

1. What is a variable?

A variable is a container that can hold anything: a number, text, or almost anything else.

2. What is a handler?

A handler is a structure used in Director to define a group of related commands. Handlers are also known as methods, functions, or subroutines in other programming languages.

3. What is an **if...then** control structure?

A special test used to determine if a given condition is true or not, and to make a decision on what to do next based on that evaluation.

4. What is a **repeat with...** loop?

A counter loop that starts from one number and automatically goes through a series of cycles until another number is reached. In many other languages, a for...next loop is used for the same purpose.

5. What is a **repeat while...** loop?

A testing loop that cycles endlessly until its test condition evaluates to true.

6. What is a keyword?

A special Lingo term that has a predefined meaning to Director itself.

7. What is important about **end if**?

An end if must always be matched with an if...then.

8. What is important about **end repeat**?

An end repeat must always be matched with either a repeat with... or repeat while...

9. How do you make one handler run from another handler?

By calling that handler; that is, by entering the target's name in the Lingo script you are writing.

Module 4: Well-Written Lingo

1. Categorize the following as variable names or handler references:

sContents

ValueOfItem()

gnValueOfItem

A variable name; a handler reference; a variable name.

2. If you were writing a program, what names would you give to the variables that contained the following information?

> The user's name, employed throughout the program
>
> A session ID number, employed once and accessible no place else in the program
>
> Local sales tax, used frequently for calculating prices

Possible variable names could include:

> gsUserName, gsName, psUserName, etc. (this could be a property or a global variable)
>
> nSessionID, nTransactionNum, etc.
>
> gfSalesTax, pfSalesTax, gfLocalTax, etc. (this too could be a property or global variable)

3. What is the purpose of whitespace in a program's code?

To break the code up visually and make it more readable; to visually imply logically related or discrete sections of the code; etc.

4. What set of characters does Lingo use to denote the beginning of a comment?

A double hyphen (--) indicates the beginning of a comment.

5. Is the 'end' strictly necessary at the conclusion of a handler definition?

The Lingo interpreter does not require it; however, it's extremely poor practice to exclude it.

6. If 'end' is not strictly necessary, what is one good reason to include it anyway?

It makes it immediately obvious where a given handler definition has actually ended and where the next one begins.

Module 5: The Debugger

1. Why click the Debug button when you get a script error?

To cause the Debugger to open in an attempt to get a better idea as to what went wrong.

2. What is a breakpoint?

A position you manually set in a script (by clicking in the grey bar on the left side of any script window) that will cause the Debugger to open.

3. What result will you likely get from the following mathematical operations in Director?

3 / 4

2.0 / 7

2.0 / 3.0

0, some decimal number less than one, and 0.6667, respectively.

4. How do you force Director to work in decimal arithmetic?

By using the float keyword.

5. What does the Watch expression button do?

It causes a variable to be loaded in the Watcher window where its value can be checked more closely.

6. How do you change a variable's value in the Watcher?

By typing in a new value, selecting that variable from the list, and clicking Set.

7. How do you toggle a breakpoint while the Debugger is running?

By clicking the Toggle breakpoint icon.

8. How do you step into another handler in the Debugger?

By clicking the Step into script button when the call to that handler is the current line in the Debugger.

9. How do you step out of a handler into previous ones in the Debugger?

By clicking the name of the desired handler in the stack list in the upper-left pane of the Debugger's window.

Module 6: Preparing to Create a Program

1. When preparing to create a Director program, what are some considerations for the audience you must have?

Whether you're making a utility program, or something for entertainment or education, or sales support; the likely age of the audience is also a factor.

2. What's an important consideration if you're creating software for educational purposes?

Whether your program will have to be ADA compliant, or in other ways account for and accommodate special needs users.

3. What does the term *port* mean as it pertains to making programs in Director?

Transferring a Director movie from one computer operating system to another platform entirely is referred to as *porting* the movie.

4. Describe one way in which choice of Xtras can affect portability of a Director movie.

If an Xtra relies on certain features of a specific operating system, it might prevent your Director movie from being ported to any other computer platform at all.

5. What is an important consideration regarding Xtras when you're planning a Shockwave distribution?

Whether that Xtra is Shockwave safe or not. If it's not, it can't be used.

6. Can external media files be used in Shockwave?

Yes, provided they are a type Director or one of its Shockwave safe Xtras can handle.

Module 7: Creating Programs

1. Of 8, 16, or 32, which monitor color depth would display the most colors?

32, which displays about 17 million colors plus 256 levels of alpha-channel effects. 16 bit displays about 65,000 colors, and 8 bit displays 256.

2. If you look at **the deskTopRectList** and see [rect(0, 0, 800, 600), rect(800, 0, 1600, 600)], what does this tell you about the display settings for that computer?

That there are two monitors attached and they are both set to display 800 by 600 pixels.

3. In terms of computer graphics, what is *dithering*?

Reducing the number of colors in an image from a higher number to a lower number, and attempting to perform some kind of blend operation to make the effect less noticeable.

4. If your Director program uses MIAW and users report crashes with errors in either IML32.DLL or DIRAPI.DLL, what is a likely cause?

A MIAW is being closed without also being correctly cleared from memory.

5. If your Director movie plays a lot of MP3 audio and AVI video, and the video sounds don't work, what do you know already about the kind of computer on which the movie is running, and what the likely cause is?

That it's running on Windows, and that you forgot to set the soundKeepDevice to false.

6. What is the difference between **QUIT** and **HALT**?

QUIT causes a *projector* to stop running, but it also causes *Director* to quit. **HALT** simply stops playback in Director, but will quit a projector.

7. What is a *hybrid* CD?

A CD that is designed to work on at least two different operating system types, as in a disc that works on either Mac or Windows.

8. What is an advantage of making modular programs in Director?

Making patches, improvements, and upgrades can be easier because you only have to release updates to the modules that have been changed or improved.

Module 8: Integrating Lingo and Sprites

1. What is the difference between locH and the mouseH?

locH is a sprite property, describing the horizontal position of any sprite. the mouseH is the horizontal position of the mouse pointer.

2. If you see a Lingo command that reads "puppetTempo 120", what is happening?

In theory the movie in question is either refreshing the screen 120 times per second, or is playing back at a rate of 120 frames per second.

3. What is happening here?

sendSprite (22, #ExecuteReset, 7)

A command is being sent to a behavior attached to sprite 22 to run the handler called ExecuteReset, with the number 7 being passed as a parameter.

4. Why won't this script work?

```
on beginSprite me
 nSpeed = 15
end

on exitFrame me
 puppetTempo nSpeed
end
```

nSpeed was not declared as either a property or global variable.

5. Why won't this script work?

```
PROPERTY pnSpeed

on beginSprite
 pnSpeed = 15
end

on exitFrame
 puppetTempo pnSpeed
end
```

The 'me' keyword is missing from the handler definitions even though this is apparently a sprite behavior script.

6. If I have two behaviors attached to a sprite, and the first behavior has an exitFrame event script, and the second one has an enterFrame event script, which script will execute first?

The enterFrame script in the second behavior will execute before the exitFrame script in the first behavior.

7. Even though the highest value I can set the tempo to is 30,000, why is it unlikely I'd see anything happening that quickly onscreen?

This represents a refresh rate of thirty thousand times per second, much faster than desktop computers can manage.

Module 9: Understanding the Power of Lists

1. The "breakout" game never resets. If you clear off all the bricks the ball just bounces around on the screen like it did for the racquetball game in Module 8. It would be nice to do some Lingo that determines if the player has cleared the screen, and then lets her choose to play again or quit the game.

There are many approaches to take to that. I've got one way to do it online. Before you download that file and look over its Lingo, though, try it yourself and see if your solution was the same as mine.

I'll give you two hints. I set a global variable, and I used another Lingo keyword, **count**. (Look it up in the *Lingo Dictionary*!)

After you've tried it yourself, download my version of the breakout game and see if what I did is what you did. (Note that if we tried different approaches, that's not necessarily bad as long as they both work.)

2. Suppose you wanted to allow the bricks in each row to be given random widths within a specific range, say no more than 50 pixels wide but not less than 30. What part of the "breakout" game might you modify to make that happen, and in what way?

This is another one where the answer is online. Again, try it yourself before you look at my code, though.

3. Conceptually, the differences between our "breakout" game and a "space invaders" style game are pretty small. After all, the invaders can be thought of as little more than bricks that move and shoot back. The paddle isn't that different from a little mobile rocket launcher that fires a ball-like missile each time you click or press a button.

How hard do you think it would be to revise this game to turn it into an invader shooting match? How do you think you'd go about doing that?

4. There are quite a few commands you can use to create, manipulate, and handle lists, so when you've got a little extra time why not look over your Lingo documentation and see what else you can discover? Lists are spectacularly powerful tools to have at your disposal, and if you understand them well you can do some genuinely incredible things with Director.

Module 10: External Files

1. What does displayOpen do?

It loads a system-standard open file dialog box.

2. What is happening with this command?

openFile(sExternalFile, 1)

The file located at sExternalFile is being opened with read-only permission.

3. What does this command do?

oDialog = new (xtra "mui")

It creates a new instance of the MUI Xtra and puts that instance into a variable named oDialog.

4. What is wrong with this command?

oFileObject.setFilterMask("Text files, TEXT")

The string being sent to setFilterMask is valid for neither Macintosh nor Windows. For Mac the command should be

oFileObject.setFilterMask("TEXT")

and for Windows it should be

oFileObject.setFilterMask("Text files,*.txt")

5. Why don't images appear in HTML files you've imported into a Director Cast member?

Director is unable to display embedded content in HTML files.

6. If you save a changed file using FileIO and don't delete the old file first, what might happen?

Old data from the previous file might get left behind and appear in the new version.

7. If you've created a projector from a movie that uses FileIO and users report when they click the Open file… button they get a script error, what is the likely cause?

You forgot to include the FileIO Xtra in the list of Xtras Director includes to make a projector from the movie.

8. Why should you not open some files with write permission?

In some cases, they may be system files and you could inadvertently cause damage; or, if the files are located on a network and you open them with write permission, other users won't be able to open them until you're finished.

Module 11: The Internet Revisited

1. What is a hyperlink?

Any clickable item in a Web page.

2. How do you make Director respond appropriately to a hyperlink?

You program on a hyperLinkClicked event handler.

3. What does downLoadNetThing do?

It copies a file from one location to another.

4. I've just made a Director movie I want to put online, and I use this call:

downLoadNetThing (remoteFileLocation, localFileLocation)

What's wrong here?

downLoadNetThing does not work in Shockwave, so that line of code is invalid.

5. If I make a projector that has a goToNetPage call in it and users tell me they get script errors when they click the button that makes that call, what's the likely reason?

One or more of the Net Xtras is missing from the list of Xtras to be included in your projector.

6. What does goToNetMovie do?

It loads the specified Director movie or Shockwave file off the Internet for playback.

Module 12: The Fundamentals of OOP

1. What is a code object?

In simplest terms, a smaller program running within a larger one.

2. What does **me** represent?

The address or memory location of a specific code object instance.

3. What is instantiation?

The creation of a code object in memory.

4. What should you always do before clearing a code object's variable?

The internal variables in the object should be set to zero, ideally by a destructor.

5. What does encapsulation mean?

The property of OOP design that keeps objects and their data discrete.

6. For exploration: You see that I created a food type variable, but all we ever did was set it to pizza. Consider what might be necessary to modify your program so it can handle sandwiches, spaghetti, and so on.

Module 13: Behaviors Are OOP Too

1. Place the following events in their correct order as Director responds to them:

startMovie, enterFrame, beginSprite, stopMovie, exitFrame

beginSprite, enterFrame (assuming a sprite in frame 1), startMovie, exitFrame, stopMovie

2. If you want to determine whether a variable has been given a value, what keyword would you use?

voidP, as in
  put voidP (someVariable)

3. How would you do the same thing for an object?

objectP, as in
  put objectP (oFile|OObject)

4. If you perform a math operation and get only integer numbers, what is one way you could force Director to work with decimals?

By using the float keyword to assign values to variables. Alternately, multiplying any number by 1.0 will transform it to a decimal.

5. What happens when you pass a decimal number through the integer keyword?

Director truncates the decimal, without rounding, taking only the part of the number to the left of the decimal point as the new value.

6. How can you tell if a user has double-clicked an item in your Director movies?

By using the doubleClick keyword.

Module 14: Movies in a Window (MIAWs) as OOP Code

1. What is a MIAW?

A Director movie in a window, or a movie that is running in a separate window while another one is playing.

2. What's a quick way to open a MIAW?

open window *filename*.

3. What's a disadvantage of using the quick way to open a MIAW?

It prevents you setting up parameters for the MIAW, such as its window frame appearance or location on the screen.

4. If you have two Cast members with the same names, but one is in a parent movie and the other is in a MIAW, will you have trouble when you write

Lingo that refers to that Cast member's name? In other words, will Director become confused about which Cast member you mean?

No, Director assumes that Casts are discrete entities unless it's explicitly told otherwise.

5. What is windowType?

A keyword that defines what the frame shape and controls for a MIAW will be, as well as some behavior aspects of the MIAW itself, such as modality.

6. What is sourceRect?

The original dimensions of a Director movie; the size of the Stage you set when you made the movie.

7. What is the maximum value that might be returned by (the systemDate).seconds? How do you know that?

86,400. That's the number of seconds in 24 hours, and (the systemDate).seconds returns the time since midnight for any particular day.

Module 15: Communication with MIAWs

1. What does **tell** do, and which movie runs the commands issued in **tell**?

It causes the movie specified in the **tell** call to execute the commands sent along. The movie receiving the **tell** command always runs the code sent by the **tell** command.

2. What is the ticks?

The time, in $1/60^{th}$ second intervals, since any given Director program or movie began running.

3. Explore MIAWs a little further by trying to open the same Director movie more than once at the same time as a MIAW from within the same parent movie, and from two different parent movies. What do you discover, and why do you think it's true?

The same file cannot be opened more than once at a time unless it has been marked as being read-only or sharable by the operating system; this is to prevent the file's resources from being changed by one movie while another is trying to read it, which could cause all manner of errors.

Index

INTERNATIONAL CONTACT INFORMATION

AUSTRALIA
McGraw-Hill Book Company Australia Pty. Ltd.
TEL +61-2-9417-9899
FAX +61-2-9417-5687
http://www.mcgraw-hill.com.au
books-it_sydney@mcgraw-hill.com

CANADA
McGraw-Hill Ryerson Ltd.
TEL +905-430-5000
FAX +905-430-5020
http://www.mcgrawhill.ca

**GREECE, MIDDLE EAST,
NORTHERN AFRICA**
McGraw-Hill Hellas
TEL +30-1-656-0990-3-4
FAX +30-1-654-5525

MEXICO (Also serving Latin America)
McGraw-Hill Interamericana Editores S.A. de C.V.
TEL +525-117-1583
FAX +525-117-1589
http://www.mcgraw-hill.com.mx
fernando_castellanos@mcgraw-hill.com

SINGAPORE (Serving Asia)
McGraw-Hill Book Company
TEL +65-863-1580
FAX +65-862-3354
http://www.mcgraw-hill.com.sg
mghasia@mcgraw-hill.com

SOUTH AFRICA
McGraw-Hill South Africa
TEL +27-11-622-7512
FAX +27-11-622-9045
robyn_swanepoel@mcgraw-hill.com

**UNITED KINGDOM & EUROPE
(Excluding Southern Europe)**
McGraw-Hill Education Europe
TEL +44-1-628-502500
FAX +44-1-628-770224
http://www.mcgraw-hill.co.uk
computing_neurope@mcgraw-hill.com

ALL OTHER INQUIRIES Contact:
Osborne/McGraw-Hill
TEL +1-510-549-6600
FAX +1-510-883-7600
http://www.osborne.com
omg_international@mcgraw-hill.com